Investing For Beginners 2021:

6 Books In 1:

Day Trading, Forex, Options & Swing, Dropshipping Shopify, Real Estate Investing. Discover The Psychology And The Best 7 Strategies To Become a Profitable Investor

ROBERT ZONE

© **Copyright 2021 by Robert Zone - All rights reserved.**

The content contained within this book may not be reproduced, duplicated or transmitted without direct written permission from the author or the publisher. Under no circumstances will any blame or legal responsibility be held against the publisher, or author, for any damages, reparation, or monetary loss due to the information contained within this book. Either directly or indirectly.

Legal Notice:
This book is copyright protected. This book is only for personal use. You cannot amend, distribute, sell, use, quote or paraphrase any part, or the content within this book, without the consent of the author or publisher.

Disclaimer Notice:
Please note the information contained within this document is for educational and entertainment purposes only. All effort has been executed to present accurate, up to date, and reliable, complete information. No warranties of any kind are declared or implied. Readers acknowledge that the author is not engaging in the rendering of legal, financial, medical or professional advice. The content within this book has been derived from various sources. Please consult a licensed professional before attempting any techniques outlined in this book.

By reading this document, the reader agrees that under no circumstances is the author responsible for any losses, direct or indirect, which are incurred as a result of the use of information contained within this document, including, but not limited to, — errors, omissions, or inaccuracies.

Table of Contents

Day Trading for Beginners:

Introduction……………………………………….13

Chapter 1 Basics of Day Trading & Qualities of a Day Trader……………………………………………15

Chapter 2 Concepts of Day Trading…………………20

Chapter 3 How Day Trading Works ………………33

Chapter 4 How to Reduce Your Risks When Day Trading ……………………………………………50

Chapter 5 Finding and Picking Stocks and Trading Strategies …………………………………………56

Chapter 6 Day Trading Tools………………………67

Chapter 7 Understanding Trading Orders…………80

Chapter 8 Money Management ……………………90

Chapter 9 Dos and Don'ts……………………… 109

Chapter 10 Managing Risk in Trading and the Role of Journaling …………………………………… 119

Conclusion……………………………………… 131

Forex Trading for Beginners:

Introduction 137

Chapter 1 How to Start Forex Trading................ 153

Chapter 2 Technical and Fundamental Analysis ... 159

Chapter 3 Forex Trading Strategies 177

Chapter 4 Choosing A Broker............................ 189

Chapter 5 Forex Market 197

Chapter 6 Forex Trading Psychology 206

Chapter 7 Money Mistake to avoid..................... 217

Chapter 8 Trading the Breakout 235

Chapter 9 Systems and Techniques for Beginners 243

Conclusion 251

Options Trading for Beginners:

Introduction 257
Chapter 1 Understanding Option Trading 260
Chapter 2 How to Start Options Trading 271
Chapter 3 Brokers 281
Chapter 4 Platforms and Tools for Options Trading 292
Chapter 5 Basic Investment Strategies 304
Chapter 6 How Options Are Priced 314
Chapter 7 Risk Management 324
Chapter 8 The Basics Of Technical Analysis 335
Chapter 9 Trading psychology 350
Chapter 10 The Best Strategies to Make Money ... 360
Chapter 11 Tips for Success 369
Conclusion 385

Swing Trading:

Introduction 389
Chapter 1 Basics of Swing Trading 391
Chapter 2 How Swing Trading Works? 401
Chapter 3 Platforms And Tools For Trading 420
Chapter 4 Financial Instruments for Swing Trading 439
Chapter 5 Candlestick Chart Patterns and Technical Indicators 448
Chapter 6 Swing Trading Rules 464
Chapter 7 Fundamental and Technical Analysis ... 473
Chapter 8 Money Management 480
Chapter 9 Swing Trading Strategies 498
Conclusion 507

Dropshipping Shopify 101:

Introduction.. 513
Chapter 1 Understanding Dropshipping 515
Chapter 2 Setting Up A Successful Dropshipping Business... 535
Chapter 3 Dropshipping ebay, Amazon and shopify... 545
Chapter 4 Pros and Cons 559
Chapter 5 Tools That You Need for Your Store..... 576
Chapter 6 What Factors To Look At When Analyzing The Target Market 587
Chapter 7 Marketing 597
Chapter 8 Dealing With Your Competitors 603
Chapter 9 Establishing Your Brand Through A Marketing Plan 613
Conclusion... 628

Real Estate Investing for Beginners:

Introduction 633
Chapter 1 Fundamental of Real Estate Investment 636
Chapter 2 Real Estate Investment Groups 655
Chapter 3 What To Expect In The Real Estate Business 672
Chapter 4 Types of Rental Properties to Invest ... 683
Chapter 5 Choosing the Best Location for Your Real Estate Investment.. 692
Chapter 6 Financing Investment Properties 701
Chapter 7 Getting the Right Property to Sell 712
Chapter 8 How to Get The Best Offer................. 724
Chapter 9 Common Mistakes to Avoid In Real Estate Investing 736
Conclusion 750

Day Trading for Beginners

The Ultimate Penny Stocks, Options and Psychology Swing Strategies For a Living Like a Rich Dad, Using The Tools, Tactics, Money Management, Discipline and Bases

ROBERT ZONE

Introduction

The stock market is a vast place and there are millions of trades that take place all over the world, within a single day. There are both buyers and sellers in the market and they will all have the same motive in mind; to increase their wealth potential.

Of all these trades, not everything will be of the same nature. Some will be long-term investments and some short. Long-term investments refer to those that are held for a long period of time. They are preferred by those who are not in a hurry to make money. Short-term investments on the other hand are those that are liquidated within a short period of time. They are not meant to be held for a long time, as the owners will be interested in disposing them off early.

Short-term investments can be of many types based on the time that they are held. Some can be held for a month, some for a week and some will be disposed off on the same day. This book will focus on the last option.

Better known as Intraday trading, day trading is one of the most preferred ways to trade in the stock market. Preferred mostly by those willing to part with their investment within a single day and realize a profit, or loss, from.

Intraday traders are interested in realizing a profit by capitalizing on the difference in the rates of these securities as opposed to long-term investors who will be in it for the Dividends.

Intraday trading has the capacity to help you attain a big leverage, as the rate of return on your investments can be quite high. However, it can also go the other way and cause you to lose out on a lot of money owing to poor investments. It is up to you to make the right choices and invest your money wisely.

You have to understand that the stock market is a very volatile place and anything can happen within a matter of a few seconds. You have to be prepared for anything that it throws at you. In order to prepare for it, you have to make use of risk capital. Risk capital refers to money that you are willing to risk. You have to convince yourself that even if you lose the money that you have invested then it will not be a big deal for you. For that, you have to make use of your own money and not borrow from anyone, as you will start feeling guilty about investing it. Decide on a set number and invest it.

You have to conduct a thorough research on the market before investing in it. Don't think you will learn as you go. That is only possible if you at least know the basics. You have to remain interested in gathering information that is crucial for your investments and it will only come about if you put in some hard work towards it. Nobody is asking you to stay up and go through thick texts books. All you have to do is go through books and websites and gather enough information to help you get started on the right foot.

Chapter 1 Basics of Day Trading & Qualities of a Day Trader

Before the invention of online trading platforms, people could only engage in stock market trading through brokerage firms, financial institutions, and other trading houses. As more inventions related to the internet were made, it became easy for individual traders to invest in the stock market. One way you can make money on the stock market is through day trading.

Day trading is one technique that can help you gain a lot of income if used properly. However, it becomes a challenge for those who have little information or those who lack the right trading strategies. Sometimes, even the most experienced traders end up losing a fortune because of inadequate knowledge and planning.

Definition
Day trading refers to a technique of stock trading that involves buying and selling of security or assets within a single day. Although day trading takes place in most marketplaces, it is more common in forex and stock trading platforms. For you to succeed in this kind of trade, you must have enough capital. The main goal is to leverage the profit on every slight price movement.

When day trading, you must ensure that each position you open closes by the end of the same day. This means that you cannot hold a position overnight.

Instead, you must close the position in the evening and reopen it the next day. It is the opposite of long-term trading where you purchase stock, hold it for some time then sell it off at a profit. That is why day trading is not considered as a form of investment.

Individuals who engage in this kind of trade are known as day traders. As a day trader, you must master how prices move in the marketplace. This is important if you want to make a profit from each short term price movement. A trader can make an unlimited number of trades within a single day. However, beginners can limit themselves to one or a few trades depending on the amount of capital and time available. If a trade does not seem quite profiting at the end of the day, you may decide to let it continue to the next day. However, you will be required to pay some fee to your broker for this to happen.

How long each transaction lasts depends on the trader. Some complete trades in a matter of seconds or minutes while others take several hours. Traders who purchase and sell multiple times within the same day usually end up with high-profit volumes. Some traders prefer selling their stock as soon as a good profit has been realized. Others prefer to wait until the close of the day to end their positions.

Qualities of a Good Day Trader
Day traders who engage in the business as a career always seek to improve their skills each day. They possess in-depth knowledge of the market as well as the strategies required to make good cash from the market. So, who is the right person to engage in day

trading? Let us look at some of the characteristics one should possess.

1. *Market Experience* - if you happen to engage in day trading without the requisite knowledge of the market, you may lose all your capital. You must be good at reading charts and carrying out technical analysis of the prices and market trends. You must also be able to carry out all the due diligence required to ensure you maximize the profits you realize from the trade.
2. *Adequate capital* - like any other trade, you need sufficient amounts of money to day trade. You must understand that this should be risk capital that you are ready to lose in case the market does not perform in your favor. Preparing yourself this way will save you the emotional torture associated with loss of cash In the trade. You must invest large capitals if you want to make more significant returns.
3. *A good strategy* - several strategies are involved in day trading. You need these strategies to stay ahead of other traders on the market. Before you start trading, you must understand how to apply these strategies in your transactions. When used correctly, these strategies ensure more consistent returns and fewer losses.
4. *Discipline* - it is essential to be disciplined as a day trader. Without discipline, it becomes difficult to record any successful transactions. Day trading depends on the volatility of stock prices. Traders are often interested in stocks whose price changes a lot in the course of the day. However, if you are

not disciplined enough in the way you select your shares, you may end up losing a lot despite the substantial price changes.

This trait is particularly crucial because the stock market has uncountable trading opportunities. You may decide to trade on several industries, products, and assets, but the truth is - not all these opportunities are good for making a profit. If you are disciplined enough, you will spend time analyzing opportunities before investing in them. You will also open and close trades at the right time, and this will ensure that you minimize losses.

5. *Patience* - day trading involves a certain level of waiting. You need to time when to enter the market and when to exit. Getting into the market blindly always results in a lot of problems. You must be patient enough to get into trades in good time.

Besides being patient, you also need to adapt to the changes taking place in the market. For instance, how a market appears at the beginning of the day is not the same way it will be at midday. You must be able to adjust your strategies to accommodate market changes accordingly.

Most successful day traders always seek to acquire these characteristics as a way of improving their business. Doing this requires a high level of mental as well as financial flexibility. You must be thick-skinned enough to risk your capital and accept any losses that come along. Remember, the main difference between successful and unsuccessful day traders lies in the profits. More profits depict you as a successful trader while less profits display you as one that is on the losing end. However, losing trades should not make you focus less because even professional day traders started by losing.

Chapter 2 Concepts of Day Trading

Traditionally, most of the people who used to trade in the stock market were those who work in brokerages, trading houses, and financial institution. Thanks to the influx of technology and the internet, there has been a rise in online trading places. Brokers have taken advantage of that and individuals are able to play the games online. This is also the reason why many people are aware of day trading. This has turned out to be a rising and lucrative business. The secret is to make sure that you completely understand what it entails, practice and learn more. For the newbies, it can be a little bit challenging. You do not need to worry since with the right strategy, approach and plan you are bound to succeed. What you should know is that even the most experienced day traders have their failures and a bad day. First, you need to know how day trading works.

How Does Day Trading Work?

What you should know is that day trading is not an investment. It involves purchasing an asset stake hopefully to make a profit over a set period. The length of time to anticipate the profit is subjective. This is because most investors are always open to the idea of holding their assets for many years, which can end up to decades. The secret is to be aware of the industry you are investing in. Always look for firms that are known to make great profit margins. They are the best since your profitability and great returns are guaranteed. Look for firms that are debt-free, have a strong product line, and do not have any pending lawsuits.

Day traders will buy and sell financial securities within a day. Traders will look for different sources of funds to buy the securities. Most of them will borrow funds and buy when the security prices are lower anticipating them to rise later in the day. The basic principle is to always buy when the cost is low and sell when it is high. That is where you will get the best profit margins. This s always managed at a compressed time limit.

An example is when a trader buys around 500 shares at 9:00 am. After 30 minutes, the price goes up, and he decides to sell. He will end up making a profit for that day less the commission chargeable and any applicable taxes. You need to know that when you sell a stock or investment that you have owned for less than a year. It is normally taxed against your personal gains. They are taxed at 35% as opposed to the long-term ones that are taxed at around 20%. It is evident that when day trading, you should put into consideration the taxation concept.

The beauty of day trading is that you have the ability to have at least 25 trades per day. The profit margin will increase based on the number of trades. Day traders always limit their risks, by not owning their stock overnight to avoid drastic price changes. The main reason could be market volatility hence the need for immediate response. Day traders will act quickly and make fast decisions, unlike other traders who will take time to make any decision.

What does a Day Trader do?

Day trader's typical day involves participating in financial markets purchasing and disposing of stocks, forex, and other securities. Their work also involves closing positions in order to make small and regular profits. There are different types of traders. The small-scale ones, the independent ones with their home space, and the ones based in institutions. Apart from trading, they also manage and maintain different markets and do research. They also do an analysis of financial notes based on securities and exchange information with the other traders.

This type of trading is considered to be on the fast lane and requires someone who can handle a lot of challenges and stress. You will need a deep and clear understanding of how the market works. You will also need to possess the required trading skills to be successful. One of the skills includes the ability to analyze different price charts.

A day trader always starts its day before the financial markets open. They will check all the financial information to help in economic development, analytical reports, market data, and any political news. They also check and do an analysis of the technical indicators and any results from the trading. The information they rely upon is from their subscription and analyst. This information is crucial and helps in decision-making.

The other duty for a day trader is to check any confirmations from trading. The confirmation is from the trading from the previous day. Then they check any activity notes and the overnight position that they hold. In case there are any errors, they need to be fixed immediately. Since all the charges are billed to the trader.

Then they will ensure that the trades have been successfully settled. The next thing will be to check the cash that the got and the profit in their trading account. What they confirm is if there is a purchase that was not sent to their accounts. Or a third party to a sale who has not paid for the security. They need to immediately address that since it is bound to affect their trading ability.

The most important part of a trader's life is when the market opens. The trader will put all the orders in the open that is entirely dependent on their style and plans. Then they will enter follow-ups on the trades that they intend to sell or buy. They spend the most part of the day doing analysis. Analyzing financial reports and charts with price movements.

An hour before the market closes; the trader will then close all the positions before leaving for the day. This is to ensure that there are no overnight risks.

Making a profit is any trader's goal. When they are private traders, they will bank all the profit. For the employed ones, they earn a percentage of the gains since they trade under customers' accounts. When there is a loss, nothing is paid. In fact, they need to refund the cash advances to the trading account.

Other duties of a day trader include doing market analysis and observation. Trading strategies formulation and completing a trade with brokers. They ensure that they sell all assets by the close of the day and have the investment as cash and profits. They also cut losses when there is a failure in investment. They are required to complete tax returns and do transaction recording.

Techniques Used in Day Trading

You need to have the best techniques when it comes to trading. Day trading can be considered simple or complicated based on the techniques and approaches that you use. Ensure that you are familiar with the concept and all that it entails. The best techniques are the ones that will help in maximizing profit and minimize price movements. In order to have effective approaches, you will need to depend on in-depth analysis, use price charts, and price indicators. The patterns will help in predicting price changes in the future.

This chapter will illustrate the best strategies and techniques to adopt that will help all traders on a different level; from beginners to experts. You will be able to know how to position yourself and know about the resources that are useful. The important thing to note is ensuring that you pick a technique that will perfectly fit with your preference, requirements, and style.

When you are starting out in the world of trading, do not be n a hurry to master all the technical terms and processes. Starts with the basics first; do not think that having a complicated technique is what will make you successful. You should know that the simpler your plan is the more effective it will be.

- You need to understand all the components of money management. You need to know the amount of money you are ready to risk as your capital. Note that it is not advisable to put down anything above 2% of your capital for each trade. Ensure that you are aware that you are also bound to make losses.

- Ensure you know how to manage your time. Day trading will need you to input a lot of your time. And you should also know how to strike a balance between your professional and personal life. Do not expect to allocate like an hour or two, and expect to have great returns. Be attentive in monitoring the financial markets and looking for new trading chances.

- Start small, do not be in a hurry to invest a lot of capital. Learn a lot, master the skill then invest more. You can start with at least 3 stocks daily. It is considered wise to start with fewer stocks and make great returns that investing in more and not gaining anything.

- The only way to understand the market and master it is by learning a lot. You need to keep yourself informed on what is happening. Be updated on what is happening, any news or occasions. Ensure you know about asset implications especially when there is a shift in economic policies.

- Be consistent with your trading. Deliver work with the same morale and spirit. Depend on logical facts and a strategic plan. Always ensure that your timing is always right. This is because when the market opens, it becomes volatile. Experts will be able to read the patterns, you should be able to bide the time. You can hold on in the first minutes of trading.

There are several components that each trader is s meant to know. Be it a beginner or experienced, you should master the components.

Volatility: This component will illustrate the potential gain in each trade. Great volatility means greater gains or losses.

Liquidity: This component makes a trader enter and exit the trading period and still manage a stable and attractive price.

Volume: Volume is a component that will indicate the number of times a stock has been traded over a certain time. It is commonly known as the average daily trading volume. When the volume is high, it indicates higher gains or interest in the trade. When the volume increases, it means that there is a change in price.

What is the Market to Day Trade?

There are three different markets for day trading. They are forex, futures, and stock market. Most people are aware of the stock market and not future and forex.

Stock Market: When people think of day trading, stock market comes into their mind first. It is considered the best when it comes to buying and selling company shares. And you'll need to exit all positions by the close of the trading period. There is a requirement to hold at least $25k in your account, anything less will not be accepted in day trading. The required capital to start is $30k.

Future Market: This is another market for day trading. This is where there is an agreement between a seller and a buyer. They agree to sell or buy at an agreed amount at a certain time. Traders make their gains from price fluctuations. This is from the difference computed between what is bought or sold and when the position closes. For this market, you do not need too much capital, a minimum of $3500 and a maximum of $5k is enough to start. The opening hours vary, you need to be careful and ensure that before the trade closes, you are out. You need to consider access to the future market and know of the requirements. Usually, there is a limit on the minimum balance; it is set at $2k.

Forex Market: This is considered a common and accessible market; it trades for 24 hours in a day. They are allowed to start with a minimum capital of around $100, what is recommended is at least $500 to start with. They only deal with one currency and that could be a limitation when it comes to the investment currency. There are also specifications and requirements for this trading platform. As a trader, you need to be careful of the platform that you choose, ensure it is something that fits your preferences and needs. There are demo accounts that can be used to practice and apply the techniques you have learned.

Several factors will affect your choice for a trading market. They include your financial position, the trading technique that, interests and personality. An example is when you want to start trading and your capital is below $25k. You will not be able to trade unless you continue saving up. When your capital is adequate, you can choose any of the trading markets listed above. You need to know that there are other techniques that will work in one market and not the other.

And others will work in a certain time and others not. Always When you have a technique to adopt, choose one market and stick to that. When you are new to day trading, do not flip between markets but maintain a market. You are allowed to shift between trades based on the time you are trading.

All three markets are considered great. You will choose a market based on your preference and interest. However, it is recommended to stick to one market, as you know more about the others.

What is the Expected Monthly Income from Day Trading?

Most people start day trading for different reasons. To some it is just a lifestyle, others business and others love the challenge. The amount of money that day traders make vary, some will lose capital will others will use it to gain more income. How the trader makes their income is influenced by the approach they use and how they manage their risk. The secret to more income is to have a better approach, ensure you are able to manage your risk and work hard.

Most traders will ensure that their risk is small, equivalent to at least 1 % of the capital they use to trade in with. If you are trading with stock worth $3000, ensure that your risk is not more than $30.

The strategy that is used in trading is normally in two categories: the win rate and the profit that is relative to losses. The win rate is described as the number of times a trader wins. And then you need to divide that by a number of trades. For instance, when a strategy wins at 60 trades from 100 trades. That will be at 60%. Having a high win rate is every trader's wish.

But that will not make you profitable if your wins are high, but fewer winners that are not considered profitable. The win rate is expected to be at least 50%. And the reward to risk ratio is a factor that needs to be considered. In any given time, traders will expect to have bigger winners than losers.

Even though day trading is the most common and known, it also requires more capital investment. Let's assume a day trader starts their trading at $40k, and you use a 4:1 ratio. It will give a buying power of $160k (4 x $40k), ensure you have a reward to risk ratio is 1.5:1. This will be in terms of $0.15 as winning trades and $0.10 as losing trades.

This means that the maximum loss you can encounter is $400, which is 1% of $30k. To achieve that, you will need to trade with stocks that have high volatility and volume.

When you choose a good strategy in your trading, you are guaranteed 50% of the profit. So if you have 5 trades daily, and you trade 20 days per month; that is an equivalent of 100 trades monthly. So that will be computed as 50 x $0.15 x 4000 = $30,000. And if the other half was a loss, that will be 50 x $0.10 x 4000 = $20,000. So your gain will be $10,000 and you'll need to deduct commission chargeable and some other fees.

Another example is when the trade cost is $10, the commission will be 100 trades by $10= $1000. Your take-home will be $10,000 - $1000 = $9,000 per month.

Day Trading Hardware Requirements

For you to be a successful day trader there are several tools of the trade that are required. You might already possess some of them. Modern trading is mostly done online, and you will be able to view and access financial markets on the internet and have access to the trades. Therefore, the first equipment you will need is s a laptop or a computer. Then organize how you will be accessing your internet. There will come a time when you will need to call your broker for clarification or update. At that point, you will need a phone to be able to do that.

You will also need access to brokerage, market data in real-time, and chart for trading. All this will enable you to run your trades effectively and smoothly. Day trading needs advance and updated technology. So when getting a laptop or computer ensure you get one with enough memory and a faster processor to avoid any lagging or crashing. Ensure that the machine s faster when it comes to loading information. If you get that your workload is constantly increasing, you can invest in two desktops.

When you have a problem with your internet, the only way you can communicate with your brokers will be via a phone call. Ensure you invest in a phone or landline for trading purposes. As a backup tip, ensure you program your broker's number on your phone. So that when you do not have access to the internet or your computer breaks down, you can access their number.

To succeed in day trading, you will need a broker; a company that helps in the facilitation of the trades. Day traders do a lot of trades on a daily basis, this is why they need a broker who will charge low commissions and the best trading software. There are brokers that are known from banks, but the problem is they charge high commission and do not have solutions tailor-made for day traders. Day traders are advised to always seek services of brokers who are small scale and regulated. Make sure if you choose software that is compatible with the brokers.

You will need to have access to accurate financial information and data. Most of them are derived from price movements and changes from the assets and markets they are trading in. You'll need to request the information that you need from the broker. You will get some brokers giving information free but in return, the commission charges are high. The basic requirements are a quick and reliable laptop or desktop, a working telephone, and software for trading. You should consider getting a smartphone that can use backup internet. Plan for reliable and fast internet connectivity and find a broker who is regulated. One who charges commissions that are low and will provide trading software. The last thing will be to subscribe to market information of your choice based on the trading market.

Day Trading Software Requirements

The trading charts require a processor and a memory component; they should be of high speed and updated. Do not go for software that will make your screen to freeze once you become busy analyzing your trades. Look for internet connectivity that is fast enough to help in loading web pages. If that is not possible, consider your internet slow to do any day trading. When there are price movements and changes, you will be getting thousands of information to your computer. The streaming is done per second. Therefore, that means it is a lot of data per hour for a day.

When it is too slow to do all that, you will have a lag experience. Lag simply means, receiving old data instead of new. You will have data backlog and not able to see any current prices. Take a test from all the internet providers before making a choice.

Always consider having internet access with a backup plan. This will help when there is an internet outage, you will still be able to access the internet. This can be done easily using a smartphone, via hot spot or mobile data. The backup plan should be outsourced from a company different from the internet provider. So that when the internet connectivity goes done, it will not affect the backup plan.

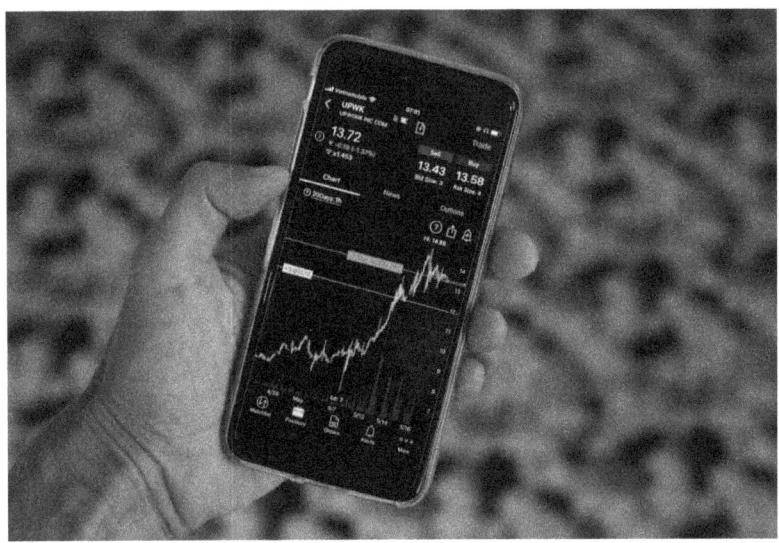

Chapter 3 How Day Trading Works

There was a time when the only people able to trade in financial markets were those working for trading houses, brokerages, and financial institutions. The rise of the internet, however, made things easier for individual traders to get in on the action. Day Trading, in particular, can be a very profitable career, as long as one goes about it in the right way.

However, it can be quite challenging for new traders, especially those who lack a good strategy. Furthermore, even the most experienced day traders hit rough patches occasionally. As stated earlier, Day Trading is the purchase and sale of an asset within a single trading day. It can happen in any marketplace, but it is more common in the stock and forex markets.

Day traders use short-term trading strategies and a high level of leverage to take advantage of small price movements in highly liquid currencies or stocks. Experienced day traders have their finger on events that lead to short-term price movements, such as the news, corporate earnings, economic statistics, and interest rates, which are subject to market psychology and market expectations.

When the market exceeds or fails to meet those expectations, it causes unexpected, significant moves that can benefit attuned day traders. However, venturing into this line of business is not a decision prospective day trader should take lightly. It is possible for day traders to make a comfortable living trading for a few hours each day.

However, for new traders, this kind of success takes time. Think like several months or more than a year.

For most day traders, the first year is quite tough. It is full of numerous wins and losses, which can stretch anyone's nerves to the limit. Therefore, a day trader's first realistic goal should be to hold on to his/her trading capital.

Volatility is the name of the game when it comes to Day Trading. Traders rely on a market or stock's fluctuations to make money. They prefer stocks that bounce around several times a day, but do not care about the reason for those price fluctuations. Day traders will also go for stocks with high liquidity, which will allow them to enter and exit positions without affecting the price of the stock.

Day traders might short sell a stock if its price is decreasing or purchase if it is increasing. Actually, they might trade it several times in a day, purchasing it and short-selling it a number of times, based on the changing market sentiment. In spite of the trading strategy used, their wish is for the stock price to move.

Day Trading, however, is tricky for two main reasons. Firstly, day traders often compete with professionals, and secondly, they tend to have psychological biases that complicate the trading process.

Professional day traders understand the traps and tricks of this form of trading. In addition, they leverage personal connections, trading data subscriptions, and state-of-the-art technology to succeed. However, they still make losing trades. Some of these professionals are high-frequency traders whose aim is to skim pennies off every trade.

The Day Trading field is a crowded playground, which is why professional day traders love the participation of inexperienced traders. Essentially, it helps them make more money. In addition, retail traders tend to hold on to losing trades too long and sell winning trades too early.

Due to the urge to close a profitable trade to make some money, retail investors sort of pick the flowers and water the weeds. In other words, they have a strong aversion to making even a small loss. This tends to tie their hands behind their backs when it comes to purchasing a declining asset. This is due to the fear that it might decline further.

How to Start

People who want to start Day Trading should do several things to put themselves on the right path. Firstly, they need to step back and ask themselves whether this form of trading is really for them. Day Trading is not for the faint of heart. It requires a high level of focus and is not something people should risk their retirement plan to do.

Actually, beginners should consider opening a practice account before committing their hard-earned money. Reputable brokerage firms provide such accounts or stock market simulators to aspiring traders, through which they can make hypothetical trades and see the results.

In addition, aspiring day traders need to have a suitable brokerage account before they begin trading. Some brokers charge high transaction costs, which can erode the gains from winning trades. In addition, good brokers provide research resources that are invaluable to traders.

Aspiring traders who discover that Day Trading is not for them should do what smart investors do, which is engaging in long-term investing in a diversified fund or stock portfolio. They should regularly add more funds to their accounts and let the magic of growth expand their investment portfolio. This may not be as thrilling as Day Trading, but it is better than doing something that will clean out one's savings.

Consider Constraints and Goals

Before investing the time, energy, and effort in learning or creating and then practicing Day Trading, prospective day traders should consider their constraints and goals. For example:

1. Traders need to determine whether they have enough capital to engage in Day Trading. If they lack the capital, they should wait until they have it while they are learning about and practicing different trading strategies.
2. They should understand that achieving consistent gains takes several months to a year, even when practicing several hours each day. For those who practice intermittently, it will take longer to achieve success; therefore, prospective traders should put in the time and effort required to achieve their goals.
3. Once they start trading, they need to commit to trading for at least two hours a day, depending on their commitments.
4. Until their trading profits match or surpass their income, new day traders should not quit their day jobs. They also need to determine the ideal time of day to trade based on their other commitments. In addition, they should ensure that their

trading strategy fits that time of day. Essentially, their trading strategy needs to fit their life.

5. People who want to venture into Day Trading need to determine whether they want to do it with the aim of quitting their regular jobs. To get to the point where they can replace their day jobs by Day Trading, prospective traders need to understand that they will probably need to practice and trade for a year or more, depending on their dedication.

Aspiring day traders should consider the factors above before investing their time and money in learning this line of trade.

Choose a Broker

While new traders are practicing and developing their trading strategies, they should set aside some time to choose a good and reputable broker. It may be the same broker they opened a demo or practice account with, or it may be another broker. Actually, choosing the right broker is one of the most important transactions day traders will make because they will entrust the broker with all of their capital.

Capital Needed to Start Day Trading

How much capital people need to start Day Trading depends on the market they trade, where they trade, and the style of trading they wish to do. There is a legal minimum capital requirement set by the stock market to day trade; however, based on the individual trading style, there is also a recommended minimum.

A day trader needs to have enough capital to have the flexibility to make a variety of trades and withstand a losing streak, which will inevitably happen. Traders also need to determine the amount of money they need, which requires them to address risk management. In addition, they should not risk more than 2% of their account on a single trade.

Capital is the most important component when it comes to Day Trading. By risking only 1% or 2%, even a long losing streak will keep most of the capital intact. For day traders in the United States, the legal minimum balance needed to day trade stocks is $25,000. Traders whose balance drops below this amount cannot engage in Day Trading until they make a deposit that brings their balance above $25,000.

To have a buffer, U.S. day traders should have at least $30,000 in their trading accounts. Stocks usually move in $0.01 increments and trade in lots of 100 shares; therefore, with at least $30,000 in their accounts, day traders will have some flexibility.

Day traders can usually get leverage up to four times the amount of their capital. A trader with $30,000 in his/her account, for example, can trade up to $120,000 worth of stock at any given time. Essentially, the trade price multiplied by the position size can equal more than the trader's account balance.

Day traders can trade fewer volatile stocks, which often require a bigger position size and a smaller stop loss, or stocks that are more volatile, with often require a smaller position size and a larger stop loss. Either way, the total risk on each trade should not be more than 2% of the trading account balance.

Day Trading Basics

Day Trading, on the surface, looks like it should be relatively easy. New day traders think it is all about making several simple trades as the price moves, making a little money, and repeating the whole process tomorrow. However, many dangers lurk in the Day Trading markets; unfortunately, a large percentage of new day traders are not aware of these dangers.

Some of the pitfalls for day traders include:

>Lack of Risk Management

Often new day traders often lack risk management protocols, which is a huge danger. Sometimes, they have an incomplete strategy for managing risk. Nevertheless, they are usually optimistic about their Day Trading abilities, which often causes them to overlook critical risk management steps. Establishing a basic risk management strategy involves the following steps:

- **A Stop Loss**

    Traders should place a stop-loss order in each trade they make to control their risk. People who are starting out on Day Trading should limit their risk on each trade to 1% of their trading account balance. The difference between their entry price and stop-loss price, multiplied by their position size, is their risk.

- **A Daily Limit**

    A daily-stop loss limit can help day traders by limiting how much money they can lose in a day. If day traders suffer multiple losing trades each day, they may still find themselves down more than 10% in a single day. A typical daily-stop loss limit should not be more than about 3% of a trader's account.

Therefore, if the trader loses 3% on any given day, he/she will stop trading for that day. As day traders develop a profitable trading record and gain experience, they can adjust their daily-stop loss limit to be equal to their average profitable trading day. By placing this limit, a typical winning day will recoup the losses from a single day.

Improperly Tested or Untested Trading Strategies

New day traders are often so eager to start trading and make money that they start using untested or improperly tested trading strategies with real money. Others, however, try out their strategies on demo accounts, and if they make a few successful trades, they immediately start trading with real money. Unfortunately, both of these approaches will probably lead to future disappointment.

Successful day traders, on the other hand, test their strategies on many different market conditions through demo trading to learn the pros and cons of their strategies before using them with real money. They demo trade for several months until they are comfortable with their Day Trading strategies before risking real capital with their strategies.

Broker

Choosing the right broker is one of the most important trades for a day trader. Day traders deposit their capital with their brokers, and yet some of them do not take the time to research their broker until a problem arises. Scam brokers, for example, can pop up anywhere.

Traders who find themselves working with such a broker will find it very difficult or even impossible to withdraw their money and any profits. Fortunately, scam brokers usually do not last long thanks to forum complaints. Therefore, a careful online search will reveal any problems with a broker.

A more subtle broker problem is constantly slow quotes. Day traders need direct and uninterrupted access to their broker, who then sends their orders to the appropriate exchange. They should test their broker's trading software because poor software will make it hard to execute trades in a timely manner.

Technology

No one is immune to technology problems. For example, computers can crash, power can go out, the internet can go down, and much more. Day traders cannot get out of a losing trade quickly if technology fails; therefore, they need to place a stop-loss order on every trade.

In addition, they need to program their broker's phone number into their cell phone and landline phone, so they can call them quickly in case of a problem. It is a good idea to have a mobile version of their trading platform on their internet-enabled mobile devices, which might still be operational if their computer crashes.

Order Types

The profits and losses day traders make come from the orders they place. Day traders should know their order types for getting in and out of a market order or a limit order. They also need to know how to set profit targets and stop-loss orders, both for going short and long.

For professional day traders, placing orders is automatic, like switching on a car's turn signal, when about to change lanes. Day traders who do not know their order types will have slow and clumsy trading or even place the wrong order type, which will cost them money.

It is normal for some trading mistakes to happen; however, compounding such mistakes with order-related trading mistakes is a recipe for disaster. Before they start trading, new day traders should know their order types.

Trader Personality and Tendencies

Another hidden danger for a new day trader is his/her personality and tendencies. In the beginning, Day Trading will be confusing, infuriating, and stressful in a way a new trader never thought it could. There are endless possibilities in the markets, and no one cares what anyone else is doing.

This freedom, however, can be unnerving and dangerous for many traders, which is why many of them lose money. When people are starting out, they do not know how they will react under different stresses and pressures. Some choose to quit, others to overtrade, and others still are too afraid to trade.

Many distractions keep people from staying focused and trading effectively. Traders should take a critical look at their personality to identify their shortcomings and then work to develop these six important Day Trading traits.

Volume, Price, Technical Indicators

Day traders can use technical indicators to provide trading signals and assess the current trade. Keltner Channels, a popular technical indicator, use average prices and volatility to plot lower, middle, and upper lines. These three lines move with the price to create the appearance of a channel.

Chester Keltner introduced these channels in the 1960s, but Linda Bradford Raschke updated them in the 1980s. Today, traders use the later version of the indicator, which is a combination of two different indicators, which are the average true range and the exponential moving average.

Created by J. Welles Wilder Jr. and introduced in 1978, the average true range is a measure of volatility. The moving average, on the other hand, is the average price for specific periods, with the exponential variation giving more weight to recent prices and less weight to less recent prices.

Keltner Channels are useful to day traders because they make trends more visible. When a certain asset or stock is trending higher, its price will frequently come close, touch, or even move past the upper band. In addition, the price will stay above the lower band and middle band, although It might occasionally barely dip below the middle band.

When an asset or stock is trending lower, on the other hand, its price will regularly come close to the lower band or reach it; however, sometimes it will move past the lower band. The price will stay below the upper band and often below the middle band.

Day traders should set up their indicators so that these guidelines hold true, at least most of the time. If the price of a stock is moving constantly higher but not reaching the upper band, the channel may be too wide, and the trader will need to decrease the multiplier. However, an asset that is trending higher but constantly touching the lower band shows that the channel is too tight, requiring an increase of the multiplier.

For their indicator to help them analyze the market, day traders need to adjust it correctly. If they fail to do this, then the guidelines for trading will not hold true, and the indicator will not serve its intended purpose.

Once they set up the indicator correctly, day traders should purchase during an uptrend when the price of the asset pulls back to the middle band.

They should place a target price somewhere near the upper band and a stop-loss order halfway between the lower and middle bands. On the other hand, if the price of the asset is hitting the stop-loss too often, and the trader has already made the necessary adjustments, he/she should move the stop-loss a bit closer to the lower band.

This will give the trade more wiggle room and reduce the number of losing trades the trader has. During a downtrend, when the price of the asset rallies to the middle band, day traders should short sell, which means selling the asset with the hope of buying it back at a lower price.

It is also important to place a target near the lower band and a stop-loss order about halfway between the upper and middle bands. This trading strategy leverages the trending tendency and provides trades with a 0.5 risk to reward ratio. This is because the stop-loss point is approximately half the length of that of the target price.

However, traders should not trade all pullbacks to the middle line. If a trend is not present, this strategy will not work effectively. Sometimes, the price of the asset moves back and forth between hitting the lower and upper bands. This method will not be effective in such situations.

Therefore, day traders should ensure the market's pattern is following the trending guidelines. If it is not doing so, they should use a different strategy. The Keltner Channel strategy tries to capture big moves that may evade the trend-pullback strategy. Day traders should use it near the opening of a major market when big movements happen.

The typical trading strategy is to purchase when the price breaks the upper band or sell short when it drops below the lower band within the first 30 minutes of the market opening. The middle band, however, acts as the exit point. This type of trade does not have a profit target. Traders simply exit the trade whenever the price touches the middle band, whether the trade is a winner or a loser.

Introduction to Investing in Stocks, Options, and Forex

When most people hear the term Day Trading, they think of the stock market. However, day traders also participate in the forex and futures markets. Some day traders, for example, trade options, but most traders who do so are more likely swing traders who can hold positions for weeks or days, but not fractions of a trading day.

People who want to be successful day traders should initially focus on a single market, such as the stock market. Once they master that market, they can try to learn and practice trading other markets if they choose.

Day Trading Stocks

Those who are thinking of Day Trading stocks should consider a few important factors. These are:

1. Under U.S. law, the minimum starting capital for Day Trading stocks is $25,000. However, they need to add a buffer above this amount and start with a capital of at least $30,000.
2. Market hours for Day Trading are from 9:30 am to 4 pm Eastern time. However, traders can still place trades one hour before the market opens.
3. The ideal periods to day trade stocks are from 8.30 to 10.30 am and 3 to 4 pm ET, when volatility and volume are high.
4. Day traders can trade a wide variety of stocks. They can also trade the same stock or a small number of stocks every day, or find new stocks to trade each week or even each day.

Based on these factors, prospective day traders will determine whether the stock market is a good option for their Day Trading. If they do not have the initial capital required, for example, they should consider the futures or forex markets, which require less starting capital.

In addition, if they cannot trade during the most ideal trading hours, their efforts will not produce as much fruit as they would have if they were available during those optimal hours.

Day Trading Futures

Some of the important things to consider about Day Trading futures include

1. There is no legal minimum starting capital required to begin Day Trading futures. Experts, however, recommend starting with $2,500 to $7,000 if one is trading the popular futures contract. The more money one starts with, the more flexible one will be when it comes to making trading decisions.
2. The official market hours for trading the S&P 500 and E-mini are from 9.30 am to 4 pm ET.
3. The optimal time to day trade ES futures is from 6.30 to 1030am and 3 to 4p Eastern time.
4. Commodities futures contracts also provide reliable Day Trading opportunities.
5. Most day traders who deal with futures often focus on one futures contract; however, others choose futures contracts seeing significant volume or movements on a particular day.

Day Trading Forex

Things to know about Day Trading forex include:
1. The minimum starting capital required is $500; however, experts recommend starting with $5,000 if one wants a decent monthly income stream.
2. Forex trades 24 hours a day; however, certain times are ideal for Day Trading than others.
3. Day traders can trade any different currency pairs, but beginners should stick to the

GBP/USD or EUR/USD. These two currency pairs offer more than enough price movement and volume to generate a good income.

Based on these three factors, day traders will likely determine whether this market is appropriate for them to day trade. Those with limited capital should consider Day Trading the forex market, which is more flexible than other markets.

Social Trading

Social trading works somewhat like a social network. However, there is a big difference, which is that instead of sharing pet photos, dinner photos, and selfies, people use social trading networks to share trading ideas. Essentially, traders use this platform to interact, brainstorm and watch the trading results of other professionals in real-time.

Some of the benefits of social trading include:

1. Access to reliable and helpful trading information
2. Ability to earn while learning
3. Quick understanding of the trading market
4. Ability to build a trading community of investors

Since social trading networks cater for both professionals and beginners, they create a reliable trading community, which allows day traders and other types of market traders to generate an income as they learn.

The allure of this form of financial trading is undeniable. It is more exciting for a trader to earn a living working from the comfort of his/her home, rather than working a regular 9 am to 5 pm gig. However, inexperienced or careless day traders can destroy their portfolios within a few days.

Chapter 4 How to Reduce Your Risks When Day Trading

Like any kind of investment, day trading does come with some risks. And day trading is often considered an even riskier option compared to some of the other investments you can choose. As a beginner, these risks may seem overwhelming and you may worry that this is not the right investment vehicle for you. There are a few things that you can do to help limit your risks as much as possible, including the following.

Only Trade What You Can Afford to Lose

When you enter a trade, make sure that you only trade the amount of money that you are comfortable with losing. There is a chance, especially when you are a beginner, when you may pick a bad trade and can lose money in the process. If you bet too much money on this, if you used leverage, or you made false assumptions about how the market would go, you could end up in big financial straights in the end.

Before you enter into day trading, consider setting aside a savings account. Take some time to put some money in savings before you get started, and add to it as you make profits. Only use the money in this account when you are trading. That way, when it is gone, you stop. And you didn't put your regular income or regular savings in jeopardy in the process.

Set up Your Stop Loss Points

Before you go into a trade, it is important to set up your entry and exit points. These are going to help maximize your profits like minimizing the potential losses that you could have. You need to have an idea of what price point the stock needs to be at for you to enter the trade. And then you need to have stop points for both ends of the spectrum for your profits and your losses.

Setting a stop point for losses can ensure that you only lose so much money. There are times when the market will plummet very quickly. If you don't have this in place, the market could slip down and you could lose a ton of money in a short amount of time. This stop point tells the brokerage account when you want to leave the market so you can limit your losses as much as possible.

You also want an exit strategy when it comes to how much money you want to make as profits. While this may seem silly as a trader, you want to earn as much as possible. But since there is a lot of variability in the market during the day, the market can often reach a high point and turn, without going back up again. Setting this point helps you to earn as much profit as possible without you staying in the market too long.

Work with a Broker

As a beginner, it is often best to work with a broker if you can. This can open up a lot of different resources to you that can make day trading more profitable. The right broker can be someone you bounce ideas off, someone you can ask questions to, and someone who can give you advice on the best stocks to follow for your trading.

You can also pick your broker based on the fees that they charge. Each broker is going to be a little different. Some charge a flat rate based on how many trades that you want to do. If you plan to do a lot of trades here, which is common for day trading, you may not want to go with that option. If you are spending $4 for every trade you do, this is going to add up quickly when you do a bunch of trades through that broker.

Another option is to work on commission with the broker. This way, you only pay a percentage of the profits that you earn on the trades you do. This can be helpful as long as you make sure that you earn enough on the trades that you can cover the commissions and fees, and still have some money left over for profits in your pockets.

Stick with the Strategy You Chose Through the Whole Trade

After you take a look through some of the strategies we will discuss in this guidebook, you should have an idea of which one will work the best for you. Make sure to pick one that makes sense for you, has the number of risks that you are willing to take, and that works with your trading profile.

Once you pick a trading strategy, you need to stick with it, at least during that trade. Many beginner traders end up failing and losing a lot of money because they enter a trade using one strategy and then they move into a second strategy at some point during the same trade. Sometimes this is because they see they will lose money and they want to make changes to prevent this. Other times, they do it simply because they didn't fully understand the strategy they chose. Either way, it can result in disaster for that trade.

If you start with a trading strategy and find that it is not the right one for you, then finish of the trade and try a new strategy on the next trade. You may lose some money on that first trade, but you will limit the loss quite a bit compared to switching strategies right in the middle.

Take a Break from Trading When You Need It

Sometimes, you are going to run into a trade that is bad. You may not have put in the right exit points, or you may have picked the wrong strategy and it didn't work out well for you. This can be hard especially if you are a new trader and it is one of your first trades.

After this bad trade happens, or if you seem to be making bad trade after bad trade, it is time to take a break. At this point, if you stay in the market, you will let your emotions take over and you will continue to make bad trading decisions. You may want to make a lot of income from day trading but sticking in the market when your emotions are involved, and after having a bad time with trading, it's just going to make things worse.

The break doesn't have to be a long time. Even a few days to a week can be enough to help you refocus and come back with a fresh look on your trading. It can be hard to take a break. You want to try a new idea, you want to make the money you lost back, and you don't want to give up. But taking a break doesn't mean you have given up. It simply means that you are giving yourself time to think critically the next time you trade.

Learn How to Keep the Emotions out of the Game

With any type of trading, if you let your emotions get into the game, then you have lost. This can be hard for many people especially if they put more money than they can afford to lose into a trade. With day trading, emotions can be an even bigger issue because the market changes so rapidly and you have to get in and out as quickly as possible.

When you allow your emotions to start coming into play, you are basically losing all of your control to make smart decisions. No one can make good decisions when the emotions are involved, and with all the stress and issues that can come with day trading, those emotions will hit some extremes pretty quickly. This is why it is so important to go through and pick out a winning strategy and to stick with it. This will keep the emotions at bay and you can make the decisions ahead of time before the emotions of being in the market come into play.

If you are in a trade and find that your emotions are starting to get in your way, it is time to make some changes. In some cases, you will be able to stick with your stop points and be safe for the rest of the trade. But if you have already gone through and left the stop points behind, it is time to leave the trade, no matter where it is going, and restart. You may even need to take a little time off from day trading, especially after a trade that did not do that well, so that you can regroup and get back to the critical thinking.

Don't Follow the Trends

If you are jumping onto a stock that everyone else is as well, then you are already getting to the party too late. As soon as others start purchasing or selling a stock, the price has already changed and you are too late. This could result in you paying too much for a stock, or selling it for too little because you got caught up in the trend.

As a day trader, it is your job to learn to spot trends before they happen. If you read the news, look through the right charts, and use your knowledge about the market, you can easily jump onto a stock before the trend happens. When you do this successfully, you would then purchase the stock while the price is lower, before others catch on. Then, when others catch onto the value of that stock, the price will go up where you can sell it for a higher price than you originally purchased it.

You can use this idea when selling the stock as well. If you know that a stock has a price ceiling of $55 and the stock is currently at $54.99, or even above $55, then it is time to sell. In the short trading period that you get with day trading, you won't really see the price of a stock go much above its ceiling price ever. You can see this trend and sell the stock at that high point before the market drags it back down and you lose money.

Day traders do not jump onto a trend because they know it means that they are too late for the party on that particular security. They learn how to read the trends through their own research and can accurately predict the best times to purchase and sell the stock to make the most profit.

Chapter 5 Finding and Picking Stocks and Trading Strategies

In this chapter, we get down to the actual work of day trading. We will cover how to read the market by discussing the types of charts used by day traders and how to read them. We'll also discuss strategies for picking stocks and what to look for in stocks for day trading. Finally, we'll cover the most common trading strategies and how to execute them.

Reading the Market
We've already discussed charts and charting software in passing. Now you need to know how to read the charts your software or your broker provide to you. There's three basic types of charts you're likely to look at when you're reading the market: line charts, bar charts, and "candlestick" charts.

Line Charts: line charts are the simplest type of chart you are likely to use while day trading. A line chart tracks only the closing prices for your selected time interval and will display as a jagged line from left to right. This is the type of chart you are probably most familiar with outside of the world of trading, and it provides the least information of the common chart types. However, many traders still use line charts for certain trading strategies. Since a line chart is less cluttered, it can make inflection points in the market more obvious to the eye and can be useful for drawing lines to identify ranges or trends.

Bar Charts: bar charts, also known as OHLC bar charts or HLC bar charts, include information on the open (O), high (H), low (L), and close (C) price of an asset over a given time interval. The chart will appear as a series of horizontal lines following the same sort of jagged line you would see in a simple line chart, with a small line jutting from each side at the open and close. There's a lot of information in these charts, so it may take quite a bit of practice to get used to reading them.

Open: the open on a bar chart is the opening price for the time interval and shows on the chart as a small line sticking out of the left side of the bar.

High: the high price during the interval is indicated by the top of the bar.

Low: the low price for the interval is indicated by the bottom the bar.

Close: the closing price for the interval shows as a small line sticking out of the right side of the bar.

Direction: you can tell the direction of the market during the interval by comparing the positions of the opening and closing prices for the interval. If the open is higher, the market is moving down. If the close is higher, the market is moving up.

Candlestick Charts: candlestick charts contain the same information as bar charts but presented in a different fashion that many traders find easier to read. At a glance, the candlestick chart will look similar to a bar chart, but more colorful. Each time interval will display as a colored bar (the "body" of the candle), red or green, with a line (the "tail") extending some distance above and below the body of the candlestick.   Here's how the information is represented:

High: the high price for the interval is indicated by the top of the tail above the candle.

Low: the low price for the interval is indicated by the bottom of the tail below the candle.

Open: the opening price for the interval is indicated by the bottom of the body of the candle.

Close: the closing price for the interval is indicated by the top of the body of the candle.

Direction: the direction of the market is indicated by the color of the body of the candle - red if the market is moving down, green if the market is moving up.

Chart Parameters: when generating a chart, you will need to pick the interval that will be represented by each point in your chart. The interval could be based on time, "tick", volume, or price range.

A chart generated by time is the most intuitive, and will generate a new bar, candle, or point based purely on the passage of time - even if very few or even no transactions occurred during the interval. This is the most useful way to generate a chart if you are looking to see how a stock or asset performs in real time.

A chart generated by "tick" uses an interval based on a set number of transactions. For example, if you generate a 200-tick chart, the graph will produce a new point every time 200 transactions occur. This can be useful for comparing trends between stocks with different levels of activity.

A chart generated by volume will generate intervals based on a set number of shares exchanged.

You will also need to define the scope of the chart. Depending on your strategy, you may want to look at a chart for the entire trading day, or a chart that covers the last minute.

Trend lines: most trading software allows you to draw your own trend lines on charts or will have options for displaying trends such as the simple moving average automatically.

While you can get a lot of information just from your chart without trends, most of the decisions you will make in executing your trading strategy will come from looking at trend lines.

Picking Stocks

Now that you know the basics of reading the market and looking for trends, you're ready to learn about how to pick stocks for day trading. The type of stock you will be looking for depends on a lot of different factors, and you may be looking for different types of stocks to fit different trading plans and different trading strategies. We'll cover this topic in three parts: (1) things you should look for every stock you plan to trade while day trading; (2) some broad-based picking strategies for different trading plans; and (3) the distinct characteristics of stocks that are suitable for specific day-trading strategies.

(1) Things to Look for in Every Stock You Plan to Day-Trade: while what you're looking for will be different depending on what strategy you're planning to execute, there are a couple things you should always be looking for when picking stocks.

The first is volume: you should always look for stocks that have a high level of daily activity. If you buy into a stock with insufficient volume, you can easily find yourself stuck - the asset price won't move enough for you to take profit and you'll lose out on other trading opportunities until you can move out of your position. Typically, you should be looking for a stock that has an average daily volume of at least 1 million shares.

The second is volatility: you are looking for stocks that will move enough in a typical day for you to make a profitable trade. Set your stock filter to look for stocks with an average day range above 5% over the last 50 days. It's important to remember that volatility is not necessarily the massive up or down swings that can follow breaking news - it can also be the regular and constant turbulence that exists in all exchange traded markets.

(2) Broad Strategies for Picking Stocks: you need a broad strategy for picking stocks beyond simply looking for the desirable characteristics discussed in this chapter. How you go about researching and picking stocks depends on how much time you have available to trade and how much research you are willing to do.

If you don't have much time to trade, you may wish to specialize. That is, pick one or two stocks, or a single industry sector (such as healthcare), and only trade in those stocks or that sector. This lets you become an expert in those stocks: you know how they usually behave, where the opportunities will be, and what news events will cause swings and how. This means that you don't have to spend a lot of time sifting through charts or learning the basic facts about new companies - you already know what's likely to happen. A popular way to execute this strategy is to target an ETF, such as the S&P 500 SPDR (Ticker symbol SPY). Specializing like this works well with a range-trading or "trade the news" strategy.

If you're looking for a little bit more flexibility, you might choose to pick a set of stocks to trade each week. Each weekend, run a stock screener to identify a set of 2-4 stocks that have good volume and volatility for your trading strategy. After you have picked your stocks for the week, trade those stocks, and only those stocks following your trading plan. If you've achieved good results, you could choose to remain on the same set of securities for multiple weeks in a row. This strategy is suitable for a trader who has a little more time to dedicate to day trading but isn't prepared to trade full time.

If you're looking to pursue a full-time career as a day trader, you might choose to run a stock screener every single day. This is probably what you want to be doing if you are pursuing a momentum strategy - as you will be trying to identify stocks that have a strong current trend, instead of trying to capitalize on small movements caused by underlying volatility. Obviously, this strategy is very time consuming, and may require additional tools to execute effectively.

(3) Distinct Characteristics Suitable for Specific Strategies: depending on your strategy, you may be looking for more specific factors than simple volume and volatility.

If you are looking to trade on a momentum strategy, you should look at stocks that are close to 52-week highs and lows. Stocks that have reached extreme price points are more likely to be volatile or to be close to an inflection point that can afford a big trading opportunity.

You may also want to keep an eye out for stocks that have a gap against the trend. That is, if you look at your chart of the stock's current price, you'll see that there is a space (a "gap") between the price and the trend-line. This is a good way to identify stocks that have been overbought or oversold, or where the stock price has failed to adjust to breaking news. The moment when the gap closes is the moment when you have an opportunity to make a profitable trade.

Finally, you can set up a scanner to identify specific situations where there is an opportunity to trade based on a specific pattern in the market. One example of this is a method commonly referred to as "sniper" trading, which was originally implemented on the FOREX market.

An Overview of Common Day Trading Strategies
By sticking to your strategy, you maintain a stable level of risk and can reliably make your expected earnings goals. Here's a quick overview of some of the most common strategies for setting entry points and price targets.

Scalping: Scalping is one of the most common strategies for day trading, and with good reason - it's incredibly simple. When you are using a scalping strategy, your target price is essentially whatever price is high enough to make your trade profitable over commission. It's as easy as that: pick your asset, pick your entry point, and sell as soon as it's profitable for you. As always, make sure you have set a stop-loss if you have misjudged the buy and bought into a downward trend.

Fading: In many ways, a fading strategy is the opposite of scalping. When you are scalping, you are looking to profit on an upward trend - while fading, you are looking to profit on a downward trend. Scalping is absurdly simple, while fading requires a fairly high degree of sophistication to be really successful. Here's a basic overview: a trader who is using a fade strategy looks for a stock that has risen very quickly. Having identified a potential trade, the trader shorts the stock. The price target is a predicted low inflection point where buyers begin to step in after profit-takers exit.

This probably seems counter intuitive to a trader starting out, since it requires you to bet a stock that has been on an upward tear is going to fall in the same day. So, here's a quick explanation of the reasoning behind a fade strategy: (1) a stock that has risen very quickly is probably overbought - the price has been driven higher than demand can justify; (2) early buyers are probably ready to start profit taking - you can expect that traders who bought into the trend early are ready to unload stock, dropping the price; and (3) existing buyers may be scared out of purchasing at the current, inflated price - creating an opportunity to short the stock at a point below the peak, but above where the upward trend started.

Fading is a risky strategy, since it requires you to identify a very specific situation - but, as always, higher risk can yield higher rewards than a low-risk strategy like scalping. You may wish to consider a fading strategy after you have gotten comfortable reading the market if you can afford the additional risk.

Momentum Trading: generally speaking, momentum trading is a simple sounding strategy that can get complicated fast. When you are using a momentum strategy, you are looking to identify an existing market trend that you expect to continue for some time. While trading using a momentum strategy, use your tools to look for a consistent upward or downward trend - but not, for example, the sort of extreme upward trend you would be looking for under a pure fading strategy.

If you have identified an upward trend, under a momentum strategy, you buy in while the stock is rising, much like under a scalping strategy. Unlike scalping, however, you aren't looking to sell at the minimum point where you can make a profit. Instead, you're aiming to set your price target at the inflection point where the price will begin to fall. This can be done either by monitoring the current prices and charts and selling as soon as you observe momentum shifting, or by setting a price target at a point where you are making a reasonable profit.

If you have identified a downward trend, you can also short under a momentum strategy. Like a normal fade strategy, you are looking to set your price target at a low inflection point where seller volume will decrease, and buyers will begin to re-enter the asset.

Trading the News: trading the news is a specific form of momentum trading that tries to identify an upward or downward trend before it even begins. If you are looking to execute on this strategy, you will be monitoring news headlines for events that will have an effect on a specific stock, a specific business sector, or even the market as a whole. Your goal is to correctly identify a market trend at the point it begins based on that news. This can allow you to increase your profit margin compared to a normal momentum strategy where you are simply buying into an existing trend.

There are regularly occurring, scheduled events that can be helpful to watch out for when trying to execute a news-based strategy. One example would be a publicly traded corporation's quarterly earnings calls. By listening in on an investor earning call, you can try to ascertain whether a company has done better or worse than it was expected to by market analysts. Depending on earnings performance, this can help you identify an upward or downward trend and set your positions early. Another example would be Federal Reserve meetings - the chairman's comments on the market or interest rates can put the entire market into an upward or downward trend on a dime.

Of course, everyone who is trading - especially the large, institutional investors - keeps an eye on scheduled events like this. This means it's hard to get a jump on the news - and big investors will get trades to go through faster than yours ever can. The real opportunities for profit come from unexpected events, or events whose market consequences aren't immediately obvious. If you think you're smarter than the market, maybe you can identify a rise or fall before it happens by taking in all the news you can find. However, betting on uncertain news or nascent trends is risky, and keep that in mind before you take action on an unusual news item.

Range Trading / Daily Pivots: All of the strategies we've discussed so far are somewhat dependent on market conditions where you can discern clear up or down trends in a given asset. However, you can still make money in a very stable market with the strategy of range trading, by taking advantage of the natural, low level volatility that exists in the market - the "noise" or "turbulence" that is always present. Here's a three-step summary of how to execute a range-based strategy:

(1) Identify the daily range of an asset. Your goal in a range strategy is to identify the daily high and low points of the target asset that are caused by natural

market volatility, identifying the points of support and resistance that cause price inflection. The easiest way to do this is to pull up a longer-term chart, such as the 4-hour simple moving average, and draw a horizontal line across matching peaks and troughs. The peaks should exist at the point of resistance, where the asset is overbought and demand cannot sustain a higher price. The troughs should exist at points of support - where the asset is under bought and the supply is insufficient to meet demand at a lower price.

(2) Time your entry so you are buying into the asset when it is priced in the support zone. This is what you expect to be the market low for the day.

(3) Manage your risk. Even though this strategy is looking to take advantage of the predictable volatility in a stable market, you still need to appropriately manage your risk by setting a stop-loss in case you have misjudged the low and set your price target at the expected zone of resistance.

Chapter 6 Day Trading Tools

For you to carry out day trading successfully there are several tools that you need. Some of these tools are freely available, while others must be purchased. Modern trading is not like the traditional version. This means that you need to get online to access day trading opportunities.

Therefore, the number one tool you need is a laptop or computer with an internet connection. The computer you use must have enough memory for it to process your requests fast enough. If your computer keeps crashing or stalling all the time, you will miss out on some lucrative opportunities. There are trading platforms that need a lot of memory to work, and you must always put this into consideration.

Your internet connection must also be fast enough. This will ensure that your trading platform loads in real-time. Ensure that you get an internet speed that processes data instantaneously to avoid experiencing any data lag. Due to some outages that occur with most internet providers, you may also need to invest in a backup internet device such as a smartphone hotspot or modem. Other essential tools and services that you need include:

Brokerage

To succeed in day trading, you need the services of a brokerage firm. The work of the firm is to conduct your trades. Some brokers are experienced in day trading than others. You must ensure that you get the right day trading broker who can help you make more profit from your transactions. Since day trading entails several trades per day, you need a broker that offers lower commission rates. You also need one that provides the best software for your transactions. If you prefer using specific trading software for your deals, then look for a broker that allows you to use this software.

Real-time Market Information

Market news and data are essential when it comes to day trading. They provide you with the latest updates on current and anticipated price changes on the market. This information allows you to customize your strategies accordingly. Professional day traders always spend a lot of money seeking this kind of information on news platforms, in online forums or through any other reliable channels.

Financial data is often generated from price movements of specific stocks and commodities. Most brokers have this information. However, you will need to specify the kind of data you need for your trades. The type of data to get depends on the type of stocks you wish to trade.

Monitors

Most computers have a capability that enables them to connect to more than one monitor. Due to the nature of the day trading business, you need to track market trends, study indicators, follow financial news items, and monitor price performance at the same time. For this to be possible, you need to have more than one processor so that the above tasks can run concurrently.

Classes

Although you can engage in day trading without attending any school, you must get trained on some of the strategies you need to succeed in the business. For instance, you may decide to enroll for an online course to acquire the necessary knowledge in the business. You may have all the essential tools in your possession, but if you do not have the right experience, all your efforts may go to waste.

Day Trading Pricing Charts

Charts are used by traders to monitor price changes. These changes determine when to enter or exit a trading position. There are several charts used in day trading. Although these charts differ in terms of functionality and layout, they typically offer the same information to day traders.

Some of the most common day trading charts includes:

1. Line charts 2.
Bar charts
3. Candlestick charts

For each of the above charts, you must understand how they work as well as the advantages/disadvantages involved.

Line Charts
These are very popular in all kinds of stock trading. They do not give the opening price, just the closing price. You are expected to specify the trading period for the chart to display the closing price for that period. The chart creates a line that connects closing prices for different periods using a line.

Most day traders use this chart to establish how the price of a security has performed over different periods. However, you cannot rely on this chart as the only information provider when it comes to making some critical trading decisions. This is because the chart only gives you the closing price. This means that you may not be able to establish other vital factors that have contributed to the current changes in the price.

Bar Charts

These are lines used to indicate price ranges for a particular stock over time. Bar charts comprise vertical and horizontal lines. The horizontal lines often represent the opening and closing costs. When the closing price is higher than the opening price, the horizontal line is always black. When the opening price is higher, the line becomes red.

Bar charts offer more information than line charts. They indicate opening prices, highest and lowest prices as well as the closing prices. They are always easy to read and interpret. Each bar represents rice information. The vertical lines indicate the highest and lowest prices attained by a particular stock. The opening price of a stock is always shown using a small horizontal line on the left of each vertical line. The closing price is a small horizontal line on the right.

Interpreting bar charts is not as easy as interpreting line charts. When the vertical lines are long, it shows that there is a significant difference between the highest price attained by a security and the lowest price. Large vertical lines, therefore, indicate that the commodity is highly volatile while small lines indicate slight price changes. When the closing price is far much higher than the opening price, it means that the buyers were more during the stated period. This indicates likelihood for more purchases in the future. If the closing price is slightly higher than the purchase price, then very little purchasing took place during the period. Bar chart information is always differentiated using color codes. You must, therefore, understand what each color means as this will help you to know whether the price is going up or down.

Advantages of bar charts
- They display a lot of data in a visual format
- They summarize large amounts of data
- They help you to estimate important price information in advance
- They indicate each data category as a different color
- Exhibit high accuracy
- Easy to understand

Disadvantages

- They need adequate interpretation
- Wrong interpretation can lead to false information
- Do not explain changes in the price patterns

Tick charts

Tick charts are not common in day trading. However, some traders use these charts for various purposes. Each bar on the chart represents numerous transactions. For instance, a 415 chart generates a bar for a group of 415 trade positions. One great advantage of tick charts is that they enable traders to enter and exit multiple positions quickly. This is what makes the charts ideal for day traders who transact volumes of stock each day.

These charts work by completing several trades before displaying a new bar. Unlike other charts, these charts work depending on the activity of each transaction, not on time. You can use them if you need to make faster decisions in your trade. Another advantage of tick chart is that you can customize each chart to suit your trading needs. You can apply the chart on diverse transaction sizes. The larger the size, the higher the potential of making a profit from the trade.

When used in day trading, tick hart works alongside the following three indicators:

- *RSI indicators* - these are used when trading highly volatile securities. They help you establish when a particular security is oversold or overbought since these are the periods when stock prices change significantly.
- *Momentum* - day traders use this together with tick charts to show how active the stock price is and whether the activity is genuine or fake. If the price rises significantly, yet the momentum is the same, this indicates a warning sign. Stocks with positive momentum are ideal for long trades. You should avoid these if you wish to close your positions within a day.
- *Volume indicators* - these are used to confirm the correct entry and exit points for each trade. Large trading positions are often indicated using larger volume bars while low positions with little volatility are displayed using small volume bars.

Candlestick Charts
Candlestick charts are used on almost every trading platform. These charts carry a lot of information about the stock market and stock prices. They help you to get information about the opening, closing, highest, and lowest stock prices on the market. The opening price is always indicated as the first bar on the left of the chart, and the closing price is on the far right of the chart. Besides these prices, the candlestick chart also contains the body and wick. These are the

features that differentiate the candlestick for other day trading charts.

One great advantage of candlestick charts entails the use of different visual aspects when indicating the closing, opening, highest, and lowest stock prices. These charts compute stock prices across different time frames. Each chart consists of three segments:

- The upper shadow
- The body
- The lower shadow

The body of the chart is often red or green in color. Each candlestick is an illustration of time. The data in the candlestick represents the number of trades completed within the specified time. For instance, a 10-minute candlestick indicates 10 minutes of trading. Each candlestick has four points, and each point represents a price. The high point represents the highest stock price while low stands for the lowest price of a stock. When the closing price is lower than the opening price, the body of the candlestick will be red in color. When the closing price is higher, the body will be colored green.

There are several types of candlesticks that you can use in day trading. One is the Heikin-Ashi chart that helps you to filter any unwanted information from the chart data, ending up with a more accurate indication of the market trend. Novice day traders commonly use this chart because of how clear it displays information.

The Renko chart only displays the changes in time. It does not give you any volume or time information. When the price exceeds the highest or lowest points reached before, the chart displays it as a new brick.

The brick is white when the price is going up and black when the price is declining.

Lastly, the Kagi chart is used when you want to follow the direction of the market quickly. When the price goes higher than previous prices, the chart displays a thick line. When the price starts to decline, the line reduces in thickness.

Each of the above charts works using a time frame which is represented using the X-axis. This time frame always indicates the volume of information represented by the chart. Time frames can be in the form of standard time or in the form of the number of trades completed within a specified period as well as the price range.

Charting Software

Each of the above charts is created and viewed using specific software. This can be found in a brokerage firm, although you may also purchase this online depending on the type you want to use.

The software helps you identify the right opportunities by indicating when and how you should start and close positions. They always display the necessary patterns required to estimate future changes in stock prices. Using stock patterns, you can also establish continuations as well as reversals in the stock prices.

Chart software is available in many forms. You may find those that are in the form of mobile apps or others that are web-based. Getting the right software enables you to generate correct charts. This explains why you also need to incorporate technical analysis in your trades.

Most day trading chart tools are available free of charge. Some have a forum where you can learn from experienced traders as you use them. They also come with demo accounts that enable you to master day trading techniques before investing your capital in the business.

How to Choose Day Trading Charts

Before selecting any charts for your day trading engagements, you must consider a number of factors. These include:

1. *Responsiveness* - This refers to how quickly the chart can display information about the changing market features. This is the first and most important factor you should always check out for. Any delay in the way a chart displays data means that you will not receive vital information in real-time. You may end up acting on old information to make your decisions, and this can lead to significant losses on your part. Most charts may freeze or crash when your computer runs out of memory. This explains why you need a fast processing machine for your day trading business. You want to ensure that the whole process remains as efficient as possible. When testing a chart for responsiveness, wait for a time when the stock market is busy. For instance, you may try using the chart during a critical financial announcement or news session. If the chart freezes at this point, then you will understand that it is not the best for your needs.

2. *Cost* - every trader wants to invest in tools that cost less to acquire and maintain. Years back, trading charts used to cost a fortune. This limited the number of traders that could engage in day trading. For instance, traders could buy market data from stock exchanges, and this would also cost a lot of money. Nowadays, all information required for any kind of trading is cheaply available. This means that charts should also not cost as much. There are several alternatives available on the market today for you to select from. As you do this, always have the price in mind.

3. *Stability* - a good chart is one that remains online and up to date all the time. For you to succeed as a day trader, you must remain on the market most of the time. If your chart keeps disconnecting from the stock market or fails to display market information on time, then it will make you incur more losses. You must, therefore, ensure that you remain connected to the market continuously. If you experience instability as a result of the chart software you are using, feel free to change it. If the instability is resulting from a poor internet connection, you may need to replace it too.

4. *Type of Indicators* - if you have ever engaged in day trading before then you understand the importance of technical indicators. Having the right indicators plays a vital role in ensuring you predict the right price movements in the future. Indicators

help you to save a lot of capital. They prevent you from making important investment and financial mistakes that may lead to losing your capital. You may create your own indicators, or you may get charting software that has in-built indicators. If you decide to use your own indicators, you must ensure that the charting tools you purchase can be used together with these indicators. If not, you might need to stick to those indicators supplied together with your charting software.

5. *Compatibility with your computer* - before settling for any charts, check whether it will work well with your current computer resources. This is an important factor as it will determine whether you will continue to use your old machine, or if you will have to purchase a new one. Some charts require a lot of RAM space. If your computer does not have this capability, you will end up adding more RAM. This translates to more yet unnecessary costs. When you are looking around for a chart, ensure that you check how much resources the charts will need. Most chart packages have an indication of the minimum requirements you need for the charts to work well. If this is not clearly stated, make sure you ask your provider about it so that you do not make a blind purchase.

6. *User-friendly* - a good chart should be easy to use, read, and interpret. A complicated chart will only make your trading days

difficult. Get a chart that simplifies the work of interpreting data. Take your time and research on the available options then choose the best in terms of simplicity and layout. You may consider getting recommendations from other traders, although this does not necessarily mean that the said chart will work for you. Having a complicated chart can make you lose your confidence. You must, therefore, avoid it if you want to have a smooth trading experience

7. *End-user support* - once in a while, your chart software may experience a problem that needs technical assistance. As you continue using the software, questions may arise that need the attention of an expert. If the provider is not available to assist or respond to your questions, you may get stuck using the package. Before making a purchase, ensure that you find out the kind of technical support you will receive and how this will be done. Is it via live chat, email, or telephone contact? You can also go through some customer reviews just to understand if the service provider has a history of supporting its clients on technical matters. In case you need a highly responsive system, you may need to avoid those platforms that use the support ticket criteria. Companies that use this criterion to solve customer problems always take a long time to respond to even the most critical issues.

Charts play an essential role, and you can use timed as well as ticked charts for successful day trading. Always remember that different tools are designed for different kinds of trades. You must understand the kind of tools you need as a day trader so that you do not struggle on the market.

Chapter 7 Understanding Trading Orders

As a trader, you will need a broker through whom you will place buy or sell orders for any asset. You can decide whether you are going to buy or sell any stock, then place an order accordingly on your online trading platform.

Usually, Exchanges use a bid and ask process for fulfilling orders placed by traders. This means that there must be a buyer and seller to complete a single order, and they both should agree on the price. For example, if a trader wants to buy a stock at X price, there must be a seller willing to sell that stock at the same price. No transaction can occur unless a buyer and a seller agree at the same price.

The bid is the highest price a trader is willing to pay to buy an asset, and the ask is the lowest price, that trader is willing to accept to sell that asset. In stock markets, the price moment is directed by a tussle between the bid and ask prices. These prices keep constantly changing. As trading orders get filled, the price levels also keep changing, which is reflected in the technical charts.

While day trading, one must keep in mind this bid and ask process, because this will determine at what price the order will be executed. When markets are moving slowly, the change in price is also slow and one can wait to get the trading orders filled at the desired price. However; when markets are highly volatile and sees big up or down moves happen within split seconds, the order may get filled on a higher than expected rate. This can cause losses to day traders as the price changes quickly and can reverse by the time their orders are filled.

Different markets have different methods of matching buyers' and sellers' prices. These methods are called trading mechanisms. There are two main types of trading mechanisms; order-driven, and quote driven. In markets that use quote driven trading, a constant stream of prices (quotes) is available to traders. These prices are decided by market makers, therefore; these types of trading systems are better suited for over the counter (OTC) markets or dealers. There is a considerable spread between the bid and ask prices, which constitutes the profit of the deal maker or the market maker.

Exchanges mostly adopt the order-driven trading mechanism. Here, orders are executed when buy orders match with a sell order. In this type of trading mechanism, dealmakers are not involved.

Mechanism of Trading Orders

In the electronic day trading, orders are placed on the online trading platforms. These orders are the trader's instructions to the broker, or the brokerage firm, for buying or selling some security. When you are trading stocks, you place orders to buy or sell a stock, which is fulfilled by the brokerage firm with whom you have a trading account. The ease of electronic trading has given traders the freedom to initiate various types of order, where they can use different restrictions in order conditions. By these restrictions, traders can control the price and time of order execution. Such instructions help increase traders' profits or restrict the losses.

In systems, where the trading mechanism is order-driven, traders can also control the timeline of any specific order. For example, a trader can place an order which will remain open until its execution. Traders can also place orders that last till the end of the session, or one day, or a specific time.

Understanding how trading orders are placed, and how they can impact one's day trading, is important because it can affect once profit or loss in day trading. For example, a novice day trader may not be aware of the slippage between the bid and ask prices. There is always a difference between the bid and ask price is called slippage. It occurs in every trade, and every trader faces it whether buying, selling, entering a position or exiting from a position. This is also called the spread between a bid and ask price. So, when you place an order to buy a stock at $4, the slippage may increase its cost to $4.05 when your order is filled. Likewise; when you are existing any position, you place an order to sell at $3, but the slippage causes it to get filled at $2.98, thus chipping away at some of your profits.

Professional traders advise beginners to stay away from highly volatile market situations because the slippage risk increases during those choppy moments. For example; on a central bank policy declaration day, stock prices become highly volatile and move with big numbers within seconds. In such a situation, the ordered price and executed price may be different, causing financial harm to the day trader. From the outside, such big moves may look tempting to day traders and make them greedy, thinking they can make big profits with such huge price moves. But the reality is, the slippage between the bid and ask price is equally big and it can change considerably by the time the trading order gets filled, or immediately after the order is executed, creating a loss-making situation for the trader.

Different Types of Trading Orders

Most individual traders use a broker or dealers' trading platforms to place their trading orders. These platforms provide the facility of placing various types of orders, which are helpful in trade planning. Placing an order on the trading platforms is instructing the brokerage firm to buy or sell a financial asset on behalf of the trader. Based on the execution type, here are some common order types:

Market Orders: These orders do not have any specific price. A market order is an instruction to the broker to complete the trade at the available price. Because there is no fixed price, these orders almost always get executed, unless there is some liquidity problem. Traders use market orders when they want their trades executed quickly and they are not bothered about the execution price.

These orders are good if there is not much slippage between the bid and ask price. But a big slippage can cause loss to the traders, especially those who day trade in options.

Limit Orders: Traders place limit orders when they want to buy or sell stocks (or other assets) at a specific price. For example, if Apple shares are trading at $220, and traders expect the price to dip low, they can place a limit order to buy the shares at $219 or lower. Limit orders can be used for both buying and selling. Traders use these orders when they are trading with technical levels and are sure of price touching those level. For example, if a trader has bought Apple shares at $220, and thinks it can touch $222, he can place a limit order to sell his shares at that higher price. When the share price reaches that level, his sell order will get executed.

Stop Orders: These are also known as stop-loss orders and make a part of traders' money management techniques. A stop-loss order can stop the trade from going below a specific price, thus restricting losses for the trader. These orders are used for both buy and sell trades. The price specified in a stop-loss order is called stop price; and once that price is reached, the order is executed as a market order.

Day Order: This order Is valid only in the same trading session where it is placed. If the specified price is not achieved by the end of the session, the order is automatically canceled. This saves day traders from carrying forward their orders to the next day.

Preparations for Placing an Order

When preparing day trading plans and strategies, many day traders forget to pay attention that how they will place orders for trades. Believe it or not, the simple act of placing a trading order can have a big impact on the success of your day trading business.

Successful day traders always give importance to order processing techniques and plan their trades around the stock price they will focus during the trading. The trading plan itself means planning at what price you will enter a trade and when you will exit. Online trading platforms provide many methods of placing your orders around your planned trade prices. You can prepare charts of your trade, mark entry, and exit points and place orders for both trades together, or separately.

A good trading plan always includes trade entry, exit, profit booking, and loss stopping points. The margin trading facility provided by various brokerage firms also includes placing a stop-loss order together with the primary buy or sell order. This ensures that your trade will never suffer a loss beyond a specific price level. Here is an example to illustrate this:

Suppose a trader has bought stock 'A' at $10. He is expecting the price to go up, so he'll make some profit. However; anything can happen in stock markets and in case the price reverses, he wants to restrict his losses to $3 only. So, he will place a stop-loss order at $7, which is $3 below his buying price. If the price keeps moving up, the stop loss order will remain inactive. In case, the stock price falls, nothing will happen till it reaches $7, at which time the stop loss order will be triggered, and automatically sell the stock he has bought.

A stop-loss order makes sure that even if the trader is not available to check prices, his position will be safe till a certain price.

Similarly, traders can also use limit orders to exit their positions after earning a profit. Taking the above example once again, if a trader has bought a stock at $10, and believes that the price will move up to $15; he can place a limit order to sell at $15. When the price reaches his target ($15), it will be automatically executed, and the position will be squared off with a profit of $5.

These examples show that day traders can use a combination of different order types for money management and managing the risk and reward ratio. By technical analysis of any stock chart, day traders can find at what price the stock will make a big move, and be ready to place their orders near that price level.

Some other Order Types:

Apart from the basic orders, some other order types are not so common but can be used for money management or specific trading strategies.

For example, some day traders are more active during the market closing hours, as they create trading strategies for the next session. To take advantage of the price movement during the closing hours, they can place 'Limit-On-Close' (LOC) orders. As the name shows, it is a limit order and is specified for getting executed when markets close. As you know, a limit order controls at what price any security will be bought or sold. LOC has an extra parameter of 'on close', which adds another condition to this order, that it should only get executed if the closing price matches the order's price limit. For this order, both the limit price and the market's closing price are important.

Expert day traders use this order to take advantage of the closing time volatility in the stock markets, where they expect the price to reach a certain level. The LOC order has a drawback; if the closing price does not reach the limit price of the order, it is not executed. Also, this order must be placed within a specific time, before markets close for the day. The LOC order is valid only through the same trading session and is not carried forward to the next session.

Sometimes when the trader places this order but its requirements are not met for a while, the trader decides to wait till it gets executed. In that situation, it will be called an open order. The order will remain open until the trader does not actively cancel it. All open day orders get canceled automatically at the end of the session. During the session. If traders do not wish to wait further for the trade to take place, they will have to cancel all open orders manually. The open orders are often caused by buying or sell limit orders or stop orders. Traders can use GTC (good till canceled) option for their open orders, which will carry forward their orders until it is executed. Traders have the option to cancel the open order at any time.

When traders open any order and then decide not to get it executed, they can cancel it and it becomes a canceled order. This can happen when they mistakenly place a wrong order and upon realizing their mistake, immediately cancel the order. Or sometimes, they place a limit order, wait for it to get executed, then decide not to complete the trade and cancel the order. Market orders usually get immediately executed, so it is difficult to cancel a market order after it has been placed. But limit and stop orders have a time gap before getting executed. Therefore; traders can cancel these orders before their execution.

Overview

For stock trading, one needs to place buy or sell orders through a broker. There must be a buyer and seller to complete any order and they should agree on a specific price to complete the trade. Stock prices move through a process of the bid and ask. Day traders must keep this in mind when they are placing an order because the difference between the bid and ask price can cause slippage, which is harmful to a day traders' profits. Different markets have a different trading mechanism.

Online trading platforms facilitate order execution. Traders place their orders through the platform, which is executed by the brokerage firm. The time and method of order placing can impact one's day trading profits and losses. The spread or the difference between the bid and ask price can change at what price any trade is executed. Therefore; beginner day traders should stay away from volatile markets because, in those market conditions, the slippages can cause them considerable financial harm.

Day traders can use different order types to execute the trade. Market orders are executed almost immediately at the latest available price. These orders are good to use when markets are trending. Most of the time, day traders prefer to place limit orders where they can control the buy or sell price of their trades. Traders also used stop-orders to control the loss or to decide the profit booking levels in their trades. For intraday trading, traders can use the day order, which, if not fulfilled, gets canceled at the end of the session.

Order placing has an important place in traders' money management and trading strategies. Traders can pre-plan their trades and decide at what level they will buy or sell any stock. Technical analysis can help them find levels where the stock price will make considerable moments. They can place different orders near these price levels to manage their trades. Day traders can combine various orders to manage their risk and reward ratio.

Apart from the basic order types, there are many other orders, which expert traders use for their trading strategies. LOC or 'Limit-On-Close' Is one such order that traders can use to buy or sell stocks at the market-closing price. They can use this order type to take advantage of the closing hours' high volatility in markets, or if they are planning any strategy for the next day's opening session. Any order that is not filled is called an open order. Sometimes traders cancel their orders for various reasons, and these are called canceled orders.

Chapter 8 Money Management

What is Money Management?

Money management is not a new aspect of the financial management world. It started when there was a rise of capitalism. When the economy was under a system that was dominated by private owners, they had their private properties and gained on the profits. Money Management started in around 1600, and individuals only survive by depending on how effectively they get their income. In the present age, to be successful financially involves having the ability and the zeal to save more, and lean on investing any surplus.

Money management is a term to refer to the many ways people manage their financial resources. It ranges from budget planning in regards to their income. Money management involves planning and purchasing items that are important to you. Without planning well and lack of money management skills, the amount a person has will always not be enough for them.

Before anyone starts on the money management journey, you need to be aware of the assets and liabilities that you have. Some of the examples of Personal assets and properties are cars, home, retirement, investment, and bank accounts. On the other hand, personal liabilities are loans, debts, and mortgages. To be able to know your net worth, you should see the difference between your assets and liabilities. When the liabilities are higher than the assets, then you have a lower net worth. Having excellent money management skills, you will be able to avoid this.

Goal setting helps in Money management. Without goal setting, you will be worried about daily bill management; this can adversely affect your long term goals. With goal setting, you can have a clear view of the expenses needed to, and which needs to be cut out. A perfect example is when you have a goal of getting a car worth $30,000, your goals will be to cut down your expenses. Similar to someone whose goals are to get a $20,000 car?

After planning and knowing your goals, start creating your budget. A budget is an estimation of income for a defined period of time — a tool which will assist you in managing your money well. With a budget, you will be able to save some cash and be able to minimize impulse buying. An example of a reasonable budget will be to allocate $250 for entertainment and miscellaneous expenses a month after settling the basic needs. If your income increases, it would be advisable to add the extra income to your savings plan and not adding it to the expenses budget.

When budgeting, you will have multiple accounts to manage. For example, you may have an emergency fund and saving accounts. By doing this, you will avoid the temptations of spending the funds on impulse buying. The retirement plan should be kept separate from the other accounts. There are different software that you can use to assist you in money management. An example of a money management software is Quicken; it helps in tracking your various accounts and ensuring your saving and spending goals are on the right track.

The different aspects of money management include analyzing, planning, and executing a financial portfolio. The financial portfolio includes investment types, taxes, savings, and banking. In business management, there are economic variables that might affect your business finances. The best Money Management skills are to be able to access and control all the factors that might affect your financial position.

You can achieve your set goals through excellent money management. A dream of owning a home without using student loans, and be able to have a stress-free life from debts. Have a better plan to be able to deal with unpredictable events that can affect your finances; like loss of employment, serious illness. With Money Management, you will be able to have some savings that will cover your unexpected events.

Internet is a global computer network that contains information and provides communication. Banking, investment, and insurance needs did not exist before. In the past days, customers had restrictions on decisions making in their financial matters, with less information on their options in their local areas. With the lack of internet connection, there was limitation and restrictions on where to find the right information. People had to go shopping for different items, like furniture and electronics. And also the purchasing of mortgages and insurance policies.

Money Management Skills

Do you know your income expenditure? Do you know your shopping, clothing and entertainment expenses?

Money Management is a life skill which is not in the school curriculum. Most people learn it from our parents on how to handle money.

Since most people didn't learn about financial skills in school, you can still learn them now. Here are some of the Money management skills that you can follow to improve your skills.

Set a Budget

Track how you spend your money. Do you spend on food, movies, entertainment, and clothes? Do you frequently have an overdraw of your bank account? If this is true, then set a budget. Check your bank statements and note down how much is your expenditure categorically. You will find out how much wastage of money you are not aware of.

Spend wisely

Have a shopping list when you go to the grocery store? Do you first check the price of an item before putting the item in your basket? Use coupons if available. Use online resources and mobile apps to stay focused on your expenditure.

Monitor your spending! By not being attentive to these small tips, you will keep on losing money. It takes time to get coupons, and It takes some effort to find coupons and writing a shopping list and checking the price of an item before buying, it will all be worth it in the long run.

Balance your books

Most people rely on going online to look at their bank balance. By doing this, you won't be able to know how much you are spending at the moment. The best advice is to be accountable by recording all your expenses; you will have avoided over-spending.

Set a plan

You must have a plan for you to accomplish anything. For you to go from location A to B, it won't be possible without a GPS to show the routes. You will end up driving aimlessly going nowhere.

This is similar to not having a financial plan. You will always be broke and not knowing where your money is spent on.

"Where did that money go?" With a great plan, you will be able to track your money and expenditure.

Think like an investor

The education system does not teach about handling money, mainly how to invest in growing your wealth. The rich people did not just save $500 a month; they learned how to grow their savings and invest. Turning that $500 into $1000, then into $10,000 and eventually into $100,000 and more.

By investing and growing your money, you will have secured a stable financial future. Think like an investor, and see your money grow.

Have the same financial goals with your partner/spouse

If you're married and you have a joint bank account, then learn to work together. You must both agree with the financial goals.

Make a budget and also see a financial adviser to learn how to invest your money. You must ensure that you have the same financial goals and stay focused.

Save Money

Have a strong commitment to saving your money and securing your future. You can improve your financial situation and make it better! But you need to start with the decision to do so. Make a decision to start saving your money and improving your management skills.

Importance of Money Management

Sticking to a budget and living within your means - is proper money management. Look for great price bargains and avoiding bad deals when purchasing. When you start earning more money, understanding how to invest will become an essential way of reaching your goals like having down payment for a home. Understanding the importance of excellent money management will help you achieve your plans and future goals. Some of the importance of Money Management are:

Better Financial Security

Being cautious of your expenditures and saving, you will be able to save enough for the future. Saving will give you financial security to deal with any unexpected expenses or emergencies like loss of employment, your car breaking down or even saving for a holiday. Having savings, you will not have to use a Credit card to settle crises. Saving is a crucial part of money employment as it helps you build your financial security for a secured future.

Take Advantage of Opportunities

You may encounter opportunities to invest in a business to make more money or an exciting experience like a good deal on a holiday vacation. A friend may inform you of a great investment opportunity or get a great once-in-a-lifetime dream holiday vacation. It can be frustrating not having the money to jump right to these opportunities.

Pay Lower Interest Rates

With excellent money management skills, you can determine your credit score. The highest score means you pay your bills on time and with low-level total debt. Having a higher credit score, you can save more of what you have and have a lower interest rate for car loans, mortgages, credit cards, and even car insurance. And there is the chance to brag to your friends about your high credit score at the parties.

Reduce Stress and Conflict

Paying your bills on time can have a relieving feeling. But on the other hand, being late in paying your bills cause stress and have a negative impact like shutdown in your gas and water supply. Always being broke before your next paycheck can bring conflict and, a significant amount of stress for, couple. And, as we all know, stress brings health problems, experts say, like hypertension, insomnia, and migraines. Being aware of how you can manage your finances, so you have extra cash and savings can put your mind at ease. You will enjoy a stress-free life.

Earn More Money

With your income growing, your financial planning will not only include budgeting for monthly expenses but also figuring out where to invest the extra cash that has accumulated. Knowing different kinds of investments for example stocks and mutual funds, you can earn more money from the investments than what you could have made by leaving the money in your savings account in your bank. But be aware not all investments are recognized as a good investment idea, for example, offshore casinos. One of the best benefits of having investments, you can be at work earning monthly income, and your investments, on the other hand, are making more money for you.

More saving and time

Excellent money management can assist in avoiding your finances from spiraling out of control. It is easy to be in debt if you are unaware of how all your income it's spent monthly. Effective money management means better use of your spare time. You can spend time with your family and friends, by having a clear budget, you will be able to plan for fun days out as you will have available cash to do so.

Peace of mind

Excellent money management gives you some level of calm and peace of mind. With your income and the savings, you can handle any financial demands with the confidence that you have the resources to handle any need that will arise.

Best Money Managers

When developing your investment strategy, you will find yourself seeking some assistance. A well-chosen money manager can help you achieve your financial goals. Research is vital, find the right money manager who will be the perfect fit for your financial goals. There is a lot of information you can get to be able to find a money manager. You can rely on referrals, the internet, or financial companies to get the right money manager for you. In this segment we will go through what a money manager is. How does it work? What is the difference between a money manager and a financial advisor? What is the role of a money manager? What are the pros and cons of having a money manager? And what are the fees required?

Who is a Money Manager?

A money manager, also known as investment managers or portfolio managers. It's an individual or a firm which manages investments portfolio and provide personalized financial advice to an individual or institutional investor. Money managers offer advice to clients about the steps they should take to increase their returns.

How does it work?

Money managers earn a fee for their services and not a commission. In some cases, a client will pay a percentage of the managed assets to their money manager. In this way, both the client and the money manager will work hard towards the success of the portfolio. Here is an example illustrating how money managers work:

Suppose Mary has $20,000 and she wants to invest the money. She will find a money manager to manage her new portfolio. Then she schedules a meeting with the money manager. The money manager inquires about Mary's investment goals, the risk if the investment is a short-term or long-term, etc. Based on Mary's feedback, the money manager will choose a set of securities that will help Mary achieve her financial goals. The money manager will monitor Mary's portfolio on a monthly fee basis, the performance and the value of the portfolio.

What's the difference between a money manager and a financial advisor?

When it comes to your finances, doing it alone can be intimidating as you try to understand the game plan. You need to find the right professional to assist you in meeting your goals.

A financial advisor and a money manager have a lot in common, the two jobs are different, and they can't be handled by one person. A financial advisor is also known as wealth managers. A financial advisor understands the specifics of the client's economic life and creates a detailed investment plan, that is is also known to help the client meet their financial goals. A money manager focuses on managing the strategy your portfolio is invested in.

The role of a money manager:

> A good money manager focuses on successfully managing your portfolio strategies, and should be able to meet the following expectations:

To consistently manage investments portfolio with their stated investment objectives

√ Appropriate risk management

√ Avoid unnecessary turnover within the management team

√ Operate transparently

What are the pros and cons of having a money manager?

When you have a financial goal, you want it to be a success. One of the ways to achieve that is by getting an expert to help you achieve your goals. Do you have some savings which you are thinking of investing? Then you need a money manager for you to achieve your goals of investing. You need a trustworthy and focused money manager. Consider a lot of things before hiring one. To be able to make the right choice, here are some of the pro and cons of having a money manager:

The pros:

Your money manager knows the financial environment

Your money manager can assist you in constructing an income statement and help you understand the market competition. With a great money manager, you can get an excellent customized financial plan and gain essential insights that will help you in your journey.

Your financial manager will make sure your money financial wisely

If there ever a time that you needed to make sure that your cash made the most significant impact, it's now. With a strained economy, there is no room for errors. Your money manager will assist you to avoid the risks and make sure your money it's spent in a way that will bring the best returns. Wondering whether to expand? If you are also thinking of increasing your investment, a money manager makes the smartest and best-informed decisions and assist you with any questions that you might have.

A money manager will free up your time to do what's most important

Your money manager will take away the stress of financial oversight, and this allows you to focus on other vital parts of life.

Your money manager can help your business function well

If you run a business, the money manager can help you with your business. To find out why invoices taking too long without getting paid, why your business is losing cash, and you are not sure where the wastage is happening. The money manager can implement control measures that allow you to easily track your money movement.

The cons:

Your money manager could be expensive

The main reason for not hiring a money manager is the cost! Your concern is a valid one. Money managers are highly qualified and experienced and usually request higher charges. Who can afford an expensive money manager when you have come a long way without him or her up to this point? The solution here is to do your research to get an affordable money manager who will give you the best quality results as well.

Performance Not Guaranteed

Although your money is managed professionally by the money manager, there are still no guarantees. In a bad market day, even the best money manager may lose money.

Lack of Control

You might not have the time or the knowledge to wisely invest your money; it will not be 100% comforting to some people to hand over control of their money to a stranger.

What is a Money Management Rule?

Investing doesn't necessarily need you to be an expert in the field. As a matter of fact, you don't need to be rich to begin investing. However, most people fail to manage their money because they don't know where to start. Here are some of the rules of money management to guide you through your journey:

- Have a plan

How much are you planning to invest? When do you want to invest? When do you plan to exit? You can start from the end and determine how much money you need to invest. Plan for the future, towards financial freedom.

- Time is money

The earlier you start investing, the better advantage you will have. Time is the biggest asset you have. For every time you invest include retirement savings too. There isn't anything that can make up for the effect of compound interest. If you end up losing money in the market, there is enough time for you to recover when you need it. For example, if you invest $1k for five years, you can make equal to $1.8k or $2k in 6 years, assuming the rate of return is the same. It amounts to a 10% difference if you invest one year later.

Do you sincerely think the 10% difference is worth falling off your investment? Never use the "it's too early to start investing" phrase as an excuse to keep your money under the mattress. It's much better to begin late than never.

- It's emotional

We usually make most of our money decisions emotionally like greed, nervousness, and fear. To be able to focus on your long-term investment plan, do not check your account on a daily basis. There are regular fluctuations in the market and individual stocks. If to are making long-term investments, you don't need the stress of constant checking.

A lot of investors get fear after checking the media, and they end up buying or selling their investments at the wrong time. To avoid making such a mistake, be ready, and try to stay calm.

- Financial Goals

Set short term and long term financial goals. Grow your goals and adjust them monthly. Correct your failures and enjoy the success.

- Save Money

Saving for regular expenses like home maintenance and car expenses. It's advisable to save 5-1o percent of the net income. Save 3 to 6 months of your income to an emergency fund.

- Financial Status

Set different expenses and include your debt payments too. Compare the amount of money coming in and what's going out. Know your debts and net income.

- Set a Budget

Budget and closely monitor your spending plan.

- Record Expenditure

Carefully monitor your money. You can note down and adjust appropriately.

- Know the Difference Between Needs and Wants

To quickly know the difference, a need is something that is required for survival. For example, food, shelter, clothes, and water while a want is everything else. Wants to make life a little bit enjoyable. Put more fused on Needs first. And spend on the Wants only after you have taken care of your needs.

- Use Credit Sensibly

Consider credit for planned purchases only. Take the amount that you can comfortably afford to purchase on credit. Credit payments shouldn't exceed 20% of net pay. Don't borrow from a creditor to settle debt to another creditor.

- Settle your bills on time

Keep a higher credit score. Talk to your creditors in advance to explain your situation, if you won't be paying your bills on time.

Tips Used for Money Management

Money management is a delicate topic. For most individuals, it can be overwhelming and intimidating. You may have retirement savings, or not having enough emergency savings. Whatever your concern is, having a good handle of your finances is the best option. Here are some money management tips to get you started.

Manage Monthly Pay

Know your monthly income to better manage your money. Monthly budget, including rent or mortgage payments, gas bills, and other expenses like student loan payments, can be stressful to keep track of. However, making small changes can help you reduce your debts and expenses. Add extra into your monthly payments. Another advice is to increase payments over a year, or another option is to sign up for an automatic payment program. This will assist you to save time and money every month, as payments are deducted automatically from your savings account.

Track Your Spending Habits

Play detective with your finances. You will need to check the financial status by yourself. It might be overwhelming by limiting yourself to monthly expenses. Check out credit card statements, utilities bank account statements and also electronic payment records. Create a spreadsheet or use a pen and paper and track your expenses.

You can also categories your expenses. For example, labeling purchases as Needs wants savings and debts. You can be more detailed and categories like transport, food, and clothing. It all depends on an individual, how much weeds you want to get. After you have compiled everything in one list, get the total of every category to see how you spend. You will be shocked by the amount of money you spend on a particular expenditure.

- Design a budget

When you track your spending, it will naturally lead to the next step: creating a budget. With the numbers you have from tracking your spending, you can now decide how much money you want to go into each item in your budget. You can also scale back some areas of your expenses that you discover you're overspending. You can write a budget as detailed as you like. Everybody's budget is different. Keep the budget relatively simple.

For proper budgeting, guideline uses the 50/30/20 rule — a strategy to help you divide and allocate your monthly income. The fifty percent will go towards fixed costs example, mortgage or rent, taxes, debt and car payments. The thirty percent will go towards spending, for example, vacation and eating out. And the 20% should go towards savings including emergency fund or investing. Regularly monitor your budget. It's better to start with a basic budget than not having a budget at all. Always save more than you're spending.

- Set Financial Goals

Once you have attained your emergency savings account, you should work towards establishing financial goals. The financial goals can be short term goals such as holiday and long term goals such as saving for college, a house or a retirement plan. The mistakes most people make with their budget is they're short-sighted. Have a long term focus, have a five or ten-year plan. For example, it's easy to get money and buy that fancy car but, you can easily forget that you have a long term plan to have kids, and this can bring new expenses. Try to anticipate those long term goals and how to achieve them.

- Set an Emergency Fund

You never know what the future will be. You could be unemployed or get an emergency. Whether you like it or not, life happens. Your emergency funding will be determined by your budget. Most financial expert's advice is saving 3 to 6 months' worth of expenses. Having an emergency fund to handle unplanned problem will help you feel more secured and prepared. Take away stressful emergencies with a financial cushion. Put your emergency fund in a savings account that is liquid and accessible, but only to be used for emergencies.

Apps Used for Money Management

Times are tough. Whether you earn a high net income or you get by, monitoring where your money is spent. There are many ways to track your spending, how you invest and more. We use our cell phones daily, and we always have our phones in our pockets all the time, using apps to help you manage your money is the best option.

Having a good understanding of your cash flow is very vital in managing your finances. How much of your income is coming in? When does the money get to your bank account? How do you spend the money? These are essential aspects of your financial success. Fortunately, there are a lot of money management apps in the market designed to help you check your bank balance, track your expenditure and, analyze your spending habits. Plus, there are apps that will assist you in making better financial decisions based on the data from your accounts.

And the best part? You can access your financial situation on the go. A lot of these money management apps can be checked online and also on your mobile device. It's very convenient as you can take care of your finances no matter where you are.

What do budget apps do? There are two main types of budget apps. One is an expense tracker — it best-fit people who deduct a lot of items from their taxes. For example, business owners who travel a lot, people who track their meals, transportation, and, all other professions who use expenses trackers. This app will help you track how much money you spend. You also have all the info you need when tax season rears its ugly head. The other type of budget app is the one which helps you track your bank budget, expenses bills, and utilities. These help you track your money, especially for people who manage multiple accounts and pays bills online.

Here are some of the best money management apps you should consider:

- Personal Capital

Personal Capital has excellent features to track your budget and also include information about your investment accounts. And you can easily view on tablets, laptops, desktops and your mobile. It also shows graphs of your investments, that are easy to read and track down your investment performance.

- Mint

Mint is one of the popular budgeting apps. Mint offer features like access to your investment accounts and budgeting tools. The budgeting portion is the main feature, and the investing part is little like an afterthought. The best app if you want to keep a very detailed budget. Mint also has a reminder feature to when your bills are due, and you can also pay your bills from the app.

- Acorns

Acorns take virtual change out of your account. Instead of saving it, the app invests the difference. The app helps you start investing with virtually no effort. You can use Acorns on your transactions. The app has a new shopping type function, Found Money.

- YNAB

YNAB is an acronym for You Need a Budget. YNAB cost $6.99 per month, but they waive the first month's fee. The philosophy for YNAB is " a job for every dollar." YNAB also offers a bank syncing and support feature. YNAB can also help you set your financial goals and make the most of each dollar earned.

- Honeydue

Many couples use spreadsheets to manage their household finances. Honeydue is the best app for couples as it helps couples best co-manage their money. Honeydue helps to track shared bills; the pair can see their accounts in one spot, comment on the transactions, and build bigger and better financial goals. Honeydue has the main feature; couples can decide on how much they can share information with their significant others. This feature helps them to remain focused on their goals and not get caught in the weeds, arguing over the small stuff.

- PocketGuard

PocketGuard will help you find savings in your spending. This app sync with your accounts and enables you to track and analyze your spending, which you can use that data to help you build an excellent budget. You can identify a pattern in your monthly spending, track your bills, and save some money.

- Dollarbird

Dollarbird is an app that assists people who have issues with budgeting. This is a free app; however, it has premium add-ons. Your budget is put in a calendar form, and you can view any upcoming expenses. Other features are, you can color code transactions by category and pay you bills through the recurring transaction. Dollarbird lets you see the projected balance, so you are aware of how much money you can safely spend. The limitation that comes with this app is that the app does not sync with your bank account. With this app, you can quickly enter your transactions manually, and this means you will be more involved with the approach to your money.

- Credit Karma

Credit Karma offers you access to your Credit Report. There are several uses of this app, for example, a company can use the app to determine whether to employ you or to estimate your credit score so as a business can be able to figure out the rates that they will charge you. This app can also be used to determine your loan applications and credit cards. Credit Karma is free to users however, the app earns money by offering targeted ads based on your credit score.

Chapter 9 Dos and Don'ts

Now let's distil the information above into more digestible bites. These tips will be your guideposts along the path to success, and light the way so you avoid the pitfalls new investors are susceptible to.

Seven Tips For Always

1. Don't let your emotions get the best of you. You have a wealth of information at your fingertips, and now you have the wherewithal to turn all that info into actionable steps. Don't let pride, or wanting to be right, or fear derail you.

2. Trust Yourself

This is the key difference between an okay trader and a great one. It might seem like this contradicts the previous piece of advice, but if you've done your homework and come to a fact-based conclusion, don't let the opinions of others turn you from the path you've decided on.

3. Don't Worry About What's "Hot"

This builds on Tip 2. When you get into the world of investing you'll be getting tips left and right from people who may or may not have an ulterior motive, and almost certainly won't have as much insight into your particular needs as you do. It's easy to let excitement carry you along, but it's almost always dangerous. If you're hearing that a stock is "hot" at a dinner party everyone already knows about it, and it's probably overvalued by this point.

4. Remember Context

Investing doesn't happen in a vacuum. When you hear horror stories about someone losing their house in bad trades, it's always because they forgot about the context of their life. You have to have income that pays the bills and forgetting that to chase the next big windfall is just another emotional mistake that you must avoid.

5. Never. Stop. Diversifying.

Diversification isn't a one-time process. As you sell off parts of your portfolio, you'll reinvest that money in other ways. Make sure your portfolio remains diverse.

6. Be Patient

Making money on the stock market takes a cool head and a steady hand. If you jump out of the water every time it gets a little warm you don't stand a chance. You'll take losses, but you now know how to deal with them. Don't let a small loss become a drain on your assets or on your focus.

7. Respect The Time Limitations of Your Investments

Say you invest in a fund or bond that requires you to hold it for a specified amount of time. During this time, the market spikes, and you realize you'd still make a little bit of money if you sell now and pay the fee for exiting early. While you didn't lose anything in this transaction overall, you've lost the opportunity for that money to make as much as it could have if properly invested. If you know you'll need cash to hand during the time an investment requires, pick a different investment.

Seven Tips For Never

    1. Over-Diversification

After all this time drilling the importance of diversification into your head, this may come as a surprise. It's true, though, that there is a thing as too much diversification. If you only have a small amount to invest, and you spread that too thin, you're only leaving yourself the option of buying extremely inexpensive stock. This may cause you to miss opportunities you wouldn't otherwise. In this case, the advice should be: Diversify Wisely.

    2. Ignore Fees At Your Own Peril

Even with a discount broker, trades aren't free. Remember to calculate the fees into the price of stocks you buy and to subtract them from your profits on stocks you sell. It seems obvious, but you can trade yourself out into a hole if you're not careful to monitor how much of your money is going to fees and commissions.

    3. Don't Think In Dollars

You must think in percentages. For a simple illustration of why, imagine this scenario: You hold 10 shares each of Stock X and Stock Y. Stock X, you bought for $100 per share and it's gone up to $110 in the first quarter you own it. You paid $6 per share for Stock Y, and now it's gone up to $9. While obviously Stock X has gone up $10 and Stock Y has only gone up $3, Stock X has increased 10% while Stock Y has skyrocketed up by 33%. That's quite a difference. Looking at percentages ensures that you're making your money work for you as hard as you can.

4. Analysis Paralysis

You can't noodle over forms and charts forever. At some point, you have to pull the trigger and enter the marketplace. Do your homework, but make sure you get to the real work once that's done.

5. Paying Someone Else To Do Your Job

You've obviously come this far, so you are willing to do the work of investing yourself. Don't pay a full-service broker or advisor to make decisions you can make yourself. Not only is this a waste of money, it removes your ability to use your special knowledge to choose stocks and investments that you believe in.

6. Stay Off The Style Merry-Go-Round

If your goals are lofty and your risk tolerance high, jump in with both feet. If you're a less aggressive investor and want to build a safe "buy and hold" portfolio, choose cautious investments from Day One. Part of learning to be successful on the stock market is practice. You'll need to get used to the swing of the market, and you won't do that if your style is jumping around erratically.

7. Don't Use Real Money Your First Time Out!

There are many sites that offer "virtual stock markets" that will let you get a feel for how buying and selling stocks works without investing a dime. It's absolutely worth your time to spend a few hours on these sites getting your feet wet. Beware, though: this is a particularly easy place to get hung up in your homework, leading to #4: Analysis Paralysis. A few hours is good, but a few hours is enough.

Obviously, there is a lot more depth in some of these areas, but you are now well rooted in a foundation of knowledge that will allow you to get started as in investor. Keep your head clear, focus on facts, and you're well on your way to investing success.

Beginner's Mistakes to Avoid

Playing out of your depth: Scared money never wins.
Fear freezing thinking: Analysis Paralysis

While doing your practice trading, pay close attention to how much your trades vary in profit/loss during each 5-minute segment, how much it varies in 15 minutes, half hour, hour and so on. Don't do this just one day or one hour but over several days or even a couple of weeks. The reason to do this is quite simple: You are, so-to-speak, "testing your risk tolerance." Admittedly, there is a difference between paper trading and using real money. Still it is better that you get this experience than not. If you feel these variations are not acceptable for any reason, this type of trading may not be for you.

It is quite natural for you to have some 'analysis paralysis', especially the moment as you switch to trading real money instead of practice trading. If your brain is overwhelmed so completely with all you are trying to learn, be patient with yourself. Give yourself enough time for your brain to assimilate the process. With practice your thinking and reactions become faster. You will also notice the points at which you start stressing during losing trades; take some notes on this because you need to know how this amount to determine your risk tolerance and experience the point where your decisions are triggered by emotions. By the time you can practice trade and accomplish 25 consecutive "successful" (error free whether winner or loser) trades, you will be able to get some idea of what risk level you can handle.

Using a Blind System and Using Technicals Blindly

By "blind system," I mean those get-rich-quick scams that promise lots of money with very little work, risk, or thought. Buyers beware. No one who would ever sell you such a system will ever agree to pay your losses. Trading blind on promises from unproven sources - is risky territory.

Remember that technical indicators are tools, not foolproof trading systems and must be used in the context of market concepts, trends, and patterns.

Impatience and Not Preparing Well Enough

Think of trading as owning your own business. You invest a few bucks for information and supplies, then a research period to test feasibility as best you can, and then risk your hard-earned money. In an earlier chapter, I strongly suggested you practice trade with a ledger, keeping notes, until you can string together 25 consecutive trades with no errors. It can take a while to do this successfully. Be patient and take time to learn by doing, not just reading about it. Remember no two traders are identical; find what works for you.

Ignore Brain Pattern Dominance

When you trade using technical charting and indicators, you will notice that you start to "see" a lot of potential patterns that can be forming. This is apophenia; your brain working hard to find patterns and project outcomes. This is normal. Wait and let the "market tell you" what is going on, and don't allow your attention to stray when your brain sends you all the possible outcomes of things that are not yet in your charts and indicators. Until you gain some experience, this is one of the most difficult things to learn. Trading with technical indicators and charts is not a perfect science by any means. The indicators will sometimes lead you astray no matter how long you study them. It is quite common for inexperienced traders to think that if only they find the right technical indicators, they will win the vast majority of trades. This is a very popular myth. It is something almost everyone wants to believe.

It is a rookie mistake to think that just because you got a good night's sleep, got up early, read the day's financial news or financial channel, and have spent hours of practice - that the market will send you a perfect technical indicator trade in the first ten minutes of your trading. You must have patience. Sometimes, you see a trade instantly. Other times you can go more than an hour and see no chances at all. Other days, you'll have almost too many good signals. These things do not happen on a schedule. You will see some days that are volatile and fast, maybe too fast for your risk tolerance. Other days will be so slow, you might feel bored and that you've wasted time. Over time, you learn to recognize those time periods - when trying to trade at all is impossible; so don't. Some days as the saying goes, "You get all dressed up and there is just no place to go." Hope is not a strategy. Let the market tell YOU what's happening, not the other way around.

Over-using Genius of Hindsight

This is another of the "most common" mistakes new and veteran traders make. I've already written extensively about this. You can learn from genius of hindsight, but you should never judge your ability to trade with information you did not have during the trade. This may seem counter-intuitive so I want to be perfectly clear about this: You can LEARN from hindsight; it can be a debriefing. Recognize that judging your decisions with hindsight is always a hypothetical matter, never based on the same facts you had before or during a trade.

Trying to Guess Reversals

There are times when you may have a strong bias about what the market "should" do. For example: The market may have extended time periods of remarkable gains or losses. You come to feel the market should be ready for some reaction, retracement, or some adjustment. Times like this will give you a strong bias and it is too easy to forget that you could be considering trading on that bias, even though the technical indicators or other market action is telling you otherwise. Over time, you will learn to use your technical charts and indicators much like a night aircraft pilot uses instruments to navigate. It is quite common to 'over read' your indicators like the MACD. By that, I mean you will naturally start to anticipate what might happen next and trade on this speculation, rather than waiting for a more reliable signal. As discussed often in this book, humans have a very strong predilection to find patterns where they do not really exist. To allow yourself to follow this inclination is to run the extra risk of ignoring your charting and indicators. Avoiding this mistake, takes an enormous amount of patience and a bit of experience.

Letting recent experience skew your thinking

So what does "your recent experience" really mean? To a stock trader, it could mean last year or last month. To a day-trader, it could mean 15 minutes ago, yesterday, or two hours ago or even five-minutes ago. When a day trader has a string of consecutive losses, it can result in the trader being less aggressive and overly cautious. This can materialize into a reaction of: a) taking profits too quickly to "make up" for the losing trades, b) perhaps letting the losses accumulate due to being hopeful, or c) exiting a trade in a small drawdown too quickly to avoid more losses. Any of these three reactions as a result of recent losing trades can be directly categorized as letting your emotions influence your trading decisions.

The solution to this problem is learn to rely on the experience you gain using the candlesticks and MACD. Over time, you will gain more confidence in your ability to read market news, to be aware of scheduled reports and major events that occur during a trading day and will better understand how to interpret the various intensities of trading signals. As you gain experience with reading candlesticks and using the MACD indicator - you will learn to rely more on these things - than to listen to that voice in your head that brings emotional reactions as well as its ability to find patterns that are really not there, those optical illusions due to apophenia and pareidolia. Each trade you make is no more related the last trade than is one coin toss that follows another. They are mutually exclusive even though your brain is hard-wired to relate them. This first step in avoiding this is to be aware of it.

Not Evaluating Your Trading as a Business Plan

You must keep a clear and accurate trading log. You'll be using it to evaluate your methods and results. It will be the equivalent of a business ledger that records expenses (losses) and profits and it will detail your methods.   It is easily possible to   over-think everything. The ledger you keep will show you truthful results and it can be used to identify both mistakes and to help find improvements you can make. At the end of the day, you will be your own business manager and can inspect your books to see how your business is doing. Your account balance won't lie, it will tell you if you are doing things right.

There is No Such Thing as a Winning Streak

There is a certain amount of euphoria when you make money trading. There is always a temptation to think you are on a roll, but this is only an illusion. Each of your trades must justify its own risk-reward.

Chapter 10 Managing Risk in Trading and the Role of Journaling

The first thing you need to know as a trader is that you will run volumes of trades and experience a lot of risks. Trading the markets is one of the riskiest investment techniques, and many people go for day trading because they have the potential for higher gains over a short period. If you have a small account, day trading gives you the chance to grow small accounts in such a short timeframe.

Risk comes about because you have to execute hundreds of trades in such a short time. You also have the capacity to place any trade you want, for as low as $500 or as high as $25,000 in a single trade. The trades are also at high speed, which means the market can swing any way - up or down. The direction of the market determines whether you make a loss or a profit.

Day trading gives you two realms of strategies to go with - high risk trading strategies or Lowe risk strategies. The goal of a successful trader is to maximize profit while lowering risks. Every time you place a trade, you need to evaluate the risk of the trade and then weight it against the potential reward. Often times this is made worse by our emotional reaction to various price directions. For instance, since you experienced a loss recently, the next logical step would be to take a higher risk on the next trade so that you can compensate on the loss. Experienced traders have a heightened level of awareness that they use to recognize a loss and reward and will make sure they take the right decision. However, you have to learn the skill over time.

You can develop a sense of decision making by keeping a journal as you trade and then reviewing the notes after the close of the market.

Different Types of risk

When talking about risk, you need to consider the different types in order for you to understand what we are saying. As a day trader, your primary role is to know the distance between the entry and the stop. Stop loss needs to be based on a resistance area on the chart or recent support.

Majority of your losses need to happen when a trade hits the stop price. This means you won't make any profit on whatever you are trading.

The second type of risk id the volatility of the market. As day traders, volatility is a friend to all of us, but it is also risky because markets that are extremely volatile tend to result in higher losses than what you actually planned for. Since there is a sense of inherent risk in trading, you need to try and avoid placing a trade when the volatility cannot be predicted, for instance when there is breaking news.

The other type of risk is exposure risk. Exposure results when you multiply the price of shares by the number of held shares. As an investor, you increase this risk when you hold on positions for a very long time. To mitigate this risk, you need to hold onto shares for a short time.

If you are holding onto large positions for a long time you stand to experience stock halts. Halts can take hours or days, though they are rare. The most common halts are those waiting for the release of news or volatility halts. Anytime a stock halts, it can lead to a different price. The biggest risk is that the stock might reopen at a very different price, which might be lower than the current price of the stock. You can take steps to reduce the effect of the halts by understanding what leads to the halts in the first place.

Journaling

If you are looking at a routine that is easy to implement and that can change the way you trade, then think about keeping a journal. The journal is a little black book that details what you do each day.

The aim of keeping a journal is to help improve your setups so that you use your experiences to analyze and help refine your trading while you improve the whole experience.

Here, we look at all you need to come up with a journal and maintain it.

What is A Journal?

A trading journal is a way to keep track of what you are doing o daily basis as a day trader. You jot down notes of what you do each day especially the different trades (or lack of) and the results of any action you take.

The trading journal needs to be tailored to your trading styles and preferences. You can keep the journal in a physical notebook or a detailed digital document on your computer. Regardless of the format, when maintained with due diligence, the trading journal can be the best way to make you a better day trader.

How Does the Trading Journal Help You Achieve Better Trades?

There are a number of ways in which a trading journal will help you become better at what you do.

Many traders attribute their success to creating and maintaining a trading journal. By noting down the different trades, you are able to check the progress over time. This allows you to find out what is working or not and change or modify them to succeed.

Helps You develop discipline in Trading

Having a trading journal helps you develop discipline as you trade. How does it do so? Well, it forces you to follow the guidelines that you have set down.

The sense of accountability that you get when you have a trading journal makes sure you are responsible for research and trading. If you know what you need to keep a log each day, you do it without fail. Making sure you log your trades and whatever happens requires a lot of discipline. Good habits such as these require you to go straight when executing trades.

Helps You Master Your Emotions

One of the top suggestions to help you run trades the right way is to trade like you are not human. Machines do not have emotions and approach all the processes in a scientific way.

However, this is easier said than done. When you get in a position to lose money, usually you find it tough getting emotion out of the way.

Keeping a journal can help you keep the emotions out of the way. With a journal in place, you get to keep track of how you feel emotionally in various trading stages. This is just to keep the emotions in check.

With time, you realize that there is a pattern that is emerging, for instance, you might find yourself getting calmer and taking orders the right way each time.

Improves Your Risk Management Practices

Day trading comes with a high level of risk. This is something that you cannot change at all because it is the nature of the market for things to run this way. However, there are various ways in which you can mitigate these risks. For one, you need to invest a large amount of research and study to give you the knowledge that you need to choose the least risky trades possible.

With a journal, you can learn things about risk tolerance. For instance, you might find that you have consistently been able to hold positions for longer and you have been losing profits as a result. You might also find that you have issues getting out of trades because you have been taking positions that are too big for your stage.

By looking at the risks that you have been taking and how they affect the results you return, you get to make adjustments.

For instance, you might exit trades sooner or you might end up taking smaller positions based on the results you return. This way you help reduce risks and improve risk management.

Creating the Perfect Trading Diary

Now that you know how effective the trading journal is, you need to know how to come up with the best one. Here are a few tips for success when coming up with a journal:

• Be consistent

Trading needs you to have a routine. You will probably get the most out of the journal if you have a routine that you follow religiously.

You also need to follow the routine to the latter. This means that you are consistent with what you do day in day out. For instance, you need to wake up early each day to prepare for trading. This allows you to get errands and tasks out of the way early and gives you to do research so that you are ready to roll when the market starts.

This is a directive though because since many traders are doing other responsibilities, you need to come up with the right schedule that works for you. Choose the routine that will work for you and that you can stick to easily.

• Analyze the Market

The more the trades that you track, the more data you have to deal with and the more you get to learn and the faster you do it.

By recording the trades, overall thoughts, market observations and more, you aren't just learning from the mistakes that you are doing, but you are also gaining a sense of how to perform the right market analysis.

For instance, with the right trading data, you get to notice gains and losses in a particular industry or sector. This can give you clues on the trends in the market that you might have missed out.

Once you see what is working and what isn't, you get to have a targeted market analysis.

- Analyze and Come Up with Your Own Setups

A trading journal allows you to come up with the right setups. Here is how this works out:

- Find the setups that trigger trade entry

When do you enter the market? The trading journal helps you figure everything out. You need to go into each trade with a plan. However, if you realize that you are entering trades too soon or too late based on the journal, you can then decide to try something different.

With the perfect trading journal, you have the capacity to determine the setups that trigger the entries.

- Gain Insight into the Market

When you record your own setups, you have the ability to gain insight into the market that you are trading in. you get to notice market trends and how they might end up affecting the setups.

As a trader, understanding the way the market runs is ideal because it helps you to keep up to date. The market is dynamic, and the setups that work in one market condition might not work for other conditions. When you understand the market, you get to navigate around and acclimatize to new markets.

- Know the Appropriate Lot Size

In any market, the lot size means the number of shares which you buy in any transaction. The theory of size allows you to regulate price quotes. It is basically the size of the trade that you place in the financial market.

With price regulation being a part of every market, you need to always be aware of the number of units that you purchase eon contract, and determine the price you pay per unit.

Make sure you keep track of the lot sizes that you deal with in any trade, as it helps you to decide the types of approaches that you take in the future.

- Determine the Style of Trading

Many traders choose to be one type of trader or another. Many of them do it by force, which is a fact that isn't the best. As a trader, you need to naturally gravitate towards a specific trading style, and not force it.

Rather than chasing after what is trendy or what you have seen other traders do, it is advisable to focus on a style of trading that gives you profit, whether you go after long or short positions.

A trading journal can help you determine the type of trade that is best suited for you by giving you a summary of the trades that gave you money.

- Understand Profit Placement

Trading is a probability game, with so many moving pieces that make it work. With so many parts that are needed to make everything work, you need to make sure you get everything right the first time. This isn't easy at all.

Here are a few specifics that you need to master:

• Cut losses fast: you need to learn to cut losses quickly, which means you pull out of a position earlier than later, even if it means missing out on a few profits. It is always good to be safe than sorry. Having a trading journal helps you determine when to get out of a trade. If you notice that you are losing constantly, then journaling can help you learn how to cut losses fast. Additionally, if you notice that you are getting out of trades too early, then you can start staying gin the game a little bit longer.

• Stop losses: you need to learn how to come up with the best stop loss order. The order can help you release the order when you reach a particular price. With the right stop loss order, you can buy the security rather than selling it when you reach a certain price. Make sure you record the different entry and exit positions; how much you have risked and the results of everything. As the information collects over time, you can determine what your best setups are so that you can focus on replicating the profits you gained in the past to eliminate losses.

Apart from this information, you also need to record other things so that you make the most out of each entry:

• The date: this shouldn't be left out of the journal. Not only does it help you to track what you were doing and when you were doing it, but it allows you to go back and look at the performance of the stock on that date in future. Never assume that you will rack everything in your brain!

- The Time Frame: do not just record the date, but make sure you know the perfect time for each entry. In the world of trading, minutes matter. Trading in the morning can make a huge difference compared to trading in the afternoon. For instance, the setup that works for you during the morning hours might not work the same way in the afternoon.

- Price in: this is the point where the journal starts working well with the trading plan. When coming up with a trading plan, you set the key tactics such as the entry point, the exit and what you plan to gain from this trade. This helps you to stick to the plan and then keep emotions out of things. In the journal, make sure you note the price at which you entered a successful trade.

- Price out: don't just mark the time that you entered the trade - also take note of the price that you exit the trade too. The exit is also as vital as the entrance. Keeping this data allows you to analyze whether you are staying in a position for the right amount of time. Note any difficulties that you encounter getting out of the position, as this might affect the level of risk next time.

- Amount you are risking: before you enter a trade, you need to determine the amount of money you plan to put into the trade. Note: The money you put tin should be an amount you can risk losing. So, how much money should you risk on a trade? The answer is that you need to always take a cautious position, and never try to risk what you can't lose. You do not want to enter into a trade and blow up the account as this might trigger emotional trading.

Tips for Creating an Efficient Trading Journal

1. Identify the Patterns That lead to Losses

As a trader, you can't eliminate the risk of making losses. For many traders, the success rate is 70 percent, and many of them know that the 100 percent win rate is a myth.

You can never control how much you win, but you can at least control the amount you can lose by cutting losses fast.

You also get to learn from the losses. Once you have a trading journal, you begin to identify patterns that lead to losses and assess what is happening.

2. Identify the Patterns That Have Made You Profit

As a trader, you not only focus on the things that went wrong, but also look at what went right as well. You need to chart patterns in the trades to help you analyze what make you the most money. Many successful traders base their success on being able to identify patterns. Many depend on stock charts, but later realize that even the trading journal gives them an insight into what they need to do.

3. Go for Professional Assistance

Trading classes give you an asset that you will never regret in your trading life. Even with the right data, you might find yourself failing to make profitable trades because you do not have the mechanics to make things work for you. When you take time to learn the mechanics of trading, you find that you have the basis to identify key indicators and add them to the journal.

Just like any other trade, the more you get prepared to execute trades the more successful you become. The knowledge originates from previous traders that have become successful in their efforts.

4. Work With templates

Templates make it easy for you to come up with a plan. There are many platforms online that offer you both paid and free templates that you can use to create the perfect journal, all you need to do is to choose the one that suits you then customize it to your liking. As you become more adept, you find that the journal becomes your best friend, and it also becomes more detailed.

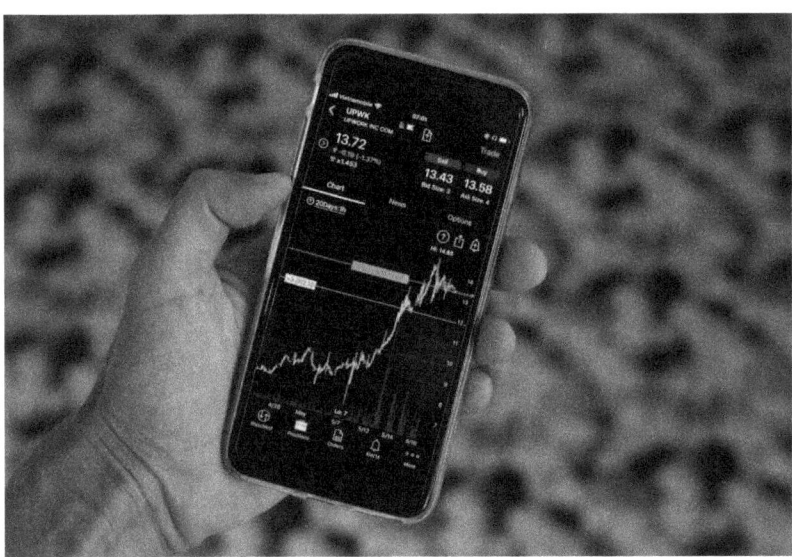

Conclusion

Now that you have made it to the end of this book, you hopefully have an understanding of how to get started day trading forex, as well as a strategy or two, or three, that you are anxious to try for the first time. Before you go ahead and start giving it your all, however, it is important that you have realistic expectations as to the level of success you should expect in the near future.

While it is perfectly true that some people experience serious success right out of the gate, it is an unfortunate fact of life that they are the exception rather than the rule. What this means is that you should expect to experience something of a learning curve, especially when you are first figuring out what works for you. This is perfectly normal, however, and if you persevere you will come out the other side better because of it. Instead of getting your hopes up to an unrealistic degree, you should think of your time spent with the forex market as a marathon rather than a sprint which means that slow and steady will win the race every single time.

This book has been able to give you all the information that you will need to become a successful day trader. We have also given you all the information that you need to avoid the classic mistakes that people make when they attempt to be successful with this. Through this book you will have gained knowledge on the rules and strategies of day trading while making sure that you are being able to be aware of losses and the management of risk. We've also explained the reasons behind why you should be aware of these things in the first place as it is a very important issue.

Loss is a part of this business and it's something that you should recognize and learn about right away so that you know how to avoid these issues and to make smart decisions instead of decisions that are unwise and that can lead you into bad decisions. Because we want you to be able to be successful we explain the rules of taxes and the plans you will need to understand as well. This will ensure you have the best chance of moving forward with the best information possible as well.

We have also given you the best information on the platforms that you can use for trading as well as the many tools at your disposal. There are many different software that you can use and that you can utilize for your benefit. The best part of this is that you can use your computer and get down to business. When you understand the ins and outs of this business you can move through it and past people easily to maximize your own success.

One of the key things that we have taught you in this book is that you need to exercise the art of patience. Being patient with the market, the plans, the people and your marketing and decision making is going to let you have more power financially and more power in this field. You need to make sure that you have the patience to be able to push through and reach your goals. This takes time and work and if you have the patience you will be able to do this successfully.

Remembering that this is a hot commodity in today's society will serve you well as well. When you realize how many people are in this field and how many people are wanting to do the same thing and have a great level of success like you are is going to help you give the motivation you need to push past them and keep moving toward your own success. However, this also gives you a good idea of what you're up against which is an important part of this as well.

If you use the tips and information in this book to your advantage, you will be able to make sure that you can be successful and that you will be able to trade with ease earning yourself the experience and income you desire.

Forex Trading for Beginners

The Best Techniques to Financial Freedom for A Living and Work From Home Using Simple Strategies, High Probability Method, Psychology For Forex Market bases, In The Zone

ROBERT ZONE

Introduction

The most important thing to take note before starting your Forex trading journey is that this particular endeavor is not a get-rich-quick scheme. Do not expect to make a lot of money doing this for a living. Unless, of course, you are handling large amounts of money, such as those who handle hedge funds and fund managers. However, even then there are a lot of risks involved, and some people with large capitals can lose a huge amount in the Forex market. With a correct system and of course some luck, traders can make a decent and steady profit from the Forex market. A reasonably successful trader can expect to make a monthly return of around 1 or 2 percent of his or her capital. This may also result in around a 25 percent return annually. Of course, this will only happen if the market conditions are favorable and there are no other unforeseen circumstances, such as war, political upheaval, large natural disasters, and other events that will occur.

Using these figures, a person who invests around US$100,000 in the Forex market can expect an annual return of around US$25,000. This is definitely a good chunk of change, but most will likely not want to make Forex trading a full-time job. Recent data has also shown that only a quarter, or 25 percent, of traders in retail Forex end up earning any profit in three months. A good chunk of these traders are day traders, while the rest only take a small number of positions and hold them for longer periods.

Currency pairs will more often than not only move by minuscule amounts throughout a few days. These pairs typically rise and fall by around 10 percent over a year. Some people view the Forex market as a form of gambling. However, traders would argue that the odds in Forex are much higher than any casino game out there. This form of analyzed betting gives traders a big advantage as they have a lot of clues and data to go on to make informed decisions. It has to be noted that similar to traditional gambling, people may experience a string of bad bets. No matter what method you follow or how strict you are with your analysis and trading, there will be some days where you just can't win. On average, one out of three trades will be a losing trade. In reality, this could be much worse depending on how lucky you are.

Then again, if you work hard, and focus on your strategies and charts, it is possible to make a modest amount of money in the Forex market. Now that I have given the clear picture of Forex expectations one must understand that it is possible to become a successful trader if you are truly dedicated to it. If you think Forex expectation is the problem, then, you must find solutions to overcome the expectations that aren't healthy to your trading journey. Let us dig deeper into the concept of managing expectations in Forex trading.

Do you know why it is important to manage Forex expectations? Well, as I mentioned if you are not aware of Forex expectations, you'll become one of those traders who quit even before beginning the trading journey. Hence, you must try to manage your Forex expectations. First of all, what are the expectations? Let's be honest, and it is impossible to set aside expectations because everything in this world is based on expectations. Even the most successful Forex trader would have entered the market with some expectations. However, the important point is related to the way you handled the market expectations. If you let your expectations play the game, then, you are not going to win the game. Hence, setting reasonable expectations is crucial. You must consider the factors that will impact your expectations so that you can get a clear view of it.

Emotion is the triggering factor that controls your expectations. When you set reasonable expectations, and when you get the opportunity to meet them, it feels great, right? But then, how does this relate to trading? Basically, human beings are born with the ability to avoid pain. We have it in our body. But, your pain-avoidance ability works differently in trading that it links with emotions. When you set a trading expectation, you try to avoid all the information that invalidates your expectation. Somehow, you find reasons, rationalize, and even worse, you make yourself feel great about avoiding the information. This isn't healthy. You might end up blowing your trading account as a whole, so think about this!

If you have been to a foreign country, you know that you cannot buy your favorite food and drinks in the country you are visiting with your home country's currency. To avoid such a predicament, individuals have the option to convert their money into the currency of the country they are visiting at the airport.

In addition, you may have received some payment for services in a foreign currency, and you needed to exchange the money into your country's currency for you to use it. Regardless of the situations you had interacting with foreign currency. It is likely highly you have participated in forex in one way or another. A person can participate in Forex Trading whether he or she is traveling to a foreign country, or doing business in his or her country.

What Is Forex Trading

The word 'forex' is short for 'foreign exchange.' It involves the process of converting one currency into another currency for reasons including tourism, trading, and business.

Although a person can participate in foreign exchange by traveling to a different country and exchanging his or her currency for the foreign country's currency, the foreign exchange market is more significant than that. The foreign exchange market is a global forum for exchanging substantial national currencies against each other.

Due to the international spread of finance and trade, the forex markets experience high demands for foreign currencies, which makes the market the most significant money market in the world.

When multinational companies intend to buy goods from other countries, companies need to find the local currency first. That exchange will involve vast amounts of currency exchange. As a result, the local currency value will move up as the demand for that currency increases. With that exchanging going on around the world, the exchange rate always changes.

When global traders exchange currencies, currencies have a specific exchange rate, the price of currency changes according to the law of supply and demand; the higher the demand, the higher the supply and the higher the exchange rate.

The foreign trading market has no centralized marketplace for foreign exchange. Foreign exchange bureaus operate electronically through computer networks between traders all over the world.

Therefore, foreign trading goes on for 24 hours a day, six days a week in leading financial centers of major capital cities around the world. Investment and commercial banks carry out most of the Forex Trading in the international marketplaces in place of clients and investors.

Principles of Forex Trading

1. Learn the Market's Trends

It is essential for one to be able to predict the changing nature of the foreign exchange market in order to be successful in Forex Trading.

Accordingly, a person should understand the general direction of the marketplace. Trends can be uptrend, downtrend, or sideways trend. Identifying a pattern can profit a person in that he or she will be able to trade with the trend.

Uptrends are trends that move upwards, indicating an appreciation in currency value. Downtrends move downwards as an indication of depreciation in currency value. Sideways trends show that the currencies are neither appreciating nor depreciating.

2. Stay Focused and Control Your Emotions

Forex Trading is a challenging marketplace that can cause a person to lose confidence and to give up in the toughest of times. That is understandable given that traders put in their hard-earned money.

As a result, when a person experiences loss, he or she can lose focus when negative emotions become overwhelming. Some of the negative emotions a person may experience include panic, frustration, depression, and desperation.

It is, therefore, essential for one to become aware of the negative emotions that result from Forex Trading so that he or she may minimize the emotional effects of loss and remain focused.

3. Learn Risk Mitigation Tactics

In order to achieve the profits that a person anticipates, the person needs to minimize the likelihood of financial loss.

Since the forex market keeps on changing, the risks, therefore, keep on changing. The most crucial risk management rule is that a person should not risk more than he or she can afford to lose. Traders who are willing to invest more than they make, become very susceptible to Forex Trading risks.

Consequently, a person can mitigate potential losses by placing stop-loss orders, exchanging more than one currency pair, using software programs for help, and limiting the use of financial leverage.

4. Establish Personal Forex Trading Limits

A person should know when to stop Forex Trading. One can stop Forex Trading when he or she has an unproductive trading plan, or when he or she is continually experiencing losses.

An ineffective Forex Trading plan may not bring trade to an end, but it will not function as well as a trader may expect. In that case, the trader can consider stopping the trade, constantly changing markets, and the decreasing volatility within a particular foreign trading tool may also cause a trader to take a break from Forex Trading.

In addition, when a person is not in a good physical or emotional state, he or she may want to think about taking a break to deal with personal issues.

5. Use Technology to Your Benefit

Being up-to-date with existing technological developments can be gratifying in Forex Trading.

Given that forex markets utilize the online forum, high-speed internet connections can increase Forex Trading performance significantly. In order to make the most of Forex Trading, a person must take it as a full-time occupation, and he or she must embrace new technologies. Similarly, receiving forex market current information with smartphones makes it possible for forex traders to track trades anywhere.

Forex Trading is an aggressive enterprise that needs a trader to have an equally competitive edge. Therefore, a forex trader needs to maximize his or her business's potential by taking full advantage of the available technology.

6. Make Use of a Forex Trading Plan

A Forex Trading plan comprises of rules and guidelines that stipulate a forex trader's entry, exit, and money management principles.

A trading plan provides the opportunity for a forex trader to try out a Forex Trading idea before the trader risks real money. In so doing, a trader can access historical information that helps to know whether a Forex Trading plan is feasible and what outcomes he or she can expect.

When a forex trader comes up with a Forex Trading plan that shows potentially favorable outcomes, he or she can use the trading plan in real Forex Trading situations. The idea is for the forex trader to adhere to the trading plan.

Buying or selling currencies outside of the Forex Trading plans, even if a trader makes a profit, is poor trading, which can end any expectation the plan may have had.

Different Types of Forex Traders

Because foreign markets become flooded with the constant demand for currency exchange, four types of currency traders facilitate the smooth operation of forex markets.

1. Scalpers

Forex scalpers are dealers who buy or sell currencies, hold on to the exchanged currencies, and then wait for them to have higher and favorable exchange rates before the dealers can change their new currencies back to their original versions.

The scalpers hold deals for seconds to minutes and open and close several positions within a single day. In other words, scalpers go in and out of positions several times each day.

Scalpers trade currencies based on real-time analysis. Scalpers aim to make a profit by selling or buying currencies and holding on to them for a short time before buying or selling the currencies back to the forex market for small gains.

Therefore, that means that scalpers should love sitting in front of their laptops or computers for the entire forex session without taking their eyes off the screen.

Scalping is widespread moments after essential data releases and interest rate announcements. That is because high-impact reports generate significant price moves within a short period.

However, while profits can accrue rapidly with profitable trades, huge losses can also accumulate if the scalper is using a faulty system or if the trader does not understand what he or she is doing.

2. Day Traders

Forex day traders control trading positions during each trading day. Day traders close the trading positions at the end of the trading day and ensure that there are no positions that remain open during the night.

Forex day traders use currency day trading systems that regulate whether to buy or sell a currency pair in the foreign exchange market. A currency pair is the quotation of two different currencies where the trader quotes the value of one currency in comparison to the other.

Day traders target day currencies that are very liquid to leverage their capital as soon as investment prices change in favorable directions. The traders pick a price position at the start of the day, act on their assessments, and finish the trading day with either a profit or a loss.

Forex day traders avoid holding positions overnight because that may result in stock price gaps, a consequence, which can be very costly.

3. Swing Traders

Swing traders take hold of a position over a few days to several weeks. They hold places for more than one trading session, although not longer than several weeks or a couple of months.

Swing traders aim to capture huge potential price moves. Some swing traders may look for volatile stocks with constant movements, whereas others prefer stock prices that are more predictable.

Swing traders have exposure to overnight and weekend risks, where prices could rift and open the following forex session with markedly different rates. However, swing traders can generate profit by using established risk or reward strategies that will help them to determine where they will enter assets, where they will place stop-loss orders, and to know where they can make profits. Stop-loss orders help to limit the loss when stock prices fall.

Swing traders come up with plans and strategies that will give them an advantage over may trades. The traders do that by looking for trade arrangements that facilitate predictable price movements in the price of the asset. However, no trade arrangement works every time.

4. Position Traders

Position traders hold on to investment positions for long periods, anticipating the investments to appreciate. The periods can extend from weeks to months. In that regard, position traders are less concerned with short-term changes in price movements.

Position traders follow trends, believing that once a pattern starts, it is likely to continue. As such, position traders incline toward obtaining the bulk of a trend's move, which would generate profit in their investment capital.

Position traders use both fundamental and technical analysis to help in making trading decisions. They also depend on macroeconomic influences, old trends, and overall market movements to get to their anticipated end.

For a trader to have success in position trading, the trader has to know the entry or exit points and have a strategy to mitigate risk mainly by placing stop-loss orders.

Advantage of Forex Trading

1. Easy to Modify

Forex Trading markets put no restrictions on how much money a forex trader can use. Forex traders can trade a variety of goods and services.

In addition, the forex market does not have many rules and regulations for the forex trader to follow. The regulations that exist guide forex traders on when to enter and when to exit a trade.

2. Individual Control

Nobody controls the foreign market. Therefore, a forex trader has complete autonomy concerning making a trade. The forex market regulates itself and levels the playing field.

There are no intermediaries involved - a forex trader trades directly in the open forex market, and a retail forex broker eases that process.

3. Lucidity of Information

The Forex Trading market gives information straightforwardly to the public about the rates and price movement forecasts. The forex market traders have free and equal access to the market's information, and that makes it easy for the traders to make calculated and risk-free trading decisions.

Forex traders also have access to past information that helps in analyzing the market tendencies and forecasting the direction, which the market will take.

4. Widespread Options

The forex market provides a variety of options to forex investors. As a result, forex investors can take advantage of the available options to trade in different currencies in pairs.

An investor has the option of getting into foreign exchange spot trade or trading in currency futures to make the most of his or her investment.

5. High Liquidity and Volume

The forex market trades in large amounts of currencies at any given time because of how active the foreign exchange is. Therefore, there are high chances for forex traders to trade currency pairs on demand.

Under normal market conditions, a forex trader can buy and sell quickly with the anticipation that there will be another forex trader on the other end who is willing to trade back.

6. Money-Making Gains

The forex market provides Forex Trading measures that guard against financial loss. To ensure that a forex trader maximizes of gaining profits, the forex market has provisions for minimizing loss through making stop-loss orders.

Stop-loss orders enable forex traders to determine the closing price of their trade and thereby avoiding unforeseen losses.

7. 24-Hour Market

Foreign exchange markets remain open for 24-hours a day and 6 days a week. That means that the market stays open most of the time, and it is not subject to external factors that may affect it.

Consequently, forex traders are flexible to work during the hours that suit them best.

8. Low Operation Costs

Operation costs in the forex currency markets are competent in trading in the forex market. The cost of operation in the currency market is in the form of spreads measured in pips. A pip is the fourth place after the decimal point of a percent.

For example, is the selling price was 2.5887, and the buying price was 2.5889, then the transaction cost is 2pips. Brokers may charge commissions on a fraction of the amount of the trade.

9. Chief Financial Market

The forex market is the biggest financial market in the world. That is because global corporations and big financial institutions participate dynamically in the foreign exchange market.

The foreign exchange market empowers major financial institutions to retail stockholders to seek out profits from currency variations connected to the global economy.

10. One Can Use the Leverage

The forex markets allow forex traders to capitalize on the advantage. Leveraging enables forex traders to be able to open positions for thousands of dollars while investing small amounts of money.

For example, when a forex trader trades at 40:1 leverage, he or she can trade $40 for every $1 that was in his or her account. That means that the forex trader can manage a trade of $40,000 for every $1,000 of investment.

Why Forex

The foreign exchange market is open to all types of traders, and it is more accessible than any other online trading platform in the world. Similarly, one can start trading with as little as $100. Therefore, foreign exchange markets have lower exchange capital prerequisites compared to other financial markets. A person can quickly sign up to open their trading account online, where most forex retail brokers operate.

Forex Trading is easy to learn, although it may be challenging to master. However, once an investor understands how the forex market works, he or she will be open to a world of vast opportunities that include becoming a foreign exchange account manager. A foreign exchange account manager can accumulate profits from trading as well as earning commissions for managing the Forex Trading accounts.

Foreign exchange markets make provisions for forex brokers to develop considerable trading volumes because of the leverage that the forex markets offer. That explains why forex traded get rewards like deposit bonuses when creating a Forex Trading account. Likewise, forex brokers give several incentives and promotions to financial institutions that enter Forex Trading. As a result, the forex market becomes a stimulating marketplace for Forex Trading.

Forex traders form international social communities as more people sign up every day. The social networks help forex investors to encounter an entire community of foreign exchange traders, thus making the forex market an interactive market to trade. In addition, forex traders can find many international forex experts, contributors, critics, and educators, among other members, in every conceivable language.

Moreover, forex traders can buy and sell risk-free, using a demonstration trading account. The account prevents traders from putting their investment at risk, and the traders can, therefore, move to the live forex markets whenever they please. The trading accounts enable forex traders to have access to real-time market information and the latest trading wisdom from foreign experts.

The forex market infrastructure is sophisticated, causing the performance of traders to be even more level. The forex market also has low spreads and commissions, thus making the transaction costs relatively small as a result. Besides, the foreign exchange market educates forex traders on global events, as the traders continue to trade online. Favorable trading conditions are crucial for foreign exchange traders.

Heavy security measures guard the foreign exchange markets, and several authorities control every forex broker. The bodies exist to make sure that forex traders have a safe space to carry out Forex Trading activities. However, forex traders are only with regulated brokers. Therefore, one must conduct a background check on available brokers in order to ensure that he or she works with the regulated brokers.

Online Forex Trading makes use of advanced trading software that generates regular updates that help forex investors to make real-time Forex Trading decisions. Consequently, Forex Trading becomes a rewarding way to buy and sell online, also due to third-party software developers who provide add-ons and plugins for popular trading platforms.

Finally, the forex markets allow traders to buy low and sell high. What's more, forex traders can trade assets without owning them, a practice that is called short selling. Furthermore, the use of leverage enables Forex traders to buy or sell more substantial amounts than what they have in their deposits.

Chapter 1 How to Start Forex Trading

Forex trading is not a trade that one can pull off without breaking a sweat before exchanging currencies. There has to be prior preparation, studies done and analyzation of the market patterns to make the first trade. Below is discussed the steps that a trader has to make so as to start trading forexes and be successful while doing so.

Forex Trading Terminology
There are a lot of terms used that are new to a trader who is just starting off and are vocabularies to them. It would do well to an aspiring trader to acquaint themselves with the new terms and understand the meaning behind them and how to use them appropriately when trading. This will prove essential to avoid miscomprehension of certain concepts when trading. To new traders, the terms may be a little bit difficult and also have a completely different meaning than the expected one from its word-formation. The following words discussed below are some of the new vocabularies that will be encountered by a new trader, which are common in the language of trading.

A pip. A pip is the lowest measure of the value of movement of currency under observation. The term pip is, however, an abbreviation of the term- percentage in point. A pip, as the lowest measurable value of the movement that the currency makes, always measures ad 1% of the currency that a trader wants to exchange. When in the forex market a currency increases or decreases by a single pip, the inference has the meaning that the currency either increased or decreased by 1%. A great example is when the market analysis tools show that the US dollar has increased by a pip. This is to mean that the US dollar has increased in its value by $0.0001.

That is how a pip is inferred and it's meaning. Trade is always made in terms of pips, and a trader can make trades with many pips as possible. This is because the pips are the lowest value that is measured by the currency.

The base currency. The base currency is the type of currency that a trader has and is currently holding. The base currency is likely the currency of the country that you're from. If a trader is from the US, his or her base currency will be the US dollar. If the trader is from the UK, the base currency of the trader will be the pound. The base currencies of traders therefore different across many traders around the globe due to different geographical differences.

The asking price. The asking price is a term that is used to refer to the amount of money that your broker firm will demand from or will ask from you when you are making a trade. A broker always demands this price, or this amount of money when they are accepting the pair of currencies to be traded from you. The price id for buying the quote that you've made of the pair of currencies. A note to be made is that the asking price; made by the brokerage firms, is always higher than the bid price, as will be discussed immediately below.

Bid price. The bid price is mostly used in reference to the brokerage firms, where it is the amount of money that the brokers will be willing to buy or to bid the base currency that you are currently holding. The broker firm sets the bid price according to their ability to bid on the base currency that has.

Quote currency. The quote currency, unlike the base currency, is the currency that a trader wants and is willing to purchase, in exchange for his or her base currency. If a trader wants to exchange US dollars to get South African Rand, the currency of South Africa; the Rand is the quote currency. It is always stroked against the base currency when trading and when the currencies are made into pairs.

The spread. This is the commission that the broker firm receives from being a platform where forex trading can take place. When referred to, the spread means the difference in value between the bid price made by the broker and the asking price, also quoted by the broker.

These are but a few but the major terms that are used in the forex trading world. Knowing this alone will not be enough, you have to be familiar with more words and phrases that can be found in books concerning forex trading. Not only in books but also videos, forums and such where forex trading is discussed.

Finding the Right Broker Firm
So as to trade forex, you will have to have a brokerage firm that will be an online platform from which you'll open and close trade. Finding the right broker firm is an important process for other brokers can be a sham out to cheat people of their money. It is therefore paramount that a trader carries out research on the available broker firms and picks out the best and one that is highly recommended for its services. When deciding on which broker firm to go with, look at the ask and the bid price that the broker quotes, and other important aspects including the margin and the leverage level that they offer. The customer service should also be top-notch for the broker, which will be

great for a trader who is just starting off. Most of the broker companies also offer studies on how to carry out forex trading and those come in handy to the new traders. Reviews by other forex traders is a great place to start on choosing the quality of a broker.

Making an Analysis of the Worldwide Economy
To make gains and profits and gains in trades that you are going to make, analyzing the economic trends of the worldwide economy is of great import to be fully aware of the factors that may trigger the currencies to increase or decrease in value. This is important in making a correct prediction on the pair of currencies you're exchanging, whether they will make a profit or a loss. Factors that are important to look into when evaluating the global economy are like the political climate of countries whose currencies have a strong value, natural factors that may influence the economy of countries, the Gross Domestic Product of the country whose currency you want to exchange with your base currency, and other minor factors such as the investment rate of the said country. Evaluating which countries are looking up to growth and development opportunities is also important in determining the quote currency to use impairing up currencies to make a trade. Also on the analysis of the worldwide economy, when the currency of the country you seek to purchase in exchange of your base currency is doing well and is set to increase in its value, convert your base currency into the quote currency. On the other hand, convert the quote currency into the base currency in case its value increases. There are various online sites that have analysis tools on the economic performance of different countries that you may seek for them to be your quote currency. Others rank counties in terms of their GDP that makes it easier for you to choose the

countries that are projected for growth and development. Being in touch with the trending news globally is a plus in getting information relevant to trading forex. A new forex trader may subscribe to a few forex trading channels and outlets to be constantly on toes of events and happenings that may trigger the value of currencies to either increase o decrease, which may result in the reversal of the outlook of the trade made. Having relevant information at all times is key in making gains and preventing the loss of your money and probably your account is cleared.

Opening the First Trade
Pairing currencies and making the first trade; opening and closing a trade happens when the quote currency to be paired by the base currency have been paired and there is an opportune trading window. Opening a trade is making an order to purchase a certain currency and in exchange for your base current through your broker firm. You'll have the analysis tools, that are commonly offered by the brokers in software programs. The execution of making an order in some platforms might be instant while in some other platforms, it might be a tad bit slower. Nonetheless, most brokerage firms offer live prices and values of the currencies that are to traded and their exchange rates and the instant changes to their values are displayed. The first trade for a new trader might just be one or others might open up new trades over a short period of time. It is advisable that just several enough trades be opened, which the new trader is comfortable and at ease in trading.

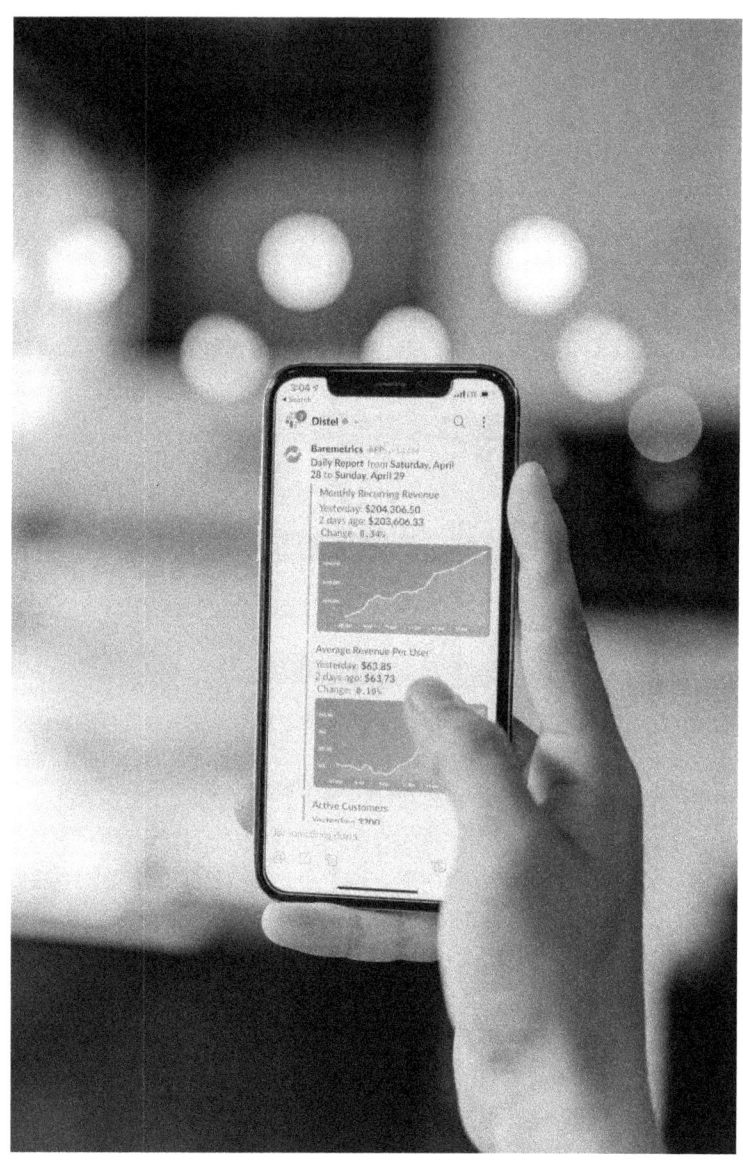

Chapter 2 Technical and Fundamental Analysis

After reviewing the strategies that are used in Forex trading, we will discuss the tools that are used in Forex trading. We are going to keep it relatively simple because frankly, it's not necessary to overcomplicate things. The main tools that we are going to focus on are tools that will help you keep track of pricing trends and help you find signals of trend reversals.

The first thing to consider is technical vs. fundamental analysis. If you are someone who has done trading on the stock market, you will have some idea of what these two concepts are about. In the Forex markets, there are some general similarities and some differences. When it comes to technical analysis, there are more similarities to be found than differences, however. Technical analysis involves the use of tools that can be applied to any financial instrument that is traded on a marketplace. The tools of technical analysis can be used to get information about trading volume, pricing trends, and pricing trend reversals. There are three main tools that are used by most traders. The first tool that is used is the candlestick charts. Candlestick charts divide up a graph of pricing of a financial asset into short time intervals, using a graphical representation (in the form of a "candlestick") that gives you pricing information for each time interval. The candlestick will let you know what the high and low prices were for the time interval, what the open and closing prices were for the time interval, and whether the closing price finished above or below the opening price, indicating whether traders were "bullish" or "bearish" on the financial asset for the given time period. Moreover, candlesticks help you see how trends are developing and possibly reversing. We are going to talk about candlesticks more in a bit.

The other tools that are frequently used include moving averages, which smooth out pricing data by averaging them, Bollinger bands, which help you see the one standard deviation pricing rage for a financial asset, and the relative strength indicator which helps you determine whether an asset is "overbought" or "oversold." You can also look at the average pip movement.

What technical analysis comes down to, is it's a set of tools that helps you determine the buildup of trends and pricing shifts as supply and demand for a given financial asset changes in the marketplace. Technical analysis is not concerned with what is causing those price movements, or even what the underlying financial security is.

Fundamental analysis is an entirely different ballgame.

Fundamental analysis for Forex markets is far broader, and actually quite a bit simpler. The main components of fundamental analysis when currencies are the subject of interest are the interest rate of the central bank, the interest rate of the central bank for the country that is the other party to a given currency pair (and so we are really considering the interest rate differential between the two countries), and the overall economic health of each country. For example, the exports that a country relies on are important, and therefore changes in commodity prices are something that needs to be considered. GDP growth rates, unemployment, and other factors are things to look at where fundamental analysis is concerned. If one member of a currency pair is performing in a much better way in comparison to the other when it comes to these metrics, that can mean that it is the better choice for the currency pair.

You want to look for both positive and negative news events, but a bad event can drive investors out of a country, such as a terrorist attack, or a political upheaval. It's important to keep up with the news even if such events seem unlikely in current circumstances; many quiet years can go by before the international situation deteriorates or becomes chaotic. A large-scale terrorist attack could hurt an economy or drive tourism away, at least temporarily. An economic recession can also cause problems if it is localized to one country.

- Factors to Consider in Technical Analysis
  - Candlestick Charts

Now, let's turn our attention to the specifics of technical analysis. The first tool of technical analysis that a new trader needs to learn is candlestick charts. A candlestick is a representation of price movement over a specific time period that you set for your chart. For example, you can set the time period to a minute, 5 minutes, or even one day. This is the trading session. The candlestick will have a body, and two upper and lower shadows or wicks.

Image from Wikipedia, courtesy of Probe-meteo.com

The upper wick represents the high price for the trading session. The lower wick represents the low price for the candlestick. The body of the candlestick represents the opening and closing prices for the trading session. There are two general types of candlesticks. They can be bullish, in which case they represent a trading session where prices were pushed upward. In that case, the top of the candlestick body is the closing price for the trading session, while the bottom of the candlestick would be the opening price for the trading session. Bullish candlesticks are either solid green in color or outlined green on trading charts. If the chart is black and white, the candlestick will be an outline for the bullish trading session.

If the asset price dropped during the trading session, then you have a bearish candlestick. On charts with white backgrounds, they are colored red—and in most cases with charts, with black backgrounds. Bearish candlesticks are colored white—on a black-and-white chart. A bearish candlestick will have a solid black body. For a bearish candlestick, the top of the candlestick body represents the opening price for the trading session, while the bottom of the candlestick body is the closing price - so this represents a case where the price dropped. In both cases (bearish and bullish), the meaning of the wicks or shadows extended out from the candlesticks is the same.

GREEN:RED:

Image from Wikipedia, courtesy of Probe-meteo.com

The trader studies candlestick patterns in order to look for signals that trends are going to reverse. A candlestick pattern, by itself, is not a reason to enter or exit a trade. The trader will "confirm" the signal seen in the candlesticks with at least two other methods that we will discuss below.

Many trading platforms use black backgrounds for Forex charts. In this case, the white candlesticks are bearish, and the green outlined candlesticks are bullish.

There are many patterns that you need to become familiar with in order to be successful using candlestick charts to help you make the right trades. The first thing to look for is called an engulfing pattern. This happens when the candlestick of one type (bearish or bullish) is followed by a candlestick of the opposite type. The second candlestick will have a much larger body, indicating that the price was driven upwards by a large amount during the trading session. The candlestick would "engulf" or completely cover the previous candlestick. This type of pattern is shown below. It indicates a coming upward trend in price.

The next pattern that we are going to look at is called "three white soldiers." The name is historical and comes from the old black-and-white charts where the bullish candlesticks would be white with black outlines. Today we might call it "three green soldiers." This is three bullish candlesticks in a row, with higher highs in succession. This indicates a coming upward trend. This is shown below.

Next, we come to a "doji" indecision candle. This candle has a thin line for a body, indicating that the opening and closing prices for the trading session were the same. The candle will also have long wicks, indicating that the prices were pushed up high and down low during the trading session, but they ended up back at the opening price. This is the "indecision," traders were neither bullish or bearish during the trading session.

Another signal that an upward trend in price is coming is called an inverted hammer. In this case, you will see a bullish candlestick with a relatively narrow body, but with a long upward wick, indicating the prices were pushed up high during the trading session. Even though the high was not maintained, the price closed higher than the open, and the opening price is the low price for the trading session. It should be confirmed using technical indicators like a moving average crossover.

A hammer is this pattern in reverse, and if a hammer occurs at the top of an uptrend, this may indicate a coming downward trend in price.

There is also a pattern known as a shooting star. In this case, there is a bearish candle in the form of an inverted hammer, appearing at the top of an uptrend. So it will have a long wick shooting upward, the "shooting" part of the star, but it will close at a lower price than the open.

The same types of patterns that form with bullish candlesticks can form with bearish candlesticks as well. In these cases, they indicate a coming downward trend in prices. For example, we can have three bearish candlesticks in a row, indicating declining prices, with lower lows for each closing price. This is called three black crows, a historical reference to the time when the charts were black and white, and the bearish candlesticks were solid black in color.

Next, we consider an evening star. This is a pattern that can indicate a coming downtrend. When there is an evening star, you first see a large upward push in prices with a large bullish candlestick. This is followed by a hammer that is a bearish hammer, so the price closed below the open. That indicates that although the price had been pushed up, it wasn't possible to keep finding buyers.

The abandoned baby pattern appears at the end of a downtrend. In this case, there is a large bearish candle that ends a streak of bearish candles. Then, there is a doji indecision candle, indicating that sellers are not coming to the table anymore. This is followed by a bullish candle indicating a buying spree is coming up:

The terms bullish and bearish used with candlesticks come from the stock market, where rising prices are desirable. Keep in mind that on the Forex markets, rising or falling prices are not framed in the same way, because you might be betting on the secondary currency and so you are hoping for falling prices. So for the Forex markets, bullish means that the primary currency is rising against the secondary currency, while bearish means the secondary currency is rising against the primary currency. So whether something is really "bullish" or not depends on what side of the trade you are on.

There are many other candlestick patterns that you can use. An entire book could be written on this topic, and we don't have space to cover them all. But you should be educated on them all before you start trading, so you should look for videos, articles, and even Udemy courses about candlesticks online.

- Strength Indicators

Another technical indicator you may want to use is the relative strength indicator. This indicator helps you get an idea if a financial asset is overbought or oversold. This helps you determine the momentum in a trend. When we say an asset is overbought, this means that the price has been pushed too high with respect to the actual value of the asset. In other words, the price is pushed higher than the fundamentals would indicate is valid. When this happens, the price can continue increasing, but the momentum of the price increase is probably going to peter out, and the price trend will peak out and eventually reverse. At this point, in short order, people holding the asset are going to recognize that it's overpriced, and they will start dumping it on the market so they can exit their positions at a relative high pricing point.

This can happen on the downside as well. In this case, we are talking about an oversold asset. This means the price that is driven down lower than the fundamentals would indicate a valid price. At this point, momentum to push the price down is going to be decreasing, even if, for a while, prices continue to drop. This probably indicates that a trend reversal is coming, and prices will start rising again. It's just a matter of time before buyers recognize that the asset has now become available at a bargain price, and so they will start moving in to buy the asset and push prices back up.

The RSI runs over 0-100. There are different conventions used with the relative strength indicator, but the standard is using 70-80 as the cutoff point for overbought. That is, if the RSI is above 70 or 80 (70 is probably too conservative), you should consider a rising price trend as overbought, and it will probably reverse soon. For oversold conditions, and RSI less than 20 is typically used.

- Bollinger Bands

The next technical indicator that you should at least be aware of is called Bollinger bands. This is a more complicated indicator that brings three pieces of information together. It consists of three curves. In the center, there is a moving average curve. You can set the type of moving average that you want to use, but by default, it will be a simple moving average. There are curves above and below the moving average that show the one standard deviations above and below the moving average. This helps you to determine levels of support and resistance as well as signs that a breakout may occur.

During a timeframe that the financial asset is ranging, it will have price fluctuations that are contained within the Bollinger bands. Therefore, if you are buying a currency pair, you can wait for the price to drop to the lower Bollinger (or alternatively, you can buy when the price touches the moving average if there are other signs it will begin rising in price). Then, you sell when the price moves to the upper Bollinger band.

When the candlesticks move outside one of the outer Bollinger bands, this can be a sign of a coming breakout. If the wicks, or especially the body, go above the upper-level Bollinger band, this can be taken as an indicator that the price is going to start moving upward, until it establishes a new higher level of pricing support.

Alternatively, you can look for instances of the candlesticks going below the lower Bollinger band, which can indicate the possibility of a break to the downside in prices, which can be a start of a new downward trend.

- The Depth Line

You may also take a look at the market in-depth in order to determine the supply and demand for a given currency pair. This tells you the number of open buy-and-sell orders for the currency pair. The larger the number of buying and selling orders, the more the depth of the market. The importance of this value is the higher the depth line, the more liquidity there is in the market for the given currency pair. It will also give you an idea of how likely it is that your order will be filled in a timely fashion at a given price. Of course, for major currency pairs such as the EUR/USD, liquidity is never going to be an issue. However, even in that case, you can use market depth so that you can see how many open orders there are at different price points. There will be an ask volume and a bid volume. The ask is the asking price from sellers, and the bid is the price that buyers are bidding and willing to pay. You can also see the total ask less total bid on your charts so that you can get an estimate of how different these values are - giving an indication of how quickly orders are going to be filled. If there is a large difference in value between the bid and ask prices, then that can indicate that there is going to be some difficulty in filling orders. On the other hand, if the difference is small, orders will be filled quickly.

- Factors to Consider in Fundamental Analysis

In this section, we are going to briefly examine the main factors you should consider when using fundamental analysis as a part of your toolkit to determine which currencies you want to invest in.

- Interest Rates

Interest rates are an important metric to consider. There are many factors that will determine the strength of a currency, but all things considered equal, higher interest rates mean the currency is going to be more in demand, and therefore it will rise against other currencies. If the interest rate in the United States rises, outside investors will be more interested in buying bonds and other interest producing assets inside the United States, and they are going to need dollars to do it. Therefore, this means that the demand for dollars will rise, and prices will be pushed up. But the key thing for Forex is the fact that currencies are traded in pairs, and so you also have to consider one interest rate against the other. So fundamental analysis will, in part, involve knowing global interest rates, or at least the interest rates of the majors.

Inflation

Inflation is another key factor. A high inflation rate means that inside the country, the currency is losing value. High inflation rates may make investing in the currency of a given country a bad proposition. Once again, when looking at a given currency pair, you are going to want to make relative comparisons for the inflation rates in the two countries.

- GDP Growth Rates

When the GDP growth rate for a company is strong, this is going to attract more investment, generally speaking. Of course, there are many factors involved. If inflation is out of control, then high GDP growth rates may not be that attractive. But if all other indicators are good, a solid GDP growth rate is going to bring people to the table, which means that demand for the currency will be high.

Unemployment

The unemployment rate is another indicator of the health of the economy. High unemployment rates will make the currency unattractive, while lower unemployment rates are going to make the currency more attractive. Again, this is something that has to be seen in a relative context; you are going to compare the unemployment rate to the other partner in the currency pair. You will also want to look at the labor force participation rate if this data is available, as well as the number of people working full-time or part-time.

Trade

Trade issues can be important, too. When there is a lot of trade, there is also a lot of exchange of currency. For example, consider Japan, dollars flowing into the country need to be exchanged for Japanese Yen so that Japanese companies can use their profits at home. Besides trade, you will also want to look at any monetary flows between countries by large corporations, which eventually can mean having to exchange the currency into the local variety.

Indicators Of Forex Trading

Before we begin an in-depth discussion of the strategies used by Forex traders, you need to have an understanding of charts. The charts used in Forex are similar in a superficial sense to the charts that you may have seen on the stock markets. Typically, Forex traders are going to be using candlestick charts. In fact, this is almost a universal practice. That is the topic that we are going to cover in this chapter.

Remember What the Chart Is Charting

This sounds like a crazy statement, but you have to remember that the currency pair A/B means that if the value shown in the chart increases, this favors the currency A. What this means is that the value of currency A is increasing relative to the value of currency B. You can also look at it in the sense that if the graph on the chart is increasing, the value of currency B is decreasing.

So if you buy the currency pair A/B, and the increasing graph or upward trend is a trend that is working in your favor.

Now consider a downward trend. When the trend is going downward, you are losing money if you had bought the currency pair A/B, because this means that the value of currency A is decreasing relative to currency B.

Where some new traders get confused is when you sell the currency pair A/B. In this case, the meanings on the chart are reversed, because if you sell the currency pair A/B, this means that you are betting on the currency B. So when the chart is un an upward trend, if you had sold the currency pair you are losing money. This is easy to understand. For the sake of simplicity, let's say that you had sold the currency pair for $1. To exit the position, you have to buy back the currency pair. But if it increases in price to $2, then you would lose $1 buying it back. The values given here are for illustration only, but it nicely illustrates the general concept.

Now consider the opposite situation. That is, we are still talking about selling the currency pair A/B, but this time we see a downward trend on the chart. This means that the price of the currency pair is decreasing. We can, of course, frame this result in many ways. One of the ways that we can do so is to say that the currency B is increasing in value, with respect to currency A. Now let's say that once again we sold the currency pair A/B for $1. Now we imagine that is has decreased in price to $0.50. Then we can buy it back, and we make a $0.50 profit.

Of course, these prices are not realistic for a Forex trade, but it clearly shows the concept of how this actually works. If you understand the concept explained here, and you've understood how to read the change in pips from the chart and how to convert that into dollars moved based on your position size, then you are well on your way to becoming a Forex trader who at least understands what is going on.

What Is a candlestick

The next thing to come across is the use of candlesticks, which you always see on Forex charts. A candlestick is a graphical way to represent price action. By price action, we simply mean how high did the price go, how low did it drop, and what the opening and closing prices were. The candlestick charts also give a visual representation that we can eyeball, in order to see at a glance whether the price went up or down for a given time period.

So what each candlestick represents is a "trading session." The trading session can be one of many different lengths of time. Different traders are going to choose different lengths of time used for the trading sessions shown on the chart, depending on what their needs are. Some traders are interested in very short time frames, so they may use one-minute trading sessions. Others are going to use 5- or 15-minute trading sessions. You can also use 4-hour trading sessions or even one-day trading sessions. It's up to you to decide what time interval to use, and this is going to be decided in part by your trading style.

Before we show the basics of a candlestick, you need to understand how and why these are used. The basic idea that is behind the candlestick is to have a visual way to look at the chart and determine whether or not there is going to be a price reversal. Price reversals and trends are the bread and butter of this business. The first thing you are going to want to look for when you are trading currencies is if there is a trend one way or the other.

If there is a strong upward trend and there are signals that the trend is going to continue, then this is a currency pair that you want to buy. Conversely, if there is a downward trend, this could be a currency pair that you want to sell. This little fact that we have described is one important way that Forex trading differs from stock market trading, at least for most people. Granted, there are many people who trade options or who short stock, and they will make more complicated market plays. But you see with Forex that it automatically offers you ways to make money, no matter which way the market is moving. It's always in pairs, and you don't have to be wedded to one single currency.

That means that you don't have to be focused only on the dollar and hoping that it's going to always rise with respect to the Euro. As a Forex trader, you really should not care which direction the currency is moving. You can earn profits either way. The only time you care about which direction it's moving is after you've entered a position. Then and only then is the time that you need to be concerned about this issue.

Trend reversals are really the important thing to look for. If the market has been in a downward trend for some time, and you have been sitting on the sidelines, you are going to be looking for a trend reversal. It's never a good idea to get involved in a trade when it's too late. If you have been following the currency pair A/B and the currency pair has been in a long time downtrend, even if you like the currency B, you are probably better off waiting for a reversal, and buying the currency pair, rather than joining the trend late in the game. So in this example, when the candlesticks gave you the signal that the trend was reversing, you would buy the currency pair. The trend reversal signal would indicate that the downward trend has come to an end, and now is the time to get in a position in order to take advantage of the coming upward trend.

Structure Of A Candlestick

The candlestick has three parts. The first part is the rectangular area that is found in the center of the candlestick. This is called the body. The body of the candlestick tells you the opening and closing prices of the trading session. However, there are two types of candlesticks. Traditionally they are black and white, but I am going to skip over that because who uses black and white charts anymore. I can assure you that almost nobody does.

The background of most charts these days is either black or white. We are going to take the latter possibility, first because most Forex traders actually use black background charts. But you can use white backgrounds and some traders too.

There are two types of candlesticks. A candlestick can indicate that the price dropped for the trading period, in which case it is called a "bearish" candlestick. Or the candlestick can indicate that the price increased over the trading period, in which case it's a bullish candlestick.

On a chart with a white background, a bearish candlestick is red in color. A bullish candlestick will be green in color. On a black chart, the bearish candlesticks are usually solid white, and the bullish candlesticks are the green outline.

That is all pretty basic to understand. Now let us use a basic fact to explain the price action described or illustrated by a candlestick. If there is a bearish trading session, that means that the opening price was higher than the closing price. As a result, the top of the candlestick body - which is a higher pricing point - represents the opening price for the trading session. In contrast, the bottom of the candlestick, which is the lower price on the chart, represents the closing price for the trading session.

A bullish candlestick works in the opposite way. A bullish candlestick indicates that the price went up during the trading session. So the top of the candlestick is the closing price for the trading session. The bottom of the candlestick is going to be the opening price for the trading session.

A candlestick has lines that come out of the top and bottom of the body. These lines are called shadows or wicks. They have the same meaning whether or not the candlestick is bullish, or whether it's bearish. The wick or shadow coming out of the top of the candlestick body tells you the high price of the trading session.

The bottom wick tells you the low price of the trading session. The basics of candlestick setup are shown below.

Reversal Signals

Now we need to be able to look for certain signals that indicate a coming change in price trend. The signals are in the price action that tells us that traders are adopting a different sentiment, and the price is about to change direction. This is something you can spend a great deal of time educating yourself about. However, there is only a small subset of indicators that you need to be aware of.

Drawing Trend lines

Drawing trend lines is a simple method that can be used to determine where pricing is going to end up, if the market appears to be moving strongly in one direction or the other. No matter which direction the price is moving, there are always going to be fluctuations. So let's consider a downward trend first. A part of the fluctuation is the fact that on the way down, there are always going to be peaks that occur, that is the asset will drop in price, then rise back up for a short time, then drop in price again, and repeat the process, with each peak as it rises up again getting smaller and smaller. This natural feature of declining prices makes it easy to estimate trends. Starting at the top peak, draw a straight line from the top of the peak, passing the line through all the peaks on the way downward. You want to extend the line past the current price so that you can get an estimate of future price levels, if the market continues to decline. This will be a downward sloping line.

If you are looking at an upward trend instead, you start at the first dip or trough in price. Then draw a straight line, with an upward slope, that connects the bottoms of all the dips on the way up to the right of the chart. This will allow you to get an estimate of where the price is heading if the trend continues.

Most trading platforms allow you to draw trend lines right on their charts on the screen, so you don't actually have to print out a chart and do this on a piece of paper, to estimate where the price is going. You will simply have to position the line in the right locations.

Simple Moving Averages

One of the most popular of the other types of moving averages is called an exponential moving average. This moving average tends to give more accurate information. The reason that it's able to do so is that the exponential moving average weights the prices. The mathematical details aren't important for traders to know, you only have to note that when you use an exponential moving average, prices that are closer to the current trading period are given higher weights than long ago prices. This means that an exponential moving average curve is going to emphasize recent prices, as opposed to long ago prices.

The use of moving averages is so common that trading platforms, like metatrader, are going to show them below your pricing chart by default. An example is shown below, with crossover points indicated by the white arrows.

The way to do your analysis is to combine what you see with the candlesticks with what the moving averages are telling you. In my experience, the moving averages tend to be very accurate indicators of upcoming trends.

However, it remains to be seen if the trend reversal is strong or long-lasting.

You can use a two-step process. The first step is to closely follow the candlestick patterns to look for indicators that a reversal is coming. If you see that the candlesticks are showing signs of a trend reversal, then you can check the moving averages to confirm or deny. If they confirm what you see on the candlestick charts, then you can make a move on a position, whether it is opening a new position or closing an existing position. So you can eyeball them with the candlesticks in real-time.

It can be good to practice with this before actually entering trades and putting real money at risk. Just spend a few days closely watching a currency pair, and begin to identify the patterns seen in the candlesticks in real-time.

Another chart option that you can look at is called the relative strength index or RSI. This can be used in conjunction with your other tools. The purpose of this indicator is to tell you if there are "overbought" or "oversold" conditions. Overbought means that there has been too much buying and that the price is higher than it should be. When there are overbought conditions, chances are there is going to be a trend reversal.

Oversold is the opposite situation; there has been too much selling off of the asset. In the case of oversold conditions, too many people sold the asset off, and as a result, prices have gone down to levels that are lower than conditions really justify.

The value of the RSI will tell you if conditions are neutral, overbought, or oversold. If conditions are neutral, the RSI will be ranging between 20 and 80. If conditions are overbought, this is demonstrated by an RSI that is higher than 80. Finally, if conditions are oversold, this is demonstrated by an RSI that is lower than 20. These values are not fixed, however. Some traders who are more conservative use a narrower range, such as 30-70.

Just like other indicators, you should not use the RSI in isolation, or take action based solely on what the RSI is telling you. Let's take the case of a rising price trend. If the RSI is telling you that the asset is overbought, you see a crossing of the short-term moving average below the long-term moving average, and the candlesticks are indicating a trend reversal, this is a strong selling signal.

Now consider in a downtrend. If the RSI falls below 20 indicating that the asset is oversold, and you see the short-term moving average crossing above the long-term moving average, with signals of a trend reversal coming from the candlesticks, then you have evidence that is strong enough to take as a buying signal. So you can see that we will take multiple signals together, to confirm what we see in the candlesticks. If the candlestick patterns are not confirmed, then you might want to hold off on making a buying decision.

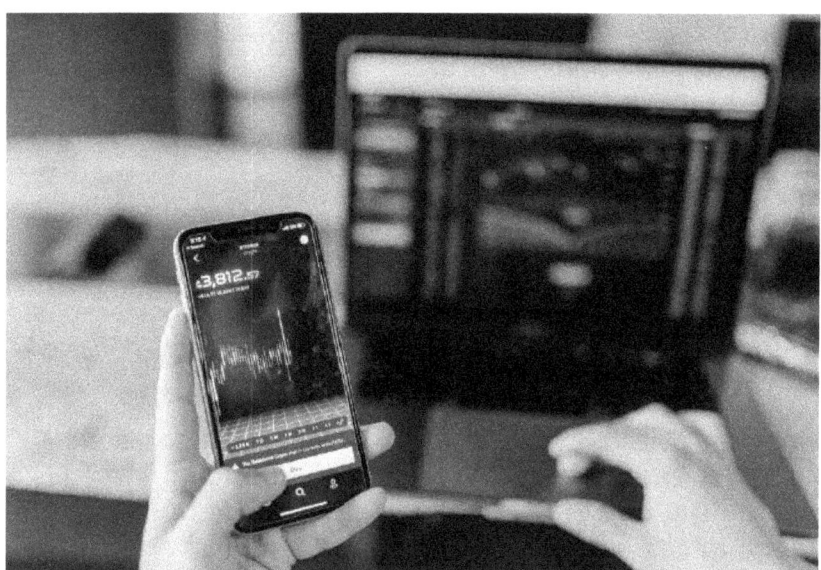

Chapter 3 Forex Trading Strategies

There are several types of forex strategies; however, it is important to choose the right one based preferred trading style to trade successfully. Some strategies work on short-term trades as well as long-term trades. The type of Forex strategies you choose depends on a few factors like:

• Entry points - traders need to determine the appropriate time to enter the market

• Exit point-trader need to develop rules on when to exit the market as well as how to get out of a losing position

• Time availability

If you have a full-time job, then you cannot use day trading or scalping styles

• Personal choices

People who prefer lower winning rates but larger gains should go for position trading while those who prefer higher winning rate but smaller gains can choose the swing trading

Common Forex Trading strategies include:

1. Range trading strategy

Range trading is one of the many viable trading strategies. This strategy is where a trader identifies the support and resistance levels and buys at the support level and sells at the resistance level. This strategy works when there is a lack of market direction or the absence of a trend. Range trading strategies can be broken down into three steps:

- Finding the Range

Finding the range uses the support and resistance zones. The support zone is the buying price of the security while the resistance zone price is the selling price of a security. A breakout happens in the event that the price goes beyond the trading range, whereas a breakdown occurs in the event that the price goes below the trading range.

- Time Your Entry

Traders use a variety of indicators like price action and volume to enter and exit the trading range. They can also use oscillators like CCI, RSI, and stochastics to time their entry. The oscillators track prices using mathematical calculations. Then the traders wait for the prices to reach the support or resistance zones. They often strike when the momentum turns price in the opposing direction.

- Managing Risk

The last step is risk management. When the level of support or resistance breaks, traders will want to exit any range-based positions. They can either use a stop loss above the previous high or invert the process with a stop below the current low.

Pros

- There are ranges that can last even for years producing multiple winning trades.

Cons

- Long-lasting ranges are not easy to come by, and when they do, every range trader wants to use it.
- Not all ranges are worth trading

2. Trend Trading Strategy

Another popular and common Forex Trading strategy is the trend trading strategy. This strategy attempts to make profits by analyzing trends. The process involves identifying an upward or downward trend in a currency price movement and choosing trade entry and exit points based on the currency price within the trend.

Trend traders use these four common indicators to evaluate trends; moving averages, relative strength index (RSI), On-Balance-Volume (OBV), and Moving Average Convergence Divergence (MACD). These indicators provide trend trade signals, warn of reversals, and simplify price information. A trader can combine several indicators to trade.

Pros

• Offers a better risk to reward

• Can be used across any markets

Cons

• Learning to trade on indicators can be challenging.

3. Pairs Trade

This is a neutral trading strategy, which allows pair traders to gain profits in any market conditions. This strategy uses two key strategies:

• Convergence trading - this strategy focuses on two historically correlated securities, where the trader buys one asset forward and sells a similar asset forward for a higher price anticipating that prices will become equal. Profits are made when the underperforming position gains value, and the outperforming position's price deflates

- Statistical trading - this is a short-term strategy that uses the mean reversion models involving broadly diversified Security Portfolios. This strategy uses data mining and statistical methods.

Pros

- If pair trades go as expected investors can make profits

Cons

- This strategy relies on a high statistical correlation between two securities, which can be a challenge.

- Pairs trade relies a lot on historical trends, which do not depict future trends accurately.

4. Price Action Trading

This Forex Trading strategy involves analyzing the historical prices of securities to come up with a trading strategy. Price action trading can be used in short, medium, and long periods. The most commonly used price action indicator is the price bar, which shows detailed information like high and low-price levels during a specific period. However, most traders use more than one strategy to recognize trading patterns, stop-losses, and entry, and exit levels. Technical analysis tools also help price action traders make decisions.

Pros

- No two traders will interpret certain price action the same way

Cons

- Past price history cannot predict future prices accurately

5. Carry Trade Strategy

Carry trade strategy involves borrowing a low-interest currency to buy a currency that has a high rate; the goal is to make a profit with the interest rate difference. For example, one can buy currency pairs like the Japanese yen (low interest) and the Australian dollar (high interest) because the interest rate spreads are very high. Initially, carry trade was used as a one-way trade that moved upwards without reversals, but carry traders soon discovered that everything went downhill once the trade collapsed.

With the carry trade strategy:

1. You need to first identify which currencies offer high rates and which ones have low rates.

2. Then match two currencies with a high-interest differential

3. Check whether the pair has been in an upward tendency favoring the higher-interest rate currency

Pros

- The strategy works in a low volatility environment.

- Suitable for a long-term strategy

- Cons

- Currency rates can change anytime

- Ricky because they are highly leveraged

- Used by many traders therefore overcrowded

6. Momentum Trading

This strategy involves buying and selling assets according to the strength of recent price trends. The basis for this strategy is that an asset price that is moving strongly in a given direction will continue to move in the same direction until the trend loses strength. When assets reach a higher price, they tend to attract many investors and traders who push the market price even higher. This continues until large pools of sellers enter the market and force the asset price down. Momentum traders identify how strong trends are in a given direction. They open positions to take advantage of the expected price change and close positions when the prices go down.

There are two kinds of momentum:

- Relative momentum - different securities within the same class are compared against each other, and then traders and investors buy strong performing ones and sell the weak ones.

- Absolute momentum - an asset's price is compared against its previous performance.

Pros

- Traders can capitalize on volatile market trends

- Traders can gain high profit over a short period

- This strategy can take advantage of changes in stock prices caused by emotional investors.

Cons

- A momentum investor is always at a risk of timing a buy incorrectly.

- This strategy works best in a bull market; therefore, it is market sensitive

- This strategy is time-intensive; investors need to keep monitoring the market daily.

- Prices can shift in a different direction anytime

7. Pivot Points

This strategy determines resistance and support levels using the average of the previous trading sessions, which predict the next prices. They take the average of the high, low, and closing prices. A pivot point is a price level used to indicate market movements. Bullish sentiment occurs when one trades above the pivot point while bearish sentiment occurs when one trades below the pivot point.

Pros

- Traders can use the levels to plan out their trading in advance because prices remain the same throughout the day

- Works well with other strategies

Cons

• Some traders do not find pivot points useful

• There is no guarantee that price will stop or reverse at the levels created on the chart

8. Fundamental Analysis

This strategy involves analyzing the economic, social, and political forces that may affect the supply and demand of an asset. Usually, people use supply and demand to gauge which direction the price is headed to. The Fundamental analysis strategy then analyzes any factors that may affect supply and demand. By assessing these factors, traders can determine markets with a good economy and those with a bad one.

Forex Strategies for Beginners

When starting on Forex Trading, it important to keep things simple. As a beginner, avoid thinking about money too much and focus on one or two strategies at a time. The following three strategies are easy to understand and perfect for beginners.

1. Inside Bar Trading Strategy

This highly effective strategy is a two-bar price action strategy with an inside bar and a prior/mother bar. The inside bar is usually smaller and within the high and low range of the prior bar. There are many variations of the inside bar, but what remains constant is that the prior bar always fully engulfs the inside bar. Although very profitable, the inside bar setup does not occur often.

There are two main ways you can trade using inside bars:

- As a continuation move - This is the easiest way to trade inside bars. The inside bars are traded in trending markets following the direction of the trend.

- As a reversal pattern - the inside bars are traded counter-trend

When using this strategy, it is important to look for these characteristics when evaluating the pattern:

- Time frame matters - avoid any time frame less than the daily.

- Focus on the breakout - best inside bar trades happen after a break of consolidation where the preceding trend is set to resume.

- The trend Is your friend - trading with thc trend is the only way to trade an inside bar

- A favorable risk to reward ratio is needed when trading an inside bar

- The size of the inside bar in comparison to the prior bar is extremely important

2. Pin Bar Trading Strategy

This strategy is highly recommended for beginners because it is easy to learn due to a better visual representation of price action on a chart. It is one of the easiest strategies to trade. Pin bars show a reversal in the market and, therefore, can be useful in predicting the direction of the price.

There are various ways traders trading with pin bars can enter the market:

- At the current market price
- Using an on-stop entry
- At limit entry, which is at the 50% retrace of the pin bar

To improve your odds when using the pin bar strategy:

- Trade with the trend
- Wait for a break of structure
- Trade from an area of value

Some of the mistakes pin bar traders should avoid include the following:

- Assuming the market will reverse because of a pin bar
- Focus too much on the pin bars and miss out on other trading opportunities
- All pin bars are not the same and should not be treated as such

3. Forex Breakout Strategy

A breakout strategy is where investors find stocks that have built strong support or resistance level, wait for a breakout, and enter the market when momentum is in their favor. This strategy is important because it can offer expansions in volatility, major price moves, and limited risk. A breakout occurs when the price moves beyond the support or resistance level. The breakout strategy is good for beginners because they can catch every trend in the market. Breakouts occur in all types of market environments.

Traders establish a bullish position when prices are set to close above a resistance level and a bearish position when prices close below a support level. Sometimes traders can be caught on a false breakout, and the only way to determine if it is a false breakout is to wait for confirmation. False breakout prices usually go beyond the support and resistance level; however, they return to a prior trading range by the end of the day.

Good investors plan how they will exit the markets before establishing a position. With breakouts, there are two exit plans:

• Where to exit with profit-traders can assess the stock recent behaviors to determine reasonable objectives. When traders meet their goals, they can exit the position. They can either raise a stop-loss to lock in profits or exit a portion of the position to let the rest run

• Where to exit with a loss - breakout trading show traders clearly when a trade has failed, and therefore they can determine where to set stop-loss order. Traders can use the old support or resistance level to close a losing trade

Pros

• You can catch every trend in the market

• Prices can quickly move in your favor

Cons

• Traders can get caught in a false breakout

- It can be difficult to enter a trade

Tips for trading breakouts:

- Never sell on breakdown or buy on breakout both carry extreme risks
- Trade with the trend
- Wait for higher volume to confirm a breakout
- Take advantage of volatility cycles
- Enter on the retest of support or resistance
- Have a predetermined exit plan

Note

Beginners are more likely to be successful in trade than their experienced counterparts are because they have not yet cultivated any bad habits. Experienced traders have to break bad habits and put aside any emotions built over the years.

Chapter 4 Choosing A Broker

A broker refers to a firm or somewhat an individual who charges a certain fee or rather a commission for executing the buying and the selling process. In other words, they play the role of connecting the customer and the seller of the product. Thus, they are generally paid for acting as a link between the two parties. For instance, a client might be willing to buy shares from a particular organization. However, he might be lacking enough information about the places that he can purchase these shares. Thus, he will be forced to seek a person who understands well the stock exchange markets. The broker will, therefore, educate the client as well as link them with the right sellers. The broker will thus earn by offering such a connection. Other brokers sell insurance policies to individuals. In most cases, the individuals earn a commission once the clients they brought in the organization buy or renews the system. Any insurance companies have utilized the aspect as a way of increasing their sales.

List Of Common Brokers

IG

It is rated as one of the best forex brokers in the world. It was one of the pioneers in offering contracts for difference as well as spread beating. The organization was founded in the year 1974 and had been growing as a leader in online trading as well as the marketing industry. One of the aspects that have boosted its growth is the fact that it has linked a lot of customers, hence gaining more trust. In other words, a duet to its large customer base, a lot of clients prefers selling and buying their services. The other aspect worth noting is that this organization is London based, and it is among one of the companies that are listed on the London Stock Exchange market for more than 250 times. The aspect is due to the fact that it offers more than 15,000 products across several asset classes. Such classes include CFDs on shares, forex, commodities, bonds, crypto currencies as well as indices. Another aspect worth noting is that the 2019 May report, the firm is serving more than 120,000 active clients around the globe. Also, there are more than 350,000 clients that are served on a daily basis. The aspect has been critical in boosting its expansion as this group of individuals does more advertisements.

Some of the benefits that one gains by working in this industry are the fact that it allows comprehensive trading and the utilization of tools that enhance the real exchange of data. The other aspect worth noting is that it has a public traded license that allows a regular jurisdiction across the entire globe. In other words, one can acquire the services of this organization across the whole world with ease without the fear of acting against the laws of the nation. Also, the premises offer some of the competitive based commission that enhances pricing as spreading of forex. There is also a broad range of markets that are associated with the premises too, there several currencies and multi assets CFDs that are offered by the organization. The aspect has been critical in the sense that it allows the perfect utilization of all the services as well as the resources available across the globe. Some of the services that are offered by the organization are permitted globally, such that even after traveling from one nation to the other, one can still access their services. Since the year 1974, the organization has joined more than 195,000 traders across the entire globe. The aspect has allowed the selling its shares as well as services hence its fame.

Saxo Bank
The forex broker was established in 1992and has then been among the leading organization in offering forex services as well as the multi-asset brokerages across more than 15 nations. Some of these nations include the UK, Denmark, and Singapore, among others. One of the aspects of the organization is that it offers services to both retailers as well as institutional clients in the globe. The character has allowed the premises to provide more than one million transactions each day. Thus, it holds over $ 16 billion in asset management. The Saxo bank also offers more services to all of her clients. Such services include Spot FX, Non-deliverable Forwards (NDFs), contract difference as well as all the stock exchange options. The aspect has been critical in increasing its customer base across the globe. Some of the services such as crypto and bond services that are offered in the premises has allowed its expansion in the sense that they are sensitive and essentials.

Some of the benefits that one gain by assessing the services of the premises are that it enhances diverse selection of quality, it increases competitive commissions and forex spread as well as an improved multiple financial jurisdiction function that is allowed across the entire globe. In other words, the premises offer services that are allowed in the whole world, and that considers the rules and policies provided in each nation. The aspect has enhanced its continued growth despite the increased competition. One is required to pay a minimum deposit of about $2000 and an automated trading solution for all the traders. There are times when the premises offer bonuses of 182 trade forex pairs to all its clients. The aspect has also been the key reason behind its increased expansion. In other words, there are various services offered at a relatively low price hence the widening of its customer base.

CMC Markets
The premises were founded in 1989 and since then, it has grown to be one of the leading retail forex as well as a CFD brokerage. The premises thus serve more than 10,000 CFD instruments that cut across all the classes such as forex, commodities as well as security markets. The aspect has allowed the premises to spread its services to more than 60,000 clients across the entire globe. The premises have more than 15 offices that are well distributed in the nation; it offers the services. Most of its actions are thus related in UK, Australia as well as Canada. The aspect is due to the fact that the premises have it is customer bases in some of these nations. In other words, its serves are well are accepted in Canada and the UK.

There are various benefits that one gains by joining the premises. One, the premise offers some of the best competitive spread to all her customers. In other words, there are a variety of services that one can choose from. Also, the premises offer some of the largest selection of currency pairs in the entire industry. There are more than one hundred and eighty currencies that one can access by joining the premises. The other aspect worth noting is that the premises offer some of the best regulated financial agents in the entire globe. In other words, there are policies as well as rules that govern the provision of services in the world. Also, it is easy to identify the premises as there are potent charts as well as patterns that are used as recognition tools.

City Index

The forex broker was founded in 1983 in the UK. Since then, the premises have gained popularity and has turned out to be one of the leading brokers in London. It is worth noting that in 2015, the premises acquired GAIN Capital Holding Company that enhanced its increased customer base. Since 2015, the premises have been providing traders with services such as CFDs and spreading-betting derivatives. The premises have been further expanding the forex services with the acquisition of markets as well as FX solutions before gaining the capital market. Nowadays, the City Index has been operating as an independent brand under GAIN Capital in Asia as well as the UK. The aspect has allowed a multi-asset solution hence offering traders access to over 12,000 products across the global markets.

Some of the benefits that one gains part of the capital holding, a large selection of CFDs as well as regulated in several jurisdictions. The organization has tight spreads as well as low margins and fast execution. In others, the premises have been time from time, offering average ranges to all the clients; hence its increased customer base.

XTB Review

The organization was founded in Poland in the year 2002. Since then the organization has been well known for its forex and CFDs brokerage. Since then, the organization has maintained its offices in several nations; it offers its services. The premise has been working as a multi-asset broker that is regulated in several centers, hence increasing their competitive advantage. The premises have been trading as multiple financial centers offering a lot of services to all her traders. With a wide range of more than 2000 functions, the premises have been trading in almost all nations hence an increase in its customer base. The premises also offer excellent services that have been the reason behind its expansion. One of the aspects that have made the forex broker be thriving in such a competitive environment.

Signs Of Illegitimate Brokers

Although numerous brokers have been working in the forex industry, the aspect of legitimacy has been an issue affecting the progress of some these premises. One of the elements that are considered is the vulnerability of the clients. In most cases premises illegitimate brokers tend to rob of their customers. Most of them are self-reliant and optimistic. Most of them operate above their financial knowledge, hence making numerous mistakes. Most of these organization record big loses as they are relatively weak in term of management. The organization offers a lot of transactions that tend to be cumbersome in terms of management. It is worth noting that most of their operations aren't legitimate and never approved by the necessary authorities. Thus, when deciding on the kind of forex premises to seek services from, it is essential to consider some factors. Avoid assumptions that are exaggerative in terms of offering services that are above their knowledge. The aspect is harmful in the sense that they provide services that are not well planned hence recording a number of loses that befalls many clients in the long run. In other words, the drops recorded in the organization

Signs Of Legitimate Brokers

Although there are numerous illegitimate brokers in the market, there are legitimate brokers who offer excellent services. Most of them provide a few unique functions. In other words, they don't give a lot of transactions. Thus, they are able to manage their operations and command profits on their premises. The other aspect worth noting is that most of the services are approved by both the clients as well as the governing bodies in the organization. The other issue worth noting is that most of these premises have employed excellent knowledge in a range the progress of the customers. In other words, all their services are focused on advancing the clients.

In a nutshell, when selecting a forex broker, it is good to consider several factors. It is critical to find whether the premises are approved by both the governments as well as the clients. It is good to view the number of services as well as the transactions that are offered by the premise. The aspect is due to the fact that most of the wrong assumptions tend to provide numerous services that are poorly managed. The reviews offered by the clients of each of these premises need to be considered as they reflect whether the brokers are legitimate or not. Clients of consistent clients tend to offer reviews that are good as the services they receive manage to be excellent. The financial reports of these organization tend to be considered. The aspect is linked to the fact that they tend to reflect whether the brokers are making loses or profits. It is critical to find premises that record gains since the benefits tend to be high.

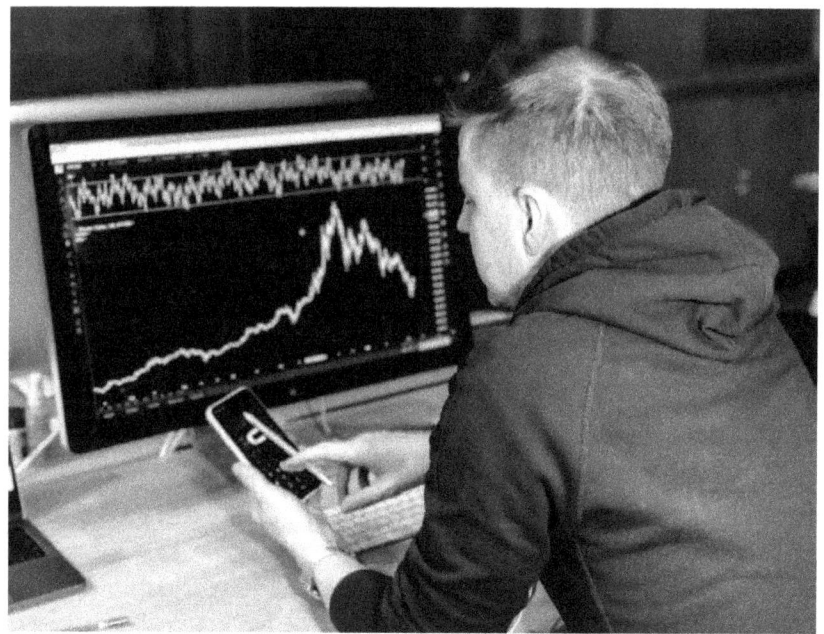

Chapter 5 Forex Market

Forex market is a market where you will buy, sell, exchange as well as speculate on the currencies. The market comprises of banks, retail forex brokers, hedge funds, central banks as well as investors. The currency market tends to be a financial market that has a tremendous amount of transaction, exceeding the combination of equity markets and futures. It is the most liquid of all the markets and the currencies traded against each other. Exchanging currencies is one of the most crucial things since that has to be there if people need to do foreign trade as well as business.

Despite being among the most significant market, there is no central place that the exchange takes place. All the transactions are done over-the-counter. The market is always open, and it is so in the entire world. You will find that the market is still active during day time and the price quotes change from time to time. The transactions will happen so that one can have a financial advantage. The fact that individual currency varies is what that will make the need for foreign exchange to raise.

When it comes to conducting trade, commercial as well as investment banks are in charge of doing that on their client's behalf. There are cases when individual and professional investors have the opportunity to trade in currency. But it is challenging for them, and it gives them a tough time. The internet has been a way that individual traders know more about the forex market.

For someone who is getting into the market for the first time, they will find it risky as well as complex to handle. There are different regulations, and there is standardization of the forex instruments. You can find cases where the market has no rules in some parts of the world. The banks that are in that trade will determine and be in a position to accept any risk that will come with the deal. They need to make sure that they are safe so that they will not suffer huge losses. That will be possible when they put an internal process in place. The bank will impose the regulations that it feels will work the best for them. The protection they require will be a determinant of the kind of riles that will put in place.

Any bank that is willing to participate in the forex market will provide an offer and a particulars currency bid. The way they will determine the prices will depend on the demand that there is in the market and the amount they and afford to supply. The traders cannot manage to influence any prices because the system has large trade flow. The method is vital in terms of creating transparency, and the investors can have access to the interbank dealing.

When you are a small retail trader, you are likely to have brokers who are not regulated and will re-quote the prices any time they wish. In some cases, they will even trade against you and take advantage of you. There may be some regulations, but that will depend on the area that your dealer is. The rules are not consistent in the whole world. So that you will know whether a dealer is under regulation or not, you need to take a thorough investigation. When you do that, you will get to know even where they are regulated. Seek to see the kind of protections that are there in case a crisis arises or the dealer's insolvency.

I a trader and you want to get in the trade and have no enough funds, day trading or swing trading is a comfortable option. If you have no issues with the limitation of funds, you can get in carrying trade or long-term fundamental-based trade. That will give you maximum profit, and you will find it worth investing your time and energy in the deal. For you to have high yields, you need to have a focus and understand the macroeconomic principles that drive the currency value. You need to have an experience with the technical analysis so that you will not be subject to losses. Know that the historical price will play a significant role in determining future rates. There is enormous data that is available out there in the market since it is done during the day and the night. That data will be useful for you to be in a position to determine the price movement in the future. For traders that like to use the technical tool, they will thrive in this market.

The prices in the forex market have a quotation of four decimal places since they have spread differences that are naturally very small. That makes it impossible to have a definitive rule on the number of decimal places that will be in forex quotes. You need to consider the risk that will come along with the trade before you get into the real currency trade. The trade-in currency is likely to be conducted in pairs. The pairs need to have low volatility as well as high liquidity. They are stable, add has well-managed economies having low chances of manipulation and smaller spread compared to other pairs. Some pairs consist of currencies from a small economy and those from a significant economy

Forex trading works in a way that the likelihood of making a profit is higher than that of making losses. Apart from benefit, numerous advantages will favor you when you get into a currency trade. The advantages of the forex market include and not limited to;

Flexibility

You are flexible when you get into the currency trade, and there are no restrictions and limitations of the capital that you will invest. The amount of money that has so that you can get into currency trade will not be a big issue. You can start small, and that will not hinder you from going to greater heights as time goes on. Some markets have a lot of rules that discourage people from getting in, and this is not the case in the currency market. The excess t=regulations are not present when it comes to the forex market.

The fact that it operates for twenty-four hours makes it a good idea since you can choose to trade at any given time. There are no restrictions, and you can even make the trade as a part-time job. Doing it as a full-time job is not a bad idea as such, and it will make you reap huge profits. The market is always open, and you do not have to wait for a specific time for it to open. You are free to hose the time that you want to do business which is different from other markets. In some markets, you have to wait for a particular session so that you will do trade. There are no situations likely to affect the forex market, and so you can trade at any time when you have the opportunity to do so. The market updates are available for you anytime you need to know how the market is doing. You will have a view of the trends that the trade is taking, and you will be in a position to decide wisely. You can trade at your convenience since there are numerous trading styles. For someone who wants to get in trade for a short time, the forex market is an excellent idea for them. You will have easy access to the forex market than any other market out there.

High Liquidity

There are vast numbers of people that are in foreign exchange in comparison to the ones in the financial market. It is highly liquid regardless of its size, and a lot of people get into the market every day. The big money orders that are out there will when the big players get into the market. There is only a small, or at times no price deviation at all even after the money gaps are filled by the big prayers. There being no price manipulation, efficient pricing is likely to be achieved, and there are no substantial deviations from the original price. Some people are ready to get into the business, and you can get someone to trade with any time you wish to purchase. Considering the levels of volatility, the price patterns remain constant. The market is efficient because of its high levels of liquidity, and the chances that competition will hit you hard are meager. Even with the large numbers of participants on every side, competition is not that severe. There is no likelihood of there being hitches, and transactions are always happening since the number of traders is relatively high. When you secure a position in the market, you stand a better chance since prices never change with a blink of an eye. That will help you to project the profits that you are likely to make when you make several transactions. The costs that are associated with the sales that you will make are not that high. The deals are done quickly, making it simple to have as many transactions as possible in a short period. You can predict the move that the prices are likely to take from time to time.

Highly Volatile

In the forex market, you can change from one currency to the other without much that from you. When you feel that specific money is having a considerable level of profit, you can shift to that so quickly. Since the aim to get into the trade is to make enough profit, that will be a good thing to do. When you know that a particular currency is likely to lower the price, you can leave that and go to the one that is a bit promising. Money-driven markets are likely to experience substantial losses. Due to the volatility level, some benefits come along with changing to a different currency which will give you good profits. Speculating on price changes from time and again will help you to stand in a safe position. Forex trading is satisfying when you compare to any other market. That is an added advantage and a sign to show you that your investment is safe in one way or the other. Short duration is there between opening and closing positions, and that means that significant opportunities to attract good profits are on the road.

Limited Entry Barriers

For you to invest in forex trade, you do not require a considerable amount of money as opposed to the requirements of other markets. Just a small initial capital is all you need to start trading currencies. There are no high amounts of deposits that you need to make for you to have an account. That is a unique advantage since some other markets need vast amounts of capital for you to start operating. It is cheap, making it simple for anyone willing to trade have the freedom to do so. If you are an average person, you will not find it hard to venture in the forex market. The market will attract people of all kind regardless of the amount of experience you have and the exposure. You do not have to worry that you will probably have many risks to deal with since there are low risks that come with forex trading. You need to organize and improve the skills you pose, and it will be a future benefit. Maturing the skills you have will not cost you much, and so that should not be the reason you why you do not want to invest in the forex market.

Great Tools to Help You Trade are at Your Disposal

When you get in the forex market, you will have great choices on the approaches that you will put in use to make sure that things will run smoothly. You can as well consider involving a specialist who will help you elevate your trading levels. They will equip you with fantastic knowledge on how to go about the forex market. When you have a full understanding of any market, you are likely to find it simple to find your way out. Different trademarks are there designed purposely for you to upgrade your trade and also consolidate news feeds. There are limits that you do not need to reach, and knowing them will help you manage risk in the right way. When you are financially unstable, there is a demo account that serves as an excellent resource. With time, you will establish whether it will be of any importance for you to own your account. Sharpening the trading that you pose from time to time will help you go a long way in the forex market.

There is Transparency

The transparency levels that are there on any information that you will access will draw you closer to the forex market. You have the freedom to access the rates any time you need to. It is made sure that the public access to such information, making you have confidence in the market. When you require any information, you do not have to wait for eternity even though the market size is big. The transparency in the entire thing will create goodwill, making you invest all that you have. You have your total control over any transaction that you want to make, and no one is there to follow you. If you do not agree with a specific transaction, you do not have to do that, and you have the free will. It is you to decide whether you want to trade with an individual trader or not. No one is in charge of accessing to what extent you are willing to risk and make a profit. That will solely depend on you and the zeal that you have to make money.

In case you are trading on behalf of an organization, make sure you do not invest your emotions as well. Take care of yourself, since the organization may find someone to replace you, making it unworthy the emotional investment you made. When things do not go the way, you desire them to go, take your time, and find out what went wrong when in the forex market. You will not invest your emotions, and you will have a successful trade. When a gap comes up, do not deal with it by hurting yourself. It will do more harm than ethical making you to hate forex trade which is an excellent experience to have.

Even though there are transaction costs that you will incur in the natural market conditions, they are of a considerate amount. Since there are no brokers in the middle, you are not going to deductions of commission when you realize a profit. That will mean that just a few expenses come along with forex trading. The fee you need to pay to a forex broker is relatively small when you compare to other securities. No clearing fees or any government deductions that you need to put into consideration. That means that the positive difference that you will make when you trade currencies will purely be profit.

Chapter 6 Forex Trading Psychology

Psychology and trading, most people might think that these factors don't relate to one another. Well, it very well does. As I mentioned earlier, most trading mistakes occur because the traders don't understand the importance of trading psychology. However, most traders don't trade successfully, mainly because of emotional problems. Especially, naïve traders don't handle emotions well, so they don't remain in the market for long. But, it is not something good which is why educating naïve traders is important. Even before they enter the market, it is important to spend the time to learn the market. However, the most common issue with trading is fear. But, fear is commonly seen when the trader moves into the live trading account. But, initially, the temptation is often found in naïve traders. When they enter the market, they enter with the thought of trading as much as possible to make money. Hence, this thought will not let them achieve what they actually should achieve. Therefore, when a trader is tempted to trade, he or she may trade even without analyzing or anticipating the trades.

However, as mentioned fear can also create a lot of issues in a trader's journey. Many traders give up trading completely because of fear. But, the fight or flight reaction is a human thing, that is commonly seen in traders. But actually, this reaction cannot be changed that easily, but of course, traders can handle this reaction wisely. If you study trading psychology, things will become simpler when trading the Forex market. Anyway, when you fear to trade, it will impact your trading behaviors negatively. Most of the time, you will look for a safer method to trade and, perhaps, it is not possible to find safer trading methods in the Forex market.

As you already know, the Forex market involves a lot of risks, so as traders, you must learn to handle them carefully. For example, when you enter into a trade, your instincts point out the chances of losing and you will eventually exit from the trade, and it might have been a profitable trade. So see, your mind has a direct connection to the way you trade.

Even if you have a defined plan, you can still steer away from trading because the power of psychology is immense. You might even become anxious and consider short-term positions because you are afraid to enter into long-term positions even if they seem profitable. Well, yes, fear, greed, and all the other emotions can cause a lot of problems to your trading journey. Hence, you must understand trading psychology. If you do, you will be able to assist those emotions wisely and handle trading successfully. Normally, if you overcome fear, it will be beneficial to your trading journey as well as life.

Typically, traders don't fear the market when they are preparing to enter into a trade, but when the market opens, their emotions play the role. As humans, you can never get rid of emotions because it is a part of humankind. But, you can always learn the methods to control your emotions when excitement is a dangerous emotion when trading the Forex market. When you are excited, you might make mistakes when entering a trade or anticipating market movements. Thus, when you are trading, you have to try to keep your emotions neutral.

Most traders succumb to accept that they are making trading mistakes that are related to psychology. But normally, when people can't accept, denial is the first reaction. Over time, they tend to accept the truth. Just like that, even the naïve traders will learn to accept the truth. However, Forex trading is not only about trading system and strategies. You must accept that mindset is an important part of Forex trading. The way you anticipate the Forex market has a lot to do with trading. Also, only if you understand the trades will you be able to enter into it. Thus, a trader's mindset has a lot to do with trading.

If you look at certain websites that advertise robotic trading systems, you might find trading psychology as an absurd thing. But, remember, those trading systems will not provide benefits as they portray. Nothing is as best as trading manually. You must use your knowledge and skills to trade the market; only then will you be able to trade successfully. Also, those websites are doing their duty to market their product, and if you rely on them and purchase it, you might have to pay them for using their product. Hence, when you come across something like this, make sure to think logically. As a beginner, you must try to settle for a simple yet effective strategy, so that you will be able to trade peacefully.

Anyway, why do you think most naïve traders struggle to make money? You might have seen many people who fail in trading the Forex market. Well, there are many reasons why traders fail, but the major reason is the ones who enter the Forex market don't really know the market. A higher percentage of traders enter into the Forex market by believing the fabricated ads. And it makes them set unrealistic goals. Eventually, they struggle to meet those unrealistic goals and end up quitting trading. But the worst part is that there are traders who quit their day job after they enter the

Forex market. Well, it is not a wise move because they must test to check whether trading works for them. Or some other traders believe trading is easy money and no matter how many times I repeat it, some people still believe it is possible. These thoughts create tension and stress, so eventually, the trader becomes emotionally unstable. Thus, when traders trade with an emotionally unstable mindset, they lose money.

Psychology Of A Successful Trader In The Forex Market

So, how can a trader develop a trading mindset? If you want to develop a trading mindset, you need to do your part. It is important to put the required effort to accomplish what you are looking for. Well, you can't build a trading mindset that quickly because you have to learn and accept the Forex market as it is. If you try to deny facts about the Forex market, you will not be able to create a trading mindset.

You must start developing your trading mindset by handling the risks in trading. First of all, understand that risk management isn't for one trade, preferably it is applicable for all the trades that you enter into. You must make sure to calculate the risk for each trade before you enter into it. When you are managing risks, certain emotions might try to confuse you, but you must not let it happen. Once you start handling your emotions wisely, you will be able to manage trades also. However, the simplest way to control emotion when managing risks is to risk ONLY the amount that you can lose. You must create a mindset that enters into a trade while knowing the probability of losing trade. If you follow this, you will be able to remain in the trading world for a long time. But, it takes practice and patience to create a trading mindset that accepts losses. Also, you must master your trading edge. No matter what trading strategy you are using, you must know it completely to trade successfully.

And, remember, overtrading will never create profits. Instead, overtrading will blow all your hard-earned money. You must trade only when you actually see a profit signal. Don't try to trade just because you feel like trading. Or don't try to guess trade because that doesn't work in Forex trading. If you overtrade, it can be challenging to stop, and you'll become an emotional trader.

If you want to build a trading mindset, you must have an organized mindset. So, basically, when you have an organized mindset, you will think about the trading plan, journal, and much more. You must accept the fact that Forex trading is a business. Hence, don't try to gamble in the market. When you are making trading decisions, you must remain calm and steady; only then will you be able to think clearly.

But then, after you build a trading mindset, you must not let emotions play their role. However, the most common emotions that you must avoid are:

Euphoria

You might argue that euphoria is good, yes, it is good. But when it is related to the Forex market, it becomes dangerous. For example, if a trader wins a few profitable traders, he or she might become confident when trading the next trade. Well, it is good to feel confident when entering the next trade, but feeling overly confident is not a good thing. When traders become overly confident, they don't watch or study the market as they did before. The consecutive profitable trades should not get into your mind and increase the level of confidence. When trading Forex if you are overconfident, you will not be able to accept the loss if the trade doesn't react the way you wanted. Hence, it is better to remain calm even if you make profits continuously.

Fear

Most traders who enter the market with no knowledge about trading tend to fear the market. Also, some traders might fear because they cannot effectively trade using any specific strategy. However, usually, when a trader continuously experiences losses, he or she may tend to fear to trade. Perhaps, it is understandable because losing hard-earned money isn't easy. But, you can avoid the mistake of risking more than the amount that you are comfortable with. Most naïve traders don't follow this rule even if we keep repeating it. If fear persists, you will not be able to trade better trades or become successful. It has the power to keep you away from good trades as well. Hence, try to overcome fear by limiting the amount you risk in trading. For the naïve traders, start your journey on a demo account without directly entering the live account. If you do so, you'll be able to learn to control emotions.

Greed

You might have heard that people say only bulls and bears make money, but pigs get slaughtered. If you don't understand what it means, it means greed. If you are greedy, you will not be able to make money in the market. Instead, you will be kicked out of the market. Mostly, traders become greedy when they don't have self-discipline. Most traders make quick decisions when the market shows profitable trade signals, but it is not recommended. Instead, you must be calm and collected. Take some time to understand the market, focus on the risk ratio, set a plan, and then enter into the trade. Also, remember, if you are risking more than what you are ready to lose, it apparently shows your level of greed to make money. Thus, you must overcome greed if you don't want to lose your account.

Revenge

This is one of the funny behaviors of traders because what is the point in revenging the market? For the Forex market, you are just one amongst the millions, and it doesn't make sense. However, if you are trying to revenge trade just because you lost a few trades, remember, this might lead to further losses. When you are emotional, you will not be able to make wise decisions. Hence, you must wait for some time until your mind is stable and ready to trade.

So, when learning the psychology of trading, you might find it exciting. But, success can decide when you take these things into practice. You don't have to try these tips and ideas on the live account, instead use the demo account. The Forex market is one of the best markets because it has provided solutions for almost all the issues. So, as traders, if you solve your personal trading issues, you will be able to become a successful trader.

Mass Psychology And Its Measures

Following are a list of things required for becoming a successful Forex trader

Trading plan: A forex trader should have a trading plan that should be prepared well in advance. The trading plan should list out his entry and exit conditions as well as his money management rules.

This is of utmost importance and he should religiously follow his trading plan to the tee. In order to become a successful forex trader, he should never deviate from the trading plan.

Discipline: This is one of the most important qualities needed to be a successful forex trader. A trader should be disciplined and methodical in the way he goes about with forex trading. He should not only meticulously plan his trading, but should also be disciplined enough to follow it.

Ability to do analysis: A forex trader should have the ability to analyze the technical charts and other financial data in order to become a successful forex trader. He should invest in himself and learn how to use the financial tools that would help in becoming a better trader. Trading is a very competitive job and one needs to be always one step ahead of others in order to be successful.

Emotional stability: It is very important to keep emotions and trading separate. In order to be successful, the trader should be able to trade like a machine and not let emotions affect his trades. He shouldn't let losses affect him nor should he get overly excited about the winning trades.

Hard work: Nothing beats hard work for becoming a successful forex trader. The trader should be prepared to put in a lot of hours and research the forex market thoroughly before each trading day. Most successful forex traders have a pre-trading session wherein they analyze the global markets, check charts, read various financial newspapers, note down key economic events of the day etc. before they start their trades.

Good knowledge of charting and analysis tools: In order to be a successful forex trader, it is very important to have good knowledge on the usage of charting and other analytic software. The usage of these trading software's raises the odds of success considerably, so it is important to have a good understanding of them.

Constant Learning: Trading field requires constant learning. The trader should be prepared to learn throughout his trading career. Something that might work now might not work after 5 years. So it's very important to constantly adapt and keep learning in order to be a step ahead of others. A good trader should be on the constant look out of learning new things that might help him with his trading be it the usage of a trading software or a new way of analysis.

Mastering fear: It is very important to master fear in order to be a successful forex trader. The trader should be prepared to take losses now and again and should understand that it's a part and parcel of the game. The inability to book losses and holding on to a losing position can result in more losses. The trader should also be ready to take a trade when a good opportunity arises and should not allow fear to hold him back.

Thinking on your own: It is very important to think on your own and make trading decisions and to not just blindly follow the crowd. As the saying goes, "buy into the fear and sell into the greed!" Now, this does not mean to always do the opposite to what others do. It just means that the trader should have an open mind and should have the ability to think on his own and make decisions accordingly.

Awareness of the global events: Forex markets are affected by the major international events that occur. So it's important to have an understanding of the key economic events happening globally as the forex markets are traded globally and affected by these economic events. A few examples of the key economic events are Federal Bank interest rate decision, ECB rate decision, GDP data of key economies, job data of key economies, inflation data of key economies etc.

Never blame the market: The market might behave irrationally but the trader should be responsible for reading the market cues and making trading decisions. Instead of playing the blame game he should learn from each mistake and learn from it. The trader should understand the risks associated with trading and have a proper money management rule in place.

Trading journal: It is important to maintain a trading journal and make an entry of all the trades he makes. The reasons for taking that particular trade should also be noted down. This would help in analyzing the trades later and help in avoiding the mistakes made. This would also help in identifying the good trades made and look for similar patterns later on.

Choosing the right broker: It is important to choose the right broker. Some of the factors that should be considered while selecting a broker should be a) low brokerage b) fast and reliable trading terminal c) ease of trading and good research and charting software's that the broker provides.

Money management rules: This is perhaps the most important among all things that are mentioned till now. A money management rule is basically the rules that define the maximum loss a trader can afford to take per trade or at a point of time. Most forex traders never risk more than 2- 5 % per trade. They also never risk more than 10-20 % at a particular point across all trades. It is very important to follow these rules; else you run the risk of wiping out your entire trading account in a matter of days, if not hours! It is always better to limit your losses and live to fight another day!

Chapter 7 Money Mistake to avoid

Now we'll turn our attention to giving some tips, tricks and advice on errors to avoid in order to ensure as much as possible that you have a successful time trading.

Avoid The Get Rich Quick Mentality

Any time that people get involved with trading or investing, the hope is always there that there's a possibility of the big winning trade. It does happen now and then. But quite frankly, it's a rare event. In many occasions, even experienced traders are guessing wrong and taking losses. It's important to approach Forex for what it really is. It's a business. It is not a gambling casino even though a lot of people treated that way so you need to come to your Forex business-and it is a business no matter if you do it part-time, or quit your job and devote your entire life to it-with the utmost seriousness. You wouldn't open a restaurant and recklessly buy 1 thousand pounds of lobster without seeing if customers were coming first. So, why would you approach Forex as if you were playing slots at the casino? Take it seriously and act as if it's a business because it really is. Again, it doesn't matter if you officially create a corporation to do your trades or not, it's still a business no matter what. That means you should approach things with care and avoid the get rich quick mentality. The fact is the get rich quick mentality never works anywhere. Unfortunately, I guess I could say I've been too strong in my assertion. It does work on rare occasions. It works well enough that it keeps the myth alive. But if we took 100 Forex traders who have to get rich quick mentality, my bet is within 90 days, 95% of them would be completely broke.

Trade Small

You should always trade small and set small achievable goals for your trading. The first benefit to trading small is that this approach will help you avoid a margin call. Second, it will also help you set profit goals that are small and achievable. That will help you stay in business longer.

Simply put, you will start gaining confidence and learning how to trade effectively if you get some trades that make $50 profits, rather than shooting for a couple of trades that would make thousands of dollars in one shot, but and up making you completely broke. Again, treat your trading like a real business. If you were opening a business, chances are you would start looking for slow and steady improvements and you certainly would not hope to get rich quick.

Let's get specific. Trading small means never trading standard lots. Even if you have enough cash to open an account such that you could trade standard lots, I highly recommend that you stay away from them. The large amount of capital involved and margin that would be used could just get you into a lot of financial trouble. For beginners, no matter how much money you are able to devote to your trading, I recommend that you start with micro lots. Take some time and learn how to trade with the small lots and start building your business earnings small profits at a time. Trading only with micro lots will help in force discipline and help you avoid getting into trouble. Make a commitment only to use micros for the first 60 days. After that, if you have been having decent success, consider trading a mini lot. You should be extremely cautious for the first 90 days in general.

Be Careful With Leverage

Obviously, it's extremely beneficial. It allows you to enter and trades that would otherwise not be possible. On the other hand, the temptation is there to use all your leverage in the hopes of making it big on one or two trades. You need to avoid using up all your leverage. Remember that you can have a margin call and get yourself into big trouble if your trades go bad.

And it's important to remember there's a high probability that some of your trades are going to go bad no matter how carefully you do all your analysis.

Not Using A Demo Account

A big mistake the beginners make, is jumping in too quickly. There is a reason that most broker-dealers provide demos or simulated accounts. If you don't have a clue what that reason is, let's go ahead and stated here. Brokers provide demo accounts because Forex is a high-risk trading activity. It can definitely be something that provides a lot of rewards and it does for large numbers of traders. But there is a substantial risk of losing your capital. Many beginners are impatient hoping to make money right away. That's certainly understandable, but you don't want to fall into that trap. Take 30 days to practice with a demo account. This will provide several advantages. Trading on Forex is different than trading on the stock market. Using the demo account, you can become familiar with all the nuances of Forex trading. This includes everything from studying the charts, to placing your orders and, most importantly, understanding both pips and margin. The fact that there is so much leverage available means you need to learn how to use it responsibly. You need to know how to experience going through the process and reading the available margin and so forth on your trading platform while you are actually trying to execute trades. A demo account let you do this without risking real capital. It is true that it's not a perfect simulation. The biggest argument against demo accounts is that they don't incorporate the emotion that comes with trading and real money. As we all know, it's those emotions, including panic, fear and greed, that lead to bad decisions. However, in my opinion, that is a weak argument against using demo accounts. The proper way to approach it is to use a demo account for 30 days and then spend 60 to 90 days doing nothing but trading micro lots. Don't worry, as your micro trading lots you can increase the number of your trades and earn profits. While I know you're anxious to get started, keeping yourself from losing all your money is a good reason to practice for 30 days before doing it for real.

Failing To Check Multiple Indicators

There is also a temptation to get into trades quickly just on a gut level hunch. You need to avoid this approach at all costs. Some beginners will start learning about candlesticks and then when they first start trading, they will recognize a pattern on a chart. Then in the midst of the excitement, they will enter a large trade based on what they saw. And then they will end up on the losing end of a trade. Some people are even worse and they don't even look at the candlesticks. Instead, they just look at the trend and think they better get in on it and they got all anxious about doing so. That means first checking the candlesticks and then confirming at least with the moving average before entering or exiting a position. You should also have the RSI handy and you may or may not want to use Bollinger bands.

Use Stop Loss And Take Profit Orders

Well, I hate to repeat myself yet again, but this point is extremely important. I am emphasizing it over and over because it's one of the tools that you can use in order to protect yourself from heavy losses. One of the ways that you can get out of having to worry about margin calls and running out of money is to put stop-loss orders every time you trade. This will require studying the charts more carefully. You need to have a very clear idea where you want to get out of the trade, if it doesn't go in the direction you hoped. But if you have a stop-loss order in place, then you can avoid the problem of having your account just go down the toilet. Secondly, although the temptation is always there to look for as many profits as possible, in most cases, you should opt to set a take profit order when you make your trade. That way you set as we said, distinct boundaries which will ensure that you make some profit without taking too much risk. The problem with doing it manually is that excitement and greed will put you in a position where are you miss the boat entirely. What inevitably happens, is people get too excited hoping to earn more profits and they stay in the trade too long. The Forex market changes very fast and so what eventually happens is people that stay into long inevitably and up with a loss. Or at the very least they end up missing out on profits.

There is one exception to this point. There are some times when there is a distinct and relatively long-term upward trend. If you find yourself, by doing the analysis and determining that such an upward trend is here, that might be an exception to the rule. In that case you want to try to ride the trend and maximize your profits.

Remember Price Changes Are In Pips
Beginners often make the mistake of forgetting about pips. If you have trouble with pips and converting them to actual money, go back and review the examples we provided. Remember that pips play a central role in price changes, you need to know your dollar value per pip in order to keep tabs on your profit and losses. This is also important for knowing the right stop loss and take profit orders to execute.

Don't Try Too Many Strategies Or Trading Styles At Once
When you are a beginning Forex trader, it can be tempting to try everything under the sun. That can be too much for a lot of people. The most advisable thing to do is to stick with one strategy so don't try scalping and being a position trader at the same time. The shorter the time frame for your trades, the more time and energy, you have to put into each trade. Scalping and day trading are activities that would require full-time devotion. They are also high-pressure and that can help enhance emotions involved in the trades. For that reason, I don't really recommend those styles or strategies for beginners. In my opinion and to be honest it's mine alone, I think position trading is also too much for a beginner. It requires too much patience.

Perhaps the best strategy to use when you're beginning Forex trading is to become a swing trader. It's a nice middle ground, in between the most extremely active trading styles and something that is going to try people's patience such as position trading. When you do swing trading, you can do time periods longer than a day certainly, but as long or short as you need to meet your goals otherwise. Swing trading also takes off some of the pressure. And it gives you more time to think and react.

This does not mean that you can't become a scalper or day trader at some future date. What I am advising is that you gain some experience using more relaxed trading styles before taking that path. And believe me, swing trading is going to be challenging enough.

Market Expectations

Life as a forex trader can sometimes get lonely. After all, this is the kind of career where you are completely on your own. You enjoy your profits alone, but you also suffer losses on your own. There is no one in the forex market whom you can depend on to comfort you. Therefore, it is also good if you connect with like-minded people. Feel free to make friends with other traders. After all, you are all players in the market who want the same thing. The good thing is that you are not competing with one another. In fact, you can even help one another by sharing information, insights, and strategies. Thanks to the Internet, it is very easy to find and connect with people who are also interested in forex trading. You simply have to join an online group or forum on forex trading. You can do this quickly with just a few clicks of a mouse. You can then make a public post or even send a private message to any member of the group/forum. If you have a neighbor or friend who also likes trading currencies, then you can invite him out for a coffee one of these days. Connecting with like-minded people is not just a way to learn but it can also inspire you to become a better trader.

- Have fun

Forex trading is fun. This is a fact. In fact, many traders get to enjoy this kind of life that they still continue to learn it despite their losses. It is also not uncommon to find traders, especially beginners, who spend their whole day just learning about forex trading. Like gambling in a casino, trading currencies can also be very addicting, especially if you are making a nice profit from it.

Learn to have fun and enjoy the journey. Sometimes taking things too seriously can ruin the experience and even make you less effective. In your life as a trader, you will definitely make some mistakes from time to time. You will experience losing money from what otherwise would have been a profitable trade if only you knew better. Do not get too stressed. The important thing is for you to learn as much as you can from every mistake. Take it easy, but remember to learn from the experience. Making mistakes is part of the learning process. Of course, you should try to minimize them as much as possible. Learn and have fun.

Risk Management

Risks do occur in every sphere of life. However, when it comes to trading in forex securities, these risks, more so, financial risks are enhanced. This is due to the volatility of the foreign exchange currencies.

Nature of Forex risk

Forex risk (currency risk, FX risk or exchange rate risk) is a risk (financial) that prevails when a financial transaction is monetized in a foreign currency. When it comes to multinationals, forex risk occurs when one or several of its subsidiaries maintain financial records and statements in currencies other than those of the parent entity. When it comes to a multinational, there is a risk that there could be negative movements in foreign currency of the subsidiary entities in relation to the domestic currency of the parent entity prior to the report being compiled. International traders are also exposed to this risk.

Types of forex risks

There are many types of forex risks. Nonetheless, the following are the major types of forex risk:

Transaction risk - This occurs where a firm has cash commitments whose values are subject to unforeseeable changes in exchange rate due to a contract being considered in foreign currency. The cash commitments may include account receivables and account payables.

- Economic risk - A firm is exposed to economic risk when its market value is susceptible to unanticipated changes in forex rate. This may affect the firm's share value, present and future values of cash flows, firm's market position and ultimately firm's overall value.
- Translation risk - Translation risk affects mainly multinational firms. Thus, a firm's translation risk is the susceptibility of its financial statements and reports to forex changes. This happens when a parent firm has to prepare consolidated statements, including those of its foreign subsidiaries. This largely affects the firms reported income. This also affects its stock value in the securities market.

Contingent risk - Contingent risks occurs when a firm engages in foreign contracts thus resulting in foreign-denominated obligations. Such foreign contracts may include bidding for foreign projects, commitments to foreign direct investment (for example, investing in foreign subsidiaries), and settling legal disputes involving foreign entities.

Forex risk management

Several strategies exist to safeguard against forex risks. Some of these strategies include:

- Forex hedging strategies - This covers transaction exposure. Use of money market tools and derivatives can help reduce these risks. Futures contracts, options, forward contracts, and swaps are some of these derivatives. Some operational techniques to support these strategies include payments and exposure netting, leading and lagging of receipts, and currency invoicing.
- Translation exposure strategies - These are strategies aimed at risks that are primarily due to prevailing reporting standard (or differences in reporting standards between the parent company and its foreign subsidiaries), which mainly affect the net assets and net liabilities. This can be mitigated through hedging the balance sheet. In this regard, a firm can purchase a commensurate amount of exposed assets or liabilities to balance off any discrepancy due to forex rates. A business entity can also hedge against translation exposure by using Forex derivatives.
  - Alternative strategies to manage economic or operating exposure can also be adopted. This may involve carefully selecting production sites with a clear intent to cut down on production cost, flexible approach to sourcing of supplies on the international markets, diversification in the export market. Creating product differentiation through extensive research and

development can also help in hedging against economic risks.

Forex risk management tools and techniques

Several tools and techniques that you can employ in the forex risk management. These tools and techniques include:

Forward Contract

- Limit Orders
- Stop Loss Orders

Options

Forward contract

A forward contract allows a user to hedge expected forex transactions by locking in a price today for a transaction that will take place in future. This enables the trader to eliminate or mitigate risks of exchange rate fluctuations. Forward contracts can last for as long as a year.

Limit Orders

You can use Limit Orders in transactions that do not have time-restricted payment obligations. Thus, a business can set an ideal exchange rate at which to buy a particular currency. For example, if the current exchange rate is EUR/0.72GBP, a businessperson may not wish to send £50,000 to the UK until he can get a better rate. He can make a limit order to his payment provider target a rate of EUR/0.75GBP. When this rate is attained, a transfer is triggered, and funds are automatically sent to the UK.

Stop Loss Orders

Stop loss orders guarantees a minimum rate at which a currency is exchanged by allowing a trader to lock in a deal so that it never trades below what he considers as an acceptable exchange rate. It is, in essence, an instruction to buy or sell a currency at a predetermined 'worst case' exchange rate.

Options

An option is a risk management tool in forex transactions. It protects businesses from downturns in the currency market, but also allows them to take advantage of positive currency shifts. When a business buys an option it secures the right, but not the obligation, to make an international purchase or exchange funds at a predetermined exchange rate on a chosen date. Where Options differ to FECs is that the buyer is not obligated to settle on that date. If movements in the forex market present more favorable exchange rates than the rate that was set when the Option was bought, the buyer is not obliged to settle.

Tips and hacks on risk management:

Set Orders - Limit orders, stop orders, trail orders, etc

- Set risk/reward ratio
- Set win-rate

Blend win-rate and risk/reward ratio to derive the most optimal strategy

Focus less on short-term performance targets and more on mid-term and long-term performance targets

Carry out position sizing

- Blend R-Multiple with Risk/Reward ratio to balance between performance and potential

Make spread vs. fees comparison for net profit

- Watch out for correlations - pairs that are positively correlated increase your risks

BACKTESTING

Backtesting is the process of testing your trading strategy on previous historical data to establish its efficacy and reliability in as far as establishing how accurately the strategy would have predicted the actual result. Thus, if the strategy works on historical data, then, it is expected to work on the current and future data.

Why carry out Backtesting?

The following are some of the important reasons as to why you need to carry out Backtesting:

- To test the efficacy and reliability of your trading strategy.
- To iron out flaws in your strategy so as to improve its efficacy and reliability.
- To cut down on risks that would arise due to unreliable strategy.
- To have an insight into how your intended forex system is going to work.
    - To refine your trading strategy parameters.

Types of Backtesting

There are two main types of backtesting:

Manual backtesting.

- Automated backtesting.

Manual backtesting

In manual backtesting, you largely design your own testing system. You manually enter and exit the markets.

Advantages

- You can have the look and feel of your system as you enter and exit the market.
    - You can easily customize the system to your unique needs.

Disadvantages

- Time consuming.
    - Reliability is not guaranteed.

Automated backtesting

In automated backtesting, you create a system that automatically enters or exits the market on your behalf. You take advantage of the already existing backtesting systems in the market.

Advantages

- Less susceptible to your emotions
    - Automate income generation`

Disadvantages

- A slight error in your coding can cost you heavily
    - You have to master the parameters of the system to be able to do a thorough diagnosis should it malfunction

Backtesting tools

Each type of backtesting has its own tools that you can take advantage of:

Manual backtesting tools

- Forex Tester 2
- MetaTrader 4
    - TradingView

With MetaTrader 4 and TradingView, you would need to use a spreadsheet program to track your trades. When it comes to analysis of your backtesting results, you can use the following tools:

- MetaTrader4 Reports
- Tradingrex
    - Excel

Automated backtesting tools

- MetaTrader MLQ5
- TradingView (pine scripting language)
- TradeStation
- CandleScanner
    - QuantShare

Stop Loss And Trailing Stop Loss
In this section, we will delve into more details about these very important risks management tools.

Stop loss

A stop-loss is an Order to buy or sell a forex currency once its price goes higher than or lower than a set stop price. Upon attaining the stop price, the stop order transforms into either a limit order (with a fixed or pre-determined price) or a market order (with no price limit). The stop order, once placed, is automatically triggered.

Without a price limit (market order, thus prevailing market price), the price at which the trade is executed may be different from that of the stop price (either higher or lower). This boosts chance of the trade being executed. However, at higher risk of selling lower than the stop price.

With a limit order, the trade must be executed at a certain pre-determined price or it lapses. This is because there could be lack of buyers or sellers willing to trade at the pre-determined price. It is less risky compared to a market order. However, it has lower chances of being executed compared to a market order.

Different kinds of Stop Loss Orders

1) Stop Loss Market Order

This is an order placed by a business entity to buy a security once its price goes higher than certain specified stop price or to sell a security once its price falls below the set stop price. In this regard, the trader has no control over the price at which the security will be sold. There are two types of Stop Loss Market Order:

- Sell Stop market order - This is an order placed by a seller to sell at the best market price after the price falls below the stop price. It is an order to minimize losses when the seller suspects that the price is on a falling trend. Thus, the seller is able to sell a security before the price goes too low.
    - A buy stop market order - This is an order placed by a buyer to buy at the best market

price after the price rises above the stop price. It is an order to minimize losses when the buyer suspects that the prices are on a rising trend. Thus, the buyer is able to purchase a security before the price gets too high.

2) Stop Loss Limit Order

This is an order placed by a business entity to purchase a security at no more than or sell a security at no less than a certain fixed price (limit price). There are two types of stop-loss limit orders:

- Stop-loss buy limit order - This is an order placed by a buyer. It can only be executed at the limit price or lower.
  - Stop loss sell limit order - This is an order placed by a seller, which gets transacted at the limit price or higher.

Trailing Stop Loss

A trailing stop-loss order, also known as trailing stop-on-quote order, is a stop order where the stop price automatically adjusts by a given point amount or a given percentage. Thus, the stop price automatically adjusts based on the last price of a security under consideration. For a sell order, the execution is triggered by the bid price, while, for buy orders, the execution is triggered by the ask price. Upon trigger by the stop price, a market order (to buy or sell) is sent to the market.

There are two types of trailing stop-loss orders:

- Trailing stop-loss sell order - When the difference between the security's last price and trigger price exceeds the trailing stop amount, then the trigger

price is adjusted. The new trigger price will then be established by subtracting the trail stop amount from the security's last price.
- Trailing stop-loss buy order - When the difference between the security's last price and trigger price exceeds the trailing stop amount, then the trigger price get adjusted. The new trigger price will be established by adding the trail stop amount to the last price.

Chapter 8 Trading the Breakout

<u>Downside breakouts</u>

The downside breakout, also known as the drop and stop, is a means of channel breakout trading that is particularly useful when used at the start of a specific session. It is a particularly useful strategy if you are set on trading the breakout and can't get anything else going at the moment. This means that the first thing you are going to want to watch out for is an evening star candlestick pattern which shows where the weekly pivot occurs.

An evening star candlestick pattern is a type of bearish pattern comprised of three distinct candles. The first is a large white candlestick that is found within the uptrend. The second will be red or white with a small body that closes above the first candle. Finally, the third candle will be large, red, and open underneath the second candle. It will also close near the center of the body of the first candle. If you see this pattern, then you can be confident the current uptrend is going to come to an end sooner than later.

After the price has made it through the upside breakout and then dropped into the downside breakout you were waiting for, it will then drop to a point that is lower than the weekly pivot point. This often leads to a number of price rejections before performing in such a way that it generates a rejection bar candle that is bearish which is a confirmation that the stop and drop is off to the races which means you can count on the price spiking downward to a significant degree.

While getting in once the confirmation has already happened will still generate a profit, it is going to be a situation that is far from ideal as the price is already headed towards the point where it will be exhausted. This means it will have a strong early upward movement, followed by a decline that is just as sharp. A majority of the average daily ranges will then have been used up at this point, something that the traders using this technique will be aware of. This means that if you want to use this strategy effectively you can't be afraid of a little micromanaging and also need to keep your expectations in check.

Furthermore, it is possible that there will not always be a visible rejection bar to make it easy to determine if the time is right. In these cases, you are going to want to use a polarity indicator to provide you with a better indication of when the market is moving in this direction. In a pinch, a number of bearish candles in a row that is growing increasingly severe as they move downward from the existing range. When any of these indicators occur, you should quickly determine the best entry point and do so using the next bearish candle by jumping in a few pips beneath the monthly pivot point.

Upside breakouts

If you find yourself in a situation where you are watching the price of one of your chosen currencies move into a tight range while at the same time waiting for what you believe to be a serious trend to start then the odds are high that by the time the price begins truly moving in earnest you will have already begun to miss out on profits that should be yours by right. Waiting to trade a breakout without preparing properly beforehand will often only lead to a scenario where rather than being ready for the breakout ahead of time you end up chasing the price which is a guaranteed means of minimizing profits at best or watching a winning trade turn into a losing one at worst.

Rejection bar candlestick: Many professional traders are extremely fond of the rejection bar candlestick, and with good reason, as it is one of the most useful technical analysis formations you can find.

It is a one bar formation that is known as the hammer or sometimes the inverted hammer forms when the currency has already rejected either the higher or the lower prices. This is visualized when a price opens before moving in a given direction and then reversing in the same session to close around or possibly just past the initial open. The best-case scenario then is one where both the close and the open of the rejection bar occur near one another, the closer the better.

Meanwhile, the tail of the bar needs to be a minimum of the same length as the body, with the longer tail typically indicating a stronger bar as it signifies that a low or high was previously rejected. The head of the bar is going to be the highest point of the price that was reached if the bar is bullish or the lowest if it is bearish. No matter how strong the bar appears to be, it should never be used as the sole justification for a given trade. As always, the more supplementary signals you have the better.

Specifically, if the price rejections can be tracked from a significant level, say the mid-level Bollinger band, then significant levels of resistance or support, or even a weekly pivot can tell you when you are onto a strong and reliable signal. Generally speaking, if you see a candlestick formation that starts to form by itself then the best course of action is going to be to look for additional reasons to enter the trade as they are going to be readily visible if the trade is worth pursuing.

Pop and stop: A pop and stop trade occurs when the price of the currency you are following suddenly pops out of the range it has been previously traveling in, stops temporarily and then resumes its previous movement. From this point on you will notice multiple rejection bars forming above and then rejecting nearby. If this then results in a larger than average candle you can realistically expect some retracement possibly enough for it to return to the previous range. This is due to the fact that the fast movement covered a sparse order area which can be seen via the gaps in the market. These gaps are naturally filled in by the market which means if you are going to get in then it needs to happen as quickly as possible.

Viable reasons for entering this type of trade include things like the time of day the pop occurred to begin with, especially if the price has been relatively quiet leading up to the beginning of the session when both volatility and liquidity are more likely to increase. This then often goes hand in hand with the price trading in a tight range. On the other hand, the price could previously move in a pop and stop motion, only to have formed rejection bars at previously relevant levels. If this occurs, then you will need to place a limit order that is a few pips lower or higher than the rejection bars. The stop loss will need to be placed just above or below the tail of the bars if you are an aggressive trader or below or above the highs or lows of the range if you are more conservative.

When you are looking for a pop and stop you are going to want to be aware of the fact that it is a relatively risky strategy. This is due to the fact that you are forced to rely on the gap created by the move to not be filled as quickly as what frequently occurs. The presence of rejection bars will also confirm the move to some extent but does not completely mitigate the potential for risk at the same time. The least risky time to use this strategy is when some time of news has just rocked the market. Once this happens you will have better luck trading in the direction the market sentiment is moving.

This will prove particularly useful if, prior to the news, the price was already trading at a particularly close range. It is important to keep an eye out for these types of announcements as they have the potential to reverse the sentiment and fill in the gap. You will need to be aware that this strategy requires a trend that is well supported in order to reach its full potential. This means that it is extremely important that you do your research beforehand in order to accurately determine if the session is likely to contain the level of liquidity that you are looking for in order to make this strategy into a profitable proposition. You will most frequently find the type of breakouts that you are looking for in open sessions of the forex market with London and New York being the prime candidates in most cases.

Additionally, it is important to maintain a level head when using this strategy and to never get greedy as the price movement after things take off can be substantial but is rarely prolonged. This is a strategy that relies on scalping, after all, which means that profits in the 1: 5: 1 or 2: 1 range are enough to bow out for.

NYSE Breakout Strategy

While this strategy only has a very specific use, it is worth keeping in mind as it can be quite profitable when executed on correctly. Using this strategy, you will want to be on the lookout for a breakout with a targeted resistance level to buy before waiting for a targeted support level to ultimately sell. This strategy works best with the EUR/USD, USD/CHF, USD/JPY and GDP/USD currency pairs working from a 15 minute timeframe.

To best use this strategy, you will need to create a vertical line on the 15-minute chart for the currency pair you have chosen starting at 7 am EST and a second line at 9 am EST. From there you will need to create two horizontal lines at the highs of the various candles that appeared between the pair of vertical lines. From there, you will need to set a pending buy stop order that is between two and five pips above the current high point and a pending order to sell stop order that is a few points underneath the low. Finally, you will need to place a stop loss on the opposite end of each order as well.

With this done you will then be free to sit back and wait for the breakout to occur, which your research should have already indicated will not be that long. Once the breakout does occur you can then cancel the pending order you placed that is now useless as you will clearly not have to worry about it being activated. When everything is said and done you can often expect between 50 and 60 pips of profit from this strategy before most trends fizzle out.

Don't forget, when setting up this strategy you only have nine candlesticks to work with between 7 am and 9 am EST. As such, if the price doesn't appear to be trending either low or high then this is because the market is likely ranging. As such, you will most likely be better off canceling your orders as this strategy is only going to be effective if the right movement presents itself during this precise time period.

This is also known as a common time for various types of press releases to be released which means you are going to want to remain vigilant as your trade is in play to prevent anything unexpected happening without your knowledge. It is also important to keep in mind that if you start a trade based on GBP in the UK session then it can likely continue on into the US session in most cases.

The biggest advantage of this strategy is based on the fact that the way it is constructed virtually ensures that you can't overtrade, simply because you are only ever watching a single trade. As such, it is great for those without a lot of time or for those who aren't especially committed to trading and are just looking to try something out. Generally speaking, if you find a scenario where the difference between the highs and lows are less than 60 pips then be prepared to double your daily trade amount as this is a strong indicator that the forthcoming movement will be extremely profitable.

However, the downside of this strategy is that if the difference between the highs and lows is far greater than 60 pips then it is difficult for it to result in a profitable trade. This is due to the fact that price is unlikely to receive the required momentum to get it to where it would need to be in order to generate a profit for you. If things are setting up to fall this way, then you will want to aim for profit between 20 and 30 pips each day instead.

Chapter 9 Systems and Techniques for Beginners

Trading Systems

A trading system can be referred to as a group of parameters that are made specifically to determine the entry and exit of a trade of a given currency or security. As the parameters are used to do this, the determined points are frequently recorded and also marked in real-time to form a trend on a chart, and also trigger the execution of a trade immediately. This system saved the trader the hustle of using complicated procedure and therefore saves a lot of time. Again, because the system does all of the things and you are only give the final product, trading systems have saved traders from the use of their emotions in trading and can let other people do for them through a brokerage.

The systems, however, have their own limitations, regardless of its type. Most of these systems are more complex, and therefore, the traders need to know how parameters are used to make decisions the trader should also understand the technical analysis of the system to be able to use it. Therefore, before adopting a system for use in FOREX trade, take time to learn the systems so that you can know what to do with the trades and use the parameter presented on the chart on screens to make a trading decision.

In the trading world, everyone needs to know when to make an effective move, and the system you are using should not be a hindrance. To make sure that you understand the system completely, most traders use a custom made a system that is used for a particular trading strategy. For instance, a system for day trading might not be the same as the system for swing trading. A system that uses patterns a strategy for trading is not the best for use by traders who use fundamental strategies for trading. Therefore, as a trader you should know your best strategies and the skill you have, and choose a system that suits your strategies. Again, many systems can only work for a given period because the FOREX market is dynamic: it keeps on changing. The system you are using should be able to accommodate the changes through constant updates; otherwise, it becomes obsolete and cannot be used in the new trading markets.

Most traders have come up with systems that specialize in different trading strategies. For instance, when you are a trader that uses events that affect FOREX trading, you can use the Geopolitical turmoil trading system in your trades. There is always a microeconomic indicator to affect FX markets, for instance, most speeches made by governors, presidents, conferences prepared by the central bank of a country whose currency is in the FOREX market, and many others. These macroeconomic indicators are so powerful that they strike when least expected, and they are always unpredictable. The same case is on the geopolitical conflicts, which happens and surprises the traders because the changes that it brings to the market. Therefore if you choose to use the geopolitical trading system, make sure that you are ready to follow and monitor the events in the country of origin of the currencies you are pairing, so that you make a move that you are certain and it is beneficial. It is not advisable to wait for an event to happen for you to make a decision to buy either one of the currencies that you want to pair, always buy and have one of the currencies of your pair such that in case of an event that destabilizes the exchange of the paired currencies, you are always ready to act in your favor.

Another trading system is the use of candlestick patterns and moving averages. There are many variations in the moving averages, but the most popular one is the simple moving average, which is studying for a determined period. When using this system, the best thing to do is to find a moving average that is suitable for you, and then search for candlestick patterns that are around the moving average. It is therefore good to understand the candlestick patterns that might occur around a moving average and know when it is effective to employ them. The candlestick should also meet the criteria for higher success. As a beginner, before you use a candlestick and the simple moving average, always try the move using a demo account and practice until you perfect the skill, then use it in a real investment account.

Some people choose to use scalping as their trading strategy, and therefore, they can use this system for trading. The system requires that you generate trading signals using mostly the fundamental analysis; this is a manual system. There are automated systems, which does the analysis for you and gives you the signals on when to buy and when to sell. Automated trading can be best used by beginners, as they learn how to do it manually. However, the automated system deprives you of the possibility of gaining the skill; it is sometimes good to learn the hard way, but became better in trading. The skill helps you to have wide knowledge in analyzing and determining trade signals, remember that the FOREX market is volatile and the system can become obsolete unless it is constantly updated. There are systems that have been designed to do scalping using specific currency pair, and the most common is the USD/JPY EMA scalping strategy. The pair have been chosen because they are moderately volatile and also has moderate risk. This shows that everyone can develop their own trading system that works, provided that you do your research well. For example apart from the USD/JPY option, you can always choose your pair as long as they have characteristics that will help you manage trades without making loses.

The above-mentioned trading systems are not the only systems we have, there are many, and as said earlier, they depend on the trader's strategy. The only important thing to do is to know how to read the parameters affecting the trade of a particular currency, and know when they present a good entry point for entrance in the market and exit. As a beginner trader, invest your time in understanding your trading skills, then using your skills; choose your trading strategy, which will guide you on choosing the best trading system. Some trading systems require your attention all the time, and this aspect should be considered when determining the system to use.

Trading Techniques for Beginners

FOREX market is the largest in the financial market around the globe. It has different techniques for trading, which involves the selling and buying securities of stocks, softs, indices, and metals, among others and currencies. The techniques use different systems and platforms that ensure that trading activities are executed effectively. Those who use different techniques use different strategies, as they speculate and predict what is the best move to maximize profits. The four basic techniques used are day trading, swing trading, position trading, and scalp trading.

Use the Day Trading techniques

Day trading is a technique where a trade opens trading positions and after trading with them, he or she closes all of them; at the point of closure of the trading day, no trades are open. This type of trading requires that the trader has experience and extensive knowledge on what constitutes FOREX trading and it is done. Before a day trader makes a decision, he or she employs different strategies that will guide him or her on the best strategies for success. Traders sometimes use technical indicators to make and do calculations on the time frames where exit and entry are favorable. Others use their instincts to make a decision on the best move that will yield profits. The traders that use this technique use the price action characteristics to hold position, and to trade currencies; they rarely use fundamental information. Traders only concentrate on the volatility of the currency and day range; a trade is only initiated if there is enough price movement because day traders realize their profits through price movements of the selected currency. The trader establishes a trade by moving in the trade and leaving the trade very fast, and therefore, the liquidity and volume of currency traded are important aspects of this technique of trading. This means that traders concentrate only on the currencies with a large volume and daily range. The events that will have a short term effect on the price and volume of currencies are appreciated much by day traders. For example news on certain economic aspects makes day trading good for many traders; these aspects include interest rates, release of information on the corporate earnings and economic statistics.

Use the Position Trading technique

Position trading in the FOREX market involves holding or taking a trade position longer. The period can be as long as years, months and as short as weeks. Traders that use this technique do not care much about the price fluctuation of currencies in the short terms and the daily news release. The technique does not make the trader active, because he or she can make very few positions for a whole year. They utilize the weekly or monthly price action chart analysis to determine security moves towards a given trend, and therefore, they use primary trends to make their profits. Unlike in the day trading technique, position technique uses technical and fundamental indicators analysis, which gives the trader a good look at the FOREX market before they make decisions.

Implement the Swing Trading techniques

It is a trading technique that is used by traders to make profits through taking a trading position overnight that goes for a few weeks the traders that utilize. This strategy mostly uses fundamental indicators analysis, which includes analysis of patterns, the intrinsic value of the traded currency, trends in the prices of the currency. They also use technical analysis to find short terms momentum price. The traders look for a currency that would have an extraordinary move within a short time frame. They are interested in trading with large price changes in a day, which prompts them to spend weeks or even months monitoring to find the large price move. When the price suddenly swings in the upwards direction, these traders trade their currencies by selling and when there is a halt in the swing, the traders stop selling, or they would have already left the trade. The focus on given assets help them to understand its movement, and its advantage lies in the huge returns by the traders; which is contrary to investors who buy and hold. This technique in trading can be used by traders in earning a living, as they have fewer risks compared to other trading techniques. In addition, the trader does not need to be checking real-time data and analyzing it to determine when to make a move that makes profits. The people who engage in part-time trading can use this technique as it does not need full-time commitment.

Employ the Scalp Trading

This is a type of trading where a trader trades currencies and holds on the position only for a short time, hoping that within the short time of hold he or she will get an opportunity to take another trading position bringing in profits. The traders take several positions in a day with the hope that that within the day, they would make a considerable amount from several small percentage profits in the market. To maximize on opportunities that show up in the market for a short time, the trader develops functional trading strategies such as the use of hotkeys to make desirable executions at the computer. On the other hand, those using the automated trading system uses set rules and guidelines to determine a trade signal.

In FOREX trading, traders make huge profits, but it is a market that is full of risks. It is therefore important for the trader to analyze his or her trading skills, and choose wisely whether he or she wants to be a swing trader, day trader, scalping trader, or position trader.

Conclusion

Figuring out how to exchange Forex effectively can be entangled for learners. A great many people need to get rich medium-term, regardless of how unreasonable it might sound. The universe of Forex trading can be a touch of overpowering, particularly in the event that you are new to the game, and don't have a clue about the standards yet. You have to plunge your toes in before you go any more profound. Fortunately, we have your back! We've aggregated a rundown of 20 Forex tips for apprentices to help you along your trading venture 2021. In the event that you as of now have involvement with Forex trading, it's in every case great to recall the nuts and bolts.

1. Pick Your Broker Wisely

Picking the correct agent is a large portion of the fight. Take as much time as is needed to check surveys and suggestions. Ensure the agent you pick is dependable and suits your trading character. Keep in mind, there are heaps of phony dealers out there who will just hold you up. Go for an approved intermediary with a permit.

2. Make Your Own Strategy

No rundown of cash trading tips is finished in the event that it doesn't make reference to systems. One of the most widely recognized errors novice dealers make isn't making an activity plan. Make sense of what you need to escape trading. Having an unmistakable ultimate objective as a top priority will help with your trading discipline.

3. Learn Step-by-Step

Similarly as with each new useful learning action, trading expects you to begin with the nuts and bolts, and move gradually until you comprehend the playing field. Start by contributing little totals of cash, and remember the familiar proverb 'moderate however consistent successes the race'.

4. Assume Responsibility for Your Emotions

Try not to give your feelings a chance to divert you. It tends to be troublesome now and again, particularly after you've encountered a losing streak. Be that as it may, keeping a level head will enable you to remain reasonable, so you can settle on equipped decisions. At whatever point you let your feelings improve of you, you open yourself to superfluous dangers. Practicing risks the executives inside your trading will assist you with minimizing the dangers.

5. Stress Less

This is one evident Forex tip - in light of the fact that it is. Be that as it may, prepare to have your mind blown. Trading under pressure for the most part prompts unreasonable choices, and in live trading, that will cost you cash. In this manner, recognize the wellspring of your pressure and attempt to dispense with it, or possibly limit its effect on you. Take a full breath and spotlight on something different. Each individual has their method for conquering pressure - some tune in to old style music, while others work out. Tune in to your emotional wellness and realize what works best for you.

6. Careful discipline brings about promising results

Of all the Forex deceives and tips for novices, this is the most significant. You are probably not going to prevail at anything on your first attempt. Just steady trading practice can yield reliably top outcomes. Be that as it may, you most likely would prefer not to lose cash while learning the rudiments. Fortunately for you, trading on a demo account costs nothing to liberate up and is to utilize!

7. Brain research is Key

Each merchant is a therapist on the most fundamental level. At the point when you're arranging your best course of action, you need to dissect showcase developments and audit your own brain science. You have to ask yourself inquiries, for example,

• Did I give indications of affirmation inclination? •
Did I make an exchange out of dissatisfaction?

• What caused me to pick that specific money pair?

Acing your brain science will shield you from numerous misfortunes along the trading advancement way.

8. No Risk, No Success

Not even Forex trading tips and deceives can promise you achievement. At the point when you choose to turn into a broker, you ought to have just acknowledged the plausibility of disappointment. In the event that you didn't - here's a rude awakening. You won't make productive exchanges 100% of the time. Try not to give false commercials a chance to get in your mind, either. Rather, be practical about your Forex trading techniques and objectives.

Options Trading For Beginners

Crash Day Course to Become a Profitable Investor in Your Spare Time for a Living with Strategies to Trade Penny Stocks, Bond, EFT, Futures & Forex Markets in 7 Days

ROBERT ZONE

Introduction

If you were to find an investor and ask to look at their portfolio, you will be able to see that they have a large variety of investments that they are working on. They don't just put all their money on one company all the time. Instead they have many different types of investments they can work with such as bonds, stocks, mutual funds, and more. In addition, there are times when a portfolio will include options, but it is not as likely to be there as some of the others.

This is like getting a key where once you use that key to open the front door of a house, then it belongs to you. You may not technically own the house because you have the key, but you can use that key whenever you would like and if you choose, you could purchase the house later on.

Options are set up so that they cost you a certain fixed price for so much time. This length will change based on the option that you are working with. Sometimes you will have an option that only lasts for a day and then there are some that you may hold onto for a few years. You will know how long the option is going to last before you make the purchase.

Options are nothing new. It's a well-known term in trading, and even though it might be overwhelming for some people to think about, options are not really hard to understand. The portfolios of investors are generally composed of different classes of assets, which can be bonds, mutual funds, stocks or even ETFs. One such asset class are options, and certain advantages are offered by them when used accurately, which other trading stocks and ETFs cannot offer. Like many other asset classes, options too can be purchased with brokerage investment accounts.

Options can be considered as an investment that gives you more "options."

But that does not mean that there are no risks involved. Almost every investment entails a multitude of risks. The same goes for options. An investor ought to know of these risks before proceeding with trade.

Options are a part of the group of securities called derivatives. The term derivative is many a time associated with huge risks and volatile performance. Warren Buffett once called derivatives "weapons of mass destruction," which is a little too much.

Options are a kind of derivative. Investors are often talking about different derivatives. Options derive their value from an underlying stock or security. In fact, options belong to the class of securities known as derivatives. For a long time, people associated derivatives with high-risk investments. This notion is not really true.

Derivatives obtain their value from an underlying security. Think about wine, for instance. Wine is produced from grapes. We also have ketchup which is derived from tomatoes. This is basically how derivatives function.

One can gain a real advantage in the market if they know how options work and can use them properly since you can put the cards in your favor if you can use options correctly. The great thing about options is that you can use them according to your style. If you're a speculative person, earn through speculation. If not, earn without speculating. You should know how options work even if you decide never to use them because other companies you invest in might use options.

Options are an attractive investment tool. They have a risk/reward framework, which is unlike any other. They can be used in a multitude of combinations that make them very versatile. The risk factor involved can be diluted by using these options with other financial instruments or other option contracts, and at the same time opening more avenues for profits. While many investments have an unbound quantum of risk attached, options' trading, on the other hand, has defined risks, which the buyers know about.

Chapter 1 Understanding Option Trading

Now, there are several options that will work when you are dealing with options. Some of the ones that you will come across on a regular basis include:

- Bonds: A bond is going to be a debt investment where the investor is able to loan out their money to the government or company. Then this money will be used for a variety of projects by the second party. But at some time, usually determined when the money is given over, the money will be paid back along with some interest. Most of the time you will work with a government bond and these bonds are even found on the public exchange.
- Commodity: Commodities are another choice that you can make when you are working with options. These will be any basic goods that will be used in commerce and can include some choices like beef, oil, and grain. When you trade these, there will be a minimum of quality that they must meet. These are popular because commodities are considered tangible, which means that they represent something that is real.
- Currency: Currency is going to talk about any type of money that is accepted by the government and can include coins and paper money. Of course, cryptocurrency and Bitcoin are starting to join the market as well. The exchange rate of these currencies, especially when it comes to the digital

currencies, will change quite a bit in very little time so it is important to be careful with these.
- Futures: These are going to be similar to what you found with commodities, but they have some different guidelines on how they can be delivered, the quantity and quality, and more.
- Index: An index is going to be a group of securities that are imaginary and will symbolize the statistical measurement of how those will do in the market.
- Stock: You can own a certain percentage of the share, but instead of running that company, you will let other management do that while you make some profits each quarter when the company does well.

Options may sound complex but are pretty easy to understand if you pay keen attention. You will come across numerous traders' profiles with different security types including bonds, stocks, mutual funds, ETFs, and even options.

Options are another asset class. If applied correctly, they will offer numerous benefits that all other assets on their own cannot. For instance, you can use options to hedge against negative outcomes like a declining stock market or falling oil prices. You can use options to generate recurrent income and for speculative purposes like wagering on the movement of a stock.

When Should You Use Options?

As an investor, you will have a number of opportunities to use options. However, there is a number that is truly beneficial. Here is a brief look at them.

- Options buy you time if you need to sit back and watch things develop.
- You require very little funds to invest in options compared to buying shares.
- Options will offer you protection from losses because they lock in price but without the obligation to buy.

Always keep in mind that options offer no free ride or a free lunch. Trading in options carries some risks due to their predictive nature. Any prediction will turn out one way or another. The good news here is that any losses that you incur will only be equivalent to the cost of setting up the option. This cost is significantly lower than buying the underlying security.

Differentiating Options from Stocks

While there is no expiration date in stocks, Options contract has one. This expiration period can be as long as a week or months or even years, and it is determined by the kind of options you are practicing and other related regulations.

Stocks are not a part of derivatives, while options are which means their value is derived from something else.

While stocks are a well-defined numerical quantity, options are not.

One can even profit with a drop in prices of the underlying stock, which is dependent on the type of strategy they are following.

Stock owners have a right in the company either for dividend or voting or both. Options owners have no such rights.

Types of Options

There are various types of options from which a trader can take advantage that will then allow him or her to sell or buy options. In addition to this, there are subcategories of options with different stipulations and advantages. It is important to review and be familiar with these in order to use options for maximum profit. Traders would do well to remember that options trading does take a lot of practice and only those who are well versed in options trading and aware of the movement and trends of companies and financial institutions do well in this particular sect of trading. That being said, here are the various categories of options trading.

Calls

Calls are used by buyers, meaning that if a trader has a call option, they have the right, but are not obligated, to buy an underlying asset at the strike price before a previously agreed upon expiration date. A call option is a contract or agreement that gives the investor/holder the right - but not obligation - to Purchase an asset at a specified price within a specified time. The main difference is that the call option gives you the right to buy or call in asset. When the price of the asset increases, you can gain a profit from a call.

The writer of the call option, also referred to as the seller, has an obligation to sell the security/asset if the investor exercises the option. The seller receives a premium for taking on the risk associated with the obligation.

Puts

The catch for the seller is that the price will need to drop before the expiration date. If this occurs, then the buyer will likely have paid the seller the full strike price, which will be more than the value of the asset. If the price plummets after the expiration date however, the seller will only gain the initial options premium used to secure the contract. Unfortunately, this also means the seller is probably losing money on the underlying asset, which they still own. However, if the seller writes a put as part of a strategy, they will need to keep in mind that the put can always be assigned and the investor will be forced to sell. In regards to the -in, -at, and -out-of-the-money terms, the exact opposite of calls is true of puts.

Before moving on to the other types of options, here is a quick note concerning some brief clarification regarding those who participate in options trading. There are four positions that can be held that fall into two categories. The first category is made up the "holders," and includes those who buy calls and puts.

This option gives a buyer the right to SELL an asset/security at a given strike price before the date of expiry. The writer/seller of the option has an obligation to purchase the security/asset if the strike price is exercised.

How option trading works

There are several parties involved in a trade. It isn't possible to trade directly with everyone, and it isn't even practical. This is why, for the sake of convenience, stock exchanges were formed. This is a channel where all the stocks are being traded.

You cannot work directly with the stock exchange as this would create great confusion. It would mean too many people making deals at the same time. This is where brokers come into play.

Brokers work as the mediators, as the channel of communication between you and the exchange. They charge a commission for their service. In the stock exchange industry's early stages, most of the transactions were carried out by the brokers on behalf of their clients. Brokers nowadays still carry out transactions on behalf of their clients, but the clients now have the option to manage their accounts easily. You will have to open a trading account with a broker, and the broker will give you access to that trading account.

Currently, a number of software programs have been successfully developed where you can directly trade on stock exchanges. The program recommendation, as well as the access credentials, will be provided by the brokerage firm you'll choose.

- Like a bond or stock, an option is a tradable security. You can purchase or sell options to a foreign broker or trade them on an exchange within the United States. An option may give you the opportunity to leverage your cash, though it may be high risk because it eventually expires (expiration date). For stock options, each option contract represents 100 shares.
- An instance of an option is if you want to buy a car/house, but for whatever reason, do not have immediate cash for it but will get the cash next month. You can now buy the asset at the agreed price and sell it for a profit. The value of the asset may also depreciate perhaps when the house develops plumbing problems or other problems or in the case of a vehicle, gets into an accident. If you decide not to buy the asset and let your purchase option expire, you lose your initial investment, the $2,500 you placed for the option.

This is the general concept of how option trading happens; however, in reality, option trading is a lot more complex and involves more risks.

What kind of investor are you?

Trading has its strategies, its techniques and its secrets. Different things apply to different people. What works for someone else may not work for you. Why? Because you are two different kinds of investors. Aggressive personalities invest in a completely different manner than conservative personalities. People who are not afraid to take risks are completely different investors than those who are methodical and play it safe. There is no better or worse here. It is just the style of doing business.

There are two major categories of investors:

- *The active investor* Those are also called <u>traders.</u> They do not hold on to options for a long time and their interest lies in making profit from the volatility of the prices. The trade a lot and as often as possible.

- *The passive investor* These are also called the <u>buy-and-hold</u> investors. They are the exact opposites. They are interested in making the maximum gain from each option and they do not trade often. And when they do they will trade once or twice.

Most people could find themselves at any point between those two categories. Some tend to be more aggressive, others tend to be slightly more conservative. One would think that being in the middle would offer you the best of both. But this is not always the case.

Aggressive personalities are actually impatient personalities. For them patience is not a virtue. So if you force them to trade conservatively in most cases they do not even know how. And they do not care to learn. The same holds true for the conservative people. Forcing them to trade more options than one or two, creates a chaos in their mindset.

Each one balances to whichever side they feel more comfortable. The side that will allow him or her to think straight and make the proper decisions. That would be the perfect world, but unfortunately there are always strings attached.

Even the most conservative investor may have to act fast and trade all his options should an emergency arise. An aggressive person should learn that there are cases where trading may be forbidden, or banned, or halted for some reason and they will have to hold on to their options.

The deeper you get into options trading the wiser you become. No matter what kind of investor you may be, the market itself will teach you, sometimes the hard way (i.e. it will cost you a lot of money) when it is time to hold on to an option and when it is time to trade it.

Top Reasons to Trade in Options

Limit Your Risk

A good reason to go with buying options is that you will be able to limit your risk down to just the amount of money that you pay for the premium. With other investment options, you could end up losing a lot of money, even money that you did not invest to begin with, but this does not happen when you are working with options.

Higher Percentage of Returns
As mentioned, an options trader is only going to pay a fraction of the value of the asset just to have some control over that asset. This will allow the trader to earn more money than what they would be able to earn when they purchase the asset upfront and then try to sell it.

Helps to Hedge Intraday or Futures Trades
It is common for traders to purchase or short-sell Futures contracts because they expect them to move in one direction or another. You may not be complaining when this goes the right way and you earn unlimited profits, but if you go with one of these trades and you don't hedge your position, you are going to complain when you start losing a lot of money. If you have an understanding on how trading options works, you could buy call or put options to help insure that you are not going to end up with an unlimited loss. The right options choice is going to help control your loss the moment that the intraday or futures positions starts going against what you wanted.

Options are flexible
When you are working with options, you will find that you get a ton of flexibility. You can choose to buy or sell, you can go with different expiration dates, you can pick from a variety of strategies and assets, and you can even have control over your strike price. There are even ways that you will be able to profit if the market goes down. Sometimes all this flexibility is going to make working in options more complicated, but if you know what you are doing, this type of flexibility will help you to profit, regardless of how the market is doing.

Gain leverage
Another benefit you will be able to get when you decide to work with the options market is the idea of leverage. To keep things simple, leverage is a big advantage to the trader. When you gain leverage, you are giving yourself more options because you are able to put more money into the market without needing to have more startup capital to help you out. This can be dangerous because it causes you to lose more money than you have in the beginning, but if you are careful and read the market right, it will make you earn a ton more money even with lower startup costs.

Low-risk
You will find that working with options can be relatively low risk. First, these options are more affordable than what you are able to get with some other types of investing, so you are limiting the risks that you are taking, as long as you use the right strategies as you do it. You are even able to look at some of the trades and pick the ones that have less risk so that you will lose less, even if the trade doesn't go the way that you want.

Chapter 2 How to Start Options Trading

There is always a beginning of everything we do in life. In this chapter, I will take you through on some of the ways on how to start options trading, some of the strategies needed for newbies of options trading, and also, the capital needed to start on this type of trading.

How Much Capital Is Needed?
After knowing how options trading works, do not rush to waste on your cash. There are too many risks in this type of trading. Capital is a basic requirement to start any business. Does options trading require too much capital? No. When starting on options trading, it is better to start with small capital to avoid massive trading risks.

Many are the individuals who utilize much of their cash for trading during their first days, which is so dangerous. Such individuals end up having too many risks to handle, and finally, they make up their minds to close their businesses. I do not want you to fall into such a mess. Do your thing with the right speed.

Start options trading with a reasonable small amount. Do not brag off that you got everything under control. You will lose even the only cash you had. Starting with less money has a high likelihood of fewer risks in trading. I bet you can now handle a few risks and be able to continue with your trading.

Strategies Used by Beginners for Options Trading

Options trading has a wide variety of strategies. There are simple to complex strategies that you can implement in options trading. Beginners find it tough to know the best simple strategies to utilize in their trading. You do not need to worry anymore. I have provided a detailed list below of the different simple options trading strategies you can use:

Buying calls. Buying calls is the simplest options trading strategy for beginners, investors, and even professionals. Investors prefer calls so much because this strategy provides them with the honor to purchase stock at a certain agreed price with a minimum amount of capital within an agreed time before its expiry.

Most of the bullish traders use this options strategy. When there is a rise in the price of the stock, you earn good profits. This strategy is right for any beginner who wants to generate better income, earn huge profits, and even save on the trading capital.

Its great potential to massive profits, however, makes it have a bigger exposure to the trading risks. You, as a buyer, can know the risks involved in your trading. Also, buying a call strategy has a better and secure feature, which can handle many risks.

The major drawback of purchasing calls is associated with the time of expiry and the loss of value. They always have a time of expiry, so you need to check on the timing. Call options lose their value when their time of expiry reaches. You do not earn any dividends when your options are past the date of expiry.

Buying put. Buying put is another simple strategy, which is just the vice versa of buying calls. Most investors use this expecting the stock's price will fall within that time before expiry. Investors always gain good enough profits when their prediction becomes right.

The things to put into consideration when buying put options include the time you are planning to be on trade and the amount of money you can afford to buy options. Purchase put options with at least one month remaining for them to expire. Do not purchase an option with a long duration before it expires. It will lose its time premium. You do not need to buy options with a duration like one year remaining for them to expire, because you will not wait to trade an option for a whole year. So, be wise when buying options.

The other consideration is all about buying options that you can afford. Do not torture yourself by buying expensive put options. You will get hurt at the end. Weigh the different prices of the put options available and select the one you can afford according to the risks involved and the size of your account.

In case their prediction fails, the loss associated with this strategy is so limited. Unfortunately, you become exposed to so many risks.

Short put. Short put options strategy is all about buying a stock at a lower price than its current cost in the market. You gain profits in situations where the stock's price remains above an agreed price within that time of expiry. Otherwise, you incur many losses.

Conversely, in situations where the stock's price falls below the price agreed before the time of expiration, another party on trade sells you the stock at the agreed price, and you have to buy it no matter the cost.

Selling a short put option is quite simple, look for a margin account and a stock that will not drop its value any time soon. Select a date of expiration that is not that far and agree on the right price to generate more income when selling. By the time of expiry comes, you will earn good profits as long as the price does not fall.

You should be extra cautious when implementing this strategy, or else, you may lose value in your trading when things turn out unexpectedly.

Covered call. A covered call is one of the preferred options strategies for beginners. It is mostly suitable for traders who have expectations of small changes in the price of the stock or no changes at all within the expected time of expiry. A trader using this strategy normally purchases around 100 shares (unit of capital) of the stock and sells a call option against the unit of capital.

After selling the option, you acquire option premiums and decrease the cost of the share. If the price of the asset behaves unexpectedly in the market, meaning that it becomes greater than an agreed price, there should be the sale of the asset by the owner using the agreed price.

Married put. A married put is an options trading strategy quite similar to the insurance policies we normally have at our homes. The strategy enables an investor who owns a stock, to purchase a put option on the stock to protect it against loss in value in the price of the stock.

You should buy the stock and put options on the same day. Also, you need to inform the options broker that the delivery of the stock you purchased will happen after the exercise of the put option. Marriage put strategy is normally used by bullish traders when buying their market trades who want to shield themselves from unlimited losses.

The drawback of this strategy is that it is costly to implement it on your trading portfolio.

Cash-secured put. On this strategy, traders write put options, and at the same time, put aside a sufficient amount of cash for buying stock. The benefits of this strategy are that you can decide on the price you want when you implement this strategy. Also, you receive payment of the options premiums when you sell cash-secured put options. In situations where the stock's price falls below an agreed price, the trader incurs too many losses.

Protective put. A protective put is an options trading strategy that many bullish traders implement to shield against loss of an asset, which is mostly caused by the drop in the price of an asset. A trader holds on to the long position of a stock and then buys a put option at an agreed price closer or equal to the price of the stock.

if it declines, the put options normally protect the agreed price (strike price) within that duration until the time of expiry. Remember, options have a date of expiration.

In scenarios where the price of the stock rises, the trader involved gains good enough profits. However, the profits reduce in cases of the options cost and also commissions. Another drawback of buying puts is that the total cost of the put normally surges due to the cost of the options.

You are supposed to offer the put options for sale in scenarios where the agreed price becomes greater than the stock's price after the time of expiry. However, this leaves the asset unprotected. Alternatively, a trader can also offer the put options for sale and purchase other options.

Collar strategy. Moderate bullish traders who formulate this strategy hold shares of an asset while at the same time, purchase put options and offer call options for sale. Both the put options and call options in collar strategy have a similar time of expiry.

It is also applicable to traders who are just writing covered calls to earn premiums and also want to protect themselves from the unexpected decline in the price of a stock.

A collar strategy normally limits losses in trading but also, unfortunately, limits the gaining of huge profits. You can make more profits without this strategy in cases where the price of the stock rises.

Now, with the idea of the simple options trading strategies that exist, you should sit down, think, and select the best strategy to use as a beginner. Weigh the risks and rewards of the strategy you will choose for excellent performance in options trading.

How to Start Options Trading

Now with the basic knowledge on options trading, I will provide you with a few details on how to start options trading journey.

1. You should look for an options trading broker. The key to successful options trading is your broker. There exist legit and non-legit brokers in options trading. Some of the tips for selecting a good broker include the following:

- Do some research on the broker first. You need to be keen and alert before opening a brokerage options trading platform. Different brokers will approach you with different platforms. Do not rush or assume everything is good; do some research on the best brokers. Make sure you spend your cash well by paying for a good options trading platform. It will help you a lot because your trading performance depends on your platform. Choose a broker with good ratings.
- Charges lower commissions. Some brokers tend to exploit traders by charging high commissions to beginners. You should weigh different commission offers of different brokers before settling on one. Some even charge no commission to traders. You should prefer brokers with fewer commissions. Payment of high commissions periodically can mess you up with losses, and you may find it even hard to secure your trading capital. Do not accept to pay high commissions. You also need to do some savings other than wasting money while paying commissions.
- A simple user interface platform. There is a wide variety of software with different functionalities and features. Some software has a simple user interface, while others are too complex for you to

use. You should choose a platform with a simple and clear user interface that enables you to do your trades with less struggle. Some platforms can waste your precious time when you struggle too much searching on the Internet on how you operate them. Make your work easier by handling software that is according to your level.
- Trading tools for research. You should also consider factors like tools that are present on the platform. Do not purchase a platform with no tools. It will be hard for you. Platform tools ease your trading and make your performance excellent. The tools here may include charting tools, research tools, and even tools that alert you on any market changes that may arise.
- Do some testing on the brokerage platform. Do not be that kind of a careless trader who does things for the sake of doing with no precautions. You need to be cautious enough since this is an income-generating activity. You should test on a brokerage software before making up your mind of purchasing it. Check on the reliability and stability of the software and be 100% sure that this is the platform you will use for your trading. Ensure the software is not that type of platform that crashes down unexpectedly. You might miss crucial trade while fixing your software.
    2. Be approved to trade options. You need to be approved by the broker in charge before purchasing and offering options for sale. They normally have their ways of approving you, like checking your experience and the money that you have. It aids in avoiding risks for the customers. You cannot escape this step.
    3. Get a clear understanding of the technical analysis. Options trading is a technical field.

You need to have the technical analysis techniques of trading options. The technical aspects include reading charts, know about the volume of stock, and also moving averages. Trading charts mostly analyze price behavior in the market. You will handle the aspects many times while trading. Perfect your technical knowledge and be cautious with them.

4. Take advantage of mock trading accounts. Using real accounts when starting options trading is a risky game. You can lose a lot of cash within a short time duration. Mock accounts exist for a reason. You should test your trading skills in the mock accounts, learn a few tricks, and perfect your skills. The advantage of using a mock account is that there is no loss of money since they mostly provide virtual money. It prepares you for real trading. You should take advantage of them and learn a lot. Utilize them for a while and do some evaluations on your returns. When everything works out well, face real trading and shine.

5. Utilize limit orders. It is risky to rely on market prices since price behavior change with time. You should utilize limit orders when trading. A limit order is a type of order that enables you to purchase market securities at an agreed price. Using this type of order shuns you from incurring losses in options trading.

6. Revise your strategies with time. After entering into the options trading, with time, you need to revise your strategies. Utilize the working strategies more often and get rid of unsuccessful trading strategies. You

should not have many strategies that do not bring good performance. Few working strategies are better than having multiple ones that do not help you.
7. Register and join in options trading platforms. Joining forums comprised of other options traders is another way of how to get started in options trading. Forums are platforms of different people with different experiences and opinions. You can learn mistakes made by others in trading. It is part of growing in options trading. So why shouldn't you give it a try?
8. Study and learn about trading metrics. Having your returns maximized is also another way of getting started in options trading. Traders normally use different trading metrics such as delta, gamma, theta, and vega. You should learn and practice them for massive returns.

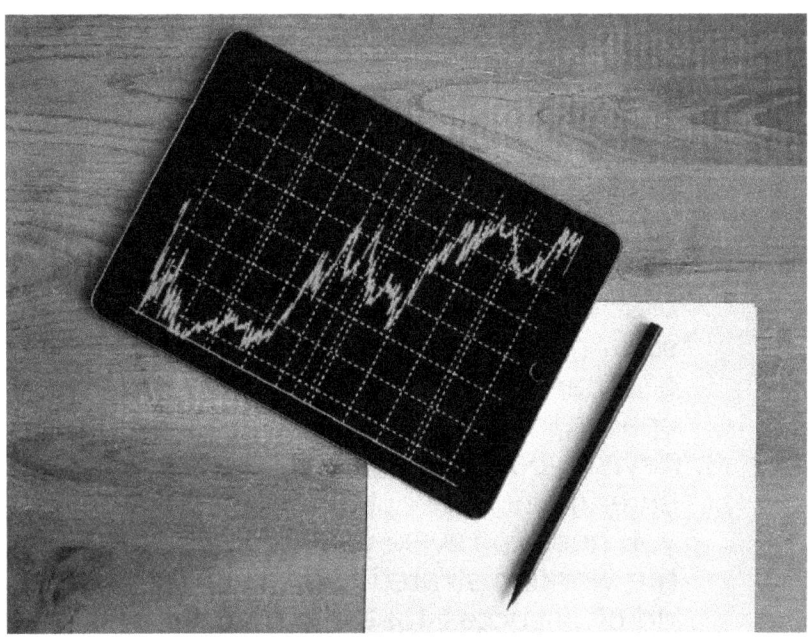

Chapter 3 Brokers

When it comes to selecting brokers, you have many options available. There are full service, discount, online, etc. Understanding the differences between them and selecting the ones best suited for your purposes is crucial if you wish to succeed. Another area that a lot of beginners ignore and then receive a rude lesson in is the regulations surrounding options trading.

There aren't too many rules to comply with, but they do have significant consequences for your capital and risk strategies. This chapter is going to fill you in on all the details.

Choosing a Broker

Generally speaking, there are two major varieties of brokers: Discount and full service. In fact, a lot of full-service brokers have discount arms these days so you will see some overlap. Full service refers to an organization where brokerage is just a part of a larger financial supermarket.

The broker might offer you other investment solutions, estate planning strategies, and so on. They'll also have an in house research wing which will send you reports to help you trade better. In addition to this, they'll also have phone support in case you have any questions or wish to place an order.

Once you develop a good relationship with them, a full-service broker will become a good organization to network. Every broker loves a profitable customer since it helps with marketing. A full-service broker will have good relationships in the industry and if you have specific needs, they can put you in touch with the right people.

The price of all this service is you paying higher commissions than average. It is up to you to see whether this is a good price for you to pay. As such, you don't need to signup with a full-service broker to trade successfully. Order matching is done electronically so it's not as if a person on the floor can get you a better price these days. Therefore, a full-service house is not going to give you better execution.

Discount brokers, on the other hand, are all about focus. They help you trade, and that is it. They will not provide advice, at least not intentionally from a business perspective, and phone ordering is nonexistent. That doesn't mean customer service is reduced. Far from it.

Commissions will be lower as well, far lower than what you can expect to pay at a full-service house. The downside of a discount brokerage is that you're not going to receive any special product recommendations or solutions outside of your speculative activities. A lot of people prefer to trade (using a separate account) with the broker they have their retirement accounts with so everything is kept in-house.

So which one should you choose? Well, if you aim to keep costs as low as possible, then select a discount broker. In fact, only in the case where you're keen on keeping things in one place should you choose a full-service broker. These days, there's no difference between the two options otherwise.

An exception here is if you have a large amount of capital, north of half a million dollars. In such cases, a full-service broker will be cheaper because of their volume-based commission offers. You'll pay the same rate or as close to what a discount broker would charge you, and you get all the additional services. Whatever additional amounts you need to invest can be handled by the firm through their wealth management line of business.

There are a few terms you must understand, no matter which broker you choose so let's look at these now.

Margin

Margin refers to the number of assets you currently hold in your account. Your assets are cash and positions. As the market value of your positions fluctuates, so does the amount of margin you have. Margin is an important concept to grasp since it is at the core of your risk management discipline.

When you open an account with your broker, you will have a choice to make. You can open either a cash or margin account. In order to trade options, you have to open a margin account. Briefly, a cash account does not include leverage within it, so all you can trade are stocks. There are no account minimums for a cash account, and even if they are, they're pretty minuscule.

A margin account, on the other hand, is subject to very different rules. First, the minimum balances for a margin account are higher. Most brokers will impose a $10,000 minimum, and some will even increase this amount based on your trading style. The account minimum doesn't achieve anything by itself, but it acts as a commitment of sorts for the broker.

The thinking is that with this much money on the line, the person trading is going to be a bit more serious about it and won't blow it away. If only it worked like that. Anyway, the minimum balance is a hard and fast rule. Another rule you should be aware of is the Pattern Day Trader (PDT) designation.

PDT is a rule that comes directly from the SEC. Anyone who executes four or more orders within five days is classified as a PDT ("Pattern Day Trader," 2019). One this tag is slapped onto you, your broker is going to ask you to post at least $25,000 in the margin as a minimum balance. Again, this minimum balance doesn't do anything but the SEC figures that if you do screw up, this gives you enough of a buffer.

Will the strategies in this book get you classified as a PDT? Well, this depends on you. Each strategy by itself plays out over a month or more so once you enter, all you need to do is monitor it and if you want, you can adjust it. However, if you're going to avoid the PDT, you're limited to entering just three positions per workweek.

My advice is to study the strategies and to start slowly. Trade just one instrument at first and see how it goes and then expand once you gain more confidence. At that point, you'll have enough experience to figure out how much capital you need. Remember that even exiting a position is considered a trade, so PDT doesn't refer just to trade entry.

Margin Call

One other aspect of margin you must understand is the margin call. This is a dreaded message for most traders, including institutional ones. The purpose of all risk management is to keep you as far away as possible from this ever happening to you. A margin call is issued when you have inadequate funds in your account to cover its requirements.

Remember that your margin is the combination of the cash you hold plus the value of your positions. If you have $1000 in cash, but your position is currently in a loss of -$900, you'll receive a margin call to post more cash to cover the potential loss you're headed for. In fact, you'll receive it well in advance. If you don't post more margin, your broker has the right to close out your positions and recover whatever cash they can to stop their risk limits from being triggered.

The threshold beyond which your broker will issue a margin call is called the maintenance margin. Usually, you need to maintain 25% of your initial position value (that is when you enter a position) as cash in your account. Most brokers have a handy indicator which tells you how close you are to the limit.

The leading cause of margin calls is leverage. With a margin account, you can borrow money from your broker and use that to boost your returns. Let's look at an example: if you trade with $10,000 of your own money and borrow $20,000 from your broker to enter a position, you control $30,000 worth of the position. Let's say this position makes a gain of $10,000 to bring its total value to $40,000.

You've just made a 100% return on this investment (since you invested just $10,000) despite the total return on the position is 33% (10,000/30,000). What happens if you lose $10,000 on the position though? Well, you just lost 100% despite the position losing only 33%. Leverage is a double-edged sword.

It is far too simplistic to call leverage bad or good. It is what it is. If you're a beginner, you should not be borrowing money to trade under any circumstances. When you're experienced, you can choose to do so as much as you want. Please note, I'm differentiating between the leverage where you borrow money, and the sort of leverage options provide.

With options, a single contract gives you control over a larger pie of stock, but the option premium still needs to be paid. It is, therefore, cheaper to trade options than the common stock. If you were to borrow money to pay for the option premium, then you're indulging in foolish behavior, and you need to step away.

There's a difference between leverage being inherent within the structure of the instrument and using leverage to increase the amount of something you can buy. The latter should be avoided when you're a beginner.

Execution
A favorite pastime of unsuccessful traders is to complain about execution. Their losses are always the broker's fault, and if it weren't for the greedy brokers, they'd be rolling in the dough, diving in and out of it like Scrooge McDuck. Complaining about your execution will get you nothing. A big reason for these

complaints is that most beginner traders don't realize that the price they see on the screen is not the same as what is being traded on the exchange.

We live in an era of high-frequency trading, and the markets' smallest measurement of time has gone from seconds to microseconds. Trades are constantly pouring in, and the matching engine is always finding suitable sellers for buyers. Given the pace of the market, it is important to understand that it is humanly impossible to figure out the exact price of an instrument.

Therefore, within your risk management plan, you must make allowance for times of high volatility when the fluctuations will be bigger. For now, I want you to understand that just because the price you received was different from what was on screen doesn't mean the broker is incompetent.

How do you identify an incompetent broker? Customer service and the quality of the trading terminal they give you access to are the best indicators. Your broker is not in the game to trade against you or fleece you. Admittedly, this is not the case with FX, but we're not discussing FX in this book. So stop blaming your broker and look at your systems instead, assuming the broker passes basic due diligence.

When it comes to placing orders with your broker, you have many options. There are different order types you can place, and each order has a specific purpose. First off, we have the market order. This is the simplest order to understand. When you place a market order, you're telling your broker to fill your entire order at whatever price they can find on the market.

A market order usually results in fast fills, unless there's a volatility event of some sort going on. The next type of order you can place is the limit order. The limit prioritizes order price over quantity. For example, if you want to enter 100 units of an instrument at $10, your broker will buy as much as possible under or equal to $10. If they can get just 90 units under $10, then that's it.

A limit order works for a lot of traders looking to enter a position. Directional risk management depends a lot on the size of the position, so it is critical not to exceed the positions limit. For such traders, this is a beneficial order. The last type of order you will encounter is the stop order. The stop prioritizes quantity over price.

Stop orders have a trigger attached to them, and once market price hits the trigger, the entire quantity of the order is executed, irrespective of what the price is. Stop orders are very useful to get out of positions quickly. Indeed, the stop-loss order is a stop order with the 'loss' in the name simply referring to the minimization of losses in case the trade goes south.

Another order you should be aware of is the Good Till Cancelled or GTC. A cousin of the GTC is the Day order. These two do not order types as much as expiry conditions for the order. A GTC is valid until the trader explicitly cancels it while the day order cancels itself at the end of the market session.

All in all, there are over a hundred different types of order your average broker offers you. Do not get bogged down trying to figure them all out.

Institutional traders use most of them for specific strategies. To trade well, you don't need to understand a single word of what those orders are about. Stick to the ones mentioned here, and you can trade successfully.

The question now is, how and where should you use these orders? Well since you're trading options, you're not going to be too concerned with stop losses and your exits are going to involve letting options expire. Thus, the biggest concern you should have is with regard to trade entry.

With options, you can choose either market or limit orders to enter. Personally, I favor market orders since it guarantees you an entry. Risk management here is a bit different than with directional trades so you can afford to enter at the market. The only exception is if there are extreme volatility conditions present.

Price Quotes

A lot of traders are stumped when they first look at their trading screens and see that there are two prices for everything. After all, every financial channel always displays one price for security but when trading, you'll be quoted two different prices within the price box. This is a small but crucial detail for you to understand.

The lower price you receive is called the bid, and this is the price you will pay if you sell the instrument. The higher price is the ask, and this is what you will pay to buy the instrument. The single price you see on your TV screen is the "Last Traded Price" or LTP. Do not make the mistake of thinking the LTP is the real price since the market moves constantly.

In fact, even the spread (the difference between the ask and the bid) doesn't accurately reflect the true state of things thanks to constant movement. There's no need to be alarmed though, as long as volatility is stable, the difference isn't much. Just remember to look at the spread to understand what you'll be paying. The spread increases and contracts constantly but if you see that it is getting too big, this is a sign that too much volatility exists and you're better off staying out.

This concludes our look at brokers and the ins and outs of it. As you can see, there isn't too much to be concerned about, but you need to be well aware since it impacts how much capital you'll be trading with. Generally speaking, the higher the capital you have, the safer you'll be since you'll have more room to make mistakes.

Being undercapitalized is one of the biggest reasons traders fail in the markets, so don't make the mistake of jumping in too soon. Also, don't try to get creative with the PDT to the detriment of your strategy. There are several gurus online who will give you 'tricks' and 'hacks' to get by this but resist the temptation.

Lastly, I've mentioned this in passing before but don't be the person who rings up their broker for investment advice. I mean, even Hollywood has figured out that this is a bad idea and has innumerable movies for you to learn from.

Your approach to trading determines how well you'll manage your risk. The real key to trading success is risk management and the simple math that underlines it. We'll look at this next.

Chapter 4 Platforms and Tools for Options Trading

A vital aspect of options trading is the platform that one uses to trade. This is because options trading requires monitoring and requires a continuous analysis of trends. Performance is also monitored, and since the trade is impacted upon by a complex of factors, one has to choose a suitable platform for trading.

A good platform for trading should offer a lot of opportunities for traders. These are opportunities to orient beginners into trading, development for the existing ones, and actualization for those with a record on the platform. A platform of trading should also prescribe the available products and any resources that subscribers on the platform can benefit from to push themselves to profitability.

With the technology developing at high speed, platforms continue to improve by the day. This is both complicating the trading itself as well as providing avenues of spreading awareness about the business. A platform should, therefore, have the ability to offer the best possible experience for the traders to do trade and grow both in experience and returns without meeting a lot of platform limitations and frustrations.

A Platform Takes Trading To the Holders

Trading involves a lot of complexities that may sometimes be scary. It makes people lose interest as soon as they develop it. They perceive it as too complicated. The impression is that it is a venture meant for the people who have higher comprehension of concepts in the economics specialty and that those who do not a background in this area will have difficulty getting on board.

However, a trading platform has to present options trading as a venture that is possible and in which anyone with interest can succeed in. The days when options trading and any other forms of trading were presented as a show of sophistication are long gone. In this era, every sector of investment is being portrayed as possible, and businesses are now being made easier in order to create a better chance for people to dare. A platform that limits investment so much and is exclusive in terms of how it carries out its trading activities is irrelevant to modern economic patterns.

Platforms, therefore, have to be interactive and user-friendly. They should have the ability to encourage users to feel like they can handle the trade. It should also have the capability to gauge the level of use and give feedback about how well they are able to use it. If it is a website, for instance, it has to be able to report the numbers as people visit it and how many eventually end up creating accounts and trading. Counting traffic is essential for feedback that can lead to the creation of a better experience for the users.

Competition

The reason for considering a good platform is because the competition is high today. Competition has led to the creation of better trading experiences through innovation. Platforms are now trying to out-do each other in being the avenues of options trading. They are doing this by striving to create ways of improving user experience. It is therefore essential to identify the various parameters of comparing the platforms.

Eventually, one has to choose a platform that offers optimal access to the trading world.

In choosing a platform sometimes, one would want to take advantage of the advantages of different platforms. This is looking at one's style of trading and how they wish to monitor their business and see if a platform is more transparent in handling the tares or whether it offers a clear lens of controlling purchases and sells of options. This is the reason why the various platforms have to be assessed in terms of their potential. Usually, platforms are related to the tools of trading. Some of the tools of trading can be found right on the platform of trading.

When a platform of trading also has various tools of aiding trading, it ensures that one can gain a lot of benefits at one place. This makes the platform a utility platform where a person can visit for more purposes than just trading. It also makes it better. For instance, if a platform has videos that offer trading tutorials. This can make it resourceful in imparting competency in participating in the very sector that the platform operates.

To best benefit from competition, one has to understand the type of trade they want to do. This is by naming their price and gauging which platform can serve better in ensuring returns and value generation. This is in order to avoid going into trading in desperation, and one has to be patient to see if the platform can also come out and meet a trader at their point of ability and also help in trading in comfort where risk is at a minimum.

Types of Trading Platforms

There are various platforms in options trading that one could consider. There is web-based trading that utilizes the power of the search engines. This platform has many operators since the building of websites in the modern age is easy. This platform is responsible for the growth in the popularity of options trading. People can trade from anyone, open brokerage accounts, make deposits, and participate in the buying and selling of assets in the comfort of their homes.

With the presence of a lot of technological gadgets such as smartphones, tablets, and computers, web-based trading has been easy and possible. Websites can be built with additional resources for learning and tools that can be an advantage for both novice and seasoned traders. On the websites, regular updates on the market can be posted to keep traders informed about trends, patterns, and even help in analyzing price movements for the subscribers.

The web is also a good platform when it comes to filtering opportunities and options based on suitability and preference in view of the various abilities of users. They can be designed to be customizable even when the options markets are standardized.

User Friendliness

Usually, websites are good as they offer various tools that aid beginners to edge into trading options. ASX, for example, offers a variety of web-based resources that guide people in their efforts to understand trading. This includes online chats that have instant feedback as a team is dedicated to the work site for correspondence purposes. The aim of this is to offer motivation and impetus to go on with the discovery of the markets trends until one becomes a seasoned trader.

Friendliness is also in terms of the efforts that are made to create peer assistance. This is through creating groups of traders that influence each other and can learn from the vast experiences in the trading of the options. This can be a positive influence on the journey to gaining competence and help support an environment where people can relate and interact as they pursue their various financial goals.

It is important to consider the fact that some of the platforms of trading offer important tools that can be helpful in deciding on options. The tools are those that help in monitoring markets and simplify the technical analysis process for the trader. This can help one to sharpen their trading strategy to align well with the ultimate goal of trading. This depends on whether the goal of trading is to earn money in terms of profit or hedge oneself against losses on the underlying asset.

Tools to Learn

Upon mastering the various basics of trading and making the initial moves to start trading, one has to use various tools that help to indicate the advancers and decliners on the market. Greeks are some kind of metrics that those involved in options trading capitalize to ensure maximization of returns. These "Greeks" include the delta matrix that measures the correlation between price movements of the underlying asset relative to the price of the option. The tools for monitoring the movements for these parameters of trading are vital as everyone is always trading with a focus on minimizing losses while geared towards profit maximization.

The gamma is another tool that can help to predict market trends in order to do good timing for decisions on exercising rights in options. Gamma is an indicator of the rate of delta variations for the option price as compared to the asset price. This goes hand in hand with the time-decay tool that indicators the value movement, either upwards or downwards, in the period of life options. This helps to signal which options to avoid given the remaining time of the life span and the value implications thereon.

There is also the aspect of the volatility of the asset underlying a particular option trade. Some of the assets or stocks do not have inherent volatility to appreciate in value due to their nature. Assets that have high market volatility usually gain a lot on the market, and hence, the value behaves better to favor the call option trade. Products with ugh volatility and high inherent value are not suitable for the put option trade since they will occasion a loss. It is therefore important to use correct tools that aid in the analysis if the technical mechanics of the options trading business.

Tools are not just concrete things that can be manipulated. Some tools, especially in trading, are conceptual in nature. This is because they are the ones by which one can trade and aid in decision making. They sample out market forces and help in mapping out market trends for the benefit of the trader. To perceive tools as only concrete in nature is a misconception of the whole options trading venture.

Professional level platforms

There is a level in trading where one attains sophistication and attains the intuition to thrive in options trading regardless of the ways market forces seem to behave. At this level, someone needs tools that can help them edge into the horizon of complexity in trading. The platforms for this professional level exist, and they have to offer tools that are an edge above the basic level. These tools have to offer strategies of competing to control the stocks and rise above the market forces. At this level, one becomes daring, and the possibilities that the platform offers should only be dared by those who have mastered trading and are sure of beating odds as they speculate about squeezing out value form trades that otherwise be perceived as highly risky.

The platform should be full of idea probing resources that lead one to gain the courage to trade more and more. Web-based platforms of this level include the think or swim platform that is categorically for seasoned traders. This is the reason why one has to know the platform to trade on based on their level of experience in options trading. Some platforms are too complicated for the starters. The tools are even out of the capacity of a beginner to comprehend the trades appear to have higher risks that may wipe away hard-earned fortunes.

Mobile Trading

Some platforms have taken advantage of the handiness of the mobile era. These entail the smartphone lifestyle and the flashier iPod, iPad, and tablet culture. This is when trading is being placed in the palms of traders to hold and run away with it. This platform usually targets traders that want to capitalize on device optimization. This is the reason why trades have classes. Some of the options could be device targeted as they can only be taken advantage of when one using the suitable device for trading, provided the relevant support tools that the device offers.

Mobile trading also comes in order to keep people abreast. This is because opportunities sometimes appear and disappear on people because they are not using a device that enables them to be precise and timely in decision making and action.

With mobile trading, apps have been developed, some with notification capability. One can customize the apps to ensure that no opportunity comes that is not taken advantage of. Opportunities' in trading have to be seized and relying on a platform that is less handy and far means that opportunities of trading are lost.

What Are We Looking For In Platforms And Tools?

First is the opportunity to learn. There is no worse platform of trading than that which targets only to admit traders who do not understand what they are getting into. The education that a platform has to offer should be free as trading is itself risky enough to prohibit any extra expenses in the process. Platform operators should understand that any interested person who visits their platform is a potential subscriber, and they should freely offer support to educate them for the purpose of acquisition of requisite knowledge on options trading.

Some of the platforms have gone as opening structures units for education on options trading.

These courses are taken online, and coaching is done through the provision of a stream of webinars transmitted live or uploading recorded ones. This is for platforms that appreciate that trading is an informed gamble that requires one to know enough. They even test the proficiency of understanding trading concepts and mechanics for the purpose of ensuring that any people who trade on the platform are doing what they understand to build the platform ratings.

It is also vital for a starter to set standards that the broker's customer service should pass. In trading, brokers should work enough to earn the commission that they charge on the options that subscribers trade on buy. This is because some brokers are obscure and may not involve the options trader who is buying options in decisions that directly impact on his capital. One, therefore, faces a lot of anxiety if the broker is not responsive and transparent on the particular mechanics that influence trade.

Excellent broker services try to suit customer needs. They ask options traders subscribed to their platform what their preferred means of reaching is. Whether a live chat or phone call suits the customer or not. They also dedicate a desk for trading communications and queries and has the discipline to listen to customers and their issues with patience. They, in fact, have feedback on the quality of customer service that those who reach out get.

Software Trading Platforms

These are more complex than web-based ones. This is because they are run on the trader's computer, and the trader is required to understand what the software does and interpret it. Even when the brokerage can offer assistance, software-based platforms require the trader to have enough technical know how to read charts, graphs, and understand patterns that represent various components of options trading.

For beginners, a complex platform has to be avoided by all means. This is because one is bound to engage in aspects of trading that they do not have an understanding of. A trading platform simply has to be simple and clear. The interface should not be too busy as to scare away those traders who are not accustomed. This is the reason why operators usually separate the platforms that as designed for basic use, which is suitable for novices, and advanced trading for the seasoned ones.

Then a broker has to offer a tutorial that guides the user on how to navigate their platform. Everything has to be explained, even those that one would deem to be obvious. Screenshots can even be available in order to be categorical and emphatic. This ensures that a broker has offered all possible assists for the trader to benefit from the offers and products on the platform successfully.

Cost Implication

It is important for the trader to know that some brokers may have charges attached to some of the services, resources, and tools that they provide on their platform. These have to be assessed in terms of their worth and whether the costs are necessary. Making some tolls premium may be an indicator of quality but not always. This is particularly the case when other platforms provide similar services toll-free.

Screening tools are particularly the ones that are bound to attract charges because they have abilities to analyze and assess market trends. They can do the thinking for the trader and help him in decision making. One has to read about the specifications of the tools and ascertain what they or cannot do. This is in order to know if they are customizable for the purpose of serving the needs and conveniences of traders.

Some charges can even be attached to the quotes update feed. Usually, the quotes can be accessed in real time for those who want to see them in real time. The quotes are important in influencing idea generation and sometimes can tip people of opportunities in the market. There is usually a delay for those who access the quotes updates for free.

It is also vital to understand platforms do not provide all the tools to everyone using their platform to trade. Some of the cutting-edge tools that can best serve the business interests of traders are premium. They have subscription charges or otherwise only appear on the accounts of traders who constantly sustain a certain threshold of account balance minimums. This is particularly the case for platforms that operate at the professional level. They require one to be active and remain active in trading since this serves the business interests of the brokerage through the commissions it earns on options contracts. In return, it offers the consultancy, expertise, and resource repository for one to realize value out of the options trades. This is why they attach a price on some of the tools.

One can only trust a platform that has a reputation for efficiency. This is a platform that ensures orders have a quick span of execution. This particularly for traders who understand the benefits of entering quick and instantly exiting from offered positions. The charges of platform subscription also matter. This is whether they are monthly or per year. It is vital to understand the way of earning waivers on platform fees. It could be through ensuring compliance with balance minimums or activity of trades per a set span of time.

Chapter 5 Basic Investment Strategies

Everyone who wants to avoid being broke or living from payslip to payslip has to have the right investment strategy. An investment strategy is a plan for making the money you already have given birth or multiply to more money.

Two Investment Factors to Consider When Choosing an Investment

Therefore, good investments have to have liquidity, meaning that whatever you invest in has to be easily convertible into cash at hand. Investments are risky, though, meaning that it's not guaranteed to get your intended profits always because, at any time, your investments can devalue. It is, therefore, essential to carefully examine your investments and see how much it's likely to yield; this is called looking at the potential returns. Looking through all these possibilities will help a person determine what type of investment to go for.

An investment strategy is best if it works to meet your needs. You should not go for investment only because it's trending; it may not work for you. Going for what works for you will ensure that you stick to your investment for long and that you are swayed away by other trends. The best way to find an investment that works for you is by getting something that defines you, and that would be something you're patient about.

It is good for young people to take more risks in investments by going for high growing stock investments. While for someone who is about to go into retirement, it's essential that they take fewer risks and distribute their assets to bonds.

Security Type

A security type is the kind of investment you hold, and it should always be diverse.

Cash and Bank Security

This type has very high liquidity because you are dealing with cash at hand that you take to the bank at any time and also withdraw at will. It has low risk because unless you need the money, it is safely kept at the bank. But this, however, means that it has no potential for growth and can even lose its value in case there is inflation. The biggest advantage with this, however, is that you have access at any needed time. Banks also offer emergency funds, and therefore in case you urgently need money, you do not have to wait for long.

Certificate of Deposit

The liquidity in this is low because you cannot withdraw cash whenever you want. You can only get the money after the agreed time with the bank. The risk is low because the money is safely kept at the bank. However, it's potential for growth is very minimal since it has a specified rate of interest. This means that your money is lying in a bank waiting for a certain interest rate instead of taking chances elsewhere. The growth rate is so low and not worth the time you waited to get the interest.

Stocks

Whenever people think about investments, they think stock. The liquidity is high because you get to buy shares from a company and share their profits. You can purchase shares from one or as many companies as you can and therefore get to enjoy a certain percentage of their earnings. The risk is medium because as much as you enjoy the profits, you are also involved with their losses. Therefore, this means that you should not expect to be paid when the company you have shared with is not making profits. However, all investments go through this uncertainty; there is no single investment that won't have a loss risk. The potential for growth in this is very high as you get to grow, the more the company grows. Every company's objective is to yield profits, and therefore companies will continue putting their best foot forward to make sure they do not incur losses. The more they work on this, the more their profits. The more the company's profits, the more your shares, therefore, the reason why the potential growth is high.

Bonds

The liquidity in this is medium because it involves you getting to give some of your money as a loan to a company or government. Then after the agreed time, your money is returned to you along with the interest you agreed on. The interest rates may be very high or low, depending on who you have loaned. If you lend big companies or treasury, you are much secured, and therefore the returns in this are small. The risk comes in because you may give loans to what is known as junk bonds, and you risk not being paid or having partial payments. However, since junk bonds do not guarantee security, they make sure to offer a little higher return than large corporate that guarantees security. The potential for growth is medium because it depends if you are paid and the profits you make from the payments.

Real Estate

The liquidity is low because it involves lands and buildings. Converting lands and buildings is dependent on the value the assets have accumulated over time. This is because if you need to have cash from these investments, then you have to make sure you are selling at a better price than you used when buying them. This makes the risk medium because they are assets and may either maintain their value or grow. If they don't grow, it is a disadvantage to the investor, but if the assets grow in value, then the investor has made it. Potential for growth is medium because of how long it takes to generate value finally.

Precious Metals

The liquidity is very high because it involves buying of precious metals like gold and silver. When you buy precious metals, you can easily convert them into cash by selling them at an even higher price than you bought it. The risk is medium because the metals need a lot of proper handling to ensure that they do spoil, and also most buyers tend to buy at very low prices. The potential growth is medium because it depends on the available market and the demand as well.

Derivatives

The liquidity is medium. You can either convert your earnings quickly, depending on how accessible the stocks you bought are. Here you get to purchase stocks from another stock instead of making a direct purchase. And for this to happen, you have to believe that the stock you are buying from will increase its value. The risk is very high because you depend on another stock to earn your profits without being directly involved. If the stock does not allow you to buy in a more valuable stock, then you are unlikely to make any value out of it. The potential for growth, however, is very high since you only get to buy from stocks that have value.

It is important to be diverse in your investments; this means that you do not settle on a particular type. If you are able to split your assets, you are in a better secure position. When there is a downfall in one sector, you can count on another industry. But if you hold all your assets in one industry and the sector goes down, you will significantly suffer as an investor because you will lose everything. Something else worth noting is that one should be careful with their investment as they get older. One mistake from such a person can lead them into a very desperate life after retirement.

Investing Strategies

Buy and Hold

This calls for thorough research before entirely going into any investment. After the research, you should settle for a long term investment of like ten years. You should then buy this investment and hold it irrespective of how many temptations that you may come through along the way to sell them. Sometimes it may be so tempting to sell it because the price at which you are being offered is a little tempting, but you should be able to resist. An investor should only sell if the rules for sticking to the stock are no longer favorable. This may happen in that either there is a sign that the stocks are no longer maintainable. This could be from the fact that the company is taking a different strategy than what you signed up for, and there you get uncomfortable to continue. You may also sell only. if you have had enough before the end of the long-term, and you want to opt-out. It should never be out of greed, thinking that what you are being offered is too good to resist because you do not know how much better you are likely to get. There is, however, a downside to this, as explained below. You may do great research and have everything correctly figured out. You may yield your investments after the long-term you had invested in. However, when retirement sinks in, you need the money urgently because that's your only survival hope. The other downside is that you may have made the wrong choice all along. Then with buy and hold strategy, you may make a lot of loss that will kick you out of the market even if unwilling to.

This type of investment is often referred to as time in the market strategy because of how investors wait until very long to avoid short term dangers. This then means that the investor does not have to keep on trading like in other strategies because they are doing it for the long-term. This strategy is the opposite of the absolute market timing strategy. The absolute market timing strategy believes that an investor should transact within short-term periods. There, an investor in the absolute market will buy and sell within small durations aiming to purchase at low prices but eventually selling at very high prices.

Several portfolios use the buy and hold strategy. They are, however, often known as the lazy portfolios. These are some of those portfolios.

Portfolios under the buy and hold strategy.

- Core and satellite - this is a time tested investment that has a core, which is the big capital, which has the most significant investment; it also has other smaller investments. This is done so that the investments are spread out in order to achieve very big returns with very low risks.

- Modern portfolio theory- This means that the investor does all he can to have very low risks in the market, while still yielding very high returns in any given portfolio of his investments. In short, what the investor does in this is that he holds one given asset, mutual fund, and security each at a time. The individual types are usually highly risky, but when they are put together with other many types, they get a balance. The balance created ensures that the risk is lower than the primary assets.

- Postmodern portfolio theory- the difference between this and modern portfolio theory is how the two view risks. The modern portfolio views risks as having several different types of investments that have many risk stages come together in order to yield significant returns. It actually focuses on risks and returns. On the other hand, a post-modern portfolio investor focuses on the behavior instead of settling on the calculations aspect the way a modern portfolio investor does.

- Tactical asset allocation - This is where an investor gets to put together all the different strategies. The investor in this will work out to ensure that stocks, bonds, and cash balance so that he gets more significant profits at low risks by comparing the index. The tactical asset allocation investment strategy differs from technical analysis and fundamental analysis in that it focuses on assets rather than on the type of investment to select.

Value Investment

This means that you go for stocks that are more underestimated than the other stocks. In short, it means going for stocks that most people are unlikely to go for. This is risky but brave because you are not following the crowd. In doing this, you go for companies that are just beginning to grow and have not attracted the big fish in the market; you can also go for companies that were only recently established. You can stick to this investment until you feel that you are doing quite well or have achieved more than you expected before eventually selling. This, however, does not come without a possible risk, as explained below.

Being an active trader makes you have easy, quick access to more significant returns. However, that also means that as quick as it is to make profits, it's also very easy and fast to make losses. Therefore, it is usually recommended that you use small investments instead of putting in too much for this kind of trading because anything can happen. It is better to lose small than to lose hugely, and therefore, not taking the risk is very important.

Fundamental Analysis

In this strategy, you analyze financial statements so that you are able to choose the best stock for you as an investor. What happens is that there is a data comparison of the financial statements of all the current and past data, for all the business within the industry which you intend to venture. This helps determine the total price of the stock and also determines if the stock is really worth the purchase.

Technical Analysis

In this, technical traders use charts that help them observe the price patterns in the present, and all the trends are happening within the market. When they observe this, they are then able to foretell what may happen in the future for these markets. From technical analysis, signals, indicators, and patterns are very important because they determine the future of the trade. These are essential for the investor because they help him make decisions based on whatever signal they give. The signals may warn that it is time to buy or sell or even stop a trade. An investor has to obey because they solely depend on these unavoidable patterns.

Growth Investing

This means going for stocks in well-established companies; companies are already doing well and attracting a lot of potential. This means that everyone is already running for these investments, and they are doing pretty well. There is even evidence of how well the companies are doing. People investing in this have a lot of faith in this investment because they expect that it only keeps growing. People buying in this type of investment do not mind buying at a high price because they know that they will sell even bigger than they bought it. Therefore, what happens here is that you go for big and well-known companies. These are companies that are well known and have been in the market for long.

The right investment strategy, however, still goes back to an individual. What works for an investor is very important instead of relying on what worked for others. It may have worked for others but not work for you. It is good, however, to involve all the strategies as you make decisions as an individual investor.

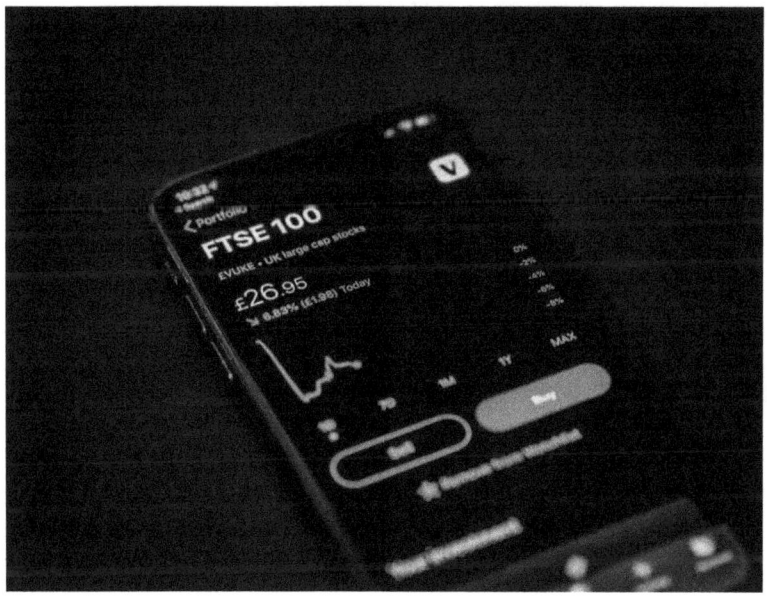

Chapter 6 How Options Are Priced

Understanding Strike Price

A strike price is a fixed price at which an options contract can be exercised. The term is mainly used when describing index and stock options.

How strike price works

The options contract has specified stripe prices. In put options, the value of the underlying asset while trading is referred to as the strike price. In call options, the holder earns the right to buy an underlying asset at the set strike price up to the expiry date. In put options, it is the price the underlying asset is traded by an option buyer up to the expiry date. In the call option, the strike price refers to the amount an investor buys the underlying asset up to the expiry date. The strike price is also referred to as the exercise price. It is an essential factor in establishing the value of an option.

Importance of Strike Price

While pricing options, this is the most crucial factor to consider. While exercising an option, the profit earned is determined by the difference between the stock's market price and the option strike price at the expiration date. A strike price can help you establish if an investment is worth your time or not. You can come out with a loss or a profit depending on the strike price involved. As an investor, you want to know the investments that bring high returns and avoid those that will result in a loss. Knowing the strike price can help you deciding on which trades to make. You also get to avoid the trades that could result in losing your investment.

The Concept of Moneyness

Moneyness refers to the quality of a financial contract. This occurs if the contract settlement is financial. It can be established by obtaining the difference between the strike price and the current trade price for an underlying asset.

Terms like out-of-the-money, in-the-money, and at-the-money can be used to explain the moneyness of options in trading.

Intrinsic Value

The intrinsic value can also be referred to as the monetary value of an asset. It is the quality of an underlying asset if it is exercised immediately. A call can get a positive intrinsic value if the stock price of the underlying asset is higher than the set price, which is the strike price. This is what we refer to as in-the-money. Out-of-the-money occurs when a put option has no value.

Time Value

This refers to the value of an option, excluding the intrinsic value. It occurs when it is difficult to establish the future price movements of an asset. Knowing the time value can aid in establishing the possible discounts that are in an option between when it was bought and when it expires. The time value is negative when it comes to European options. This is influenced by the fact that the option cannot be exercised until it gets to the expiration date.

Why Should You Care About How Options Are Priced

As an investor, it is very crucial to know how various options are priced. Knowing the prices saves one from the possibility of being overpriced or underpriced depending on the situation at hand. While evaluating the prices, you also get to identify the possible investments that you can engage in depending on your budget. This, alongside other reasons, shows the importance of knowing how options are priced. Below I have discussed a number of reasons why it's important that you have an understanding of the options trading pricing.

1. It allows you to know what to invest in.

As a beginner, you may be stranded and unable to identify the best investment that you can engage in. Before engaging in a trade, it is always good to conduct a proper evaluation. This analysis helps you know all that is required if you before engaging in business. Understanding the prices helps you know that which you can afford to invest in. You will find that some options demand that you spend a vast some money. While at it, you will identify some that need little investments.

The one that demands that you part with a small portion of your finances may appear to be very appealing. You will find that most amateur trades will prefer beginning with such. After all, you get to the part with a small piece of your income and generate profits. You forget to put all other factors into consideration, such as option strategies and end up focusing on the price. Higher chances are that you are likely to encounter a massive loss in the trade since you know very little about what you are engaging in.

This is why you should consider the pricing before engaging in any form of commerce.

While getting a brokerage account, you need to be very careful with the features and services provided by the account. By evaluating the option pricing, you will identify accounts that have peculiar pricing, and this should raise the alarm. The pricing that does not rhyme with the rest should help you know the official brokerage accounts and those that are not genuine. As the options trading markets expand, we have a lot of competition being created. This results in the creations on multiple accounts of which, some are a pure scam. Knowing the options pricing will help you identify the excellent option trading accounts.

In some cases, you may find some trades that have high pricing. You also find that the returns are equally good, and it appears like an excellent investment to make. When you decide to engage in it, you may end up getting a considerable profit. If at all, you had no information about the option and especially the pricing, it would be challenging to execute it. The fact that you have knowledge of the pricing helps you identify it as a good investment, and you decide to engage in the trade.

2. You can identify the best option strategy to use.

You find that each procedure is different in its ways, and the pricing varies. Knowing option pricing will help you identify the best strategy to utilize in every situation. While analyzing the various Options strategies, you may discover that some are more profitable than others. In some cases, one may not get any profit and remain at a stagnant point without making returns. This information becomes useful in that it guides you in investing in the right strategy.

3. You can minimize risks

It is expected that the investment in options trading comes with its risks. There are a number of challenges that you will encounter. On the bright side, some of these downsides can be predicted. Due to this factor, it becomes easy to manage them and make the right trade. If you can look into option pricing, managing some of these risks becomes easy. You can evaluate the option pricing and get to know the trades that are not profitable. Imagine the amount of trouble you will have saved yourself from if you knew how the options are priced.

4. There is room for increasing return

The dream of every investor is to get the highest possible profits. You want to see yourself running a profitable business that will unbelievably transform your income generation ability. This does not only have to be a dream, but you can make it happen. Knowing how options are priced enables you to establish the options that are profitable. Trading in such opportunities will help you earn high returns and make your dreams a reality.

5. It helps in choosing a cost-effective option

We are regularly advised to live within our means. I am a believer that people should also trade within their means. While deciding on the best option to invest in, try to aim at choosing a cost-effective strategy. By doing so, you will be able to trade in that which you can afford. If things go contrary to what you anticipated, you will get a loss, but it will not be as bad as if never invested in what you can afford to lose. The option prices play a significant role in having a cost-effective option.

From the above reasons provided, it is clear why you need to be concerned about how options are priced. The option pricing has a significant influence on options trading. It helps you identify the best options to engage in. If you have a vision of becoming an expert in options trading, you should be able to take a close look into the option pricing. You will identify the options that can result in a loss and those that are profitable and worth investing your income on. To make a fortune out of your investment, consider taking a keen look at how options are priced.

Key Influencers of Options Prices

The only way to determine the price value if an option is to establish what contributes to its value. Things are priced differently depending on their value. When you intend to purchase a car, you have probably thought of the model you intend to get. What makes a Lamborghini more expensive than a Toyota? Well, the price narrows down to the quality of the car. This applies to almost every other commodity that can be sold. The quality is usually the core determining factor while coming up with the price. When it comes to investing, the price value will discover the income you are likely to generate. If you aspire to trade in a successful venture, you may be required to use a large portion of your income equally. This is because the high quality of goods and services are highly-priced. The vice versa is also applicable. The low-priced commodities that low quality and are likely to result in a small income-generating investment. The prices will tell you a lot about the investment you choose to undertake. Below are the key influencing factors while pricing options.

The Type of Options

We have two types of options: a call option, and a put option. This is the basis in establishing the price of an item. Depending on the fact the type of option involved, the costs will differ. In a call option, the investor earns the right to purchase the underlying asset at an agreed-upon duration at the set price. In a put option, the investor has the right to trade the underlying instrument at a set price within the specified period. In a situation whereby you have the long a call or are short a put, the value of the option goes high as the market value increases. When you are short a call or long a put, the option value will increase as the market value declines.

Stock Price

This is the value of a stock. In some situations, the call option may permit you to purchase a stock at an agreed-upon price. The cost of the capital may rise in the future, resulting in the option being worth more than it already is. The same applies if the prices lack the potential to increase, this will mean that the value of the stock will go low, and as a result, you encounter a loss. For instance, you may buy the stock at $ 200 and maybe shortly it has the potential of rising to $ 220.another person may obtain a share at $ 100 and in the near future, the value of the stock decreases to $ 70. You will end up with a loss of $ 30. Ideally, one would instead go with the capital that has the probability of increasing in the future. This way, you will end up making a profit as opposed to ending up with a loss in your investment.

Strike Price

The strike price operates the same as the stock price. A strike price refers to the fixed amount of money in which a derivative contract can be exercised or bought. While dealing with stocks, this is a term that you will come across severally. In a put option, the strike price refers to the amount that the underlying asset is traded by the option buyer while at the expiry date. In a call option, the strike price refers to the price the underlying asset can be purchased by the option buyer up to the expiry. The rates will differ depending on the type of strike price.

The Expiration Date

You have heard of some contracts being regarded as worthless upon getting to the expiry date. The reason behind it is since their value is no longer in existence once the contract expires. The expiration date in options trading refers to the duration in which an option contract is of importance and after which it is considered valueless. You find that the expiry date greatly influences the option prices, and if you are not keen, you may end up making a loss.

This means that the best time to buy or sell options when the cost is high, that is any period before the expiry date is. You find that beginners are at times deceived and sold for an option that is almost becoming worthless and as a result, end up making losses.

Interest Rates

The interest rates do not have a massive impact on the option value, but they have minimal influence. The amount of a call option rises when there is an increase in interest rates, and the value of the put option falls. Alternatively, when the interest rates decline the value of the call option will also become lower, and the put options will rise. The second option becomes attractive when the interest rates increase. In a situation where the interest goes up, you will be able to earn more. This shows how interest rates influence prices.

Volatility

In determining the option prices, we use forward volatility. Forward volatility refers to the quantity of implied volatility during the duration in the future. The implied volatility refers to the implied movement of stocks. It acts as an indicator of the direction the stock moves. Some moves result from increases in the value of the capital. Also, some moves result from declining in the amount of money. When the stock value lowers its prices also decrease. In an event, the stock value increases the prices are also bound to increase. This is how the volatility influences the rates.

Dividends

A dividend refers to the regular total payment made by a company to its shareholders. It results from the profits made by a company. In most cases, options do not get dividends. If bonuses are given out, the option value will fluctuate. An ex-dividend date is provided once a company gives out profits. Dividends can be given out if you have stocks at the time of their release. When this occurs, it also influences the value of the capital, causing it to decrease with the number of dividends. The call value lowers, and the put value goes above in a situation whereby the bonuses increase. This is how profits influence the prices of options.

Chapter 7 Risk Management

Excellent risk management can save the worst trading strategy, but horrible risk management will sink even the best strategy. This is a lesson that many traders learn painfully over time, and I suggest you learn this by heart and install it deep within you even if you can't fully comprehend that statement.

Risk management has many different elements to both quantitative and qualitative. When it comes to options trading, the quantitative side is minimal thanks to the nature of options limiting risk by themselves. However, the qualitative side deserves a lot of attention. This chapter is going to give you the risk management framework that you need to succeed.

Risk

So what is risk anyway? Logically, it is the probability of you losing all of your money. In trading terms, you can think of it as being the probability of your actions putting you on a path to losing all of your capital. A good way to think about the need for good risk management is to ask yourself what a bad trader would do? Forget trading, what would a bad business person do with their capital?

Well, they would spend it on useless stuff that adds nothing to the bottom line. They would also increase expenses, market poorly, not take care of their employees, and be indisciplined with regards to their processes. While trading, you don't have employees or marketing needs, so you don't need to worry about that.

Do you have suppliers and costs? Well, yes, you do. Your supplier is your broker, and you pay fees to execute your trades. That is the cost of access. In directional trading, you have high costs as well because taking losses is a necessary part of trading. With market neutral or non-directional trading, your losses are going to be minimal, but you should still seek to minimize them.

What about discipline? Do you think you can trade and analyze the market well if you've just returned home from your job and are tired? If you didn't sleep properly last night? Or if you've argued with your spouse or partner? The point I'm making is that the more you behave like a terrible business owner, the more you increase your risk of failure.

Odds and Averages

Trading requires you to think a bit differently about profitability. In the previous paragraphs, I spoke about minimizing costs, and your first thought must have been to seek to reduce losses and maximize wins. This is a natural product of linear or ordered thinking. The market, however, is chaotic and linear thinking is going to get you nowhere.

Instead, you need to think in terms of averages and odds. Averages imply that you need to worry about your average loss size and your average win size. Seek to decrease the former and increase the latter. Notice that when we talk about averages, we're not necessarily talking about reducing the total number of losses. You can reduce the average by either reducing the sum of your losses or by increasing the number of losing trades while keeping the sum of the losses constant. This is a shift in thinking you must make.

Thinking in this way sets you up nicely to think in terms of odds, because in chaotic systems all you can bank on are odds playing out in the long run. For example, if you flip a coin, do you know in advance whether it's going to be a heads or tails? Probably not. But if someone asked you to predict the distribution of heads versus tails over 10,000 flips, you could reasonably guess that it'll be 5000 heads and 5000 tails. You might be off by a few flips either way, but you'll be pretty close percentage-wise.

In fact, the greater the number of flips, the lesser your error percentage. This is because the odds inherent in a pattern that occurs in a chaotic system express themselves best over the long run. Your trading strategy is precisely such a pattern. The market is a chaotic system. Hence, you should focus on executing your strategy as it is meant to be executed over and over again and worry about profitability only in the long run.

Contrast this with the usual attitude of traders who seek to win every single trade. This is impossible to accomplish since no trading strategy or pattern is correct 100% of the time. If we were discussing directional strategies, I'd spend a lot more time on this, but the fact is that options take care of a lot of this ambiguity themselves.

This is because you don't have to do much when trading options. You enter and then monitor the trade. Sure, it helps to have some directional bias, but even if you get it wrong, your losses will be extremely limited, and you're more likely to hit winners than losers.

Despite this, always think of your strategy in terms of its odds. There are two basic metrics to measure this. The first is the win rate of your system. This is simply the percentage of winners you have. The second is your payout ratio which is the average win size divided by the average loss size.

Together these two metrics will determine how profitable your system is. Both of them play off one another, and an increase in one is usually met by a decrease in another. It takes an extremely skillful trader to increase both simultaneously.

Risk Per Trade

The quantitative side of risk management when It comes to options trading is lesser than what you need to take care of when trading directionally. However, this doesn't mean there's nothing to worry about. Perhaps the most important metric of them all is your risk per trade. The risk per trade is what ultimately governs your profitability.

How much should you risk per trade? Common wisdom says that you should restrict this to 2% of your capital. For options trading purposes, this is perfectly fine. In fact, once you build your skill and can see opportunities better, I'd suggest increasing it to a higher level.

A point that you must understand here is that you must keep your risk per trade consistent for it to have any effect. You might see a wonderful setup and think that it has no chance of failure, but the truth is that you don't know how things will turn out. Even the prettiest setup has every chance of failing, and the ugliest setup you can think of may result in a profit. So never adjust your position size based on how something looks.

Calculating your position size for a trade is a pretty straightforward task. Every option's strategy will have a fixed maximum risk amount. Divide the capital risk by this amount, and that gives you your position size. Round that down to the nearest whole number since you can only buy whole number lots when it comes to contract sizes.

For example, let's say your maximum risk is $50 per lot on the trade. Your capital is $10,000. Your risk per trade is 2%. So the amount you're risking on that trade is 2% of 10,000 which is $200. Divide this by 50, and you get 4. Hence, your position size is four contracts or 400 shares. (You'll buy the contracts, not the shares.)

Why is it important to keep your risk per trade consistent? Well, recall that your average win and loss size is important when it comes to determining your profitability. These, in conjunction with your strategy's success rate, determine how much money you'll make. If you keep shifting your risk amount per trade, you'll shift your win and loss sizes. You might argue that since it's an average, you can always adjust amounts to reflect an average.

My counter to that is how would you know which trades to adjust in advance? You won't know which ones are going to be a win or a loss, so you won't know which trade sizes to adjust to meet the average.

Hence, keep it consistent across all trades and let the math work for you.

Aside from risk per trade, there are some simple metrics you should keep track of as part of your quantitative risk management plan.

Drawdown

A drawdown refers to the reduction in capital your account experiences. Drawdowns by themselves always occur. The metrics you should be measuring are the maximum drawdown and recovery period. If you think of your account's balance as a curve, the maximum drawdown is the biggest peak to trough distance in dollars. The recovery period is the subsequent time it took for your account to make new equity high.

If your risk per trade is far too high, your max drawdown will be unacceptably high. For example, if you risk 10% per trade and lose two in a row, which is very likely, your drawdown is going to be 20%. This is an absurdly large hole to dig your way out. Consider that your capital has decreased by 20% and the subsequent climb back up needs to be done on lesser capital than previously.

This is why you need to keep your risk per trade low and in line with your strategy's success rate. The best way to manage drawdowns and limit the damage they cause is to put in place risk limits per day, week, and month. Even professional athletes who train to do one thing all the time have bad days, so it's unfair to expect yourself to be at 100% all the time.

These risk limits will take you out of the game when you're playing poorly. A daily risk limit is to prevent you from getting into a spiral of revenge trading. A good limit to stick to when starting off is to stop trading if you experience three losses in a row. This is pretty unlikely with options trades to be honest unless you screw up badly, but it's good to have a limit in place from a perspective of discipline.

Next, aim for a maximum weekly drawdown limit of 5% and a monthly drawdown limit of 6-8%. These are pretty high limits, to be honest, and if you are a directional trader, these limits do not apply to you. Directional traders need to be a lot more conservative than options trader when it comes to risk.

Understand that these are hard stop limits. So if your account has hit its monthly drawdown level within the first week, you need to take the rest of the month off. Overtrading and a lack of reflection on progress can cause a lot of damage, and a drawdown is simply a reflection of that.

Qualitative Risk

Quantitative metrics aside, your ability to properly manage qualitative things in your life and trading will dictate a lot of your success. Prepare well, and you're likely to see progress. You need to see preparation as your responsibility. I mean, no one else can prepare for you can they?

There are different elements to tracking your level of preparation so let's look at them one by one.

Health
You can't trade if you're physically unfit. If you have a fever or if you're suffering from some condition that makes it impossible for you to concentrate, forget about trading. You can rest assured that the other

traders in the market will be more than happy to take your money.

When viewed from an options trading perspective, the risk is even more acute. All options strategies will require you to write options at some point, even the most basic ones like in this book. Even if your position is covered, making a mistake, and having an option you wrote be exercised by the buyer is an unpleasant thing that happens. Maintain a regimen of exercise and eat healthy food. Depending on how long you sit in front of your screen, you might even want to consider avoiding certain foods when in session.

Heavy meals and food that makes you drowsy will cause your performance to dip, so avoid eating them when you're in the market. Also, don't exercise to such an extent that you're completely exhausted. The idea is to be fresh and alert, not fatigued and aching for a good sleep.

You might have an image of traders as being highly wired and as people who spend their entire lives in front of a screen. Well, most traders do sit in front of a screen most of the time, but the successful ones make time for other stuff in their lives as well. So don't try to copy some false vision here. Instead, do what feels comfortable to you while taking care to not slip into habits that are detrimental to your success.

Lifestyle

Your fitness is just one part of your lifestyle, of course. Is your lifestyle conducive to profitable trading? Are you someone who loves staying up at all sorts of odd hours and considers it perfectly normal to stumble onto a work task while hungover or worse? Make no mistake, the market will make you donate all of your capital to it.

Many beginners underestimate how difficult trading is. This should come as no surprise since beginners by definition underestimate anything. What shocks most of them is the degree to which they underestimate the difficulty of trading successfully. Let me put it in writing for you: Trading is one of the most challenging things you will ever do in your life.

The reason it is so difficult is due to the ever-changing nature of the market and the mental demands it places upon you. Another key lifestyle question to consider is the hours when you'll trade. Most of you reading this probably have full-time jobs and cannot spend your whole day in front of the market.

So plan out when you'll trade and how you'll prepare yourself for the session. What routines will you carry out? If you're going to trade in the morning before work begins, how will you manage to do this? Will you work in a quiet place or in some noisy truck stop on the way to work? Options positions don't need a lot of maintenance, so there's not much need for this, but when will you check in on the market throughout the day? Will you check in a few times? Five times? Define everything to do with your routine.

Think of yourself as a professional athlete who has to show up for a game everyday. An athlete has a precise method of preparation before showing up for a game. They don't deviate from their preparatory routine and certainly don't experiment with new things during game time. Practice is when they try out new stuff.

How will you practice your skills and improve your ability to execute your strategy? When will you do this? Plan it all out and develop your success routine.

Mental States

Trading is a mental activity. You don't need to lift or push anything physically. Therefore it is crucial to ensure that your mental state is as optimal as it needs to be for you to execute properly. Having a checklist or a mental check-in list works wonders for the trading process.

Before any trading, write down what's going through your mind and ask yourself how you feel. If you find that you're tired or frustrated and unable to focus properly, step away, and do not trade. If you're planning on sitting in front of your terminal for more than an hour, make it a habit to check in with yourself every half hour or hourly. This need not be a detailed examination, just a simple check-in with yourself to see how things are going.

Take your risk management tasks seriously, and the market will reward you with profits. Do not be the trader who stumbles into the market completely unprepared and then wonders why trading is so unforgiving. Above all else, seek to eliminate all sources of stress when it comes to trading. Take regular breaks and schedule months off from the market to recap and assimilate the things you've learned and need to improve.

Trading every single day of the year does not make sense. This isn't a job where you'll be rewarded with a certain salary for just showing up. You need to produce results, and in order to do so, you need to manage your downside carefully.

An excellent practice is to actually review how you work and set aside months exclusively for trading and months exclusively for practice purposes. By practice, I mean reviewing your prior results, working on your mindset and improving your risk management abilities. This is an unconventional method of working but it will pay massive dividends down the line.

Now that you have a better understanding of the basics, it's finally time to jump in and take a look at various trading strategies you can deploy with options.

Chapter 8 The Basics Of Technical Analysis

Technical analysis is the method of using charts and other recording methods to analyze various data in options trading. Using these visual instruments, you have the chance to determine the direction of the market because they give you a trend.

This method focuses on studying the supply and demand of a market. The price will be seen to rise when the investor realizes the market is undervalued, and this leads to buying. If they think that the market is overvalued, the prices will start falling, and this is deemed the perfect time to sell.

You need to understand the movement of the various indicators to make the perfect decision. This method works on the premise that history usually repeats itself - a huge change in the prices affects the investors in any situation.

History

Technical analysis has been used over the years in trades. The technical analysis methods have been used for over a hundred years to come up with deductions regarding the market.

In Asia, the use of technical analysis led to the development of candlestick techniques, and it forms the main charting techniques.

Over time, more tools and techniques have come up to help traders come up with predictions of the prices in various markets.

There are many indicators that you can use to determine the direction of the market, but only a few are valuable to your course. Let us look at the various indicators and how to use them.

Support and Resistance

These levels occur at points where both the buyer and the seller aren't dormant. These levels are displayed on the chart using a horizontal line extended in the past to the future.

The different prices reach at the support and resistance points in the future.

How to Apply Support and Resistance

• Using these points allows you to know when to call or put.

• Support and resistance give you a way to determine the entry point to use for a directional trade.

The Significance of Trends in Option Trading

Technical analysis works on the premise of the trend. These trends come by due to the interaction of the buyer and the seller. The aggressiveness of one of the parties in the market will determine how steep the trend becomes. To make a profit, you have to take advantage of the changes in the price movement.

To understand the direction of the trend, you ought to look at the troughs and peaks and how they relate to each other.

When looking for money in options trading, you ought to trade with a trend. The trend is what determines the decision you make when faced with a situation - whether to buy or to sell. You need to know the various signs that a prevailing trend is soon ending so that you can manage the risks and exit the trades the right way.

Characteristics of Technical Analysis

This analysis makes use of models and trading rules using different price and volume changes. These include the volume, price, and other different market info.

Technical analysis is applied among financial professionals and traders and is used by many option traders.

The Principles of Technical analysis

Many traders on the market use the price to come up with information that affects the decision you make ultimately. The analysis looks at the trading pattern and what information it offers you rather than looking at drivers such as news events, economic and fundamental events.

Price action usually tends to change every time because the investor leans towards a certain pattern, which in turn predicts trends and conditions.

Prices Determine Trends

Technical analysts know that the price in the market determines the trend of the market. The trend can be up, down, or move sideways.

History Usually Repeats Itself

Analysts believe that an investor repeats the behavior of the people that traded before them. The investor sentiment usually repeats itself. Due to the fact that the behavior repeats itself, traders know that using a price pattern can lead to predictions.

The investor uses the research to determine if the trend will continue or if the reversal will stop eventually and will anticipate a change when the charts show a lot of investor sentiment.

Combination with Other Analysis Methods

To make the most out of the technical analysis, you need to combine it with other charting methods on the market. You also need to use secondary data, such as sentiment analysis and indicators.

To achieve this, you need to go beyond pure technical analysis, and combine other market forecast methods in line with technical work. You can use technical analysis along with fundamental analysis to improve the performance of your portfolio.

You can also combine technical analysis with economics and quantitative analysis. For instance, you can use neural networks along with technical analysis to identify the relationships in the market. Other traders make use of technical analysis with astrology.

Other traders go for newspaper polls, sentiment indicators to come with deductions.

The Different Types of Charts Used in Technical Analysis

Candlestick Chart

This is a charting method that came from the Japanese. The method fills the interval between opening and closing prices to show a relationship. These candles use color coding to show the closing points. You will come across black, red, white, blue, or green candles to represent the closing point at any time.

Open-high-low-close Chart (OHLC)

These are also referred to as bar charts, and they give you a connection between the maximum and minimum prices in a trading period. They usually feature a tick on the left side to show the open price and one on the right to show the closing price.

Line Chart

This is a chart that maps the closing price values using a line segment.

Point and Figure Chart

This employs numerical filters that reference times without fully using the time to construct the chart.

Overlays

These are usually used on the main price charts and come in different ways:

• Resistance - refers to a price level that acts as the maximum level above the usual price

• Support - the opposite of resistance, and it shows as the lowest value of the price

• Trend line - this is a line that connects two troughs or peaks.

• Channel - refers to two trend lines that are parallel to each other

- Moving average - a kind of dynamic trendline that looks at the average price in the market

- Bollinger bands - these are charts that show the rate of volatility in a market.

- Pivot point - this refers to the average of the high, low, and closing price averages for a certain stock or currency.

Price-based Indicators

These analyze the price values of the market. These include:

- Advance decline line - this is an indicator of the market breadth

- Average directional index - shows the strength of a trend in the market

- Commodity channel index - helps you to identify cyclical trends in the market

- Relative strength index - this is a chart that shows you the strength of the price

- Moving average convergence (MACD) - this shows the point where two trend line converge or diverge.

- Stochastic oscillator - this shows the close position that has happened within the recent trading range

- Momentum - this is a chart that tells you how fast the price changes

The Benefits of Technical Analysis in Options Trading

There are a variety of benefits that you enjoy when you use technical analysis in trading options. The benefits arise from the fact that traders are usually asking a lot of questions touching on the price of the market and entry points. While the forecast for prices is a huge task, the use of technical analysis makes it easier to handle.

The major advantages of technical analysis include

Expert Trend Analysis

This is the biggest advantage of technical analysis in any market. With this method, you can predict the direction of the market at any time. You can determine whether the market will move up, down or sideways easily.

Entry and Exit Points

As a trader, you need to know when to place a trade and when to opt out. The entry point is all about knowing the right time to enter the trade for good returns. Exiting a trade is also vital because it allows you to reduce losses.

Leverage Early Signals

Every trader looks for ways to get early signals to assist them in making decisions. Technical analysis gives you signals to trigger a decision on your part. This is usually ideal when you suspect that a trend will reverse soon. Remember the time the trend reverses are when you need to make crucial decisions.

It Is Quick

In options trading, you need to go with techniques that give you fast results. Additionally, getting technical analysis data is cheaper than other techniques in fundamental analysis, with some companies offering free charting programs. If you are in the market to make use of short time intervals such as 1-minute, 5-minute, 30 minute or 1-hour charts, you can get this using technical analysis.

It Gives You A Lot of Information

Technical analysis gives you a lot of information that you can use to make trading decisions. You can easily build a position depending on the information you get then take or exit trades. You have access to information such as chart pattern, trends, support, resistance, market momentum, and other information.

The current price of an asset usually reflects every known information of an asset. While the market might be rife with rumors that the prices might surge or plummet, the current price represents the final point for all information. As the traders and investors change their bearing from one part to another, the changes in asset reflect the current value perception.

If all this turns out to be true, then the only info you require is a price chart that gives all the price reflections and predictions. There isn't any need for you to worry yourself with the reasons why the price is rising or falling when you can use a chart to determine everything.

With the right technical analysis information, you can make trading easier and faster because you make decisions based not on hearsay but facts. You don't have to spend your time reading and trying to make headway in financial news. All you need us to check what the chart tells you.

You Understand Trends

If the prices on the market were to gyrate randomly without any direction, you would find it hard to make money. While these trends run in all directions, the prices always move in trends. Directional bias allows you to leverage the benefits of making money. Technical analysis allows you to determine when a trend occurs and when it doesn't occur, or when it is in reversal.

Many of the profitable techniques that are used by the traders to make money follow trends. This means that you find the right trend and then look for opportunities that allow you to enter the market in the same direction as the trend. This helps you to capitalize on the price movement.

Trends run in various degrees. The degree of the trend determines how much money you make, whether in the short term or long-term trading. Technical analysis gives you all the tools that make it possible for you to do this.

History Always Repeats Itself

Technical analysis uses common patterns to give you the information to trade. However, you need to understand that history will not be exact when it repeats itself, though. The current analysis will be either bigger or smaller, depending on the existing market conditions. The only thing is that it won't be a replica of the prior pattern.

This pans out easily because most human psychology doesn't change so much, and you will see that the emotions have a hand in making sure that prices rise and fall. The emotions that traders exhibit create a lot of patterns that lead to changes in prices all the time. As a trader, you need to identify these patterns and then use them for trading. Use prior history to guide you and then the current price as a trigger of the trade.

Enjoy Proper Timing

Do you know that without proper timing you will not be able to make money at all? One of the major advantages of technical analysis is that you get the chance to time the trades. Using technical analysis, you get to wait, then place your money in other opportunities until it is the right time to place a trade.

Applicable Over a Wide Time Frame

When you learn technical analysis, you get to apply it to many areas in different markets, including options. All the trading in a market is based mostly on the patters that are as a result of human behavior. These patterns can then be mapped out on a chart to be used across the markets.

While there is some difference between analyzing different securities, you will be able to use technical analysis in most of the markets.

Additionally, you can use the analysis in any timeframe, which is applicable whether you use hourly, daily, or weekly charts. These markets are usually taken to be fractal, which essentially means that patterns that appear on a small scale will also be present on a large scale as well.

Technical Analysis Secrets to Become the Best Trader

To make use of technical analysis the right way, you need to follow time-testing approaches that have made the technique a gold mine for many traders. Let us look at the various tips that will take you from novice to pro in just a few days:

Use More than One Indicator

Numbers make trading easy, but it also applies to the way you apply your techniques. For one, you need to know that just because one technical indicator is better than using one, applying a second indicator is better than using just one. The use of more than one indicator is one of the best ways to confirm a trend. It also increases the odds of being right.

As a trader, you will never be 100 percent right at all times, and you might even find that the odds are stashed against you when everything is plain to see. However, don't demand too much from your indicators such that you end up with analysis paralysis.

To achieve this, make use of indicators that complement each other rather than the ones that clash against each other.

Go For Multiple Time Frames

Using the same buy signal every day allows you to have confidence that the indicator is giving you all you need to know to trade. However, make sure you look for a way to use multiple timeframes to confirm a trend. When you have a doubt, it is wise that you increase the timeframe from an hour to a day or from a daily chart to a weekly chart.

Understand that No Indicator Measures Everything

You need to know that indicators are supposed to show how strong a trend is, they won't tell you much more. So, you need to understand and focus on what the indicator is supposed to communicate instead of working with assumptions.

Go With the Trend

If you notice that an option is trading upward, then go ahead and buy it. Conversely when the trend stops trending, then it is time to sell it. If you aren't sure of what is going on in the market at that time, then don't make a move.

However, waiting might make you lose profitable trades as opposed to trading. You also miss out on opportunities to create more capital.

Have the Right Skills

It really takes superior analytical capabilities and real skill to be successful at trading, just like any other endeavor. Many people think that it is hard to make money with options trading, but with the right approach, you can make extraordinary profits.

You need to learn and understand the various skills so that you know what the market seeks from you and how to achieve your goals.

Trade with a Purpose

Many traders go into options trading with the main aim of having a hobby. Well, this way you won't be able to make any money at all. What you need to do is to trade for the money - strive to make profits unlike those who try to make money as a hobby.

Always Opt for High value

Well, no one tells you to trade any security that comes your way - it is purely a matter of choice. Try and go for high-value options so that you can trade them the right way. Make use of fundamental analysis to choose the best options to trade in.

Be Disciplined

When using technical analysis, you might find yourself in situations that require you to make a decision fast. To achieve success, you need to have strict risk management protocols. Don't base on your track record to come up with choices; instead, make sure you follow what the analysis tells you.

Don't Overlook Your Trading Plan

The trading plan is in place to guide you when things go awry. Coming up with the plan is easy, but many people find it hard to implement the plan the right way. The trading plan has various components - the signals and the take-profit/stop-loss rules. Once you get into the market, you need to control yourself because you have already taken a leap. Remember you cannot control the indicators once they start running - all you can do is to prevent yourself from messing up everything.

Come up with the trading rules when you are unemotional to try and mitigate the effects of making bad decisions.

Accept Losses

Many people trade with one thing in mind - losses aren't part of their plan. This is a huge mistake because you need to understand that every trade has two sides to it - a loss and a profit. Remember that the biggest mistake that leads to losses isn't anything to do with bad indicators rather using them the wrong way. Always have a stop-loss order when you trade to prevent loss of money.

Have a Target When You Trade

So, what do you plan to achieve today? Remember, trading is a way to grow your capital as opposed to saving. Options trading is a business that has probable outcomes that you get to estimate. When you make a profit, make sure you take some money from the table and then put it in a safe place.

How to Apply Technical Analysis

Many traders have heard of technical analysis, but they don't know how to use it to make deductions and come up with decisions that impact their trades. Here are the different steps to make sure you have the right decision when you use technical analysis.

1. Identify a Trend

You need to identify an option and then see whether there is a trend or not. The trend might be driving the options up or down. The market is bullish if it is moving up and bearish when it is moving down. As a trader, you need to go along with the trend instead of fighting it. When you fight against the trend, you incur unnecessary losses that will make it hard to achieve the rewards that you seek.

You also need to have good ways to identify the trend; this is because the market has the capacity to move in a certain direction. It is not all about identifying the direction of the trend but also when the trend is moving out of the trend.

So, how can you identify a trend the right way? Here are some tools to use so as to get the right trend:

• Using triangles that map major swings

• The Bill Williams Fractals indicator helps you to identify the trend

• Use the moving average

• Trend lines give you an idea of the direction of the trend

Once you identify the trend, the next step is to try and mark the support and resistance levels

2. Support and Resistance Levels

You need to understand the support and resistance levels that are within the trend. Use the Fibonacci retracement tool to identify these spots on the trend.

3. Look for Patterns

Patterns need to show you what to expect in a certain market. You can use candlesticks to determine the chart pattern.

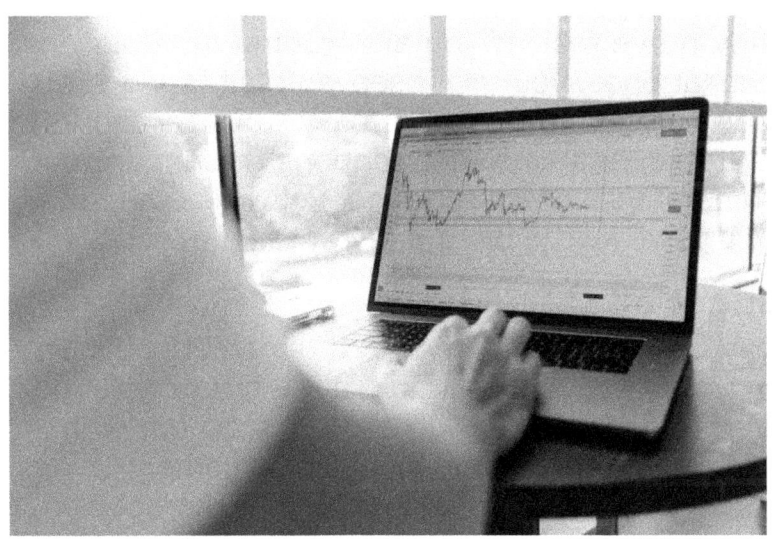

Chapter 9 Trading psychology

Options prices can move a lot over the course of short time periods. So someone who likes to see their money protected and not losing any is not going to be suitable for options trading. Now, we all want to come out ahead, so I am not saying that you have to be happy about losing money in order to be an options trader. What you have to be willing to do is calmly observe your options losing money, and then be ready to stick it out in order to see gains return in the future. This is akin to riding a real roller coaster, but it is a financial roller coaster. Options do not slowly appreciate the way a Warren Buffett investor would hope to see. Options move big on a percentage basis, and they move fast. If you are trading multiple contracts at once, you might see yourself losing $500 and then earning $500 over a matter of a few hours. In this sense, although most options traders are not "day traders" technically speaking, you will be better off if you have a little bit of a day trading mindset.

Getting it all started

You may be excited to jump into the market and start trading right away, but there are a few things that you will need to do first. You will need to start out with a good understanding of the basics that come with options and you need to know some of the option types that you can pick from. We talked about these topics a little bit before, but the more that you can learn about them before investing, the more success you will have.

After you have had some time to understand what options are all about and what you will be getting yourself into, it is time to come up with your motivation for trading. Ask yourself how much money you are looking to make from this trade and how you would like to use that money when you have earned it. This motivation is going to help you out so much when you are in the thick of the trading and you need some help staying focus.

The trading plan is going to basically list all of the things that you want to be able to accomplish while you are trading. It can include what you expect to happen, some of your goals, the strategy that you will go with, and any other guidelines that will help you be successful. Those who decide to start investing in options without having a good plan in place will be the ones who run into a lot of risks.

You don't make emotional decisions

Since options are, by their nature, volatile, and very volatile for many stocks, coming to options trading and being really emotional about it is not a good way to approach your trading. If you are emotional, you are going to exit your trades at the wrong time in 75% of cases. You don't want to make any sudden moves when it comes to trading options. As we have said, you should have a trading plan with rules on exiting your positions, stick to those rules and you should be fine.

Be a little bit math-oriented

In order to really understand options trading and be successful, you cannot be shy about numbers. Options trading is a numbers game. That doesn't mean you have to drive over to the nearest university and get a statistics degree. But if you do understand probability and statistics, you are going to be a better options trader. Frankly, it's hard to see how you can be a good options trader without having a mind for numbers.

Some math is at the core of options trading and you cannot get around it.

You are market-focused

You don't have to set up a day trading office with ten computer screens so you can be tracking everything by the moment, but if you are hoping to set up a trade and lazily come back to check it three days later, that isn't going to work with options trading. You do need to be checking your trades a few times a day. You also need to be keeping up with the latest financial and economic news, and you need to keep up with any news directly related to the companies you invest in or any news that could impact those companies. If the news does come out, you are going to need to make decisions if it's news that isn't going to be favorable to your positions. Also, you need to be checking the charts periodically so you have an idea of where things are heading for now.

Keep detailed trading journals

You don't want to get in the same situation with your options trading. It can be an emotional experience because trading options is active and fast-paced. When you have a profitable trade, it will be exciting. But you need to keep a journal to record all of your trades, in order to know exactly what the real situation is. That doesn't mean you quit if you look at your journal and find out you have a losing record, what you do is figure out why your trades aren't profitable and then make adjustments.

Take a disciplined approach

Don't just buy options for a certain stock because it feels good. You need to do research on your stocks. That will include doing fundamental analysis. This is going to mean paying attention to the history of a stock, knowing what the typical ranges are for, stock in recent history is, and also reading through the company's financial statements and prospectus.

Select a Security

This can be done by researching the finance sections of major news corporations. New options traders, and particularly those who are new to trading in general, should approach options trading cautiously. Rather than diving right in, investors should get their feet wet by experimenting with a limited number of securities and options so that they can keep track of gains and losses and avoid mistakes for future investments.

Choose OTC or Regulated

Trading While this can be decided at a later stage, it is suggested here so that new investors can refer to the boards of a regulated exchange, such as the New York Stock Exchange, when choosing a put or call that is well suited to their tastes. Practiced traders can pick up an OTC option later if desired, such as a call to cover the cost of an insurance put, also known as a married put.

Select Strategies

Before beginning trading, investors will need to be sure they are familiar with a few simple strategies that can be implemented with a stock.

Examine the Market

Investors will need to study the time frame charts associated with their underlying security selection.

Purchase Options and Trade

Based upon conclusions drawn from studying time frame charts, investors will need to buy the appropriate calls or puts. At the same time, investors should choose one or two of the strategies with which they are already familiar that they believe will work well in the present market climate. If trading via a regulated exchange, options for the strategies may be selected from a list published by the exchange.

Utilizing options for trading purposes

Options can generally be utilized for trading purposes in one of two ways. First, they can be used as a type of speculation whereby those who believe they are in the know can test out their hypothesis without committing fully to their hunch.

Alternatively, those who are already flush with underlying assets can then use options trading as a type of insurance if they are unsure how some of their other investments are going to perform in either the short or the long term. Typically, options are purchased when major losses on riskier investments are expected in the near future as they allow the holder to wait and see how things proceed before getting a fair price for their investment no matter how the market falls.

Appreciate That Options Trading Is Not Simple

It is vital at this stage to recapitulate the meaning of options trading. This is a contract that grants one the right of either buying or selling a security based on the speculative value of it in a limited period of time. However, the contract is not obligatory in nature. In understanding options trading, two forms of it have to be understood; first is a call option, and the other is the put option. The two are opposites of each other. One buys the former option when one expects an asset's value to go up over time but before the deadline of expiry of the contract expires.

Read and Understand Essential Literature Available On Options Trading

Reading is part of the process of educating one's self in business. A lot of literature is currently available on various platforms for the benefit of those seeking to understand investments and avenues of investment. Success and failure stories are also hugely available, particularly on the internet where people could acquire first-hand accounts on the options trading venture.

However, reading is only helpful if the correct material is being read. Not every account of business success stories is true. Some are exaggerated while others are written to arouse interest to influence people into making certain decisions for business purposes. The internet is full of hidden business activities, some of which are even hidden behind the sensational headlines of the literature resources striking people's eyes on their phones and computers. This means that knowledge is only good when it comes from the correct source.

Acquire an Understanding of the Basics of the Kinds of Trades

The trades are basically either a call option or the put option. These have to be understood well since they are the start of knowing this trade as an investment. The types of trade are the core part of the knowledge that a person can gain on options trading. All these can be explained with a desire to gain an understanding of how each of the two types of trades works. This can be achieved the desire for understanding can involve seeking mentorship or seeking consultancy firm. It can call for some level of schooling in order to begin to attain literacy, especially for those people who did not have prior knowledge of economic investments.

An options trading mindset

When it comes to making money trading options, it is important to remember that you must control your emotions at all times, something that is easier said than done, especially if you are in the moment and have just taken an unexpected loss. Cultivating the proper mindset can be done with practice, however, and doing so will make it easier for you to face the early parts of your options trading career with the proper expectations in regards to what sort of results you can expect from options trading. Specifically, this means that you will need to understand that investing in options isn't a quick and easy path to success and, rather, is sure to take plenty of dedication and hard work if you hope to see reap the potential rewards.

The first step to finding success via options trading is to get your emotions in check. The best traders are robotic, they only rely on the facts and they follow their trading plan 100 percent of the time. If you find yourself getting extremely emotional as far as trading is concerned then it is important that you start off by keeping a log of the emotions you have while trading, and the results of those emotions on your trading outcome. While this might seem unnecessary at first, you will be surprised how helpful having a clear outline of your personal patterns is when it comes to improving your overall trade percentage in the long term.

The fact of the matter is that if you ever hope to successfully trade options then you are going to need to know you can stick with your plan no matter what the emotional part of your mind is telling you to do. A good plan is one that remains successful, not 100 percent of the time, or even 95 percent of the time and instead manages to be successful roughly 60 percent of the time. While 60 percent is certainly enough to ensure you turn a profit, it is not enough that it allows for additional wiggle room in the terms of letting your emotions talking you into going off book at every turn. Remember, trading options is a numbers game and keeping your emotions in check is key to not working with skewed data.

Setting up a reasonable expectation

A trader who is staring up should always have the patience to wait to know a market and should not expect that he or she would large and handsome profit from their trading options. A new trader should never high expectation when they are just into the market. Rather they should be mentally prepared for losing capital rather than gaining capital. A trader should always begin to expect at least at a minimum market experience of a year or half. This can be illustrated very simply in any field. A famous successful person always bears time and patience to be the greatest achiever in their field.

Proof concept

If a trader starts off with the small trade he or she will not only gain experience but will also save time. Noises of the stock market do not affect the small traders but if a trader starts with big trading options he or she will react to these noises in the stock market. A new trader will be in a bad situation with such reactions and at the early time period. Starting with a small trade will teach a trader to manage capital which is very much necessary. A trader remembers all trades are not same in nature. A good trader will generate great ideas after the proper experience. A trader must always have records and check on them to see what idea works for them and what does not.

Proper sorting and record keeping

A good successful trader should always keep a record of few important things of the market like:

- The trader should keep a record of orders placed and quantity involved in it and money making out of it.
- The trader should keep in mind implied volatility and its reference to current condition.
- The trader should keep in mind about his competitors in the market in that particular trade.
- When the traders begin to keep a record and maintain records they begin to move towards success and chances of being in odd position is also reduced.

Good position of the trader

Once a trader has achieved his or her position in a trade or stock market, there are frequent ups and downs. A good position trader must know how to react to these situations. By small trade, he or she won't be much affected by the noise of the stock market.

The trader should keep in mind about buying stock exchange at the perfect time. When a trader does so he or she can perfectly be in the market and understand well.

Proper evaluation of the position

A trader must decide very well that that few decisions like backing out on losses must be decided well according to perfect time.

There are few other decisions like a plan suddenly executed and whether he or she should move on with the profit or go for more?

Even if the sudden plan does not work out then he or she must have a backup and move on forward ahead and not repent on his or her loss and look for a new fresh start.

Hard work is the only way to success

It's easy to advise and listen to it. But when it comes up to the execution of the advice it's not that easy as things do not turn up the way its told.

The simple way is to start with small trade and have a lot of patience. A trader should make proper planning for execution. The trader should learn about the market and get into a good position and stick well to it and work very hard to achieve success and be a good disciplined successful trader.

At this point, it is time to move on to the next step. You already know some of the basics that come with working on options as well as some of their benefits.

Chapter 10 The Best Strategies to Make Money

Good strategies of any kind of options trading are the major key to any kind of success that is about to be unfolded in any activity. Strategies are normally laid in the trading plan and should be strictly implemented in every options trading move that is likely to be involved. Let us wholly venture into the best strategies so far in options trading.

1. Collars. The collar strategy is established by holding a number of shares of the underlying stock available in the market where protective puts are bought and the call options sold. In this kind of strategy, the options trader is likely to really protect his or her capital used in the trading activities rather than the idea of acquiring more money during trading. This kind is considered conservative and rather much more important in options trading.
2. Credit spreads. It is presumed that the biggest fear of most traders is a financial breakdown. In this side of strategy, the trader gets to sell one put and then buy another one.
3. Covered calls. Covered calls are a good kind of strategy where a particular trader sells the right for another trader to purchase his or her stock at some strike price and get to gain a good amount of cash. However, there is a specific time that this strategy should be

utilized and in a case where the buyer fails to purchase some of the stock and the expiration date dawns, the contract becomes invalid right away.
4. Cash naked put. Cash naked put is a kind of strategy where the options trader gets to write at the money or out of the money during a particular trading activity and aligning some particular amount of money aside for the purpose of purchasing stock.
5. Long call strategy. This is the most basic strategy in options trading and the one that is quite easy to comprehend. In the long call strategy for options trading, aggressive option traders who happen to be bullish are pretty much involved. This implies that bullish options traders end up buying stock during the trading activities with the hope of it rising in the near future. The reward is unlimited in the long call strategy.
6. Short call option strategy. The short call strategy is the reverse of the long call one. Bearish kind of traders is so aggressive in the falling out of stock prices during trading in this kind of strategy. They decide to sell the call options available. This move is considered to be so risky by the experienced options traders believing that prices may drastically decide to rise once again. This significantly implies that large chunks of losses are likely to be incurred, leading to a real downfall of your trading structure and everything involved in it.
7. Long put option strategy. First things first, you should be contented that buying a put is

the opposite of buying a call. So in this kind of strategy, when you become bearish, that is the moment you may purchase a put option. Put option puts the trader in a situation where he can sell his stock at a particular period of time before the expiration date is reached. This strategy exposes the trader to a mere kind of risk in the options trading market.

8. Trading time. It is depicted that options trading for a longer period is much value as compared to a short period dating. The longer the trading day, the more skills and knowledge the trader is likely to be engaged into as he or she is likely to get the adequate experience that is needed for good trading. Mastering good trading moves for a while gives the trader the experience and adequate skills.

9. Bull call spread strategy. In this kind of strategy, the investor gets to purchase several calls at a particular strike price and then purchases the price at a much higher price. The calls always bear a similar expiration date and come from the same underlying stock. This type of strategy is mostly implemented by the bullish options traders.

10. Bear put strategy. This strategy involves a trader purchasing put options at a particular price amount and later selling off at a lower price amount. These options bear a similar expiration date and from the same underlying stock. This strategy is mostly utilized by traders who are said to be bearish.

The consequences are limited losses and limited gains.
11. Iron condor. The iron condor involves the bull call spread strategy and the bear put strategy all at the same time during a particular trading period. The expiration dates of the stock are still similar and are of the same underlying stock. Most traders get to use this strategy when the market is expected to experience low volatility rates and with the expectation of gaining a little amount of premium. Iron condor works in both up and down markets are is really believed to be economical during the up and down markets.
12. Married put strategy. On this end, the options trader purchase options at a particular amount of money and at the same time, get to buy the same number of shares of the underlying stock. This kind of strategy is also known as the protective put. This is also a bearish kind of options trading strategy.
13. Cash covered put strategy. Here, one or more contracts are sold with a 100 shares multiplied with the strike price amount for every particular contract involved in the options trading. Most traders use this strategy to acquire an extra amount of premium on a specific stock they would wish to purchase.
14. Long or short calendar spread strategy. This is a tricky type of strategy. The market stock is said to be stagnant, not

moving and waiting for the right timing until the expiration of the front-month is reached.
15. Synthetic long arbitrage strategy. Most traders take advantage of this strategy when they are trying to take advantage of the different market prices in different kinds of markets with just the same property.
16. Put ratio back spread strategy. This is a bearish type of options strategy where the trader gets to sell some put options and gets to purchase more options of just the same underlying stock with a similar expiration date and a lower price.
17. Call ratio back spread. In this strategy, the trader uses both the long and short options positions so as to eradicate consistent losses and target achieving large loads of benefits over a particular trading period. The essence of this strategy is to generate profits in case the stock prices tend to elevate and reduce the number of risks likely to be involved. This strategy is mostly implemented by bullish kind of options traders.
18. Long butterfly strategy. This strategy involves three parts where one put option is purchased at particular and then selling the other two options at a price lower than the buying price and purchasing one put at even lower price during a particular trading period.
19. Short butterfly strategy. In this strategy, three parts are still involved where a put option is sold at a much higher price and two puts are then purchased at a lower price than the purchase price and a put option is later on sold at a much lower strike price. In both

cases, all put bear the same expiration date and the strike prices are normally equidistant as revealed in various options trading charts. A short butterfly strategy is the reverse way of the long butterfly strategy.
20. Long straddle. The long straddle is also known as the buy strangle where a slight pull and a slight call are purchased during a particular period before the expiration date reaches. The importance of this strategy is that the trader bears a large chance of acquiring good amounts of profits during his or her trading time before the expiration date is achieved.
21. Short straddle. In this kind of strategy, the trader sells both the call and put options at a similar price and bearing the same expiration date. Traders practice this strategy with the hope of acquiring good amounts of profits and experience limited various kinds of risks.
22. Owning positions that are already in a portfolio. Most traders prefer purchasing and selling various options that already hedge existing positions. This kind of strategy method is believed to incur good profits and incur losses too in other occurrences.
23. Albatross trade strategy. This kind of strategy aims at gaining some amounts of profits when the market is stagnant during a specific options trading period or a pre-determined period of time. This kind of strategy is similar to the short gut strategy.
24. Reverse iron condor strategy. This kind of strategy focuses on benefiting some profits when the underlying stock in the current

market dares to make some sharp market trade moves in either direction. Eventually, a limited amount of risks are experienced and a limited amount of profits during trading.
25. Iron butterfly spread. Buying and holding four different options in the market at three different market prices is involved in the trading market for a particular trading period.
26. Short bull ratio strategy. Short bull ratio strategy is used to benefit from the amounts of profits gained from increasing security involved in the trading market in a similar way in which we normally get to buy calls during a particular period.
27. Bull condor spread. This is a type of strategy that is designed to return a profit if the actual price of security decides to rise to a predicted price range during a specific trading period impacting good chunks of profits made to the options trader and a limited number of risks involved.
28. Put ratio spread strategy. This strategy entails purchasing a number of put options and adding more options with various strike prices and equal kind of underlying stock during a particular options trading period.
29. Strap straddle strategy. Strap straddle strategy uses one put and two calls bearing a similar strike price and with an equal date of expiration and also containing the same underlying stock that is normally stagnant during a particular trading period. The trader utilizes this type of strategy for the hope of getting higher amounts of profits as

compared to the regular straddle strategy over a particular period of the trading period.
30. Strap strangle strategy. This strategy is bullish, where more call options are purchased as compared to the put options and a bullish inclination is then depicted in various trading charts information.
31. Put back spread strategy. This back spread strategy combines both the short puts and long puts so as to establish a position where the ratio of losses and profits entirely depends on the ratio of their two puts that are likely to be experienced in the market.
32. Short call ratio. This strategy involves purchasing a single call and later on selling two other calls at a higher price amount during a specific period of time before its expiration. This concept combines the protocols of the bull call spread strategy and the naked call strategy. The essence of this strategy is to acquire limited loss potential and mixed profits potential to the options trader involved during a particular period of time.
33. Iron albatross strategy. The particular trader gets to use this type of strategy when expecting a particular underlying stock to trade during a particular period of time before expiration. Four transactions are usually involved in this strategy and a high level of trading is called for. This implies that this measure kind is so suitable for the experienced traders, ones who have mastered almost every market move.

34. Bull call ladder spread strategy. This one is almost similar to the bull call strategy where security increasing in price is expected to source out some profits to the trader during options trading.

Chapter 11 Tips for Success

As already noted, options simply involve putting a price on the possibility or probability that a future event will take place. If an event is likely to actually happen, then that particular option related to that event becomes very expensive. Therefore, the more likely an event is, the better the profits from the option.

It is important to learn how to trade in options because it offers a reliable and long-term source of income. Many investors have generated wealth and become prosperous by simply trading in stock options. Options are a preferred means of investment because of various reasons. One of these is the relatively low cost of investment required. As an investor, you do not need large sums of money to buy options. They are very cheaply priced yet they offer rewards that are just as good as those enjoyed by investors in the stocks markets.

There have been plenty of advances made, over the last couple of decades, on how commodity markets function. One of the most notable of these advances is the development of online trading platforms and the speed at which deals are concluded. Trading online is fast, easy and convenient. It enables any interested investor to open an account through a broker and then start trading options and earn good returns as soon as is practically possible.

Options trading present a new, more advanced method of investing. To be successful in options trading, it is very important that you understand exactly what you are doing. This will ensure that you are not just an amateur groping in the dark but a true investor.

One of the most important reasons why trade in options is gaining popularity is that investors do not need to invest large sums of money as compared to those investing directly in stocks and shares. This is because traders do not need to actually buy the underlying stocks or shares but simply the rights affiliated with the options. However, the returns are just as great, if not greater, as those gotten from trade in securities.

Options require an arsenal of successful methods and tactics to be profitable. For a beginner or the average investor, a powerful and successful strategy is definitely essential. Whenever you invest money in the stock market, always diversify your portfolio and if possible, include options. This way, you will greatly increase the income that you derive from your investments.

Succeeding on Calls

Know when to go off book: While sticking to your plan, even when your emotions are telling you to ignore it, is the mark of a successful trader, this in no way means that you must blindly follow your plan 100 percent of the time. You will, without a doubt, find yourself in a situation from time to time where your plan is going to be rendered completely useless by something outside of your control. You need to be aware enough of your plan's weaknesses, as well as changing market conditions, to know when following your predetermined course of action is going to lead to failure instead of success. Knowing when the situation really is changing, versus when your emotions are trying to hold sway is something that will come with practice, but even being aware of the disparity is a huge step in the right direction.

Avoid trades that are out of the money: While there are a few strategies out there that make it a point of picking up options that are currently out of the money, you can rest assured that they are most certainly the exception, not the rule. Remember, the options market is not like the traditional stock market which means that even if you are trading options based on underlying stocks buying low and selling high is just not a viable strategy.

If a call has dropped out of the money, there is generally less than a 10 percent chance that it will return to acceptable levels before it expires which means that if you purchase these types of options what you are doing is little better than gambling, and you can find ways to gamble with odds in your favor of much higher than 10 percent.

Avoid hanging on too tightly to your starter strategy: That doesn't mean that it is the last strategy that you are ever going to need, however, far from it. Your core trading strategy is one that should always be constantly evolving as the circumstances surrounding your trading habits change and evolve as well. What's more, outside of your primary strategy you are going to want to eventually create additional plans that are more specifically tailored to various market states or specific strategies that are only useful in a narrow band of situations. Remember, the more prepared you are prior to starting a day's worth of trading, the greater your overall profit level is likely to be, it is as simple as that.

Utilize the spread: If you are not entirely risk averse, then when it comes to taking advantage of volatile trades the best thing to do is utilize a spread as a way of both safeguarding your existing investments and, at the same time, making a profit. To utilize a long spread you are going to want to generate a call and a put, both with the same underlying asset, expiration details, and share amounts but with two very different strike prices. The call will need to have a higher strike price and will mark the upper limit of your profits and the put will have a lower strike price that will mark the lower limit of your losses. When creating a spread it is important that you purchase both halves at the same time as doing it in fits and spurts can add extraneous variables to the formula that are difficult to adjust for properly.

Never proceed without knowing the mood of the market: While using a personalized trading plan is always the right choice, having one doesn't change the fact that it is extremely important to consider the mood of the market before moving forward with the day's trades. First and foremost, it is important to keep in mind that the collective will of all of the traders who are currently participating in the market is just as much as a force as anything that is more concrete, including market news. In fact, even if companies release good news to various outlets and the news is not quite as good as everyone was anticipating it to be then related prices can still decrease.

To get a good idea of what the current mood of the market is like, you are going to want to know the average daily numbers that are common for your market and be on the lookout for them to start dropping sharply. While a day or two of major fluctuation can be completely normal, anything longer than that is a sure sign that something is up.

Additionally, you will always want to be aware of what the major players in your market are up to.

Never get started without a clear plan for entry and exit: While finding your first set of entry/exit points can be difficult without experience to guide you, it is extremely important that you have them locked down prior to starting trading, even if the stakes are relatively low. Unless you are extremely lucky, starting without a clear idea of the playing field is going to do little but lose your money. If you aren't sure about what limits you should set, start with a generalized pair of points and work to fine tune it from there.

More important than setting entry and exit points, however, is using them, even when there is still the appearance of money on the table. One of the biggest hurdles that new options traders need to get over is the idea that you need to wring every last cent out of each and every successful trade. The fact of the matter is that, as long as you have a profitable trading plan, then there will always be more profitable trades in the future which means that instead of worrying about a small extra profit you should be more concerned with protecting the profit that the trade has already netted you. While you may occasionally make some extra profit ignoring this advice, odds are you will lose far more than you gain as profits peak unexpectedly and begin dropping again before you can effectively pull the trigger. If you are still having a hard time with this concept, consider this: options trading is a marathon, not a sprint, slow and steady will always win the race.

Never double down: When they are caught up in the heat of the moment, many new options traders will find themselves in a scenario where the best way to recoup a serious loss is to double down on the underlying stock in question at its newest, significantly lowered, price in an effort to make a profit under the assumption that things are going to turn around and then continue to do so to the point that everything is completely profitable once again. While it can be difficult to let an underlying stock that was once extremely profitable go, doubling down is rarely if ever going to be the correct decision. If you find yourself in a spot where you don't know if the trade you are about to make is actually going to be a good choice, all you need to do is ask yourself if you would make the same one if you were going into the situation blind, the answer should tell you all you need to know.

If you find yourself in a moment where doubling down seems like the right choice, you are going to need to have the strength to talk yourself back down off of that investing ledge and to cut your losses as thoroughly as possible given the current situation. The sooner you cut your losses and move on from the trade that ended poorly, the sooner you can start putting energy and investments into a trade that still has the potential to make you a profit.

Never take anything personally: It is human nature to build stories around, and therefore form relationships with, all manner of inanimate objects including individual stocks or currency pairs. This is why it is perfectly natural to feel a closer connection to particular trades, and possibly even consider throwing out your plan when one of them takes an unexpected dive. Thinking about and acting on are two very different things, however, which is why being aware of these tendencies are so important to avoid them at all costs.

This scenario happens just as frequently with trades moving in positive directions as it does negative, but the results are always going to be the same. Specifically, it can be extremely tempting to hang on to a given trade much longer than you might otherwise decide to simply because it is on a hot streak that shows no sign of stopping. In these instances, the better choice of action is to instead sell off half of your shares and then set a new target based on the updated information to ensure you are in a position to have your cake and eat it too.

Not taking your choice of broker seriously: With so many things to consider, it is easy to understand why many new option traders simply settle on the first broker that they find and go about their business from there. The fact of the matter is, however, that the broker you choose is going to be a huge part of your overall trading experience which means that the importance of choosing the right one should not be discounted if you are hoping for the best experience possible. This means that the first thing that you are going to want to do is to dig past the friendly exterior of their website and get to the meat and potatoes of what it is they truly offer. Remember, creating an eye-catching website is easy, filling it will legitimate information when you have ill intent is much more difficult.

First things first, this means looking into their history of customer service as a way of not only ensuring that they treat their customers in the right way, but also of checking to see that quality of service is where it needs to be as well. Remember, when you make a trade every second count which mean that if you need to contact your broker for help with a trade you need to know that you are going to be speaking with a person who can solve your problem as quickly as possible. The best way to ensure the customer service is up to snuff is to give them a call and see how long it takes for them to get back to you. If you wait more than a single business day, take your business elsewhere as if they are this disinterested in a new client, consider what the service is going to be like when they already have you right where they want you.

With that out the way, the next thing you will need to consider is the fees that the broker is going to charge in exchange for their services. There is very little regulation when it comes to these fees which means it is definitely going to pay to shop around. In addition to fees, it is important to consider any account minimums that are required as well as any fees having to do with withdrawing funds from the account.

Find a Mentor: When you are looking to go from causal trader to someone who trades successfully on the regular, there is only so much you can learn by yourself before you need a truly objective eye to ensure you are proceeding appropriately. This person can either be someone you know in real life, or it can take the form of one or more people online. The point is you need to find another person or two who you can bounce ideas off of and whose experience you can benefit from. Options trading doesn't need to be a solitary activity; take advantage of any community you can find.

Knowledge is the key: Without some type of information which you can use to assess your trades, you are basically playing at the roulette table. Even poker players show up to the table with a game plan. They can adapt to the circumstances and learn to read other players. That way, they can tell the contenders from the pretenders. Options trading is no different. If you are unable to use the information that is out there to your advantage, then what you will end up with is a series of guesses which may or may not play out. Based purely on the law of averages you have a 50/50 chance of making money. That may not seem like bad odds, but a string of poor decisions will leave you in the poor house in no time.

So, it is crucial that you become familiar with the various analytics and tools out there which you can use to your advantage. Bear in mind that everyone is going to be looking at the same information. However, it is up to you to figure out what can, or might, happen before everyone else does. This implies really learning and studying the numbers so that you can detect patterns and see where trends are headed, or where trends may reverse. The perfect antidote to that is vision and foresight. Practice building scenarios. Try to imagine what could happen is trends continue. Or, what would happen if trends reversed? What needs to happen in order for those trends to continue or reverse?

When you ask yourself such tough questions, your knowledge and understanding begin to expand. Your mind will suddenly be able to process greater amounts of information while you generate your own contingency plans based on the multiple what ifs. That may seem like a great deal of information to handle, but at the end of the day, any time spent in improving your trading acumen is certainly worth the effort.

Mistakes to Avoid When Trading Options

Inexperienced traders are often warned away from purchasing options that are out of the money as being a greater risk than the ultimate reward is likely to be. While it is true that a short expiration time coupled with an out of the money option will frequently look appealing, especially to those with a smaller amount of trading capital to work with, the issue is that all of these types of options are likely to look equally appealing which leaves them with no way to tell the good from the bad. As a more experienced trader, however, you have many more tools at your disposal than the average novice which means that, while risky, cheap options have the potential to generate substantial returns, as long as you keep the following in mind while trading them.

Mishandling early assignment: Early assignment occurs when a holder exercises an option that you are the writer upon much early that you had anticipated, and at terms that are much less favorable than you had initially hoped. If this happens, it can be easy to become flustered and simply sell as requested, taking a loss in the process. Instead, it is important to consider all the possible options, including purchasing another option for the express purpose of selling it, to ensure that you mitigate the extra costs as completely as possible.

Ignoring the statistics behind options trading: One of the biggest mistakes that most newbie options traders make is that they forget the probability is a real thing. When you check a potential stock before purchasing an option, it's important to understand that the history of an option is important when deciding whether or not you should be investing in it, but so are the odds and probability surrounding whether or not a particular event is going to occur.

For example, a common strategy that investors use is to leverage their money by investing in cheap options so that this will help to prevent big losses on a stock that they actually own shares of. Of course, this is a good strategy, but nothing works one-hundred percent of the time. Make sure that if the rules of probability and simple ratios are telling you to stay away from a deal, you listen to the facts that are staring you in the face. Wishful thinking will come to bite you later on.

Being overzealous: Oftentimes when new options traders finally get their initial plan just right, they become overzealous and start committing to larger trades than they can realistically afford to recover from if things go poorly. It is important to take it slow when It comes to building your rate of return and never bet more than you can afford to lose. Regardless of how promising a specific trade might seem, there is not risk/reward level at which it is worth considering a loss that will take you out of the game completely for an extended period of time. Trade reasonably and trade regularly and you will see greater results in the long term guaranteed.

Not being adaptable: The successful options trades know when to follow their plans but they also know that no plan will be the right choice, even if early indicators say otherwise. There is a difference between making a point of sticking to a plan and following it blindly and knowing which is which is one of the more important indicators of the separation between options trading success and abject failure. This means it is important to be aware of when and where experimentation and new ideas are appropriate and when it is best to toe the line and gather more data in order to make a well-reasoned decision.

This also means having several different plans in your options trading tool box and not just resolutely sticking to the first one that brings you a modicum of success. This is crucial as there are certain plans that will only work in specific situations and knowing which to use when, in real time, will lead to significantly greater returns on a more reliable basis every single time.

Likewise, an adaptive options trader knows that market conditions can change unexpectedly and is prepared to respond accordingly. This means understanding when the time is right to go in a new direction, regardless of the potential risks that doing so might entail. Sometimes a good trader has to make a leap of faith, and a trader who is successful in the long term knows what signs to look for that indicate this type of scenario is occurring in real time. Unfortunately, this type of foresight cannot be taught, and instead must be found with experience.

As long as you keep the appropriate mindset regarding individual trades, any new strategy that is attempted will result in valuable data, if nothing else. It is important to understand that learning not to use a specific course of action a second time is always valuable, no matter the costs. Working to build this into your core trading mindset will lead you to greater success in a wider variety of situations in the long term.

Ignoring the probability: Always remember that the historical data will not apply to the current trends in the market at all times which means you will always want to consider the probability as well as the odds that the market is going to behave the way it typically does. The odds are how likely the market is to behave as expected and the probability is the ratio of the likelihood of a given outcome. Understanding the probability of certain outcomes can make it easy to purchase the proper options to minimize losses related to holdings of specific underlying stocks. When purchasing cheap options, it is important to remember that they are always going to be cheap for a reason as price is determined by strike price of the underlying stock as well as the amount of time remaining for the option to regain its value, choose wisely otherwise you are doing little more than gambling and there are certainly better ways to gamble than via options trading.

Letting the opinions of other influence your trading: While every day trader is going to have opinions regarding the best way to trade this type of stock or when to use that indicator, the best day traders tend to avoid this advice like the plague and instead work out their own. The only thing you really need to focus on in order to make the right types of trades in the right timeframes is math and anything else is only going to get in the way. Keep in mind that you want to analyze and observe economic and political events, not get caught up in them.

Not dealing with short options properly: While, in theory, it might seem like buying back short options at the last moment is the best choice, this practice is sure to hurt your more than help you in the long run. It may be tempting to hold onto profitable options in order to squeeze the maximum return out of each investment but you need to be aware that the potential for a reversal is always lurking in the shadows. Instead, a good rule of thumb is to buy back options that are currently at 80 percent of your ideal return or higher and let the extra take care of itself. While it may hurt to leave some potential profit on the table, it will improve your overall reliability, netting you a profit in the long run.

Not considering exotic options: An exotic option is one that has a basic structure that differs from either European or American options when it comes to the how and when of how the payout will be provided or how the option relates to the underlying asset in question. Additionally, the number of potential underlying assets is going to be much more varied and can include things like what the weather is like or how much rainfall a given area has experienced. Due to the customization options and the complexity of exotic options, they are only traded over-the-counter.

While they are undoubtedly more complex to get involved with, exotic options also offer up several additional advantages when compared to common options including:

• They are a better choice for those with very specific needs when it comes to risk management.
• They offer up a variety of unique risk dimensions when it comes to both management and trading.
• They offer a far larger range of potential investments that can more easily meet a diverse number of portfolio needs.
• They are often cheaper than traditional options.

They also have additional drawbacks, the biggest of which is that they cannot often be priced correctly using standard pricing formulas. This may work as a benefit instead of a drawback, however, depending on if the mispricing falls in the favor of the trader or the writer. It is also important to keep in mind that the amount of risk that is taken on with exotic options is always going to be greater than with other options due to the limited liquidity each type of exotic option is going to have available. While some types are going to have markets that are fairly active, others are only going to have limited interest. Some are even what are known as dual-party transactions which means they have no underlying liquidity and are only traded when two amiable traders can be found.

Not keeping earnings and dividend dates in mind: It is important to keep an eye on any underlying assets that you are currently working with as those who are currently holding calls have the potential to be assigned early dividends, with greater dividends having an increased chance of this occurrence. As owning an option doesn't mean owning the underlying asset, if this happens to you then you won't be able to collect on your hard-earned money. Early assignment is largely a random occurrence which means that if you don't keep your ear to the ground it can be easy to get caught unaware and be unable to exercise the option before you miss the boat.

Along similar lines, you are going to also always want to be aware of when the earning season is going to take place for any of your underlying assets as it is likely going to increase the price of all of the contracts related to the underlying asset in question. Additionally, you will need to be caught up on current events as even the threat of influential news can be enough to cause a significant spike in volatility and premiums as well. In order to minimize the additional costs associated with trading during these periods, you are going to want to utilize a spread. Doing so will minimize the effect that inflation has on your bottom line.

Chasing bottoms and tops: There are certainly some strategies out there that are effective when used near the turning points of existing trends. These are in the minority, however, which means that picking bottoms and tops is, more often than not, a risky proposition. Unfortunately, it is an all too common mistake for traders to invest money into securities that are either too low or too high, gleefully ignoring the 2 percent rule as they do so. This impulse should be avoided like the plague and replaced with a focus on major inbound price moves instead. Sticking to one side of markets that are range-bound will lead to better long-term results at least 90 percent of the time.

Sticking with relative trends: If a trend is already well-defined in the market then it is entirely possible that it is going to continue long enough for you to make some money off of it but it is far from a guarantee. The market will naturally fluctuate up to 20 percent of its current average with very little warning, before settling back to the current standard. This means that if you recklessly jump onto a specific trend without doing the required homework you will frequently find yourself making a momentum play that is never going to go anywhere.

Before you make a move regarding a specific trend, there are three distinct timeframes you are going to want to consider first. If you are prone to trading in the short-term then you are going to want to keep an eye on the weekly hourly and daily charts. If you prefer holding onto trades for a longer period of time then daily, weekly and monthly charts are typically going to be more useful.

Conclusion

As a beginner, do not shy away from this investment. The same way you would decide to invest in a business should be the same way you should choose to engage in options trading. We can compare it to playing a chess game. Your ability to be tactical and skillful while playing is what determines the winner at the end of the game. The same applies to option trading. Your ability to reason and acquire skills will give you an added advantage over the others. How strategic can you conduct an options trading? How are you able to manage the risks involved? How do you determine the best time to carry out a trade? How do you decide on the best options to invest? How can you handle an unsuccessful business? Your answer to these questions will tell you what kind of a trader you will become. I'm making that conclusion since the concerns raised in the questions are what will determine the type of a trader you become.

We have had some people disqualifying option trading as a worthy investment. You may find that they have never engaged in any form of options trading yet they conclude it's a scam. Some may say so since they have heard from a third party, that it is not a good investment. There is a high possibility that the person invested in stocks without adequate knowledge of what it entails. As a result, they end up losing money and conclude that it was a waste of their finances. Well, I will not blame them for making such conclusions. However, their problem was based on the lack of necessary knowledge. I always say that never conclude something that you have not tried. Then again, the outcome varies among different people. You may find that a person benefits while another person does not. You never know what tomorrow hold; you could profit from an investment that another person failed in. I always encourage people to try out things by themselves and never rely on other people. If you have intended to invest in options trading, now is the time to push that desire and start trading. You might benefit significantly from it.

When you decide to engage in options trading, it is essential to note that learning never stops. There is always something new to be learned every day. There is never a time when someone can attest that there have acquired all the knowledge required. Information is diverse, and you may never manage to exhaust it fully. Take it upon yourself that you will keep learning and never get tired of doing so. As the options trading sector grows, more and more new things emerge. It will be useful if you can keep up with emerging trends. This will also influence the outcome of your earnings in options trading. You will find that the strategy that worked yesterday leads to a total loss today. If you can keep up with the emerging trends, this can be avoided. You get to adapt to the strategy that can work at that time. The constant changes will need a person who is open to change. Be willing to adapt to the changes that occur. Adopting this will enable you to maintain huge profits, minimize risks, and reduce losses.

Swing Trading

7-Day Crash Course For Beginners For A Living With Proper Money Management, Psychology, Secrets And Proven Strategies To Trade With Options, Stocks And Forex

ROBERT ZONE

Introduction

Swing trading enables you to take advantage of changes in stock prices, also known as swings to make profit. The strategy presents you with numerous benefits that are missing in both day trading as well as buy and hold investment strategies. You can make profit from both the upward and downward changes in stock prices.

As a swing trader, you can trade several instruments including stocks, options, futures and currencies. This book discusses numerous components of swing trading and teaches you how to swing trade the numerous financial instruments mentioned above. It defines the trading style and outline the basics involved in the trade. It also highlights the advantages and disadvantages of swing trading different types of stocks and options.

The book also provides you information on the tools and platforms necessary for swing trading and highlights the strategies beginners as well as professional traders can employ to succeed in the trade.

As you scan through the book, you will get to understand how to determine entry and exit points for each trade, as well as how to minimize the risks associated with the trade. The book covers all the latest topics associated with swing trading and lists some of the ways you can use to analyze the swing market for the best opportunities. If you read the whole of it, you will master every skill required to excel as a swing trader. Ideally this books is great addition to your library whether you are a new trader or an expert swing trader seeking to diversify your portfolio.

Swing trading represents an exciting opportunity for those who are interested in trading and going beyond the normal method of buying stock and holding it. And yet, many of those same people find the idea of day trading to be too extreme. We will begin the book with a discussion of the fundamentals of swing trading. We will introduce the concept, which is actually quite simple. We will discuss the advantages of swing trading and talk about risk management. We will also compare and contrast it with day trading.

Then we will talk about following a trend, which is one of the most lucrative ways to make money while swing trading. After this, we will introduce the main tools that are used by swing traders including technical indicators like Bollinger bands, and we will also discuss candlestick charts.

Then we will talk about using swing trading with the many different financial securities that are available today. This will include a discussion of swing trading stocks, which is where most people swing trade. We will also talk about using swing trading on the foreign exchange markets, swing trading with the exchange-traded funds, and will also discuss options and crypto. We will close out the book with a discussion of the psychology of swing trading in the best tools and platforms to use, including finding the right broker.

Chapter 1 Basics of Swing Trading

Before you get into swing trading, you want to ensure that it is the right trading strategy for you. You already know the basic definition of swing trading, so now it is time to discuss what makes it special.

Swing trading is a mix of other basic trading strategies. It isn't as fast-paced and stressful as scalping or day trading, but it also isn't as slow as position trading. Swing trading is perfect for anyone who wants to turn to the stock market for their career but wants to see larger profits and stay active throughout the day.

If you are comfortable with overnight risk, swing trading might be right for you. The reason why holding stocks overnight is risky is because you never know what they are going to do during the 12 or so hours you are away from your desk. The price of stocks can fall quickly, which means you can have a good standing with the stock when you close out at 4:00 P.M. on Tuesday. However, at 8:30 A.M. on Wednesday morning, you can find out the price of your stock fell due to shocking news about the company and now you have lost money. Of course, this risk increases when you hold stocks over the weekend.

Swing trading is unique because you are able to take time to research the history of the stock, which means you will look at its daily and weekly charts in order to find a pattern. This pattern will tell you when the best time to buy and sell your stock will be. You also have time to go through the news and get an idea of how the stock market is doing every day. You can spend time looking at various stocks to see which ones are the best for you. When trading strategies move faster than swing trading, you aren't able to spend as much time on these factors.

Swing traders have a variety of options for trading. While many people focus on individual stocks, you can also purchase a basket of stocks. This is a large group of shares, such as 100, that you buy for one price. Each share comes from a different company. You can also trade cryptocurrencies such as bitcoin.

Various Financial Instruments

While most people think of stocks when they are looking into trading, there are other financial instruments that you can focus on. Even if you use these instruments in a different market, such as Forex, you can still be a swing trader. Hence, you want to ensure that you understand what financial instrument you want to trade before you take your first step into trading.

Stocks

When discussing the stock market, this book focuses on stocks. In fact, you have already learned a lot of information about the stock market. Because of this, I won't spend a lot of time discussing stocks as a financial instrument.

Exchange-Traded Funds (ETFs)

ETFs are becoming increasingly popular and known as a basket of stocks, bonds, or other securities. People often make ETFs by combining various stocks from the market. This is helpful for several reasons. First, it gives you dozens of companies, sometimes in the hundreds, with one purchase. Because the stocks are smaller than individual stocks you would purchase, ETFs are a decent price.

Second, they are known to help limit risk. This happens because the securities in the ETFs will often balance each other out. For example, if you have a blue-chip stock, it will balance out any stocks that are performing poorly.

Third, ETFs can help people who can't watch the news as often as they would like to. This might be because they only trade part-time and don't have the ability to pay close attention to the stock market. While you will still want to do your thorough research just the same as any other stock, if one of your stocks receives bad news, you don't have to hurry to sell it. Instead, one of the other higher-performing stocks will help balance out your ETF.

Fourth, ETFs can automatically help with diversification. This is when you have a variety of companies and securities in your portfolio. It can help increase your knowledge of the market and often gives you a stronger look as a trader. The trick is you need to find the right level of diversification when using individual financial instruments as too many can be harmful to your portfolio. This is why ETFs are so helpful. They are not individual as they include dozens of instruments in one location.

Cryptocurrencies

This is a newer form of a financial instrument and one that is quickly growing. They are similar to currencies but are often called coins. Further, there are a variety of coins. One of the newer cryptocurrencies that is about to make an appearance is known as Libra. This is Facebook's upcoming coin that is meant to be global. Other coins that are currently popular and can be traded on the market are Bitcoin and Ethereum.

Many experienced traders say beginners should not start with cryptocurrencies because of the high risk they have. The main reasons for this are because they can be easily hacked and often receive negative press.

Currencies

Currencies are a different type of financial instrument because they have to be traded in pairs. They are bought and sold in the forex market and are typically matched a certain way. For example, you will pair the American dollar with the Euro or the Canadian dollar with the Euro. Like cryptocurrencies, experienced traders stated that beginners should not start out with currencies. They can be tougher to understand and carry a larger risk than stocks. However, they are easier to trade than cryptocurrencies.

Options

When you use options to trade, you come to an agreement with another party. This agreement tells you when the financial instrument can be bought and sold. In order to take part in options trading, you need to have these requirements.

1. You need to include an expiration date in your agreement.
2. You can walk away from your agreement at any time.

3. You need to follow the process of the strike price, which is when the owner of the financial instrument agrees to the price you set.

4. You need all the basic information on your financial instrument. This means that you don't decide on a company to trade in without doing your research and analyzing any charts.

Futures

Experienced traders feel that futures exchanges are the best way to get yourself started in the market. Like options, futures are an agreement of when a stock can be bought and sold. Sometimes there is no expiration date with futures; however, people typically include this because the stock cannot be traded until the agreed-upon price is reached. For instance, if the two parties state the stock will be traded once it reaches $450, then nothing can happen until the stock hits this price. This means you have no real idea when you will be able to buy or sell that stock.

One benefit of futures exchanges is that you are able to get real-time training in the stock market without having to spend too much time on various stocks. Instead, you can get an idea of how to analyze charts, research the history of companies you are interested in, and simply observe how the market runs. The whole time, you are still trading in the market because you have already set up an agreement.

Swing Futures Trading Tips For Beginners

There are dozens of tips that beginners can use to give them the best trading experience from the start. Here are some of the most popular tips to remember.

Research and Learn Every day

Before you start researching, it is essential that you read everything you can about swing trading. You will want to completely understand what swing trading is, it's benefits, risks, the best stocks to trade, and everything else involved in the process. Take your time researching to ensure you understand everything you are reading. Keep thorough notes and make sure they are close to you when you start trading. As you continue to learn, write down any valuable information in your notebook.

When it comes to your daily research, you will want to pay close attention to the historical charts for the stocks you are interested in. You will analyze the daily and weekly charts, so you can put together your trading plan for that stock. This plan will tell you when the best time to purchase the stock will be, depending on the stock's trends. You will also write down the best time to sell and your escape plan. An escape plan is when you set the lowest price you will hold the stock at. Once it reaches this price, you will sell the stock immediately. It doesn't matter if you haven't reached the highest point you thought the stock would reach during your analysis. In order to keep yourself from a greater capital loss, you follow your plan to sell the stock.

Treat Swing Trading Like a Career

Whether you are swing trading full or part-time, you want to treat it like you would any other job. You want to take it seriously. This means you will set up your schedule, limit distractions, and strengthen your self-discipline. You will want to follow all the rules and guidelines, including the ones you establish yourself, to the best of your abilities. Once you are able to do this, you are ready for a successful swing trading career.

Keep Your Emotions Out of Your Trades

One of the biggest steps you want to take when you start trading is to keep your emotions in check. If you need to find strategies that will allow you to control your emotions, such as meditation or deep breathing, you will want to practice these daily. You never want to make a trade because you let your emotions take control. When this happens, you are more likely to make a mistake which can cause you a lot of money.

Set Your Daily Schedule

Note the times of the stock market and make sure you are sitting in front of your computer during those times. This means you will want to start your day at least an hour before the stock market opens. You need to allow yourself time to read up on any news and get an idea of where your stocks and the stock market sits. The busiest time for trading is between 9:30 to around 11:00 A.M. and 2:00 to 3:30 P.M. Eastern time. However, you want to be cautious of making any trades before 10:00 A.M. Eastern time. This is because people are often trading their stocks between 9:30 and 10:00 A.M. because of the news they read about the stock's company. The first half-hour is a very chaotic time for the stock market, which can be very confusing for beginners. Therefore, it is best to wait to make any trades until the stock market has started to calm down but is still busy. Usually between

11:00 A.M. and 2:00 P.M. Eastern time is when people are taking lunch or spending their time researching and learning.

Once the stock market closes, you will want to take time to save any charts from the stocks you bought and sold. You will also want to make notes about your day in your journal. The notes you make can include how you were feeling and what your environmental conditions were as you purchased or traded a stock.

Don't Forget About Continuing Your Education
Sometimes one of the best ways to research is through educational courses that are available through swing trading websites. For example, "Guide to Stock Trading with Candlestick and Technical Analysis" is an online class that will help you learn how to analyze candlestick charts with technical analysis. This course is created for beginners and is only about $60 to take. There are other courses for both beginners and expert swing traders that you can consider taking as a part of your trading day.

Join an Online Community
Other than a broker, you will want to find someone who can help you learn the processes of swing trading. There are dozens of online communities such as The Trading Heroes Blog and Elite Swing Trading. Once you sign up for an account—sometimes you do have to pay—you will be able to connect with thousands of traders that will be happy to answer your questions or help you achieve your next step. Many of these community forums also keep everyone up-to-date on the news that can affect your stocks.

Keep Yourself in the Right Mindset
To reach your dreams of becoming a successful swing trader, you need to stay focused and stay in the right mindset. The basis of this mindset is having confidence in your abilities as a swing trader. You want to imagine yourself reaching your goals, whether this is building toward your retirement account or living comfortably as a swing trader.

Another part of this mindset is to have patience. It will take time to learn the stock market and be able to live off of your trades. Moreover, you need to have patience when it comes to the right moment. You don't want to purchase the stock or sell it before the exact moment in your trading plan.

By remaining flexible, you will be able to keep yourself in the right mindset. You want to understand that not everything is in your control. Focus on what is in your control, such as your actions. If something isn't in your control, accept it and move on.

You also want to keep your expectations realistic. Swing trading is not a career that will make you rich overnight. It will take time and energy to reach your desired success.

Mistakes Are Going to Happen
Part of being realistic is knowing that you will make mistakes. It doesn't matter how many years of experience you have as a swing trader, mistakes are going to happen. You can spend two weeks analyzing the charts for a promising stock, buy the stock, and then lose some of your capital because of a small mistake you made. Sometimes this happens because the stock market is unpredictable and no matter how

well you research, you can't predict the future. When you do realize you made a mistake, learn from it and move on. If you worry about your past mistakes, you are going to affect your future trades. You will find yourself lacking the self-confidence you need to stay successful. Don't allow your mindset to decline because of a mistake.

Chapter 2 How Swing Trading Works?

What Swing Trading

Swing trading is a type of forex trading that endeavors to profit on a stock or any budgetary instrument over a time of a couple of days to half a month. Swing brokers fundamentally utilize specialized investigation to search for foreign currency trading openings. These merchants may use basic investigation notwithstanding examining value patterns and examples.

Swing trading is a short term trading style that involves you taking a position in the financial markets and staying with it for a number of days, perhaps weeks.

Swing trading is different from other types of trading such as position trading, day trading, high frequency trading or scalping mainly because of the period of time that a trade is held.

On one hand, some trading styles such as position trading allow you to take a position and then hold it for a longer period of time such as a couple of months or even years. On the other hand, a style such as scalping can involve holding a position for a few minutes, perhaps even seconds.

Therefore, a good way to think about swing trading is, a style that strikes a balance between both sides, offering more flexibility.

As a swing trader, you are mainly looking to profit from short term price changes or what is known as price swings in the markets. These opportunities are typically determined by technical analysis.

Swing trading vs. Day trading

Day trading is a completely different trading style. And the difference between the two comes down to the length of time that positions are held.

Day trading is a trading style in which you execute a number of positions in a day, but at the end of the day, you close all of them out. So, you may open a number of trades, say 10 of them in a day, but at the end of the day, you are flat.

Swing trading is regarded as more of a part time activity. In swing trading, you will be typically looking at longer time frames such as 3 hours, 4 hours, daily or weekly to spot swing trading opportunities. Therefore, this type of trading can be adopted by people who are or already employed in a different job.

Day traders have the distinct advantage to take note of the price volatility that might be seen during a trading day. The volatility of prices on a daily basis is generally affected by big sellers or big buyers and has relatively less to do with the fundamentals of the company.

On the other hand, even though swing traders also use the help of technical indicators, the fundamental factors affecting the price of the security plays a very important role in the decision process for a swing trader. Swing traders look at particular chart patterns and use confirmation signals given by certain indicators to understand whether or not to enter or exit a particular trade. Swing traders as compared to day traders are not interested in the volatility in a stock price but are more bothered in understanding the underlying trend or the overall trend of the security.

Swing exchanging and day exchanging may appear comparative practices, however the real contrasts between the two have a typical topic: time.

Swing trading allows you take a more laid back approach. You can place a trade and walk away from your computer and not have to worry about it until may be the next day. So if your goal is to seek a source of income that is more passive, then swing trading is the way to go. It is also good for you if you are a person of mild temperament who doesn't like lots of action.

Truth be told, none of these trading styles is better than the other. It is just a matter of picking the trading style that fits you as a person and your current situation in life. You may want to consider the following before you make a decision:

• The amount of time that you can set aside for trading: If you are a busy person, you may want to consider swing trading.

• The amount of money that you have: Day trading may require that you start out with a lot of money since you will end up being dependent on it for your means of livelihood.

• Your personality: If you are more of a person who likes to take things nice and slow, you may want to stay away from day trading and opt for swing trading instead.

• Risk tolerance: Day trading is for you if you can withstand watching several trades going against you and still maintain your calmness. Swing trading is better if you are more of the calculating type who can only stand taking a loss once in a while.

Difference Between Swing Trading and Day Trading

The first question that you may have is how swing trading and day trading are different from each other. They both try and go after some of the trends that are going on in the market, and they are both short-term trades that you can work with.

The biggest difference that you will find with day trading and swing trading is how long you will hold your position. With day trading, you will purchase and sell the stock all on the same day before the market closes. With swing trading, you need to hold onto the stock at least overnight, if not up to a few weeks, depending on how the trend is going and how much you would like to make.

This can add in a little more risk and unpredictability to your trade. It is hard to know what gaps or up and down movements will happen in your position overnight, which is why most swing traders will be done using smaller position sizes than they would with day trading.

You get some choice in how long you would like to hold onto your position, which can reduce the risk a little bit. But it is always a good idea to have an idea of how long you will stay in the market ahead of joining.

As a swing trader, you will be responsible for looking at chart patterns over many days. Some of the most common patterns that you will find include triangles, flags, head and shoulders patterns, cup and handle patterns, and even moving average crossovers. You can also find reversal candlesticks, like hammers and shooting stars will help you to figure out the best time to join the market and make the biggest profit possible.

Swing trading has more risk than some of the longer-term options that you may choose to go with. With the long-term investments, you will find that you have the time and the relaxation to not worry about the big ups and downs in the market as much. Your account will end up evening out if you stay on the market long enough.

But with swing trading, this is not always going to work. You are only going to be in the market for up to a few weeks at the most. This means that if a trend does not go your way, you will lose out on money. You must do your research diligently before starting and make sure that you can accurately read the market. You only get a few weeks, which is more than what a day trader will get to work with, but adds in more risk, especially when you are working in an overnight position.

You have the choice of many investments, but if you would like to earn a lot of money within a week or less, then swing trading may be the option that you are looking for. Let's take a look at some of the strategies that you can use when it comes to swinging trading to ensure you are getting the best results possible.

Swing traders need to always remember that the opening of a stock might actually be remarkably different from how it closed the previous day. Swing traders often encounter issues with the wide spread between the ask and bid and the commissions which could take a great portion of their profits, however, this problem is much serious for day traders.

Also, unlike day traders that experience serious time commitment when trading since they need to pay attention to all open positions, swing traders may have few transactions in some days while they may not trade at all on other days. When you're a swing trader, you can check your positions periodically or they can be attended to with alerts especially when the price hits critical points. This is much better than monitoring the market constantly which could lead to apprehension and emotional trading.

Swing Trading vs. Position Trading

There is another type of stock trader who is commonly referred to as a position trader. Position traders are usually large institutions such as mutual funds, but individuals can be position traders as well. Position traders make investments in a company's stock for the long run. They may feel that a particular company or sector is undervalued and they are willing to take a position in the hope that eventually things will turn around and the market will value their company in line with where they see it going in the future.

Warren Buffett would be a good example of a position trader. He invests for the long term and takes positions in companies he considers to be undervalued, either because of market conditions or because he expects the companies' fundamentals to improve in the future.

Market Participants: Retail vs. Institutional Traders

More and more people are striking out on their own and doing their own self-directed investing. The

Internet, with its plethora of information and tools, has primarily driven this trend, along with the opportunity to trade online without the use of a professional broker. Many investors have discovered that with a little work they can match or better the performance of many of the mutual fund managers, especially when taking into account the at times exorbitant management fees being charged by these money managers.

Individual Retail traders do have some advantages over Institutional traders. These Institutional traders are motivated to trade often and in large volumes. In comparison, Retail traders can wait for a good setup and trade when they see a good risk to reward opportunity. Institutional traders also have large accounts and cannot move their money in and out of a position as readily as a Retail trader. An Institutional trader is not going to take a 1,000 share position in the stock of a small company that trades 250,000 shares in a day. It is just too small for them to bother.

Ironically, large numbers of individual Retail traders will not use this advantage to their benefit and for various reasons they will instead overtrade. They succumb to greed and fear and that causes them to trade unwisely. Instead of being patient and exercising the self-discipline of winners, they become losers by overtrading. Retail traders who want to be successful in trading with the professionals must be patient. They must also recognize and manage the psychology of fear and greed and how it affects a trader's actions.

As a Retail trader, you can also play stocks that other Retail investors are playing. Checking in on social media sites like StockTwits and Twitter will give you a good sense of where Retail investors are investing their money, however, do not get caught up in the specifics of all of the posts. There are lots of twits on StockTwits making wild predictions and touting how they just made $7,000.00 on a trade in XYZ Company. Take everything you read with a large grain of salt.

Benefits of Swing Trading

Swing trading has less risk: When compared to working with day trading, you will find that swing trading has less risk. This is because you get more time to work in the market. It is often hard to estimate how a stock will do throughout a single day.

You can swing trade along with other trades

Many traders will choose to work on swing trading along with day trading all at the same time. During the market hours, they will focus most of their energy on their day trading position.

Overnight trading can be an advantage

Some traders believe that trading overnight will harm them. They are worried about some of the trends that could happen to their stock while they are asleep.

More time to look at the market

Day trading has to be done really quickly. You don't get a lot of time to watch the markets, and you may need to make split-second decisions to get results. With swing trading, you can analyze the market over time, and you have more time to make your trading decisions. This takes away some of the pressure of your trades, and it is easier to earn money in this manner without all the stress.

Potential to reach the trades better

Compared to working with day trading, you are more likely to reach the trades that you would like with swing trading. You will be able to watch the market, predict how the trades will do over a few days or a few weeks, rather than a few hours, and make more money.

More daily freedom

If you are a day trader, you have to spend all day watching your trades. Little changes up or down in the market will make a big difference in day trading, and this can be really stressful if you are getting started. Many of the people who decide to go with swing trading tried out day trading in the past but didn't like all the stress that went with it and didn't like having to stare at their computer screens all day long. Swing trading can provide you with a similar profit without all the hassle.

Generating consistent income

Long term investors are more bothered with wealth creation or wealth preservation. They are not bothered about generating consistent monthly income. On the other hand successful swing traders can easily generate consistent income for themselves on a monthly basis.

Holding different securities to diversify your risk

High-Frequency Trades

There are a number of investment banks, funds and other companies that base their trading on sophisticated computer algorithms. They trade frequently and at lightning speed. To illustrate how important speed is to these firms, some have located close to the exchanges while others install dedicated fiber optic cables to gain a tiny fraction of a microsecond execution on a trade. These types of trades are referred to as High-Frequency Trades (HFT) due to how often they happen during a normal trading day.

How to Start Trading

Choosing to Buy Long or Sell Short

When you are setting up an account to trade, you will probably need to take the time to fill out some additional forms with the broker so that you can take this short position with a stock. You should also have an idea that this option can be riskier compared to just going long or purchasing a stock, so you must be actively there to manage the position.

When the stock starts to move down, shareholders are going to fear that they will have to lose their profits or gains, and they move to sell that quickly. This selling activity is going to feed into more selling as shareholders continue to take the profits and traders start to shorten. This additional shorting activity adds to the downward pressure that is there on the price. This sends the price of the stock into a strong decline, which means that short sellers are able to make a good amount of profits while long traders and other investors are going to enter panic mode and may try to dump their shares to protect themselves.

As a swing trader, when you are ready to enter into a position, you are going to have two choices. You can either go in or pay the price that the seller is asking for right away or you can place a bid that is at or below the bid price. Paying the asking price immediately can be beneficial because it ensures that the purchase transaction is completed or filled but may mean that you will pay more for it.

Picking out a Broker

During this process, we also need to take some time to discuss picking out a broker. If you have already gotten into other forms of trading in the past, then you can simply work with the same broker that you already have. But, if you are getting into trading and this is the first one you have done before, then you will need to search to find the right broker for you.

There are many different brokers out there, and many of them can assist you with swing trading. The biggest thing that you will want to look at is the commissions and fees that each broker assesses against you. Since swing trading times are relatively short and you will enter into and out of trades within a few weeks at most with each trade, you want to make sure that the profits you make aren't eaten up by the commissions to your broker.

There are different methods that the broker can use to come up with their fees. Some will charge a fixed rate for the whole year. This often works well for long-term trades and probably won't be an option available to you since you will do more trades. The two options that you will most likely deal with include a fee for each trade or a fee based on how much profit you earn.

Before you enter into any trade, make sure that you discuss the fees with your broker. They should be able to outline their fees and can discuss with you where your money will go when you work with them. This can help you to get a good idea of how much you will spend based on how much you earn, how many trades you decide to enter into, and more. Get the commissions and fees in writing, along with any other agreements that you and the broker and their firm agree to in order to protect you.

Make sure that your broker is regulated by the government. This is the first and most important aspect that you should always look for before anything. Never skip this one.

Ensure that they have quality customer service. Nobody deserves your money or your business if they have poor customer service; at least not in this competitive world.

Bad customer service is a symptom of a much worse problem. If they can't take care of how they handle you as a client, how are they supposed to do better when it comes to your money? You are much better shopping around for someone else who is more competent.

Trading is a tough business in which the risk of losing your money very fast is real. Therefore, managing risk is of utmost importance. If your broker is charging you heavy commissions on your trades, this raises your risk and you will likely be out of business in no time.

Website and account security. In this day and age of web hackers, your broker has to invest heavily in their security. Matters dealing with finance cannot be left to chance, and your broker has to show that they respect this. Remember, you will be trusting your broker to process financial transactions using your debit or credit card, among other things.

Quality trading tools. A high quality trading platform that packages all high quality indicators can really make for a smooth experience in trading.

Picking out How Much You Want to Invest

It is best to start out by putting in an amount that you are comfortable losing. No one hopes to lose money on any of their trades. But, it does happen, especially when you are a beginner. Putting in just the amount that you would be willing to lose if something goes wrong can help to reduce the amount of risk that you are taking on.

Getting started with swing trading can be exciting. This is a fun type of trading that moves quickly and can help you to earn a good profit in a short amount of time but still doesn't require you to spend all day on the computer watching how the trade is going.

Buying Long or Selling Short

As a trader, you need to learn more about long and short buying and selling. Trades usually commence via purchase first or selling first. To define the terms appropriately, we need to learn about the meaning and implication of each.

Long position: When you assume a long position on a stock, the implication here is that you own the security and it belongs to you. There is no debt on it. Therefore, when a trader buys an asset, he has taken a long position on the asset. In this instance, he hopes that the asset price will appreciate so that he can sell it at a higher price.

Short position: We also have a short position where a trader actually sells stocks that he or she does not own. These are stocks or financial instruments that belong to another. Selling short simply means selling in the hope of making money from the sale in order to repay the owner and make a profit in the process.

Short sales occur when a trader is trading the markets, sees an opportunity but lacks the funds or means to execute the trade. Many experienced traders come across opportunities they believe are profitable. In such instances, they get into an agreement with their broker to access stocks they do not own.

Day traders are often associated with short sales. They often sell stocks then purchase them hoping to benefit from the price difference. They sell stocks that they do not own at a high price and then buy back the same stocks when the price falls. While this can be profitable, it is a risky venture that should only be practiced by seasoned traders.

Short sales by traders are often settled by delivery of the "borrowed" security back to the real owner. Most stocks that are sold short often belong to investors but are held by brokers. As a trader, if you wish to short sell, then you first need to identify an opportunity in the market. You will then need to access the stock so that you can sell it without owning it. This is of course after your market analysis shows some profit potential.

Others who also engage in short selling are market makers. Market makers are also known as liquidity providers. They do this in order to mitigate the risk of a long position on the same stock or in response to unexpected demand. Market makers hope to benefit financially from a bid-offer spread.

Traders who engage in short selling can borrow stocks from brokerage firms. Brokerage firms often have an inventory of stocks lying around. Some of these belong to the brokerage while others belong to other long-term investors. It is important to note that even as you gain access to stocks that you do now own, there are certain rules and conditions attached. These include fees and other charges as well as rules. For instance, you can expect to be charged a certain fee for the privilege. You will also be required to pay any dividend due to the stock's owner while the stocks are under your control.

Short selling is an important tool for a swing trader because stock prices usually drop much more quickly than they go up. It is a commonly held rule of thumb that stocks fall 3 times faster than they rise.

Shorting stocks as a legitimate trading activity is still hotly debated today. Some feel that short sellers unnecessarily punish investors by causing stocks to drop faster and in larger moves than otherwise would have occurred. In addition, short sellers can use social media and other methods to spread inaccurate information to cause a stock price to drop.

In order to start short selling, you will open a margin account through your broker. This account will use your profits in your account as collateral, just as a car is used as collateral for a vehicle loan. This means that if you are unable to repay your broker back in any way, your broker still receives the money as he or she can take it right out of your account.

The biggest risk is that you can never really tell the future. No matter how much you analyze charts or the general stock market conditions, such as if it's a bull or bear market, you will never be able to officially tell what a stock or the market is going to do.

While short selling occurs in a way that is meant to protect the trader's account, you also want to make sure that you understand that you can still bring yourself into debt if the process doesn't work as well as it should. You will also want to make sure that you go through the same trading plan, research, and following all your rules and guidelines before you decide to short sell.

How to Enter a Trade?

These spreads in the bid and ask can vary for each stock and even for the same stock at different times of the day. If the stock does not have a lot of buyers and sellers, then the spread could be quite large (up to $0.50 or more per share). If there are lots of buyers and sellers, then the spread between the bid and ask could be as low as $0.01 per share.

When a swing trader wants to enter a position, they have 2 choices. They can pay what the seller is asking immediately or they can place a bid at or below the current bid price. Paying the ask immediately ensures that the order is filled (filled means the purchase transaction is completed). When a trader places a bid at or below the current bid price, they may get a purchase at a lower price. The disadvantage of this purchase option is that the trader may not get their order filled. For example, if a trader puts in a bid to buy an up trending stock, the bid may never get filled, leaving the trader without an entry in a profitable trade.

Investment and Margin Accounts

Investing on margin means that you are borrowing funds, in order to make deals. This also is called leveraging. Investments may be leveraged at a given ratio. For example, if the leverage on an investment is 2:1, it means that, for every physical dollar on the deal, there are two which are debt.

Investing on margin can be an amazing, tool as it acts as a multiplier. However, this strategy can backfire when the price of the asset does not go up, and the investor gets a "margin call", that is, they have to pay up. If the investor does not have the money to pay up, then they may be deemed as insolvent. This may lead the investor to be kicked out. In the case of large financial institutions, insolvency is a huge deal and may lead to the bankruptcy of entire financial institutions.

So, the moral of the story is to always have enough cash or highly-liquid assets, such as bonds, which can be liquidated fairly quickly in the case of a margin call.

Margin Trading Account

The margin trading account keeps a line of credit to your firm with helping you buy the stocks through the brokerage firm which also keeps the securities under consideration if you want to. There are numerous options to open the account with the margin accounts. You can opt out the possibility of buying the right purchase without listing out any price of a specific stock in the market. You have to consider, and without any complications, you will have the account with you to get into the stock market.

Understanding Margin

When you get the margin, it means that the brokerage offers your o have the trading account. You have to remember that the purchase of the credit is needed with the new stocks in there. In this case, you borrow the money from someone to have the investors over the trades. It also saves the interested when you are holding the position with keeping it overnight with the interest rate which is over the course. You have to follow the dependency over the time with the slight usage of 2% and how it helps in improving the right side of the margin with allowing it to be the right profit for you which you could use for putting it in the market with the market all along.

Requirements to open an account

There are some of the policies and procedures which everyone has to follow when it comes to opening the trading account. You have to provide the information and also help yourself to get familiar with it as soon as you can. The rule of the brokerage firms inquires your personal information such as your name, address, email address, SSN, date of birth, place of employment, tax bracket and much more. You may be hesitant at first with giving out such information, but that is required for you to fulfill the policies to get the trading account on your name. They require you to show the history of your work experience in some cases when there is a need for an inquiry. There are many questions which you have to, so you have to be patient through the process. It is always about the right move which you make to understand what the deal is going on another side. There are many other things which the brokerage firms will be asking from you, so you have to keep the items clear and be answerable to them. It will be about the registration and how you developed the interest in getting the account.

Chapter 3 Platforms And Tools For Trading

To be a successful trader, you will need access to reliable resources. The good news is that there are plenty of excellent resources all across the web. These resources include educational materials, online brokers, real-time securities markets data, and super-fast computer networks.

Sometimes you may not have access to all the resources necessary and you may have to choose between what is essential and what you can afford. A little research goes a long way in helping you make crucial decisions about your trades. It is advisable to know more about the kind of resources available to you. These resources are ideal for swing traders.

Swing Trading Tools

Traders are always searching for the best trading systems and ways they can develop these systems to suit their trading styles. Fortunately, there is a process that any trader can use in order to discover their preferred trading mode and system.

Identifying Best Strategies for Profitability

There are plenty of small but crucial things you can do as a swing trader to improve your success. For instance, you could begin by identifying the location of the swing low and swing high positions on a particular chart. If you are able to note the swings accurately, then you will be able to place accurate trades which will increase your profitability greatly.

Swing Highs and Swing Lows

Swing highs and swing lows are also referred to as SHSL. This refers to the price action where multiple bars and candlesticks are joined together so that they are viewed as a single move in a given direction. The movement is generally known as a leg. Sometimes it is also known as swing or a move. This is where the term swing originates from.

The swing represents a single part of the price action in a particular direction. This swing is always closely countered by a swing in the opposite direction. Sometimes this movement is sideways rather than back and forth. As it is, price moves back and forth in the market. In other words, it swings back and forth and hence the term swing. The highest point of a swing is the swing high while the lowest point is known as the swing low.

How to Identify Swings

The market is constantly in motion. A swing occurs when there are two consecutive lower highs and lower lows or when there are two consecutive higher lows and higher highs. Remember that swings appear in all manner of shapes and sizes. However, the rule on how to identify them is very simple. Simply look for consecutive higher highs and higher lows or consecutive lower highs and lower lows.

Swings are bullish if the general movement is upwards and bearish if the general movement is downwards. Sometimes a new low will appear when the trend is upwards. At other times a new high will appear when the general trend is headed downwards. When this happens, you should not be worried or concerned as these are considered false swings. Unless there are consecutive highs or lows, then ignore everything else.

Use Swings to Increase Profitability

We have learned how to identify swings in the market. Now we need to apply this knowledge in order to be profitable. The first step is to place your stop-loss points. This should be slightly above the higher high for a bearish situation and below the lowest low in a bullish situation.

Also, the correct and accurate swing highs and swing lows provide an opportunity to draw Fibonacci extensions. These lines will enable you to identify target areas of high probability. As such, it becomes possible to place our take profit and stop-loss points on our charts. Remember Livermore? The gentleman said to be one of the most successful traders ever? Back in 19 29, he managed to make about $100 million. In today's terms, this is equivalent to almost $1.4 billion. That is a lot of money even for an experienced trader.

If you learn about the best trading systems, then you too can make plenty of money in today's prevailing marketing rates. You could always trade with the market trend or against it. Remember that it is always advisable to follow the trend rather than the opposite. Only oppose the trend if you are an experienced swing trader and know exactly what you are doing. Key will be identifying the best entry points into a trade and the best places to collect profits as well as exit trades.

Before you begin your swing, trading ventures, ensure that you come up with a tested plan that you can implement. Therefore, test your preferred systems and strategies and ensure that they are working as desired. This way, you will be able to prepare appropriately and trade successfully and profitably over time.

Swing traders are always searching for conditions in the markets where stock prices are looking to swing either downwards or possibly upwards. There are numerous technical indicators that are available to enhance your trades. Indicators used in swing trading are basically essential in identifying trends in the market between certain trading periods.

These trading periods that range anywhere from 3 to 15 are then analyzed using our technical indicators in order to determine the presence or otherwise of resistance and support levels. If these have actually materialized and are clearly visible, then we can proceed to make other determinations.

At this stage, you will also need to determine whether any trend is bullish or bearish. You will also need to be on the lookout for a reversal because without one you will not be able to enter a trade. Reversals are also referred to as countertrends or pullbacks. As soon as we can clearly point out the reversal, then we can easily identify the appropriate entry point.

The entry point should be the point where the pullback is just about to come to an end and the trend is about to pick up again. Being able to determine these points is really crucial. This same approach is the very same one used by Jesse Livermore to earn his wealth.

Benefits

Swing trading offers some of the best risks to reward opportunities compared to other trading strategies. This means that for a smaller amount, you will stand to win a much larger profit. Trading is a risky venture but swing trading has a better payoff compared to others. As such, you stand to make more money at reduced risks compared to traders using different trading styles like day traders or position traders.

Another benefit is that a lot of intraday noise will be eliminated using this approach. Smart money traders are always on the lookout for big swings and this is what you will also be doing. This approach is less stressful and potentially more profitable compared to other strategies.

You will also have a lot of time in your hands compared to other traders. Day traders and others often spend hours each day glued to their screens. Their days are not just spent staring at the screen but their stress levels are extremely high. Constant stress will result in fast burn-out and emotional trading which are not good for long-term successful trading.

Best Indicators for Swing Traders

There are plenty of indicators that traders and investors use to enhance their trades. We shall review just a few of these and discover the best way of applying them to our trades in order to maximize profitability. It is crucial to understand that none of these indicators will make you profitable from the onset. Therefore, do not break your back trying to find the best or most profitable trade indicators. Instead, focus more on learning about a couple of extremely effective indicators as well as the strategies and methods used alongside them. Experts believe that trading strategies are more profitable when you apply the few indicators that you have mastered.

1. Moving Averages

Moving averages are among the most important trade indicators used by swing traders. They are defined as lines drawn across a chart and are determined based on previous prices. Moving averages are really simple to understand yet they are absolutely useful when it comes to trading the markets. They are extremely useful to all kinds of traders include swing traders, day, intra, and long-term investors.

You need to ensure that you have a number of moving averages plotted across your trading charts all with different time periods. For instance, you can have the 100-day moving average, the 50-day, and the 9-day MA. This way, you will obtain a much broader overview of the market and be able to identify much stronger reversals and trends.

How to use Moving Averages

Once you have plotted and drawn the moving averages on your charts, you can then use them for a number of purposes. The first is to identify the strength of a trend. Basically, what you need to do is to observe the lines and gauge their distance from the current stock price.

A trend is considered weak if the trend and the current price are far from the relative MA. The farther they are then the weaker the trend is. This makes it easier for traders to note any possible reversals and also identify exit and entry points. You should move averages together with additional indicators, for instance, the volume.

Moving averages can also be used to identify trend reversals. When you plot multiple moving averages, they are bound to cross. If they do, then this implies a couple of things. For instance, crossing MA lines indicate a trend reversal. If these cross after an uptrend, then it means that the trend is about to change direction and a bearish one is about to appear.

However, some trend reversals are never real so you have to be careful before calling out one. Many traders are often caught off guard by these false reversals. Therefore, confirm them before trading using other tools and methods. Even then, the moving average is a very vital indicator. They enable traders to get a true feel and understanding of the markets.

2. RSI - Relative Strength Index

Another crucial indicator that is commonly used by swing traders and other traders are the RSI or relative strength index. This index is also an indicator that evaluates the strength of the price of a security that you may be interested in. The figure indicated is relative and provides traders with a picture of how the stock is performing relative to the markets. You will need information regarding volatility and past performance. All traders, regardless of their trading styles, need this useful indicator. Using this relative evaluation tool gives you a figure that lies between 1 and 100.

Tips on RSI Use

The relative strength index is ideally used for identifying divergence. Divergence is used by traders to note trend reversals. We can say that divergence is a disagreement or difference between two points. There are bearish and bullish divergent signals. Very large and fast movements in the markets sometimes produce false signals. This is why it advisable to always use indicators together with other tools.

You can also use the RSI to identify oversold and overbought conditions. It is crucial that you are able to identify these conditions as you trade because you will easily identify corrections and reversals. Sometimes securities are overbought at the markets when this situation occurs, it means that there is a possible trend reversal and usually the emerging trend is bearish. This is often a market correction. Basically, when a security is oversold, it signals a correction or bullish trend reversal but when it's overbought, it introduces a bearish trend reversal.

The theory aspect of this condition requires a ratio of 70:30. This translates to 70% overvalued or over purchased and 30% undervalued or oversold. However, in some cases, you might be safer going with an 80/20 ratio just to prevent false breakouts.

3. Volume

When trading, the volume is a crucial indicator and constitutes a major part of any trading strategy. As a trader, you want to always target stocks with high volumes as these are considered liquid. How many traders, especially new ones, often disregard volume and look at other indicators instead.

While volume is great for liquidity purposes, it is also desirable for trend. A good trend should be supported by volume. A large part of any stock's volume should constitute part of any trend for it to be a true and reliable trend.

Most of the time traders will observe a trend based on price action. You need to also be on the lookout for new money which means additional players and volume. If you note significant volumes contributing to a trend, then you can be confident about your analysis. Even when it comes to a downtrend, there should be sufficient volumes visible for it to be considered trustworthy. A lack of volume simply means the stock has either been undervalued or overvalued.

4. Bollinger Bands Indicator

One of the most important indicators that you will need is the Bollinger band indicator. It is a technical indicator that performs two crucial purposes. The first is to identify sections of the market that are overbought and oversold. The other purpose is to check the market's volatility.

This indicator consists of 3 distinct moving averages. There is a central one which is an SMA or simple moving average and then there two on each side of the SMA. These are also moving averages but are plotted on either side of the central SMA about 2 standard deviations away.

Accumulation and Distribution Line

Another indicator that is widely used by swing traders is the accumulation/distribution line. This indicator is generally used to track the money flow within security. The money that flows into and out of stock provides useful information for your analysis.

The accumulation/distribution indicator compares very well with another indicator, the OBV, or the on-balance volume indicator. The difference, in this case, is that it considers the trading range as well as the closing price of a stock. The OBV only considers the trading range for a given period.

When the security closes out close to its high, then the accumulation/distribution indicator will add weight to the stock value compared to closing out close to the mid-point. Depending on your needs and sometimes the calculations, you may want to also use the OBV indicator.

You can use this indicator to confirm an upward trend. For instance, when it is trending upwards, you will observe buying interest because the security will close at a point that is higher than the mid-range. However, when it closes at a point that is lower than the mid-range, then the volume is indicated as negative and this indicates a declining trend.

While using this indicator, you will also want to be on the lookout for divergence. When the accumulation/distribution begins to decline while the price is going up, then you should be careful because this signals a possible reversal. On the other hand, if the trend starts to ascend while the price is falling, then this probably indicates a possible price rise in the near future. It is advisable to ensure that your internet and other connections are extremely fast especially when using these indicators as time is of the essence.

The Average Directional Index, ADX

Another tool or indicator that is widely used by swing traders is the average directional index, the ADX. This indicator is basically a trend indicator and its purpose is largely to check the momentum and strength of a trend. A trend is believed to have directional strength if the ADX value is equal to or higher than 40. The directional could be upward or downward based on the general price direction. However, when the ADX value is below 20, then we can say that there is no trend or there is one but it is weak and unreliable.

You will notice the ADX line on your charts as it is mainline and is often black in color. There are other lines that can be shown additionally. These lines are DI- and DI+ and in most cases are green and red in color respectively. You can use all the three lines to track both the momentum and the trend direction.

Aroon Technical Indicator

Another useful indicator that you can use is the Aroon indicator. This is a technical indicator designed to check if financial security is trending. It also checks to find out whether the security's price is achieving new lows or new highs over a given period of time.

You can also use this technical indicator to discover the onset of a new trend. It features two distinct lines which are the Aroon down line and the Aroon up line. A trend is noted when the Aaron up line traverses across the Aaron down line. To confirm the trend, then the Aaron up line will get to the 100-point mark and stay there.

The reverse holds water as well. When the Aroon down line cuts below the Aaron up line, then we can presume a downward trend. To confirm this, we should note the line getting close to the 100-point mark and staying there.

This popular trading tool comes with a calculator which you can use to determine the number of things. If the trend is bullish or bearish, then the calculator will let you know. The formulas used to determine this refer to the most recent highs and lows. When the Aroon values are high, then recent values were used and when they are low, the values used were less recent. Typical Aroon values vary between o and 100. Figures that are close to 0 indicate a weak trend while those closer to 100 indicate a strong trend.

The bullish and bearish Aroon indicators can be converted into one oscillator. This is done by making the bearish one range from 0 to -100 while the bullish one ranges from 100 to 0. The combined indicator will then oscillate between 100 and -100. 100 will indicate a strong trend, 0 means there is no trend while -100 implies a negative or downward trend.

This trading tool is pretty easy to use. What you need to is first obtain the necessary figures then plot these on the relevant chart. When you then plot these figures on the chart, watch out for the two key levels. These are 30 and 70. Anything above the 70-point mark means the trend is solid while anything below 30 implies a weak trend.

Trading Platforms

Trading platforms are the actual platforms or software programs that enable traders to place their trades and monitor their accounts. An electronic trading platform is a computer program of a website with a user interface where traders place financial trades.

As a swing trader, you will use this platform to enter, close, exit, and manage positions. This is often done via an intermediary such as your broker. Most traders use online platforms which are overseen and offered by brokerage firms. Brokers charge a fee when you use their platforms but sometimes, they offer discounts to traders who make a certain number of trades each month or those with funded accounts.

Basic Swing Trading Platforms

Trading platforms provide traders with the opportunity to place trades and monitor their accounts. There is a variety of platforms available to swing traders. They come with a number of different features. These include premium research functions, a news feed, charting tools, and even real-time price quotes. These additional features and tools enhance a trader's performance and make it easier to execute trades faster and accurately. Most platforms available today are designed for different financial instruments like Forex, stocks, futures, and options.

We basically have two different types of platforms. These are commercial platforms and prop platforms. Commercial platforms are mostly used by traders such as swing traders, retail investors, and day traders. They are largely easy to use and come with a myriad of features such as charts and a news feed.

We also have prop platforms. These are platforms that are customized for specific users such as institutional investors and large brokerage firms. Apparently, their needs are much different compared to those of small traders and retail investors. The prop platforms are designed to take into consideration the different needs of these special clients.

As a swing trader, you will most likely be using commercial platforms provided by different brokerage firms. Even then, there are some things that you need to be on the lookout before choosing one. For instance, what are the included features? How about costs and fees charged? Also, different traders will require different tools on their platforms. There are certain tools that are suitable for day and swing traders while others are more suitable for options and futures traders.

When selecting a platform, always watch out for the fees charged. As a small-scale, retail swing trader, you want to trade on one that charges low and affordable fees. However, sometimes there are certain trade-offs. For instance, some platforms charge low fees but they lack certain crucial features or provide poor services. Others may seem expensive but provide crucial features including research tools and excellent services. So, you will need to consider all these factors before eventually selecting a suitable trading platform.

There is yet another crucial point to keep in mind when selecting a trading platform. Some platforms are available only through specific brokers or intermediaries. Other platforms are universal and work with different brokerage platforms and intermediaries across the board. Traders also select trading platforms based on their own personal styles and preferences.

You should find out if there are any particular requirements or conditions that require to be fulfilled. For Instance, some platforms require traders to maintain at least $25, oo0 in their trading accounts in the form of equity and possibly cash as well. In this instance, a trader may then receive approval for credit which is also known as margin.

Examples of Swing Trading Platforms

1. The Home Trading System

The home trading system is an algorithm and trading software designed to improve performance. Using this system, you can expect to make smarter, faster and better trading decisions. This particular platform comes with innovative features and a custom algorithm that combines seamlessly to provide a real-time fully integrated trading platform. You are bound to benefit from this platform and experience the benefits of seamless trading complete with all the features that you need.

The platform is completely compatible with some of the most dynamic and highly reliable charting tool. It is able to work with all kinds of markets from stocks to Forex and indices. The platform is compatible with a variety of bars such as range and momentum bars as well as tick charts.

The designers of this platform took great care to consider all the different kinds of traders. This is why this specific platform is suitable for day traders, swing traders, Forex traders, retail investors, and long-term traders. The Home Trading System constitutes a modular platform that consists of different core features. A lot of these features can easily be switched off and on depending on the situation or to suit a particular requirement.

One of the advantages of this platform is that it endeavors to make trading extremely simple. For instance, the algorithm automatically colors the candlesticks or bars a red or blue color in order to provide a clear view of the market conditions and trends. The system will continue following the trends and mark any major changes in a contrasting color. For instance, whenever there is a trigger bar, these will appear in a different color so that it is clear to you the trader that there is definite variation in the trend.

This color feature not only makes trading easy but also improves your trading psychology so that you can trade with very little worry. Other desirable parameters that are essential to your trades are also provided on the platform. For instance, you need accurate and reliable trading signals delivered at the right time. Fortunately, the Home Trading System is designed to provide these signals in a timely and accurate manner.

When there is a turning point in the momentum of stock in the markets, then this will be detected and a change of color will clearly indicate the turning point. You will be able to see a blue color with contrasting orange color pointing out areas of interest. The dots will indicate the entry points, exit points, collect profit points and so on. A stop point is also indicated just in case the trade does not work out as planned and you need to exit.

2. The Entry Zone Platform

We also have a swing trading platform known as the Entry Zone. This platform has been around for a while but has recently undergone a complete overhaul. It has received a new design to specifically address the needs of swing traders. There is no trader in the entire world who wants to join an over-extended market even when it features a large stop-loss point.

One of the main benefits of this specific platform is that it helps eliminate the challenge of entering an overly extended market. It starts by first checking for a pullback. It does this by accessing the 60-minute timeframe. This way, you will be protected from accessing the markets at the worst moment. The algorithm is able to proceed and track the markets so that you eventually get to find out the best market entry points.

3. Able Trend Trading Platform

This is another platform designed with swing traders in mind. One of its most outstanding features is its ability to instantly identify changes in the trend. Trend direction is first indicated by a distinct color. When the signal is headed upwards then the color is blue and when it heads downwards it changes color to red. If there is any sideways movement then the color changes once more to green.

This platform, therefore, makes it pretty easy to observe the market trend and keep abreast with it. Additional information will then enable you to make the necessary trade moves that you need to as a swing trader. For instance, you will notice red and blue dots on your screen. These indicate the various stop points. When there is a downward trend, then the red dots will indicate your sell points while blue dots will indicate your buy points on the upward trend. These stop points ensure that you partake of the large market movements but with very little risk or exposure.

The reasons why this system is so successful is that it comes with state of the art features. It generates dot and bar colors that you can choose for the different bar charts. These include the 5-minute, 1-minute, daily, tick, and weekly charts. Many traders have termed this platform as both robust and functional. It is a universal platform that can work with different trading systems.

You are able to make large profits if you are able to enter the markets and join the trend at an early stage. Identifying the trend is easy when you have this software. Remember that the trend is a friend of any swing trader. Therefore, spend some time at the beginning of your trades to identify the trend and then move on from here. Identifying the trend at an early stage is what you wish to do. The risks to you are minimal at this stage. This platform helps you identify the trend and provide you with additional crucial information that even large investors do not have.

You are able to operate on any market so that you are not limited to trading stocks only. If you wish to swing trade options, currencies, and other instruments, then you are free to do so. The platform is suitable for all trading styles including day trading, swing trading, and position trading, and so on.

4. Interactive Brokers

This is a popular platform that has been recently revamped. It is highly rated software because of the useful tools available to traders. Some of these tools are extremely useful to sophisticated or seasoned traders who need more than just the basics.

This platform is able to connect you to any and all exchanges across the world. For instance, you may want to trade markets in Hong Kong, Australia, and so on. The software is able to seamlessly connect you so that you have great trading experience.

This platform has seen the addition of new features which make trading even easier. These are, however, more suitable to seasoned traders who are more sophisticated than the average retail investor or small trader.

One of the attractive features of Interactive Brokers is that it is a very affordable platform to use. It is especially cost-friendly to small scale traders, retail investors, and the ordinary swing trader as the margin rates are low and affordable.

The platform supports trading across 120 markets located in at least 31 countries and deals in more than 23 different currencies. It also supports traders who execute trades pretty fast.

Trading and Data

As a trader, you will be making most of your decisions based on data. You, therefore, need to have access to reliable data such as stock prices and so on. Long term investors do not necessarily worry about accurate stock prices in the short term. However, for swing traders, it is essential to have access to the latest trading data.

The good news is that most online brokers provide traders with some form of data. All this data is mostly free. The platforms consistently receive data streams throughout. This data is crucial for most traders. Sometimes real-time data is not free and as a trader, you will need to determine which data you need and which type you will pay for. Always ensure that you have access to all the data you require during trading.

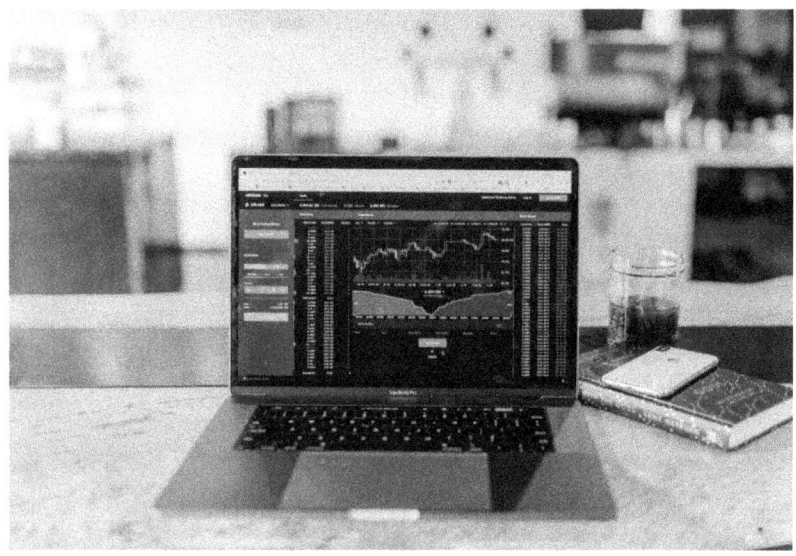

Chapter 4 Financial Instruments for Swing Trading

One of the most difficult parts of swing trading, especially for a beginner, is finding the best market for you. This includes what type of financial instruments you want to focus on when it comes to trading. There are a variety of financial instruments; such as ETFs, futures, options, currencies, cryptocurrencies, and stocks. As a beginner, it is important to try to find one financial instrument that you are comfortable with.

Stocks

Stock are probably the most common financial instrument that people think of when they start their trading career. In fact, most people probably believe that this is the financial instrument they will be trading. Part of this is because of the popularity. However, another part is because they really don't realize how many financial instruments there are when it comes to trading.

When people talk about stocks in the trading community, they will often refer to them as shares. There are several ways you can handle shares. At the same time, you want to make sure that you are focusing on stocks that are within your target companies. For example, you might want to focus on blue-chip stocks. Therefore, if you find a stock that isn't considered blue-chip, you will want to move on.

One of the biggest downsides to choosing stocks is that each stock you take on will carry its own individual risk. This means that no matter what type of negative news comes about the company for a stock you hold, such as Google or Twitter, you will have the risk of losing money due to the negative news. However, there is a way to trade stocks without having to think of each stock carrying it's own risk and this is through ETFs.

As a speculator or trader, you are not concerned with the financial stability of a company or its fundamental value of its stock because the way the activity works well, is if you look to profit in the short term, from the rising and falling of prices.

ETFs

ETFs are known as Exchange-Traded Funds. When you think of ETFs you can picture a bunch of stocks in one basket. What this group of stocks or other securities you decide to trade do is analyze the underlying index of the fund. There are a variety of ETFs. For example, you can choose an ETF that follows more of a target, such as retail companies or you could choose an ETF that has more variety within its basket. While you are looking at different ETFs, you want to keep in mind the same rules and guidelines for yourself that you do for stocks or any other type of financial instrument. While ETFs used to be focused more towards stocks, they can now focus on bonds, currencies, and even looking into cryptocurrencies.

One of the biggest pros to ETFs is you are able to have variety through purchasing one ETF because it is made up of different securities. Many people believe that this can save you money because if you decided to purchase the stocks in the ETF separately, you would be spending more money. For example, if you are interested in stocks that focus on space, you can look for an ETF that has this target instead of having to purchase a dozen or more separate stocks. In fact, most ETFs can hold hundreds of stocks.

Another positive of ETFs is you don't have to worry so much if one of the company's securities start to fall because of negative press as the other securities will help balance out the fall. Therefore, you might not even notice that price drop from one security. Because of this, many traders feel that ETFs are a good risk management instrument.

The price also tends to be more of a positive when it comes to ETFs. While most people believe that they will be expensive because they hold so many securities from different companies, this method of thinking isn't true. In fact, you might find that many ETFs are cheaper than some of the most popular blue-chip stocks on the market. On top of this, some ETFs might have a blue-chip stock within them.

Diversification is one of the terms that you will often run into as a trader. Diversification basically means that you have a variety of stock or whatever type of financial instrument you decide to trade. This is another reason why many traders look at ETFs as they will offer diversification through their variety of stocks. However, many traders and investors feel that diversification can also be a negative in the stock world. While it is highly debated, some people feel that if you have too much diversification in your account, then you can find yourself struggling to manage some risks.

Currencies

Trading currencies is just like trading money when you go on a vacation. For example, If you live in Canada and you decide to travel to Europe, you will have to trade your Canadian money in for Euros. In a sense, trading currencies in the stock market works the same way. You will always need to have two different currencies in order to trade. You will also want to watch to see what the value of the money is through a comparison. For example, some currencies receive a higher value compared to others while other currencies receive a lower value.

One important piece of advice from many experienced swing traders is that most of them agree that you should not start out trading using currencies as your financial instrument. They really believe that after you use simulation trading, you should turn your attention to stocks as these are often considered to be a base in the trading world. Stocks have been around an incredibly long time, which often helps beginners as they are learning the guidelines, rules, and how to trade in general.

Cryptocurrencies

A Cryptocurrency is a form of virtual or digital currency that can be used as medium of exchange, much like the way we use cash today. The only difference is that it relies on a complex computer network that depends heavily on cryptography (the science of secret writing) to verify and secure transactions, and also control the creation of new units.

Cryptocurrencies are one of the newest types of financial instruments available to trade. They are similar to currencies, however they are often discussed as coins and have a variety of different coins. Some of the types of cryptocurrencies are Ethereum, Ripple, Bitcoin Lite, and Bitcoin.

Just like currencies, nearly every experienced trader will tell you that beginners should not start with cryptocurrencies. In fact, most would probably see a beginner start with currency over cryptocurrencies. There are a couple main reasons for this one, both of them dealing with how risky these types of financial instruments are.

First, cryptocurrencies are newer and this means that there isn't as much research completed on them. In fact, one of the main things that experienced traders who are including cryptocurrencies in their portfolio are working hard to make sure they note everything about their trades so they can help expand the research on this type of financial instrument.

Second, cryptocurrencies are known to have high risk. They tend to suffer more than any other instrument when it comes to negative press, governmental regulations, and are even more likely to be hacked. Because of this, many traders feel it is important that the people who take on cryptocurrencies are comfortable with high risk, won't allow their mental state to be affected by the risk, and can remain calm under stress so they can continue to think rationally when having to make a quick decision to trade.

Futures

Futures are a good way to start your trading career. This is one of the most popular financial instruments among day traders but are also great for beginners who are looking to become swing traders. When you think of a future, you can think of an agreement between two people. A future is basically a contract that states exactly when stock will be sold. Typically, the agreement states that the stock will only be sold at a specific price. For example, both parties could agree that if the stock reaches $5, then the stock is to be sold. However, the stock cannot be sold to the second party until the price of $5 is reached.

Many people feel that futures are a great way to learn about the stock market. It decreases risk because you are able to create a contract that states this stock will be sold at a certain price. Of course, before you decide to agree to the contract, you will do all the research you need to do and make sure, to the best of your abilities, that you will end up with capital gain instead of a loss with the price you choose. Many beginners who state that they used futures within their first couple of months as a trader say they were able to get some more hands-on experience and learn about the stock market as they took part in futures. On top of that, they were able to gain pretty good profits.

Options

In the basic sense, options are similar to futures in there is a contract between two parties that states when the stock can be sold. However, instead of just focusing on the price, the agreement also focuses on a specific date. Furthermore, in order for the stock to become an option, there are four requirements that are needed.

1. The owner of the stock needs to agree upon the price. This process is known as the strike price.

2. You need to know the stock that the option is being applied to, such as IBM or MasterCard.

3. When it comes to options, buying is referred to as call and selling is referred to as put.

4. You also need to have a date of expiration for the option.

Like with any other type of financial instrument, there are positives and negatives associated with options. It is important to remember that all trades carry some sort of risk, no matter how well you try to manage the risk. This means that you can exhaust yourself making sure you have used every risk management technique that you can use and still have an amount of risk involved. Therefore, it is best to understand that sometimes you will lose on a trade and other times you will profit.

Forex

In simple terms, the Forex Market is nothing but a financial market, where people can trade currencies. If you are wondering what a financial market is, here is an explanation. A financial market is a place where buyers and sellers meet to exchange assets. Common assets that are traded in a financial market include stocks, bonds, currencies, commodities, options, derivatives, you name it.

The underlying principle of making profit in this market is that, if the currency you acquired, in this case, the British Pound increases in value against that of the Dollar, you make money. On the downside, if the opposite happens, you lose money. It is just as simple as that. Majority of the activity that takes place in the Forex Market during the weekdays is simply this; buying one currency in exchange of another.

Bond

As a matter of fact, the bond market is considered to be bigger than the stock market. In any event, the bond market is simply a financial market where large corporations and even the government ask for loans from the public so that they can repay them later with interest. A good way to think about it is: when you show up to the bond market to invest your money, you are basically loaning out your money to a large corporation or even the government so that they can pay it on a future date at a defined interest rate. This is very much the same way the bank lends you a loan, only that in this case, you are the bank. It is for this reason that bond investments are considered fixed-income investments.

Commodities

Another financial market that offers you an opportunity for trading or speculating is the commodities market.

The commodities are basically a financial market where buyers and sellers trade commodities. Commodities dealt in this financial market include agricultural goods such as cocoa, soy beans, wheat, cotton, rice and sugar. You also have raw materials like gold, silver, oil, copper, aluminum, lumber and gas being traded in this market.

In reality, when you trade in this market, you will not be buying and selling physical versions of these commodities. You will only be buying virtual gold or silver. Much of the activity that takes place in this market is speculative in nature, in that people will only be trading prices but on paper, you will have bought these commodities.

The way you speculate in this market is simply the same way you would trade any other market that we have just discussed. You could look at the price of wheat today or do your research and determine that in the future, there would be a shortage and therefore a high demand for it. This would imply that the price would rise in the near future.

You would then step in and purchase wheat and anticipate its price to go up. If you were right about the direction of price movement, you would make money when you sell later.

Conversely, you would do the opposite and sell if your analysis and research indicated a down price movement.

Chapter 5 Candlestick Chart Patterns and Technical Indicators

These patterns are really easy to detect when you're looking at candlestick charts while utilizing the correct technical indicator. Now, using technical indicators isn't always easy, but it's pretty much a 2-step process:

1. Apply Technical Indicators To The Price Of Your Stock- Here, you'll be applying technical indicators (which are simply math formulae) which will show you whether or not the stock is displaying buy or sell signals.

Technical indicators generally remove all subjectivity from analyzing a chart pattern. Technical indicators are one of two kinds- trending and non-trending.

- Trending technical indicators will show you the most significant changes in a given direction and mostly filter out the chart noise (irrelevant changes which don't contribute to the overall trend.) Now, this can easily happen over a few days, and the indicators will help measure the trends as well as signal when the trend is about to reverse, which will let you sell out at an ample time.
- Non-trending technical indicators tend to work with the buyers and sellers of a security. It determines how much the strength of the other investors in the market are affecting the stock movement. These indicators will often use a standardized price history by establishing the lowest and highest prices within a given time period. After that, they will be measuring the securities position in reference to that range. These indicators will also tell you when a stock is being over or under bought.

When a stock is overbought that means it's overdue for a reversal in the trend, as the stock has risen too high. Oversold means the same thing but implies the stock will rise.

While you'll find that many swing traders are looking for the one system of indicators that will always give them the correct result that just doesn't exist. Unfortunately, every indicator can be wrong, swing trading isn't just a concrete science that will always give you profits. If it was everyone would do it, and more importantly, we'd use computer programs for it.

This is why fundamental analysis is so important, it helps you figure out when the technical indicators you're observing are actually correct, rather than simply leaving it to guesswork. You'll find that many swing traders will neglect fundamental analysis even though it is what can help you really get ahead of the market.

2. Compare the Stock to the Rest of the Overall Market- This step, also known as relative strength analysis involves the comparison of the performance of a stock to its market or industry. By looking at the disparity between these two, you'll be able to tell whether or not the stock you've chosen is performing good or bad.

Divergences are extremely good signals because they show you how well the stock of your choice is performing regardless of the way the industry, in particular, is performing.

The Wider View-Fundamental Analysis

If fundamental analysis sounds like a 9-headed hydra to you, and you aren't feeling very much like Heracles, don't be afraid. We'll be using the KISS approach to fundamental analysis in this book. Which is to say we'll "Keep It Simple Stupid."

Now, I'm not going to try to set you up for your MBA in economics. What I'm trying to do here is present you the actually important bits. That is to say that we'll be looking at the most important, key parts of a firm's fundamentals. Only those that affect stock prices are really important to us. After all, we're traders, not economists.

Fundamental analysis is about constantly asking questions. You'll be asking questions like how fast is this company growing, what is its position in relation to the competition, what about the returns?

Through repeatedly answering these questions over and over again, you'll begin to have an idea of what the company's shares should be trading at. Often, you'll find that they aren't trading at that point, which is where you make your entry.

You're not going to find the intrinsic value of a stock that institutions like Wall Street are trying to calculate (the intrinsic value is the true value of the company, rather than simply being the value that the market arrives at.) On the other hand, you don't need the intrinsic value. You're not trying to find the value of the shares down to a singular cent. On the other hand, if you determine their value is between $30 and $50 but they're trading at $20 then you don't need much more to invest.

Getting To Grips With Why It Works

There's much less debate on whether or not fundamental analysis works compared to technical analysis working. After all, the whole field of investing is rooted in it. The more a company earns the more people are willing to pay to have a share of it. Let's say you rent out an apartment for $500 a month, regardless of how much you think the true value of a $500 a month apartment is, it'll be half of the value of a $1000 apartment.

Naturally, fundamental analysis is a bit more complex than this in practice. You'll be looking at quarterly earnings rather than $500 or $1000 a month. The point, however, is that fundamental analysis tries to get the value of a company from its projected future earning potential.

Arbitrageurs are a vital component of why fundamental analysis works. They are generally looking for riskless profits for themselves. For example, if a share is, say $20 a pop, and the firm is valued at $1 billion, then if the firm has $2 billion on their bank, with no debt then an Arbitrageur will pop in and buy a ton of those shares.

The Arbitrageurs taking advantage of such miss-pricings is what helps the market stay afloat. The Arbitrageur might even buy the company for $1 billion and pay for it using the money that the company had on its pricing books.

The bottom line is- fundamental analysis works because entities such as investors, firms or governments pursue riskless profits endlessly.

How to Start Trading

In this chapter, I'll guide you through selecting a quality broker for yourself and opening a trading account. In addition to that, we'll be looking at service providers, starting a trading journal, as well as how to maintain a good mentality to succeed as one.

Brokers

Much like every other kind of trader, swing traders rely on brokers. On the other hand, a swing trader needs to use a different kind of broker from the rest of them. This will depend on a variety of factors we'll be going through in this chapter.

Those factors will be broken down step by step in this chapter, in addition to a variety of details needed to open a brokerage account. After you're done with that, all you need to do is grab a few services to conduct analysis for you.

While some services are useful for conducting market screening, others will chart stocks etc. It's important to decide how much you want to invest in your setup, and I'll recommend some quality services so you can make your pick based on your needs. In addition to this, we'll be making a trading journal, which is, as you'll soon find, one of the most useful tools for a trader out there.

Now, why is the firm that's executing all of your trades being called a broker? It doesn't precisely sound like the best of names and quite frankly sounds much shadier than it should. Brokers really aren't a complicated subject.

Even though their name sounds a bit intimidating, you need a broker in order to become a swing trader...or well, to be a trader in any capacity. On the other hand, due to the wonderful capitalistic market we have, not all brokers are the same. Some will give you highly customized advice while others specialize much more in wealth-management. Some of the highest net-worth people out there participate in these trades. After all, these brokers are quite worth it. Naturally, some of these higher-quality brokers will charge massive fees, because, well, they can simply afford to do it? Generally, they'd tell you that the massive fees they offer are reflective of their advice.

You don't need this. Well, unless you're a billionaire, in which case I think you already know all you need about trading. The brokers that use swing traders use are much lower costed. They are so called no-frill brokers. The good thing about these brokers is that due to competition, even they are giving ATM card access, check-writing privileges etc.

Now, with all of those factors, how do you pick one?

The most common factor I see aspiring traders looking at is commissions. After all, nobody wants a broker to take any sum of their profits. This is a mistake.

Now, now, before you rush me down and put me on a pike, I am not trying to say they don't matter. Naturally, fees do matter. Swing trading wasn't even possible in the olden days due to the massive commissions that were everywhere.

Today, it's different. Fees these days really aren't that much, you'll be paying something like a flat $5-12 per trade that you make, which can easily be less than 0.1% of your trading volume. The difference between $5 and $12 isn't large to you, however, it might mean that you get some extra perks you otherwise wouldn't.

Now, some of the other factors are:

- Charting systems- If you rely a lot on technical analysis when you're making your trades then you'll be wanting a broker that's good at charting. The charting quality and ease of reading can make the difference between success and failure.
- Customer service- In my opinion, this is the single most important factor to look at when selecting a broker. Keep in mind these are people that will be handling massive amounts of your money. You don't want to put it in the hands of someone who you can't properly reach when you need them. Every trader will also sometimes run into problems with their broker, and in those times, this really counts.
- Ease of Deposits and Withdrawals- How easy it is to get money from your broker is only important when you're trading for a living. If it's hard, you won't have an easy time getting that monthly paycheck. On the other hand deposits are very important when making time-sensitive trades.

Which brokers you're going to choose also depends on how much you're planning to spend, fundamentally, there are two kinds of brokers:

1. Discount Brokers: These brokers are those that instead of offering quality and high-tier services, simply focus on executing trades. You tell them what you want bought and sold, they do that. Naturally, most of these trades will be made through the PC, unless you pay extra for phone support. These brokers are generally cheaper, and offer fewer services.

2. Direct access firms- Direct access firms are those companies that let you go past a broker and trade with an exchange or market without a middleman. The advantage of doing this is that you'll have way more

control due to being able to see who's offering what and for how much.

Usually, these brokers will require you to get some software that will give you very high-speed data, usually superior to streaming sites. While some discount brokers are offering direct access trading, these are generally worse at it than dedicated companies.

2.5 Full Service Brokers- This isn't really on the list because it's not for you. These are brokers like Merrill Lynch, they will offer you a bazillion different services, and charge you just about as much. A swing trader shouldn't need anyone whispering down their ear about what trades to make. Swing trading is a road of independence, you don't need someone else telling you what trades to take and what trades you shouldn't take.

I'm not going to recommend a single broker to you in this book, after all, the quality of brokers easily changes over time. Because of that, I can't really tell you which brokers are good or bad. On the other hand, I also can't know which country you're in, and while most of this book is US-driven, the fundamentals I want to apply everywhere. Just keep in mind to select quality brokers that offer everything you need!

You Need Some Standards Girl

Now, much like a girl that's just entered college, and is faced with the abundance of guys hitting on her, you'll need some standards to pick up the diamonds from the rough.

So, let me give you some baseline things to look for in a broker, like an older girl in a sorority.

Commissions: Never overpay, anything above $10 flat is a bit of a rip-off - that also shouldn't be more than 1-2c off of every share you're buying. Anything higher than this is pretty much just the broker preying on new people like you. It's also important to note that the higher your fees are, the more money you need to earn before you break even. While I've recommended some specific rates just now, too many people look only at rates and nothing else. That is the biggest noob trap in the whole world of trading, and there are a lot of noob traps. Commission rates are important but not as important as some other things.

Versatility: In this day and age, it's very important for your broker to offer to trade more securities than just stocks. Naturally, while most of us start off at stocks, trading other markets is also very popular. If your broker can figure out how to get you trading international securities, currencies etc. then that's a big plus. Naturally, you should be expecting to pay a small premium on top of the standard fee for services like this.

Various Banking Services: You'll find that some brokers are willing to give you services like check-writing or ATM transactions. These are generally just hassle-free measures to get your money. If you aren't trading seriously I'd recommend fetching one of these. With that being said, pretty much every broker will let you get your stuff to your PayPal card, so it shouldn't be all that hard getting your money.

Usability: This refers to your broker's UI and is possibly one of the most important thing about a broker. Think about it like looks in a guy, while they may not be the most important thing, everyone has a baseline of what they'll accept, and if he's pretty enough, most other things won't matter. Well, similarly to that, don't forget to check under the hood of the pretty ones, as they often don't contain everything else you need. On the other hand, a user-friendly and usable UI can make trading much easier, or even increase your profits. If it's quick and easy to place orders you're much less likely to get stressed out and make a bad trade or several. Also note that some brokers will let you test out a demo version of their platform before signing up.

Varied Amenities: Amenities are things that include services conductive to research and charting services. Let's give you an example, a discount broker may be willing to give you level 2 quotes- these will give you the access to order books for Nasdaq stocks. You will also get stock reports from Wall Street, as well as other research reports. On the other hand, these aren't really useful when swing trading due to the short-term nature of it.

Customer Service: This is the one thing I can't stress enough. It's the equivalent of a guy's core values. Sure, you can make do without them for a time, but after some time, you'll find that you're simply incompatible and nothing else can make up for them. It's very hard to determine how responsive a broker will be unless you rely on the internet, so check reviews and do a detailed analysis of every one of them when it comes to customer service. You want to be able to get your broker on the phone whenever you need them, rather than waiting for when it may be too late.

Reports and Analysis: This is the part of a broker that determines how well they can present you your data. Do they provide you year-to-date portfolio index returns? While sure, you could calculate this all yourself, having a broker do it is much easier. It's also great to have tax services in countries that have manual tax reports like the US.

The First Step-Opening An Account

After you've made your pick as to which broker you want to do business with, you'll need to decide on the kind of account you want to open with them.

Here you've got a variety of options, based on whether borrowing money to trade from your broker sounds appealing, as well as your position on trading futures or placing the account on your name or your spouse. You can even make the account a retirement account, or a traditional investing account. The next two questions will answer this, well except the spouse one, that one's to be had between the two of you...I'm not good at relationship counseling.

Cash Or Margin Account

Whether you want to get a cash or margin account will depend on you after selecting, which broker you, want to do business with. When you get this choice, keep in mind that cash restricts you to trading with funds you have available, while margin accounts allow you to borrow from your broker to trade. Picking an account is also necessary if you want trading options.

A swing trader with say, $30 000 can borrow up to $30 000 usually, now, this is a double edged sword. Let's say you invest all of it...and you lose 10%, instead of losing 3000 you'll be losing 6000 due to the money you borrowed. Margin accounts tend to make traders much more reckless. By being allowed to trade with money that isn't really yours the dealership is trying to get you to pay a fee on the money you borrowed. These can easily lead to you getting in way over your head.

If you're a new trader (as you probably are) you should be sticking exclusively to cash accounts.

Traditional Vs Retirement Account

The second account division is traditional and retirement. The difference is really quite self-explanatory.

Now, the biggest difference here is well, taxes. Traditional accounts will let you take your money whenever you want, and however much of it you want to take out. On the other hand, they also mean that you have to report this as taxable income. In the US at least, if you get classified as a full time trader you can make less taxes by turning these gains from capital to ordinary. This is important because if you aren't classified as a full time trader then you're going to have to pay the full capital tax.

A retirement account stops these problems, however, the government doesn't like this idea, and hence stops you from putting as much money as you'd like into it. Your IRA caps out at $5000 a year if you're under 49. The government also limits you when it comes to taking that money out, in most countries you can only do it after turning 59.

These kinds of inconveniences tend to be why people elect to not open a retirement account. If you just want to max out your retirement, then opening a retirement account is definitely the best idea.

Picking A Service Provider

Unfortunately, trading without a service provider is pretty much impossible. On the other hand, these are all different from each other, so a newbie might get overwhelmed by choice when selecting them.

These differ in a few ways but mainly its timelines, quality, and breadth of data that makes the final decision. What you want in one of these is all the services that you need. Primarily, you'll want charting and access to a database. You'll need those to conduct both technical and fundamental analysis. Now we're going to go over the main things you'll want to look for in a service provider.

Now, let's sit down and take a short lesson on the service provider business model first. They make money by making a deal with a data provider, and then providing you with the data that is relevant for you.

Service providers will be giving you the tools to find and chart the stocks that you want, which will increase the amount of info you have on the market. Using tools such as these is flexible enough to let you change all of your inputs. Ranging from what indicators to use to which criteria to pay attention to.

Providers are classified into two main categories. You've probably guessed it, it's those that provide technical data, and those that provide fundamental data. Those that provide both are therefore classed as unicorns.

A strong charting system is, well, pretty much necessary if you want to be a successful swing trader. They simply do way too much for you to be successful without them. That isn't to say it's straight-up impossible, but it will be far more difficult compared to just taking a provider and going with it.

You will absolutely require real time charts and quotes. Real time here means that they are of live market data, and are not being delayed by an external cause. If your plans are to trade interday, then when you enter your orders, you don't really need real time charting. After all, you'll be entering orders after-market hours. The market has a ludicrous amount of charting providers, and most of these cater to the active traders that are in their system. This is to say that most discount brokers will have connections with some charting systems. In fact, order entry is often integrated with charting, allowing you to make automatic buys and sells, which is a great feature.

While there are a lot of excellent charting services online, I can't really recommend any off the tip of the hat, because I don't know what country you're in and what the rules there might be. With that being said, I would check it out online and then determine if you need additional charting.

Now, charting systems themselves can be difficult to select from. After all, every provider will try to make themselves look different. Spoiler alert: Most of them aren't all that different. All you need to do is pay attention to what you need, the primary concern will be ease of use. After all, you won't have all day to fish out charts, you need them to be available pretty much at the snap of your fingers. Consider their visual appeal and clarity as well, you don't want to spend hours on just reading a chart.

Features such as being able to input your own indicators are excellent for advanced traders. If your plan is to stick with a single one for all of your career, then try to look for one that lets you insert custom indicators. You'll be thanking me later.

When it comes to selecting these programs I recommend checking the rankings made by Technical Analysis of Stocks & Commodities in its yearly Reader's Choice Awards. I use two charting systems: one, which is specially provided by my broker and another one in which I make the bulk of my personal research.

Fundamental analysis software lets traders who decide upon using fundamental analysis in investing as a process need to get a subscription to data providers that can assist them in their research.

It's lucky that most of a company's fundamental data, ranging from historical earnings to expected growth, is available... for free... online, God bless the internet. Honestly, it's amazing how far trading has come, and how easy it is to come across this stuff online these days.

Like seriously, just open Google Finance and look at all it gives you. Ten years ago, my broker couldn't have given me that much information. And this is all FREE, in this age of digitalization, it's important to remember that most of the things you need are available online, if you know how to look for it.

- The balance sheet of the company you're looking at

This and many other things are all available for free. Beware, though, that it does have a message board. Run away from those, for reasons we'll discuss soon, you don't want to be getting into any message boards just yet (or, well, ever really.)

Reuters is another site you can use. While sites like Yahoo! and Google will give you aggregate data, Reuters makes its own data. The main categories available on the website are Stock Overview, Financial Highlights, Estimates, Officers and Directors, Financial Statements, Recommendations, and Analyst Research. All of these have some of their uses, though as a swing trader you'll be primarily looking at Ratios.

The excellent thing about this site is the variety of data it provides. It will give you data on a company vs its peers as well as other things. Such as whether the company is going through good or bad times, as well as free research services. On the other hand, the paid subs are also quite great.

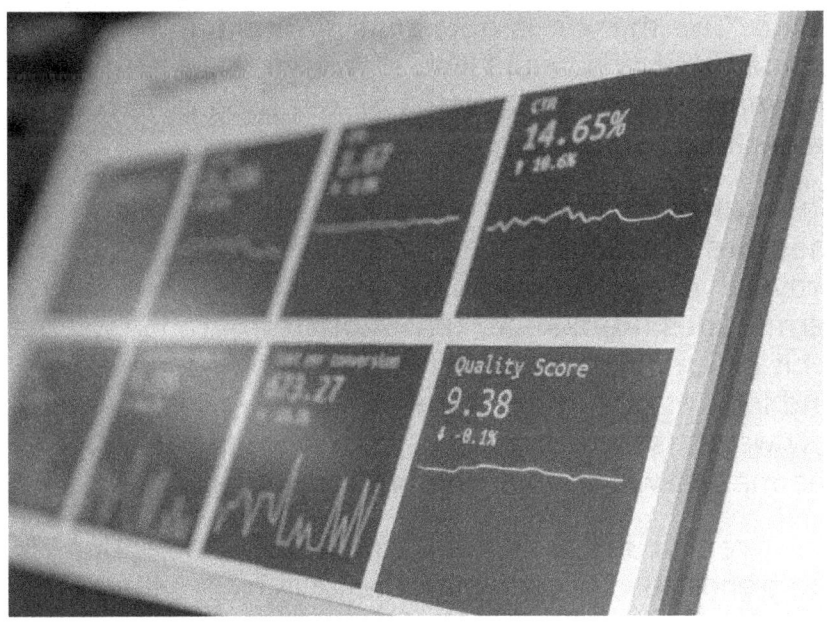

Chapter 6 Swing Trading Rules

Swing trading can take some time to master. It is easier to work with compared to working with day trading, but it is much harder and requires a lot of patience and time commitment compared to working with some of the longer-term investments that you can choose. Despite this extra work, there is the potential for you to make a big profit with limited risk if you follow the right rules. This chapter will take some time to look at some of the rules that you need to see success when it comes to swing trading.

Align the trade with the market

When you are trying to figure out what trades to do, you always need to take a look at what the market is doing. The market is not going to behave in the manner that you would like, so you need to learn how the market is about to behave and then pick your trades to go with that.

The overall direction the market will take will be measured through the S&P 500. These trends will provide you with some context for making your short-term trades. Remember that short-term trades will be a bit different than you will find with long-term trends and look at how the market will behave in the next few weeks is more important than worrying about how the market will do over the next few years.

However, you also do need to pay some attention to the trends that happen over the long-term with swing trading. These trends will often show up again and again for a particular stock and take a look at them can help to increase your profit potential. Yes, it is important to take a look at the short-term and see what is going on with the market to see if anything is about to change and then trade along with that trend. The more you can look at the charts, both long-term and short-term the more you will be able to make good decisions on your trades.

Go short weakness and long strength

You should not avoid or fight off the tape once you figure out what the overall trend is. You need to look at the charts to find long trades that will work during periods of bullishness. And then when you are dealing with periods of bearishness, you need to find the right short trades. These trends will help you to get the results that you would like when it comes to successful swing trading.

Enter at the beginning rather than the end

One mistake that some beginners will make is that they will try and enter the trend near the end of it, rather than catching the trend at the beginning. This will limit some of the money that you can make if you wait too long to enter into a trend. Of course, it is much better to get into the market at some time for the trend, before it goes down because you will be able to make some money, but the earlier you can get into the trend, the more money you can make.

When looking at the charts, it is important to look for early signs of the change. The earlier you can see these new trends, the less risk you will take with swing trading and the bigger the profits you will make. This means that you have to be active. Trends can go quickly and if you are not careful about what is going on in the market, and you are not looking at the market averages, you will end up missing out on some trends and will miss out on some money, or even lose money.

Looking at the overall market averages on your charts will help out with this. When you look at the market averages, you will sometimes see that the stocks have been oversold or overbought. When this has happened, it means that it is likely they will turn around again soon. If the trend looks like it is about to reverse, you can jump in, get the stock for a good price, and sell it over the next few weeks when things start to go back up.

You need to get some of your own indicators in place to figure out when these trends are about to happen. The Volatility Index, the Put/Call Ratio, and the Arms Index are good tools. You will be able to see, through these methods, when the market is testing a major zone of resistance and support, and it can help you to predict what will happen in the future.

On the other hand, looking at moving average crossovers and trendlines will make you fall behind. These are just going to confirm that a trend is happening and by the time you see them and join in on a trade, it may be too late to make any money. These tools can help you determine if you have made a good decision along the way, but if you are relying solely on them, you will miss out.

Never trade on one technical concept

With swing trading, things will change on a frequent basis. You need to work with trading quickly, picking up one trade and then selling it within a few weeks. You do not get the benefit of staying with the market for a very long time, or you are missing out on the profits you can make. Relying on just one technical concept will lead you to a lot of trouble along the way.

In most cases, the highly profitable trades will occur when you can find at least two (but more is much better) technical tools send you the same message. There are times when several of your tools will show the same indicators, and this means that the stock will rise or fall sharply in the near future. This is great news for you. The more indicators that show the same information, the more likely that the trend is about to occur and that you will make a large profit in the process.

However, there are times when one indicator will show that a trend is about to occur. If you only look at that one indicator, you may find out after entering the trade that it is wrong. You want to have at least a few indicators in place to help you make your decisions. The best opportunities for swing trading will show up in at least a few indicators, and when you can get three or more of these to show up with the same message over a two or three day period, this will increase your profitability.

Enter the trade with a good plan

There are a lot of different strategies and plans that you can go with. Many of them can be successful when it comes to swing trading, but you do need to pick out a good one and stick with it. One of the worst things that a beginner can do is get started with a strategy, see that it is maybe not doing as well as they had hoped, and then skipping over to a new strategy right in the middle of their trade. This is setting yourself up for failure, and you are more likely to lose money with this method than any other.

It is fine to switch out the types of strategies that you want to use if you find one is not the best for you. But you must make sure that you pick out a strategy and use it for the whole time of your trade. Even if the trade is not going the way that you would like, stick with the strategy. This will limit your risks, and you will learn more from the experience in the long run. If a strategy is not the right one for you, simply switch to a different one the next time.

Try to work the odds

You are not able to make the market work the way that you would like. The market will behave however it would like. There are a lot of different people who are in the market, and the swing trading will only take place over a few days. You need to learn how to work with the market, rather than trying to influence it.

It is never a good idea to risk a dollar just so you can make a dime. You have to pick out smart trades, trades that will lower your risk as much as possible while making your high profits. There will be some trades that may promise a lot of money if you try them, but the risk is so high that you are likely to lose all of your investment plus more without making anything.

The best trades that you can do are ones that will provide you with a strong profit if you make the right types of decisions, but where you can limit your losses as much as possible if you are wrong. The profits may not be as big as some of the trades that you can make, but it ensures that you will not lose out on all your investment either.

Learn to control the emotions a little bit

The most important thing that you can do when you get into swing trading is learning how to keep your emotions out of the game. This is important no matter which investment you choose, but it is especially important when you are working with some of these short-term investments. Once your emotions get into the mix, it is a lot harder to make smart decisions and smart trades that will lead to profits.

If you let your emotions get into the mix, you are likely to make poor trading decisions. You will make decisions that will lead you to lose money. You will stay in the market too long, hoping to earn more money, or hoping that you can recover some of your losses. Basically, when you start letting the emotions get into the mix, you are risking your money, and you will end up losing out on all your hard work.

For those who are not able to think through their decisions critically, who are not able to keep their emotions out of the trades that they will do, it is much better to just stay out of the market completely. Swing trading needs some fast decision making and the help of a lot of research. If you are not able to do this without all the emotions, you will fail in the long run.

Do your trading with a consistent group of stocks

When you first get started with day trading, it is pretty easy to jump around between stocks. You may find on that looks good and then want to jump to another once the trade is all done. There is nothing wrong with following the action, but it is always best to have your core stocks that you track on a regular basis and learn how they work.

Having a few regular stocks is a great way to see regular success with swing trading. These regular stocks will allow you to learn about the market better and can save a lot of time researching. You will have time to learn how the stocks work and understand how they have performed in the past and are likely to perform in the future. It takes some of the work out of it all when you can stick with a few core stocks over the long term.

Of course, there is nothing wrong going with a new stock on occasion if you see some big trends that are coming up. This can be a great way to increase your profit, especially if you have been in the market for some time. But chasing after those new stocks can take up a lot of work. Learn as much about your core stocks as possible, and you will save a lot of work, reduce your risk, and increase your profits.

Everyone will spend time working with different methods and strategies when it comes to swing trading. And even with different methods, it is possible to see many people make a profit. If you follow some of these rules and learn how to pick the right strategy, you will see some great results when it comes to swing trading.

Swing trading is an extraordinary way to make cash for the initiators. It is straightforward and learns. You need to learn it by following four basic rules with the end goal to get well on the way to get the best stocks for swing trading with success. Swing trading is a procedure of trading that trusts on the getting responses among the significant trends which will be either upside trend or drawback trend. This trading, as a rule, goes on for around 2-5 days in a stream. Numerous Forex traders swing trade on the daily edges. It is unsafe so don't think to attempt it.

You need to pursue four rules with the end goal to taste success:

Rule 1: Use Support and Resistance

At whatever point you are trading you should discover the territories of help and resistance on the daily Forex graph. The ones which are high on the unpredictability are great that is because they slant not to keep going longer. For this, you should use the Bollinger band and also the trend lines.

When you are trading in Forex, never make this regular blame:

A few traders sit tight at the time when the cost will reach close to the point they are expecting and believe that by then of time they will enter the trade and seek after better levels of hold. Never foresee anything or figure anything because it will prompt a snappy wipeout and the market will remove your value and won't give you any prizes.

Rule 2: Watch Momentum

If you are en route to swing trade in Forex or any money related hardware, it underpins the trading sign. There is no additional space to grasp the individual pointers. That is the reason you should start with the stochastic and Relative Strength Index (RSI). Presently you are in the way of trading.

Rule 3: Set a Target

When you enter the trade, the benefits and misfortunes come at a quick pace. You can put the stop component which is anything but difficult to apply and is obligatory. It is at the posterior of the help and resistance that you are anticipating. If you are utilizing a stop close premise at that point put the objective just before when you figure the price will go as indicated by your desires. It is encouraged to go for a basic short swing trading framework whether you are a tenderfoot or an accomplished trader or speculator. This swing trading programming causes you to track your short swing trading stocks at a superior rate than you could do.

Rule 4: Shop Spreads

While you are engaged with swing trading stock, you will trade with unstable and fluid monetary forms. In the main segments, you should be skilled to get some stupefied spreads and that addition of a few pips as it were. Every one of the intermediaries is never comparative at whatever point it goes to the spreads. You should make astute choices because if the managing costs climb up, then you need to have the tightest spreads that are workable for you.

Chapter 7 Fundamental and Technical Analysis

Fundamental and technical analysis are both techniques used by investors and traders all around the world to make decisions on the stock market. In this chapter, we are carefully analyzing the two, their differences, similarities, and where they are best used.

Fundamental Analysis

Fundamental analysis is whereby the trader, stock analyst, or investor looks at the basic fundamental financial level of business when analyzing the trade. It analyzes the trades' profits, revenues, margins, earnings, losses, among others. This analysis determines the financial health of the trade by analyzing the trades' key rations. You can have an idea of stocks in a company through fundamental analysis. it accounts for several factors; these include asset management, revenue management, the interest rates as well as the production of the trade. The goal of fundamental analysis is to identify and determine the stocks' current worth and market value.

In fundamental analysis, you measure a stock or any type of security intrinsic value. This is done by studying all possible factors that influence the value of the stock, such as the financial management condition of the company and economic conditions. A particular value is then produced and compared against the current price to help the trader figure out if he or she will buy or sell any security. The stock is considered to be overpriced if the value is lower than the current price. While the stock is labeled undervalued if the value is more than what is the current price.

Fundamental analysis involves going through both the tangible and intangible aspects of the trade. They are grouped into two aspects, the quantitative and qualitative fundamentals.

Quantitative fundamentals

The numeric characters that are measurable in a trade operation are known as quantitative fundamentals. They are obtained from the trade's financial statements, the profits, losses, revenues, and other assets. The cash flow statement, the balance sheet, and income statements. From these statements, you are able to analyze the financial status of the trade, where you are losing or gaining money.

Qualitative fundamentals

These are the intangible aspects of the trade. These are a competitive advantage, the competitive edge, the trades approach, the management quality, and the overall growth of the trade.

Limitations On Fundamental Analysis

If the management has wrongly recorded the financial details or they are was a misinterpretation, there is a great percentage that the decision you will make will be wrong as it will be based on false information, irrelevant, and data that is not accurate.

There is blind and total reliance on historical financial data to predict the future. This overreliance can prove to be fatal for the trade. Analysis should be done on recent changes in the trade and according to well predicted financial data.

Has over-ambitious, achievable assumptions that may lack the credibility of management and the industry growth areas. Assumptions may be based on future interest rates, growth rates, and other different factors. When these expectations and estimations are not archived, your whole investment can collapse.

Their prizes set on stocks might be influenced by overenthusiasm and can be set to a level that is not justified fundamentally. This can be dangerous for the trade. The fundamental analyst does analyze the business but not the stock market. There is no connection between the trades stock behavior and the progress of a stock.

Technical Analysis

The technical analysis evaluates investments and identifies opportunities by statistical analysis of tends from trading activities. These traded include volume and price movements. technical analysis majorly focuses on the trading signals, price movements, and other analytical charting tools. They are used to evaluate the securities weakness of strengths.

It uses trading data that is from past trades and price changes of security. These include futures, commodities, stocks, fixed income currencies. These are used as indicators of price movements of future securities.

Assumption Of Technical Analysis

There are two basic assumptions forming the framework for technical analysis.

The first assumption is that the market makes a discount on almost all things. There is criticism that technical analysist ignores the fundamental factors and only consider price movements. Technical analysts believe that everything is already prized to the market, from the broad market, the market psychology, and the trades fundamentals. This cancels out consideration of other factors when making an investment decision and only leaves out an analysis of price movements.

Secondly, the technical analyst believes rather than the stock price moving erratically; it is most likely to continue with past trends. This is because of the move in the long term, medium-term, and short-term trends. Most technical analysis is based on this assumption.

The market psychology tends to attribute to the repetitive nature of the prize movements; the trends tend to be very predictable. the technical analyst uses historical charts pattern to analyze previous market movements to have a clear understanding of the trades. They have a belief that history does repeat itself and that the prize movements will too.

Most traders buy and see stocks on the same day; they need to make quick decisions on the sale and purchase price. Using fundamental analysis is not possible when making such short-term decisions hence technical analysis being more preferred. This is because it helps the trader with ideas and directions of the stock price.

It should be noted that technical analysis is built on several assumptions and ignores other major factors. It focuses on the prediction of the price movements, which may not always be accurate and on point.

Limitations On Technical Analysis

The efficient market hypothesis tends to disapprove of the legitimacy of the technical analysis.it states that there is a reflection of all current and past information on the market prices, so there is no way you can use the patterns to your advantage to earn extra profit. Fundamental analysts and economists do not believe that prizes repeat themselves; rather, they move in as random movement and information contained in volume data, and the historical market cannot impact the trade.

It has been stated that technical analysis works sometimes because it is a self-fulfilling prophecy. A technical analyst can manipulate their ways of making sure that the market favors them. For instance, if many technical traders place a stop-loss order below a certain range and a larger number of traders do so with a similar range, the stocks will reach this price, increasing the number of sales orders pushing the stock down, making confirmation of the anticipated movement of the traders. Other traders will see the decrease in prize and sell their positions, making the trend stronger.

Difference Between Fundamental And Technical Analysis

The purpose of technical analysis is to focus on the internal market statics, the historical price movements, and patterned charts on such data, while the fundamental analysis focuses on the variable when making decisions on the trade. It shares prices based on financial statements, company statics, and facts.

Each system of analysis has a preferred term. For short term investment decisions, you can use technical analysis due to the short-term trends and prize changes. such investors are more interested in short term profits as they buy and keep stocks for a short period of time, a couple of years probably. While fundamental analysis is mainly used by an investor who wants to make investment decisions that are long term. This is used for a project that will last for a longer time. They purchase stocks with largely laid out dividends payouts and hold the stocks for several years before selling them.

The fundamental analysis makes intrinsic value estimates for the purchase and shares; then, sales are made when the market surpasses these values. On the other hand, the technical analyst does not make value on a stock as they believe that it is all dependent on the demand and supply from the market. The market is lead through rational and irrational factors.

The past trends or prize fluctuations do not concern the fundamentalist, technicians rare; however, affected by these trends and price fluctuations, they do believe that they reoccur. they use charts to follow to prize movements and draw conclusions from them. There are no assumptions of similar prize trends in a fundamental analysis like in technical techniques.

In fundamental analysis, decision making is through analysis of financial statements, quality management, and growth trends. They are used to make judgments based on their statistical information. Technical analysts pay more attention to pattern charts indicating prize movements and the market trends.

To properly identify the overvalued and undervalued prizes of the stocks, you use the fundamental method of analysis as it compares the intrinsic value of the stocks and the market value while the technical method of analysis is more useful in checking and calculating which is the best time to bus of sell orders.

There is a lot of investment in technical analysis. Millions are used to purchase and maintain technical analysis tools and trading software. This can be a bit difficult for the average individual trader. It is much cheaper to invest in fundamental analysis strategies.

Chapter 8 Money Management

This term is used to refer to the process of investing, spending, saving, and budgeting; it is also used to refer to the way capital is used for personal or group usage. The other words used for money management includes portfolio and investment management. When you are good with money, it involves a lot apart from just meeting your needs. When it comes to money management, having math skills is not mandatory, there are different skills needed that will be discussed later.

Money management is simply how you handle all the finances and how you handle all your long-term goals. It also involves how an individual manages their investment in order to make great profits. Most people think that great money management skills are all about saying no when you are tempted to make a purchase. What it really implies is when you are able to say yes to what is important to purchase. When you do not practice good money management skills, whatever money you have might look little for your lifestyle.

To have a good start when it comes to money management, you need to know where you are. This is in terms of your financial capability and power; like assets and liabilities. Assets include your investment and bank accounts, any properties and retirement accounts. Liabilities are the things that you need to pay like credit card balances, any loans like student loans and car loans and any mortgages and outstanding debts. Your net worth is when the value of your assets is more than your liabilities. And when your liabilities are more than your asset that is considered a net loss or negative net worth. When you have great money management skills and approaches, getting a net worth will be easy.

Ensure that you set your goals in order to achieve great money management. Your goals will create a plan on how you will manage your money. When you have your goals set, it will give clarity on which are priority expenses and which you can let go. You will need discipline and effort in order to achieve all your efforts. For instance, when you plan to buy a car worth $20k, you will need to work harder and smarter and reduce your expenses. You will need to do all that as compared to someone whose budget car is $10k.

When you have your budget drafted and set, remember to have adjustments. When you prepare a budget, you have the chance to know all the expenses that you have. For instance, you can set aside $150 that can be for entertainment and any miscellaneous expenses after payment of all expenses and managing your debts. Good advice is when you get a pay increment, do not use the additional income for your entertainment but add it into your savings.

When you have a target to meet different goals, you are likely to have the money in different multiple accounts. A good example will be to ensure that you have a separate emergency fund so as not to get tempted for any impulse buying in the future. You will also have different strategies and that will be for different goals. You will be aggressive when you start investing in different stocks that you will not need to invest money in like 20 years. You need to also have an account that has no risks like a savings account that that can be used as emergency funds when the need arises. When you have such multiple accounts, you can use a software program to help in tracking the several accounts. A good one can be Quicken; it will track all your expenses and the savings goals.

The Basics of Money Management

Money management is a term that deals with solutions and services that are in the investment field. The good thing is, in the financial market there are different resources available that can help in personal financial management. For any investor, their intention is to have a good net worth, so it will come a time when they will need the services of professionals like financial advisors. The advisors are known to offer brokerage services, money management plans, and private banking. The advice is best for retirement, estate planning and other benefits.

When you are in business, it seems complicated when there is a need to manage cash flow and different accounts. When you are able to strike a balance, you are guaranteed to be successful. If you are not able to manage all that, you will need to get the services of an accountant or bookkeeper to do all that for you. Even if you will outsource, you need to know the basics of money management and bookkeeping. You will need to know simple tasks like interpreting bank statements, understanding accounts payable and receivable, credit, and tax forms.

Money management will also involve knowing more about debit cards, checks, online payments, cash, and credit cards when it comes to payment options in your business. You will also need to have a planned and established payment plan and a debt collection system just in case of non-payment.

Opening a bank account is another way to help in money management, you need to choose a name and have an operating and registered business. Make sure you get more information on credit card facilities, a debit account, and any other additional services. Another important concept is to ensure that you have extended credit facilities in case of late payments. This can be planned for 30-6-90-120 days after a product is delivered or a service is rendered. You can motivate your customers to pay on time by extending discounts. Before the credit extension, ensure that you have done proper background check especially with large amounts. Even when there is credit extension, there are times where you will end up not being paid or not aid in time. To be able to recover your money, you need to ensure there is open and clear communication.

What Are Money Management Skills?

Before you can know of the best skills for money management, you will need to ask yourself some questions. What is your weekly or monthly income? Do you have a list of expenses that you need to pay? What you need to know is that money management is a skill used in life and cannot be taught in school. These skills cannot be learned in school but mostly from life experience.

✓   Have the ability to set a budget. This will help in tracking your expenses and the way you spend money. What do you spend a lot on, is it entertainment, clothes, or food? What is the tendency of overdrawing money from your bank account? If all that is yes, then you will need to set a budget. Look at your monthly statement and write down all the expenses in categories. You will be surprised by how much you are wasting.

✓ Spend what you have wisely. Always have a shopping list when you go shopping. Do you have a habit of looking at the product prices before putting it in the shopping basket? If you have coupons, ensure you use them. There are mobile apps and online resources that can help in focusing on your expenses. Do you know how to monitor your expenses? When you are not attentive to this advice, you will end up losing your hard-earned money.

✓ Always balance your books, do not always have a tendency of getting your bank balance online. When you depend on online information, there will be an issue when you want to know the balance on what you are spending at that particular moment. Be accountable and ensure you record all your expenses and this will help in avoiding any over-spending.

✓ Set a plan that will help in accomplishing anything that you put your mind. When you have a financial plan, you will be able to track how you are spending your money.

✓ Always think like an investor. When in school, you will not be taught how to handle money but largely on how to invest your money and have wealth growth. Learn to grow your savings and to invest at an early age. Turn that $100 to $200, $400, $800, and more. Having a stable financial future means that you have invested and grown in your money. When you start thinking like an investor, your money will grow. If you have a spouse or partner ensure that, they also know about your financial goals. If you possess a joint account with your partner or spouse, always work together and agree on the financial goals. When you are stuck or in doubt, consult a financial adviser and learn a lot of how to invest.

✓ Save your money, always be focused, and committed when it comes to saving money and this will guarantee a better future. This will help in improving your financial position and even make it better. The first step is to have the decision to do that and this will help improve your management skills.

Importance of Money Management

Money management will help any individual in living on a budget and within their means. You will be able to look for great bargains and avoid any deals you believe that is not good when making a purchase. When you start getting a stable income, you will need to know how to invest because that will help in attaining your goals. And when you practice proper money management, you will meet all your goals and plans. There is the importance of money management:

✓ You will have better financial security: When you are careful with your expenses and savings, you will end up having enough for your future. Your savings will help in giving the proper financial security and you will be able to take care of yourself in case of emergencies. With your savings, you will not need to use your credit card in case of any issues.

✓ When you have proper money management and manage to save, you will be able to get opportunities and invest in the business. It will be frustrating to know of a great opportunity and not having enough funds to invest.

✓   Your credit scores will be determined by the way you manage your money. When you have high credit, score means you have managed to pay your bills on time and you have low-level debt. A high credit score means you will have more savings and you will be charged low interest when making purchases like cars or mortgages.

✓   Money management helps in reducing stress, this will happen when you start paying your bills on time. When you are late in paying your bills, you will encounter stress. Stress will bring about health problems like insomnia, migraines, and hypertension. You need to be aware of how you will handle money management, this will help in having extra cash and manage to save and manage a stress-free life.

✓   Money management helps in earning more money and when your income increases, you need to develop proper budgeting. And know of the right places to invest the extra money you have made. You need to know of additional venues to save money like in stocks and mutual funds; this will help in earning more money unlike money laying in your savings account. Ensure you learn about the investments, not all investments are profitable. The better thing about investments is that you can be on a monthly salary and still earning from your investment.

✓   When you adapt great money management skills, you will not waste money on unnecessary things. When you do not know how you are spending your income, it will be easy to be in debt. When you use your spare time effectively, it will help in managing your money. For instance, when you spend time with your friends and family members, ensure that you are aware of your budget.

✓ Peace of mind is guaranteed when you have better money management skills. When you a stable income and better savings, you will be able to handle any financial issues with confidence that all your needs can be handled perfectly.

World Top Money Managers

These managers are known to offer management and investment advice. They manage both active and passive funds.

✓ The Vanguard Group: It is a well-known management and investment firm, they have more than 20 million clients and in more than 100 countries. They started in Pennsylvania in the '70s and they have grown their assets to more than $5 trillion by close of 2018. They hold over 300 funds, move 150 in the US and more than 400 indexes to all of their market funds.

✓ Pacific Investment Management Company: This management firm has a worldwide presence and founded in California in the '70s. They have grown their asset base to more than $1 trillion by close of 2018. They have over 700 professional managing investments and with over 10 years as experts. They have over 100 funds and they lead in the fixed income sector.

✓ BlackRock, Inc: They started with their main company as BlackRock Group, by 1988 they started another division and labeled it BlackRock, Inc. They grew their assets to over $15 billion in 5 years and by the end of 2018, they grew to over $6 trillion and they have become the largest company in investment management in the world. They have over 100k in their workforce and over 50 offices in more than 30 countries. More than 20% of their assets are equivalent to $16 trillion.

✓ Fidelity Investments: This firm was founded in the '40s and by end of 2019 their customers have grown to over 20 million and more than $5 trillion in asset base. Their mutual fund is more than 300, this includes domestic and foreign equity, money market, fixed income, money markets and allocation of funds.

✓ Invesco Ltd: This firm has been in business since 1940 in offering investment advice. They announced in 2018, that they have made over $800 billion way above their products. They have over 100 EFTs that are made from their share capital. In 2017, they had a decline and it affected their stock price. They have managed to be among the best in the world despite all the challenges and setbacks. They have become among the top and best companies in the world, in terms of money, assets, and investment management.

The Approaches Used in Money Management

Great financial skills make money management easier, and how our money is spent largely affects your credit score and your debt cycle. There are tips that can help you if you are struggling with how to manage your money.

✓ Always have a Budget: Most people do not like to have a budget because they believe it is a boring and repetitive process. That involves listing all their expenses, summing up numbers, getting everything up, and running. When you have a budget, there is less room to be bad with money. You will get to know your income and expenses. The secret is focusing on the value that the budget will bring to your life instead of the budget creation process.

✓ After making the budget, the trick is to make sure that you use your budget. It will be a waste of time when you draft a budget and you do not stick to it. If it is a weekly or monthly budget, ensure that you refer to it often, and it will help when making your spending decisions. The budget should be made in a way that, at any given time you can easily track how much you have spent and know of any penning expenses.

✓ When drafting your budget, have a limit set for any unbudgeted expenses. In any budget, what is important to know is the funds left after paying all your expenses. When you have any budget and everything is settled, you can have the balance for your entertainment purposes. The amount set for fun should be a specific amount from your income. If you are planning to have a big purchase, refer to your budget first.

✓ Start by tracking your spending habits. When you have small purchases, they will end up piling and finally, you will notice that you have gone beyond your budget. When you track your spending plans. you will be able to know the places that you are failing and how you can rectify them. If you can, ensure that you save all your receipts and have a record of your spending in a journal. Have them in categories so that you can easily track them and know of the areas that are hard to stick on a budget.

✓ When your income is steady and qualifies you for a credit facility that does not mean that you should get that facility. You do not need to commit yourself to any monthly recurring bill. Most people think that the bank will not approve of the facility because they cannot afford it. What the bank knows is just your income exactly as you have reported. And if you have given a credit report, they will use what is offered on that report and they will not have any obligations not to give the credit facility. It is a personal decision to know if you qualify for the credit facility and if you have the capability to pay regarding your monthly income and other obligations.

✓   When making a purchase decision, ensure that you are paying the right and best prices. The best way to do this is by making a comparison and making sure that you are paying the lowest prices for the products and any services rendered. Look for discounts, cheaper alternatives, and coupons.

✓   In situations whereby you are planning to make a huge purchase, ensure that you save for that purchase. When you have the ability to delay gratification, will help in ensuring that you manage your money in a better way. It is advisable to out of large purchases, instead of sacrificing important things or tying a purchase to a credit card. This will help in evaluating if you really need the purchase or more time to do a price comparison. Ensure that you develop a habit of saving up instead of having a tendency to use credit cards; this will help in avoiding any interest on the cost price.

✓   Always limit the purchases that you do use your credit card. In situations whereby you run out of cash, chances are that you will end up using your credit card even if you cannot even afford the purchase and paying the balance. Learn to resist from using your credit cards when making any purchases that you know you cannot afford and especially on this that you do not need.

✓ Develop a habit of saving regularly. Open a savings account and ensure that you deposit money regularly; you can do it daily, weekly, or monthly depending on your income. This will definitely help in developing a healthier financial habit. Another better way will be to set up a plan that the funds are automatically credited to your account. That will help reduce the responsibility of reminding yourself to do that all the time.

✓ If you need to be a good manager when it comes to money, ensure that you practice it all the time. Plan when you intend to make a purchase and always buy what you can afford. When you make it a routine and a daily habit, it will be easier to manage money and the better for your finances.

Money Market Mistakes

To be successful in your investment in the money market, you need to ask yourself several questions/statements:

• Do you have an account for emergencies?

• The account that you have will be an investment

• That the funds you are setting aside will be useful soon.

When you decide to invest, you need to know that it is a risky venture and there are factors that you will need to consider first before any investment. For instance, when you decide to invest in a stock you need to know of factors like economic volatility. In the case of bonds, there are challenges like interest rates and inflationary risks. For a brave investor, leaning on a money market account will be a brave move. This is because they are known for safekeeping for the money. There are several mistakes when it comes to money market:

✓ The mistake that most investors make is thinking that money market accounts are the same as money market funds. They are financial instruments that have distinctive differences. Most people know of the money market fund as a mutual fund, the main characteristics are low returns and risks for every investment. They invest their funds in liquid assets for example cash. When invested in debt securities they have higher returns and ratings and mature in a shorter time. Most investors make the mistake and think that their money is safer in the money market, but that is not the same as with money market funds.

✓ Most people who are in investment believe that the money that they have in the money market is safe. The biggest mistake that they make is thinking that they are even safer from investments. Another belief is that, it better to have a lower interest rate with money in the bank than no interest at all. Most investors do not know the exposure they are in regarding inflation. This is the main reason that funds that are in the money market will not beat inflation. A good example is when the inflation rate is low than the interest that is claimed. Investors would know that, even though they believe the money market is safe, they are not safe from inflation.

✓ When in investment, you always need to know how to strike the right balance. Most of the time, the money market is influenced by inflation changes and rates. When you have such an investment, do not be tempted to input higher capital. They need a higher minimum balance as compared to the normal savings accounts. The normal account needs to be in operation for at least one year and have a higher amount of capital. When you have anything more than that, then it will be sitting their idle and it will lose value.

✓   Most investors like using money as their safety blanket. They believe that when they hold onto their money, it will be the best approach for any investment. This is not true especially when it is about savings whether in their money market or standard savings. It is not right to have your money exposed to uncertainty and any risk. This is one of the reasons why investors are afraid to invest and they would rather stay with their cash.

✓   To be a good investor, you need to know about asset diversification. When you are dealing with cash that is no different at all; this is because most people believe that cash is not an asset. You need to know that from the basics of finance and accounting, cash is known as a current asset. When you decide to hold on cash, ensure you do not hold more than $200k. It is not a coincidence to find any ordinary investor who has several bank accounts, in order to secure their cash. They have an approach to divide money or cash into three categories and that is a useful thing. The first one is to ensure that you have some money set aside for at least 3 years that is considered a shorter period. Around 4 to 10 years as the average timeframe and above 10 years as the longest timeframe. This is what will help the investors to know how long they can time their projects, how much is needed, and what will be saved in the end. This approach is important because it will also help in knowing about all the risks.

The best advice is to ensure that you invest in investments that are in the long-term and on lower risks. These will include investments like bonds, treasury bonds, life insurance, and annuity. You will need to know of the options that will help to avoid losing money value, avoiding any risks and the different ways about cash diversification. You can make use of the different trading and investment tools that will help in giving more returns instead of money market accounts. You need to look for investments that will help in creating more returns in a shorter time than the longer timeframe.

✓ Any investor needs to know that the reason for the money market is to hold money. When you have your money in just one place, you will not have any earnings or benefits; you need to move the money around. You will need to get more information on the different options and invest more. You should also know that money market accounts are not to be considered as long-term investments. The main reason is that they are subject to high interest rates than what is charged on a normal savings account. Hence not the reason to consider it a long-term investment.

✓ You should not be enticed to look for accounts that offer interest rates as a promotion. The reason is the interests are bound to change after some time.

Budgeting Apps

As an investor, you need to know that, with the tough economic times you need to know the best way to invest in the financial market. And when you become successful and start making money, you need to look for apps that will in managing your money. Thanks to technology all, those apps are easily available and easy to download. They can be downloaded and installed on tablets and smartphones; hence you can use them anytime and anywhere you are due to portability. The apps help is keeping you on track regarding the way you spend and how you spend.

✓ MINT:

Mint can be downloaded as an app or used as a website; it is in the budgeting and investment category. It is compatible with iOS, Web, Windows 8, and Android. It is more of a budgeting app and it will still help in managing your money. It has a feature whereby you can categorize and customize all your expenses and transactions. It has the ability to synchronize all your transactions from investments, bank accounts, and credit cards. They have a reminder feature for all your pending bills and this helps to avoid any lateness in bill payment that should be very convenient for any investor. All you need to do is set up a free account and then include all your financial details. This will then give a breakdown anytime an activity happens and you will be able to get a report.

✓ Good Budget:

This app uses the envelope concept, when you sign up you are given 10 free envelopes when you are on standard subscription. When you have an upgrade to Plus, you will then be charged a monthly charge of $6, and then you will have unlimited envelopes. The concept works in a way that, when your envelope is empty, you are not able to shop or spend any money. The other alternative is that you can move money among envelopes; this is because the app has the flexibility to use a common budget. You can share the budget with other people, the app is compatible with iPhone and all android devices.

✓ Dollar Bird:

This app also helps in money management; it manages future expenses and will remind you when you have payment dues. To set up and activate is free and it has additional premium features. Your budget will be broken down in a calendar form and your pending expenses will be visible. You have the chance to have all your transactions in categories that are color-coded and they will keep on adding up as you have repeated transactions. When you check on your utility bill and paycheck, they will be displayed there. You will be able to see all your current balance. What you can spend and still be on a budget. The main setback is that it does not synchronize will your bank accounts. The problem is you will need to manually enter all the transactions. The app is available for iOS users, Android, and the web. You will have the privilege to know about your income, expenses, and cash flow.

✓ EXPENSIFY:

This is considered an app and tool that is used to report expenses, track all receipts, and all the expenses that you have. The main advantage is that it helps in quick data entry and saves a lot of time doing data entry. You will have the opportunity to make all the entries in one click. This app is available for Android and iOS users, you will do all the capturing automatically and using OCR; this is a smart scan. All your reports are available by taking one picture and they are all uploaded and completed within a click.

When you submit your expense, they get reimbursed faster and approvals are done very fast. When you use the app, you will be able to track all your expenses, categorize all of them, know the cost of all. All the expenses are consolidated and synchronized.

Chapter 9 Swing Trading Strategies

Like with any other version of trading, there are various strategies that you can use throughout your trading career. While most people like to stick to one or two strategies, which means they have to find financial instruments that work with their chosen strategies, other traders tend to go from one strategy to the next. However, as a beginner, it is best to realize that you should stick with one strategy as this will help you continue to learn about swing trading and how the stock market works in general. Of course, as you continue to build your trading knowledge and become more comfortable with swing trading, you can look into other strategies. While I cannot discuss all of the strategies in this chapter, I am discussing some of the most important and popular ones.

Trend Following

No matter what strategy you decide to use, you will need to make sure that you understand how to read charts and trend lines. You will use these tools in order to help guide you towards the best time to make your move to buy and sell a stock. When it comes to following a trend, there are a lot of details; such as what the opening price was, the highest price, the lowest price, and the closing price. You will analyze the trend over a period of time, how long depends on your personal preference. Through your analysis, you will start to notice a pattern in the trend line. This is the pattern that you will follow when you decide to take on a stock, see if your strategy will work for the stock, or what strategy to use.

The factors that you will look at when trend following are:

Price of the Stock
The price of the stock is one of the most important features that you will pay attention to. This doesn't just mean the price of the stock at that moment, such as what you would pay in order to purchase the stock. Even though the current price is the most important price, you will want to pay attention to all of the prices that you see for every day that you take into your analysis. For example, if you decide to look at the historical context of the last two months, you will look at about 60 days of stock pricing in order to help you find a trend. This means that you will look at the opening price for each of these days, the closing price, the highest price, and the lowest price. You will want to look at these prices in detail and in general. In a sense, this means that you will look at the larger image and the smaller pieces that make up the larger image.

Managing Your Money
Money management is thought to be one of the trickiest parts of trading. When it comes to managing your money, you want to make sure that you don't have too much money as it can give you a bigger loss. However, if you have too little money for the stock, then you aren't able to reach the full benefits when you make the trade. This is another time in swing trading when you want to find the best spot in order to make the trade.

One of the biggest tips to help you figure out how much money to put towards a stock is by evaluating the risks associated with the stock. You will be able to do this through any strategy that you will use and various other factors that are part of your trading plan.

Rules and Guidelines
One of the most important factors to remember when you are looking towards your trend line and thinking of making a trade. These rules are not only the guidelines that you will receive as you start to learn the swing trading technique, they are also the rules that you will set for yourself. For example, if you decide that your stop-loss price is going to be $10.00 lower than the price you bought the stock from, you will want to make sure that you follow this guideline.

One of the biggest reasons you need to make sure that you are following your guidelines is because the more consistent you are with your trading, the more likely you are to become successful. Furthermore, you will want to make sure that you follow the guidelines as they will help you to think systematically when it comes to making decisions. While you might find yourself turning back to your trading plan and guidelines consistently as a beginner, the more you follow the same procedures, the more you will focus on them as a way in making sure you are following the steps instead of needing them more for direct reference on where to go and what to do next. In a sense, trading will start to become more natural to you, which is a great strength when you are analyzing trend lines.

Diversity
Diversity is one of the more popular controversies when it comes to trading. While some traders feel you need to have great diversity, which is a variety of stocks, in your portfolio others feel that this isn't as important. In reality, the more serious you want to be

with your trading, the more you will focus on diversity. However, this isn't always true when it comes to investors. But, as stated before, investing and trading are two different career paths in the stock market.

You can look at diversity as what is the right feature for you. You might find that you don't need to have a large diversity because you are a part-time swing trader or you have a specific target that you focus on. However, you might also find that the more diversity you have, the better-rounded you feel as a trader. You might find that diversity is helping you learn more about investing in general.

Always Note the Risk

Another important factor to pay attention to when you are looking into trend following is how much risk is involved if you decide to take on the financial instrument you are looking at. When you are looking at the risk, you always have to pay attention to your guidelines and your trading plan. These two factors will help you decide if you should take on the stock due to the risk it carries or not. It is important to remember you need to stick to the risk level you are comfortable with. Even if you think that this stock could give you good rewards, this doesn't mean that you should agree to take on the financial instrument if you are uncomfortable with the risk.

This also doesn't mean that you can't increase your risk level as time goes on. You just want to make sure that you build your confidence and comfort level with risk as your risk grows. Furthermore, as you get more knowledgeable with swing trading, it might be a good thing to slowly increase your risk when it comes to taking on stocks. It's always good to grow in many directions as a trader, including with risk.

Trend following tends to be one of the most popular techniques when it comes to trading because it has a high success rate, providing you understand where the trend line is heading. Of course, you should always remember that the stock market can take drastic turns and no one can truly predict the future. This means, even if you analyze the trend lines to the best degree, you will still have some risk involved as the trend line could differ a bit from what you originally thought.

Using Options As A Strategy

We have already discussed what options are; however, one factor I did not discuss is how options are usually seen as a strategy when it comes to trading. Because you are able to set up an agreement which gives you the option to buy or sell the stock later, you are technically strategizing the right time to take the next step in the future.

One of the biggest ways to do this is through analyzing the various charts that you see for your stock. In fact, you will focus a lot on technical analysis, which is something I will discuss later. You will focus on the historical charts of the stock as this will give you a time-frame for when you will want to take the next step.

Options are known to be a great strategy if you are looking for leverage, which is when you increase a return on a trade through borrowed money. It is important that you need to make sure you will only use this strategy if it will help you to receive more of a profit. In fact, this is one of the most important factors of choosing a strategy. You have to make sure that it is going to help you gain a profit and decrease your risks.

Short Interest

Many experienced traders state that beginners should not take part in the short interest strategy as it tends to be more of a guessing game than other strategies. When you focus on the short interest strategy, you will compare the number of short shares to the number of floating shares.

This is a great strategy to learn as a swing trader because it can show when the stock market is about to go into bearish conditions, which means that the stock prices will start to go down. Furthermore, short interest can also warn you about short squeezing.

Pay Attention To The Float

One of the best ways that you can tell if a trade is going to help you is through a technique known as float. Basically, a float is the total number of shares that a trader will find in public sharing. This can become very helpful because, if you have the right size of float, you can see higher profits.

However, this is also the trick when it comes to the float strategy. There tends to be a fine line between having a massive float and having a float that will give you the best profits. The reason why a massive float, which would be too many shares, can cause you to lose capital instead of increasing your profits is because if you have a huge float, the price won't move as quickly. However, if you have a smaller amount of shares in your float, then you will find that the price moves a bit higher, of course this gives you a larger profit. With this said, you also don't want to have too little shares in your float. If this happens, then you won't be able to make much of a profit either as this can stop your float from increasing in price.

Breakout And Breakdown Strategies

When you focus on the breakout strategy, you are looking at the history of your stock's trend line in a microscopic fashion. What I mean by this is you will be focusing on what the trend has done over the past few days. When you are looking at the trend line, you will see every time the price has gone up and down. Stock prices are almost constantly changing throughout the day, which is what the trend line shows. Every now and then, you will notice in the trend line that you have a several high points and several low points. These high points indicated the highest prices of the stock and the lowest points show the lowest prices.

The biggest difference between the breakout strategy compared to the breakdown strategy is the condition of the market. If you notice that the stock has been going on an upward trend for a while, you will use the breakout strategy. However, if you notice that the trend shows the price has been decreasing over time, you will use the breakdown strategy.

Of course, for both strategies, there is that specific spot you need to try in order to gain your best profit. The best spot to make your next move will depend on the pattern of the trend.

News Playing

As you know by now, one of the most important parts of your day is your pre-trading portion. This is one of the first things you will do once you start your day. You will want to do this before you start trading; however, you will probably be checking out the stock market so you can see the changes in your stocks and any target stocks that you are watching.

However, one of the most important parts of this part of the day is reading the news that happened over night. This is important because you need to know what news is going to affect what stock, especially if you own the stock. You should always make note that any type of news can affect the pricing of financial instruments. For example, if you read that a company donated a large amount of money towards a nonprofit organization, people might be more likely to invest in that stock. However, if you read any negative news about a company, you will find the stock price going down because people are selling their shares.

But, you need to remember the trick of keeping your emotions out of the stock market. While News Playing is a strategy which is used all across the board when it comes to the stock market, for example all traders and investors use this strategy, it is important to remember that you should never make a decision to sell or take on a stock because of your emotions. I won't go much more into this because I discuss how your emotions can be a risk factor in the stock market in another chapter, but it is also a big part of News Playing that you have to look out for.

You always want to make sure that you think logically when you are making a decision to buy or sell a stock. Even if you find you hold a stock where the price is dropping due to negative news, you want to make sure you continue to follow your trading plan instead of going on your emotions. Therefore, you should only focus on selling the stock if the price drops to your stop-loss price. You also should not hold on to a stock for longer than you originally planned, even if they are the center of a positive news story. While you can be a little flexible when the price continues to rise, at least in swing trading, you don't want to hold on to the stock for longer than a swing trader should. You always have to keep the time-frame in mind.

Conclusion

This book should have been able to guide you through everything there is to know about the stock market and swing trade. I wish every question you had has been adequately answered by this beautiful book here. You should, by this point, know whether you would use swing trade in the process of investing in the stock market. The essential things should be ready at your fingertips and ready for usage at any point you decide to trade.

Swing trade and its aspects have been figured out in this book. Swing trade has been seen to take up a little time in the stock market. It is seen as a quick, swift, and easy way to make a profit. Most traders who have a short time in their hands use this. Something else that has been mentioned in the characteristics of a swing trade. These are the basic things that bring about swing trade to be there. They are what make swing trade. These also help to differentiate swing trade from the other types of trading that exist in the stock market.

There is also the fact about technical analysis and fundamental analysis. These two types of analysis help to look at how the stock market is operating. They help to see if you get into the market right now. You will earn some profit, or you will get loses. The technical analysis helps to look into past trades and how the trends of the market have been in recent years. As for fundamental analysis, one can look at the outside factors that affect the stock market. One does not need to look into the market.

You should also understand what simulation trading is and how important it is to make sure you complete this type of trading before you start trading for money. You should also not only understand risks which are associated in swing trading but also have an idea on how to decrease these risks once you start swing trading. Of course, this is one reason you want to make sure to practice simulation trading at first. As stated before, simulation trading will help you make sure that you understand the risks and the strategies which are associated with swing trading.

By now you should not only clearly understand what swing trading is, but also what the average time fame is for a swing trader. You should be able to remember the 11 commandments of swing trading, techniques, what the right mindset is when you are trading, know a variety of tips to help you get on your way, and also understand the many mistakes that other swing traders have made.

Furthermore, you should be able to explain how a day will go for a full-time swing trader, be able to explain the two different types of stock market conditions, and the art of short selling.

On top of all the information you need to know about being a swing trader, you also know how to get started with researching as much information as possible. On top of this, you have learned tips to help you become a better researcher, so you can gain the most out of your research time. It is important to keep these tips in mind as you will need to used them throughout your career. On top of this, you can also add your own tips, which will become useful when you begin to help other beginner swing traders in the next few years.

Dropshipping Shopify 101

The Ultimate Guide to Making Money Online With E-Commerce Business Model Creating Passive Income, Financial Freedom, Finding Marketing Products To Sell Online

ROBERT ZONE

Introduction

Dropshipping is a business model where there is no need to maintain inventory, own a warehouse, store goods or even directly ship products to the customer. This is all done by a third-party called a supplier. The store owner simply makes the products available for purchase to customers at a marked-up price. Then, the seller forwards the customer information to the supplier, along with payment, when an order is made. The seller keeps the profit.

If you want to make money with drop-shipping, you'll need the right niche for your store and the right collection of products to offer. To find a successful niche, look at the best-selling categories on Amazon. When starting out, sell products that are already popular in that niche. Then, as your store's customer base grows you can include other products. If you don't wish to pick a niche, you can run a general store. This allows you to incorporate a variety of products and you won't need to worry about being able to incorporate a specific item into the theme of your store. The benefit of a niche store, however, is that it allows you to build a reputation, or brand, within your niche and this reliability can translate into a more loyal customer base.

To sell these products, you'll need a website to serve as a store. This can be created using WordPress or a Shopify theme even if you have no coding experience, You can easily outsource this step to a professional. This store will be your business headquarters, so it needs to be neat, professional, and easy to navigate. Your website's domain name should be the same as your store name, so take this into consideration when naming your store. The products should be listed with multiple professional looking images and keyword heavy product descriptions.

Drop-shipping is one of the cheapest ways to open an online business because it doesn't require investing in any inventory. You can start a drop-shipping store for less than $100, but turning that store into a passive income stream will require investment in outsourcing and automation.

There are also some downsides to drop-shipping. The products you are selling are representing you, but you don't really get much control over what that representation looks like. Your store has no choice over packaging or presentation, although some suppliers might let you customize these things for a fee. Because you are the face of the product and the retail process, you are also held responsible if anything goes wrong with the product or the shipping. You'll have to be the liaison between the customer and the supplier, which is one of the reasons it's very important to choose the right supplier. You also have to go through the supplier if you need to contact the shipping company, which can be frustrating and time consuming. Over all, there are risks involved but drop-shipping can be a great introduction to online business and can provide a buildable source of passive income.

Chapter 1 Understanding Dropshipping

If you have ever thought in your wildest thoughts that you could make a difference in this world, you are right. You can be as successful as the leading millionaires in the world. Dropshipping is the one business opportunity that gives you a chance to rise above all your fears and discouragements. Even if you have tried business and failed a million times, there is nothing to fear in dropshipping. With dropshipping, you invest nothing, so you have nothing to lose.

What Is Dropshipping

Dropshipping is a type of retail business where the merchant does not have to hold products, store products or fulfill orders. In other words, if you are the merchant, you will not need to have a physical store for your products, you will not need a warehouse for your products and you will never be required to deliver the products to the buyer. This may sound absurd but it is true. Dropshipping is the only type of business in the world where you can sell a product you do not hold. You can sell the product and deliver it to the buyer without ever getting in contact with the product.

As a dropshipper, your work is to link the product buyer and the product seller. Now, this may sound like broking or affiliate marketing. Before you jump off the ship, first understand the concept. Dropshipping is a business; it is not an online marketing scheme. Dropshipping is different from MLM or affiliate marketing. If you have spent so much time or money in MLM schemes you might be a bit skeptical with online business models. With dropshipping, there is nothing fishy. Actually, as a dropshipper, you are in full control of your business. You are responsible for creating your business and branding it. A dropshipping business does not involve selling products for a third party. In reality, every product you sell should be your choice.

Dropshipping is also a good venture because it does not need heavy investment to start. Given that it is an online business, you will only need a few dollars to set up your point of sale. Once you are set, you will be ready to start making money. However, before you get into the business, you need to understand the key principles and concepts. You should understand what we mean by product sourcing and niche research. You need to understand how to choose the right products and where to find them. You also need to know how to market your products.

Understanding Dropshipping

To understand the concept of dropshipping, we need to understand the value of the internet first. The internet creates a whole new virtual world. The coming of the internet has turned the world into a global village. Given that all people around the world can communicate and link with each other online, it has become easier for the world to trade. This means that there is a huge potential market in most parts of the world.

Now, the internet creates a virtual world with virtual people. This means that you can also create a virtual store with virtual products. In simple terms, although you interact with people on Facebook, you do not have to talk to them face to face to prove that they are real. In traditional retail, a customer had to interact with the seller face to face. However, with dropshipping the seller does not have to interact with the customer face to face. Through online communication channels, you can sell products to individuals you have never seen. You can sell the products by convincing online users that the product is beneficial to them. You need a language that will help you appeal to the feelings and desires of your online community.

Understanding the importance of an online connection is the only way to grasp the concept of dropshipping. First, you have to learn to interact with virtual individuals. You have to know that as much as you cannot talk to people face to face, the virtual communities are actually made up of real people and they also have needs.

In this global village, there are also virtual businesses. Although the business may not be in your country or your locality, they do exist. These businesses include manufacturers, suppliers, and retailers. If you want to get into dropshipping, you have to create a connection with these businesses. In traditional retailing, you had to contact a supplier and visit their premises to discuss agreements. On the contrary, dropshipping allows you to contact your supplier and make an agreement without ever meeting face to face.

In simple words, the internet gets rid of the need to meet face to face in order to do business. The consumer can buy a product from the retailer without the need to meet face to face. In the same way, a retailer can order products from the supplier without the need to meet face to face. So, how exactly do you know what kind of products you are buying from a person before meeting face to face?

Just like everything else is virtual in the internet world, so are the products. You can see and even feel a product in a virtual state. Product manufacturers and suppliers are able to show you the product through images, videos, and words. Product descriptions and images play an important role in the dropshipping business. Without product descriptions and images, it would be impossible to sell anything online. Thankfully, any type of product can be photographed and described. With the images and descriptions, you can imagine and visualize the product you are buying without having to see it or touch it. The ability to sell virtual products makes dropshipping possible.

An online store is a virtual product store. This product store is what we refer to as the point of sale. Your point of sale is an online platform where you list products. Each product is made up of product images and descriptions. When you list products to your store, potential buyers browse through the products and pick out the ones that they wish to buy.

In traditional retailing, this type of arrangement would not be possible. Traditionally, you had to provide the actual products in your store so that the buyers could look at them before purchasing it. However, with the online space, the buyers look at product images and descriptions to get the feeling of a product. The same case applies to you as the merchant. You do not have to hold the products from the suppliers. You do not need to have a warehouse where you store the products. In dropshipping, when an order s made it goes directly to the supplier, who then supplies the product to the customer.

There are four parties that make dropshipping possible.

- The supplier
- The merchant
- The consumer and the
- Dropshipping platform

The supplier is the business that is responsible for shipping products out to buyers. There are different types of suppliers in dropshipping. In most cases, suppliers are manufacturers or wholesalers. In other cases, a supplier might be a more established retail store. The supplier ensures that all the orders that are made to the merchant are fulfilled. It would be impossible to have a dropshipping business if you get the suppliers out of the picture.

The merchant or the retailer is the dropshipper. In this case, you are the merchant. As a dropshipper, your work is to look for a market. The supplier provides the products, you provide the market. Just like traditional retailers, the merchant creates a store where they sell products. Think of a big brand like Walmart; they do not produce any of the products they sell, yet they have managed to create a global brand. They retail products across the world due to their trademark name. The same case applies to dropshipping. You do not have to produce any products but you can create a brand name. You can be known for supplying certain products and attract a certain type of people. As a merchant, you have to think about the easiest way to attract customers who need your products. Once you have the customers, the rest of the work lies with the supplier.

The product consumer in this business model is just a consumer, like any other. In most cases, people who buy products from online stores buy them for personal use. However, since online products are way cheaper as compared to those sold in physical stores, it is common to sell products to retailers. As an online retailer, you may easily find retailers who buy products from your store in bulk for the purpose of reselling them.

The dropshipping platform is the most important aspect of your online business. As the dropshipper, it is important to ensure that your business enjoys a constant flow of customers. It is also your responsibility to ensure that your customers enjoy the right products. To be able to do all these, you need a reliable dropshipping platform. The platform links you to the suppliers and the consumers. The platform helps you find the right supplier and products. Some of the best dropshipping platforms will only help you with marketing tools. Marketing and analysis tools will help you find the right market and products.

Benefits of the Dropshipping Model

The dropshipping business model is among the most profitable and one with the least risk. It has more benefits and fewer disadvantages as compared to other businesses. Some of the key benefits include:

Low Startup Cost

One of the reasons why you should choose dropshipping is the fact that you do not need money to start the business. The main reason why people procrastinate business is that they lack money. Financial capacity dictates the type of business you start and the locality you setup your business.

However, dropshipping is not limited by your financial situation. Even if you are a stay at home mum, you can start a dropshipping business with your pocket change. Some of the dropshipping platforms such as eBay allow you to start your business with zero investment.

Unlimited Market

The other reason why people procrastinate getting into business is the market. Some may say that they have the right product but cannot access the right market. If the right market is your problem, then think about dropshipping. Dropshipping allows you to target the exact group of people who may be interested in your products. Thankfully, dropshipping is not limited by geographic boundaries. Even if your target market is in a different country, you are free to start trading in that country.

Little Time Investment

You probably want to start your business while still maintaining your job. If you are afraid of the risk of quitting your job to get into business, dropshipping gives you the right opportunity. If you think that getting into business may affect your work or education, do not worry so much. With dropshipping, you will only need one or two hours per day to check through your store, respond to customer questions, and ensure that orders are fulfilled. Interestingly, you can manage your store on the road. You do not even need to stay in the same place to run it. If it turns out that you are too busy to manage the store, you can hire virtual store managers to take care of your business.

Unlimited Room for Growth

With dropshipping, you can earn as much as you wish. Nothing limits you to selling a single product or opening a single store. You can invest in as many products as you wish. After all, you are getting the products free of charge. You can play around with as many products as possible and try to find out which ones are profitable for you. You can expand your market reach at any time you feel like. There are no geographical or social limitations. If you are experiencing limitations in your country, why not move your business to another country. You can sell the same product in another geographical location without having to relocate from your country of residence.

Access to Unlimited Products

It does not matter the type of products you wish to sell. When it comes to dropshipping, you can sell any product anywhere in the world. When you use a certain dropshipping platform, you are linked with product manufacturers and suppliers from across the world. These giant manufacturers allow you to pick any product you wish to sell. It does not matter your area of specialization. You can pick any product as long as you are convinced that you have the right market for it.

Access to Affordable Marketing

Another big problem for most startups is the cost of marketing. It is very difficult for SMEs to compete with established brands based on the fact that big brands have the financial capacity to market. Established brands also enjoy a large market share since their brands are already known. However, when it comes to dropshipping, every business has a chance. The online market gives you access to billions of potential customers. Digital advertisement is the cheapest form of advertisement and it is the one with the highest ROI. You do not have to invest in expensive print media or screenplay advertisements. With simple techniques such as social media marketing, you can grow your brand and start making thousands of dollars.

High-Profit Margins

Dropshipping being an online business offers the highest profit margins. The profit margins allow you to set competitive prices for your products. Given that you do not have to undergo the cost of storage, inventory management or product transportation as it is the vase with physical retail stores, you have a lot of room to play with your profits. You will realize that most suppliers sell their products at ridiculously low prices. When you choose to have your products sold online, you have a huge profit margin. Some products give you as much as 1000% profit compared to the standard retail prices.

Limited Legal Restrictions

Another big problem that most businesses have to face in the real world is legal restrictions. The process of starting a business in most countries is complicated. You have to through a lot of paperwork and approvals. Before you are allowed to set up your business, you are forced to spend a lot of money on a venture you are not even sure that will be successful.

On the contrary, dropshipping does not require you to go through such problems. If you want to start your business, you can start even without fulfilling the conventional requirements. Many countries do not have a defined legal structure for setting up an online business. Even those that have clear structures, do not have a clear enforcement strategy. Given that the online business world is so expansive, only a few countries pay attention to online business. With that said, there are some countries that many place restrictions on dropshipping. If you realize that trading in your country is a problem, you may choose to start an online store in another country. No one limits you to a certain location. You are not limited to selling n your locality or to operate from your country.

How to Start Your Own Dropshipping Business

You are probably thinking about starting your own dropshipping business and you are wondering where do you start from. It is good that you are thinking about it. The first step to starting a dropshipping business is conceptualizing it. Before you even think about venturing into the field you have to get a clear concept. I will introduce you to some hard facts that you must consider. While dropshipping is a business that is open and one that guarantees success, you also have to very careful when getting into it. If you start your business and end up a failure, you might never gain the courage to start again. This guide is not only supposed to help you start your business but it is aimed at helping you start a successful dropshipping business.

According to Shopify, the leading dropshipping platform, 99% of all new dropshipping stores opened on the platform do not succeed. Now, these are some hard facts to swallow. Before you dismiss this business model, get the facts right. Although only 1% of the business succeeds, all the business that succeed go on to make a six-figure income. Dropshipping is the proverbial case of one hot guy having a thousand girls while plenty of average guys struggle to chase one girl. It is important to note that, there is no shortage of market or shortage of products in dropshipping. The only reason why most businesses fail is that there is a lack of strategy. Given that starting a dropshipping business is free of charge, most people only start online stores with a trial mentality. People start online stores thinking that there is nothing to lose. As a result, most entrepreneurs do not give their online business the seriousness it deserves.

Dropshipping is a business like any other. It is not just an alternative or an incase type of business. If you wish to make money from this business, you will make good money. We are talking about millions and not just pocket change. However, if you want to take this venture as a joke, it will slap you right back in the face. You must realize that given the business model allows every Tom Dick and Harry to start a store, the competition is high. Each product you chose to sell is already being sold out there. For you to succeed, you have to stand out. For you to attract the customers out there, you need to show them that your products are not just picked from another website and relisted. We will get into the deeper details of establishing your business as we progress. However, to help you start your business here is a simple step by step guide.

Step 1: Conceptualize Your Business

Before you start a business, you need to have a concept. Your concept should answer questions such as:

- Why do you want to start the business?

- What do you expect to gain from the business?
- Whom do you target to help with your business?
- What solution does your business offer?
- What should be the future of your business?

A business concept that will work is based on a problem solution approach. There is no business that is established without the aim of solving a problem. For your business to succeed, you must see a gap in a society and choose to close that gap. If you want to start a dropshipping business, first conceptualize it. Look at the people around you or those abroad. Try understanding the problems they face in receiving certain products and think about the best solution to that need. This way, you have a good starting point.

Step 2: Do Market Research

In the conceptualization stage, you only make your business plan based on your observations. However, before you start any business, you must do research to confirm your hypothesis. Research will help you determine the market potential. The research will help you know if your hypothesis is true and if the solution you wish to provide will take care of the problem. As we delve deeper, we will look at the available options in regards to market research.

Step 3: Create Your Products and Find a Supplier

Now that you are sure that there is a gap in the market, you need to create a product that will fulfill that gap. For instance, if you realize that there is a lack of good dresses for short ladies, you need to start creating a solution to that problem by providing dresses for short ladies. However, you also need to create a product that will feel unique and special. You need to make short ladies want to associate with your brand and not just any other brand that sells dresses for short ladies. In creating your product, you have to communicate with suppliers so that the short dresses may be customized to have a certain feeling.

According to your market research, you will find out what is the biggest problem affecting the short ladies dressing industry. Maybe, they only lack official dresses. Let your dresses for short ladies have an official feeling in that case. What if the dresses could be designed to make the ladies feel a bit taller than they are? It is such a minor factor that will make your business stand out from every other business out there.

Step:4 Choose and Set up Your Point of Sale

After creating the right product for your business, you need to start selling it. The only way to sell is by creating an online store. To create an online store, you have to choose the right platform. There are many factors to consider when setting up your point of sale. As we will see in the following chapters, each dropshipping platform has its ups and downs. The important point to note is that each option gives you a chance to sell your products. After deciding on the platform, you want to use, design your store according to your target market preferences. In everything you do, it is important to always think about your target market. Dropshipping is all about fulfilling the market needs. You need to appeal to the emotional side of buyers so that they give you their money.

Step5: Market Your Products and Make Money

The last and most important step is making money. Dropshipping is only sweet if you are making money. You may set up your store and list products but before you taste the money, you will never see the value. Product and store marketing are very important factors in this business. Without the right marketing strategy, your efforts may be futile. As we delve deeper, we will give you tricks that will help you market your products to millions of people without even using a cent. This is the guaranteed way of making money.

Where Do You Start

It is common for most people who want to get into dropshipping to ask where exactly the starting point is. Understanding some of the key pillars of dropshipping should give you a rough idea of where to start. In the dropshipping world, the key pillars include the dropshipping platform and the suppliers. Without product suppliers, the business may not be possible. However, the starting point should be a marketing point. Even if you have the right products but lack the market you will never succeed in any dropshipping business.

The first concept should be inspired by your market. Your concept of whatever you wish to sell should be inspired by the conversations you have with your social media friends. Of course, social media is a major player in the dropshipping business. Without social media, dropshipping could just be a shadow of what it is today. According to Shopify, 85% of Shopify store owners market their products on social media. This means that social media should be your first point of research. Through social media, you should be able to find out the types of products people are looking for in certain localities. You start realizing the constrains that people go through trying to find certain products. Social media trends and conversations should help you understand the certain constraints that marginalized groups may face.

Another important aspect that may help you find inspiration is your own life experiences. Every person belongs to one or several groups of people. As a member of a certain group, you understand the needs of that group better. This is often the most successful starting point. You start from the known and move out to the unknown. For instance, if you have six toes, you represent a community of people with six toes. You know the trouble that such communities go through in their search for shoes. This could be a good starting point for your business idea. You can start your business based on your racial affiliation, your body size, your sexuality or your religious affiliation. You can start a business targeting your professional field, your transport needs or your health needs.

Once you find a certain area of life you associate with, move to the next step, which entails linking your social issues to the real market. In this case, you start mobilizing a market by creating social media content. You start attracting people who may be interested in that specific area. Although this is not a mandatory step, you need to do some social media mobilization to gauge the possible market reception of your products. Through social media mobilization, you may create social media groups or join groups that share similar problems. For instance, you will realize that there are Facebook groups for overweight people that enjoy millions of followers. Through such groups, you can start your market research. You can post questions and start conversations that will help you know how different people deal with their weight problems.

While engaging with the potential market, you should also be doing product research. Is there any product that can provide a long-lasting solution to the needs of these people? Using top B2B websites such as Alibaba, start researching on the available products. A simple search in the Alibaba search area will help you determine if there are reliable products. You will come across the top products and read through reviews to determine the ones that are ideal for your friends.

If you come across a product that looks ideal for your friends, you are in a position to start thinking about starting an online store. Now start by trying every platform possible. Get the necessary information on the available selling platforms such as Amazon, Shopify, and eBay. Look at the advantages of each and decide how you wish to market your products. Think about the future of your business and the prospects of making money. Through your marketing efforts, determine whether it is possible to make a lasting brand from a certain online platform even before you invest in it.

Mindset

Your mindset will play an important role in your success as a dropshipper. As already mentioned, 99% of new dropshipping businesses on Shopify do not succeed. Given that the platform boasts of 300, 000 successful stores, it means that people open stores every day. For you to succeed in dropshipping, you must have a strong mentality. If you are an individual who expects things to happen easily you may give up.

If you are an individual who easily gives up, your business may not succeed. There are 5 types of mentality that describe successful dropshipping entrepreneurs

- Positive mentality
- Don't die mentality
- Go-getter mentality
- Limitless mentality
- Authentic Mentality

Positive Mentality

It is all about the positive aspects of life. A person who has a positive mentality does not look at the negative aspects of life. You need to focus on the positives to succeed in any type of business. Every business has challenges and discouragements. If you focus your mind on the challenges, you may never make a step in life. In the same way, dropshipping has its challenges. As you get into the business, you will meet store management issues that will require your mental strength. Choosing to be positive, hoping for the best and working to better your business will help you stand out among others.

Don't Die Mentality

Don't die is a type of mindset where you never give up. A person who has a don't die mentality works out in the toughest of all situations. If you are thinking about getting into any type of business, you must be ready to face the challenges that come your way head-on. Although the journey will not be easy, you should remain focused on your ultimate dream. The same case applies to dropshipping. The reason why most people fail is that they think dropshipping is a get rich quick scheme. Although dropshipping will give you money, it is not something you should get in with a faint heart. You should be prepared to do your job if you wish to make any money out of the business. Do not get into the business thinking that everything will run according to your plan. Actually, you have to put in some effort even before expecting any outcome.

Go-Getter Mentality

A go-getter mentality is the type of person who goes for whatever they want in life. In dropshipping, you must learn to go for the specific something you want. As mentioned, for you to get into this business, you must relate your needs and the needs of the people around you. A go-getter person is a person who does not settle for the status quo. If you see something is not right, you go out of your way to make it right. If you feel that your group or a certain group of people do not get what they deserve, you have to go out of your way to help them. You stand up and find a solution to problems. A go-getter person is an ideal candidate for dropshipping because the business is tough. As you think about the future of your business, you must go for whatever you want. You should be the one who determines the kind of products to sell in your store. You should be in a position to go out and find the right suppliers and pick quality products. With a go-getter mentality, you are in a position to push your brand forward and ensure that it reaches the place you are targeting.

Limitless Mentality

With the limitless mentality, you open your mind to the impossibility. A person who works with a limitless mentality has wild dreams. You should have wild dreams for your business. Dropshipping is not limited in terms of geographical reach. For this reason, you must allow your business to thrive beyond the geographical region. You should allow yourself to get into the business and thrive beyond the borders of your country or your locality. With a limitless mentality, you are able to try out different types of products. You are not afraid to try out new suppliers and introduce foreign products to your market. The limitless mentality allows you to be the leader in your niche. You become the person that other businesses look up to know what to do. You set trends and go ahead of others by introducing products that others are afraid to try out.

Authentic Mentality

An authentic mentality is a type of thinking where a person values originality. The reason why most businesses fail in dropshipping is lack of originality. As an entrepreneur, you need to be original in your ideas. Do not just copy the ideas of other people and use them to run your business. You should choose products that are original in nature. The way you package your products should also reflect originality. You should come up with your unique product ideas and collaborate with suppliers to introduce products that are unique to the market. You should choose a unique niche if you wish to succeed. Most of the niches are already saturated. However, if you are wise enough to select a unique niche, you will be able to create a long-lasting business. The originality of your idea determines how lasting the business will be. Trying to build your brand on the ideas of other businesses will not help you stay in business for long. You need to open your mind up and spot original ideas. You need to look at the available market opportunities and utilize the gaps in the market. Without originality, your products will just be like any other product out there.

It is important to ensure that you are psychologically prepared even before you start thinking about the dropshipping business. Psychological preparedness means that you should make up your mind about getting into the business. You should make up your mind that you want to do business and that you want to do it the right way. Although you may not have as much money to invest in the business, a positive mentality is better than any amount of money. You may have so much money to invest in a business but lacking a positive mentality may cost you dearly.

Chapter 2 Setting Up A Successful Dropshipping Business

Establish A Niche

What you choose to sell is critical to whether or not your dropshipping business will last longer than a few months.

You see, consumers often follow trends, and that means you need to be able to follow trends as well with your business so that you can keep the profits rolling in. Trends are always changing, so that is why you need to stay on top of it. Luckily, even though the internet is part of what makes the trends fluctuate so often, it also now makes it easier than ever to keep track of them.

Thanks to the internet you can research the worth of a niche and whether it can bring you profit overtime or not. Don't eagerly jump on the bandwagon of a popular niche because they can quickly become oversaturated, meaning many businesses are trying to focus on that niche at once so that you are less likely to make money on it.

This can make the process of establishing a niche quite confusing for people just starting out since the basic idea of sell what's popular doesn't quite work. By the end, you will one hundred percent know how to choose and establish the niche of your choice.

Establishing your chosen niche can really end up slowing your roll, no matter how excited you are to begin. That's because it isn't as simple as we would like it to be.

You will need to sit down and truly brainstorm a good niche. Finding something you are passionate about is definitely an excellent start, but it is much more than just that. Then you have to focus on ideas surrounding that niche that could not only work for you but work with the current market.

It isn't as hard as you might believe to research a niche. You can start with what you enjoy, what your family and friends enjoy, and move forward from there. It all just takes consideration on what you can find around you and what you might be able to sell. Be realistic most of all.

Then once you have a few ideas, not just one, you have to research them all and then compare them to one another. You'll have the weigh the risks and the benefits of this niche and maybe set up a few simple plan models for each one to see what might work best.

Are you starting to feel the thrill of all this information? That's great because we are really going to detail the process now so that you completely understand and will soon be able to do it for yourself. Be ready to absorb it all and prepare yourself for the success that you deserve.

Niche Evaluation And Validation

A niche is meant to appeal to a specific audience, which means you can narrow down the types of products you have listed on your online store. Narrowing down to a specific niche can help attract customers because it can often be overwhelming to find a store that sells everything and anything.

Plus, someone looking for a specific product might end up quite confused if they click on your site and find all sorts of goods that don't have an obvious relation to one another. Your brand needs to be more focused so that the attention it receives is positive.

What you need to consider when evaluating a niche is whether or not it can fulfill the needs of your consumers. This means you need to think about the answers this product can give to those needs, the prices at which you can sell it, and the profitability overall.

To get an idea of whether or not a marketing opportunity is right for you, you can research the sales volume of that market. That includes checking out how often the items are searched and then see what type of sales volume you could potentially have.

Google is a great tool to use when evaluating a sales opportunity by utilizing their keyword tool, which is accessible and free to use.

The more specific you get with your keywords the easier it will be to see how popular it is and what type of traffic you can potentially receive for it. Instead of choosing a wide category you will end up focusing on a smaller category, considered a sub-category. This will lead to your overall niche.

Try and figure out the real audience of your niche so that you know who you are selling to, and see how that follows through with other companies.

Don't be afraid to use big businesses like Amazon to help you figure out what you are doing. You can see the levels of popularity on a product easily by starting to type the name in and see what Amazon auto-fills it with. That assists in naming your subcategories and validating what you are considering.

A dropshipping business is a great idea, but you have to really get to know your audience so that the products you end up selling match what they are buying. Your research should tell you whether or not your idea is worth pursuing, so buckle up and get to it.

Amazon uses a specific algorithm to do this auto-filling, so you can see that it would be a reliable resource. Be smart and use your competition to your advantage. It's not a bad thing to take notes from those big-name retailers, because they are who you are competing hardest again.

Starting to get the idea? That's wonderful because we are about to explore more about selecting, establishing, and resourcing the right niche for you.

How To Select A Niche

Finding a niche that you can sell in without having to spend a ton of revenue on ads is very important when you're starting out. If you are beginning a dropshipping business then you probably don't have a lot of capital to start with, so you need to be as thrifty as possible.

You don't have the ability to dive into whatever harebrained scheme you may have.

We've talked about the best ways to evaluate and/or validate a niche, so now we need to discuss the criteria for selecting one. If you have brainstormed a few different niches to research and evaluated them well, then you're ready to go about the process of selecting one.

Find the price point of items and seek out the most expensive that you can find. A good place to start would be eBay, but it's not the best place to take the prices of, Just use eBay as a general and basic guide to lead you toward products that could work for you.

It's not too hard to utilize eBay to help you in your quest to selecting a niche. Find a few products that are constantly sold in multiples every day and soon you can have a list of products that you know would sell for you.

Amazon is another great way to help you find items to sell. They have categories within categories within categories for you to explore, so make sure to do that. They have a wealth of items at various prices with plenty of reviews to sort through so that you can choose what you need.

Another important factor to take into account is not selling low-cost items. I know, I know, people are always looking for great deals, but you want to sell items that can net you a profit over time, especially since dropshipping is not immediately lucrative.

Alright, so maybe you've found a niche that can work for you and a set list of products that you could possibly sell. That's a fantastic start, but there are still a few more things you should do to help you select your niche.

Start looking for suppliers of these particular products and ask about their prices and shipping, and what sorts of deals, discounts, or availabilities they have. You don't want to pick a niche where the sellers already have established buyers, because then you won't be able to break into the market.

In fact, you usually make around 20% of the price of an item back. So if you're selling a $10 phone case you would likely only receive a $2 profit. The bigger your items are and the better-selling, the more profit you'll end up with. The math isn't too difficult.

You want to find those items that are more expensive but also sell well. Once you have a good set of those you are ready to get going.

How To Establish A Niche

Finding that perfect niche means that you are ready to establish the niche, but that can take a lot of work. Niches are not always the easiest to get going because it can be kind of confusing to figure out how to sell them overall. Often the niche is a subcategory that doesn't immediately spell out what you can begin selling.

For example, here is a list of 2019's top ten most profitable niches of 2019:

- Minimalist Luggage
- Home Gaming Setups
- High-Performance Workstation
- Home Gym Equipment
- Tiny Home Furnishings
- Custom Window Treatments
- Recreational Boating
- Home Theater Equipment •
  Indoor Grow Rooms
- Kiteboarding Gear

These clearly are not niches that are simple to find profitable products for which shows how much work you really have to put into your niche to establish it. You need to know the market inside and out and have a lock on your competitors as well if you desire to make any leeway.

Make sure that you find the perfect name for your brand or store. You want it to be easy to remember and potentially unique. Stay away from anything integrating your name into, and make sure to remember that anything too long just won't be attractive to a buyer. Short and snappy is easy to remember.

One of the easiest ways to establish your brand is by utilizing Shopify, which is an e-commerce platform that makes it easy for you to set up your website and get started. You don't need to know any fancy jargon or hire someone else to work with Shopify, and it has multiple apps out there to help make shopping easy and stress-free.

Let's talk a little more about Shopify and how it can assist you when you are looking to set up your dropshipping business.

Shopify is the all-in-one that you need to get your business off the ground. Once you have that perfect name you can start working on that website, and Shopify is there to help you every step of the way with all sorts of helpful tools.

There are different themes, forms of analysis, and more on Shopify that make it easy for you to establish yourself in the niche of your choice.

You can also experiment with themes, styles, and more without throwing away a ton of money on a designer.

Shopify also offers apps like Oberlo that are a great help when you are setting up. You see, Oberlo is a great resource for amassing different products you may want to sell and is helpful when researching potential niches to choose as well.

It's lucky that these days there are plenty of ways to work on marketing yourself without having to hire any outside parties.

Ultimately, using the right marketing tools and ad selections can help bring attention and traffic to your new online store.

What Resources Do You Need?

Again, one of the most attractive parts of starting your own dropshipping business is how little it will cost. Most of the resources that you require are free to access, or at least inexpensive.

This, of course, includes Shopify and its attached Oberlo. They are indispensable when it comes to success at your new chosen profession.

This is because Shopify and Oberlo together make it easy for you to find products and add them to your store so that you can quickly become legitimate and get going.

Amazon, eBay, and Etsy are all also integral to the process of you finding the products you will end up selling because it is so simple to see what sells for them.

Google keyword analysis is another great resource to follow because it provides concrete information and numbers on searches. Market Samurai is a different product that utilizes Google's keyword process and can create lists for you to further research.

It is also important to establish yourself with a secure supplier so that your business does not suffer from the get-go with someone who is not reputable. Seriously, this is a very important step to take so be sure to do your homework properly when choosing who to work with.

A way to identify possible suppliers is by seeing what other sites use, such as Amazon, and see about partnering with them. Be sure that they can communicate effectively and have a resilient reputation so you don't end up in hot water.

If there is an issue with the product or their shipping they need to be able to respond back to you quickly and effectively, otherwise, you are just drawing out the issue with the customer which can lead to a bad review.

By choosing to work with established suppliers you are setting yourself up for more success. Even if it takes longer and you don't get the best deals it still works out in the long run for you because the reliability is so necessary when you are getting on your feet.

Utilizing the competition that exists is just as important when trying to establish yourself. You can order the same products from different competition to compare price, quality, and even packaging. This helps you get a feel for what the successful businesses are doing so that you can imitate.

Don't be afraid to see what others are doing because that's how you can take a full step forward, otherwise you are walking blindly. Even using the same suppliers means you can offer at a similar price range to your competition, that way you know you are just as likely to be considered when compared side by side.

Honestly, the possibilities are endless when it comes to your dropshipping business. It's up to you to use all these resources that are at your fingertips, just waiting to help you net that first profit.

Chapter 3 Dropshipping ebay, Amazon and shopify

How to Dropship on Amazon & eBay

If instead of creating your own website, you want to dropship on an existing platform or marketplace, Amazon and eBay should be among your top considerations. Let's discuss how you can set up your dropshipping store on these two marketplaces.

Amazon

Being the biggest name in retail e-commerce, Amazon has a lot of inherent advantages as a dropshipping platform. You can open a dropshipping account with Amazon and take advantage of their market share and stellar reputation to sell your products. Amazon buys products from suppliers in bulk, so they have massive inventory in warehouses in different parts of the world, which means that if you work with them, your small shop could grow fast and operate globally.

With Amazon, you also have access to a large market of more than 300 million users, which means that you could get large returns if you have great products and strategies. Because Amazon already has hundreds of millions of potential customers, you don't have to spend too much on advertising. In fact, you can easily advertise within the platform itself. If you optimize your page, you could get organic traffic there without needing to advertise.

Before you choose Amazon for your dropshipping platform, you should understand that they have one major downside. They prioritize merchants who use their FBA program over those who dropship with the help of third-party suppliers. If you are using Amazon's FBA program, you actually have to buy your inventory upfront and send it to Amazon's warehouses where it will be stored until it's shipped out to customers. If you wanted to limit your startup costs to almost zero, the FBA program probably isn't your best option, so stick with dropshipping. That being said, Amazon is a great place for drop-shippers because it has some of the best shipping times and quality control measures in the whole retail e-commerce business.

Many people think that dropshipping is against Amazon's terms of service, but it's actually not. Amazon doesn't allow arbitrage dropshipping (this is where people source products that are cheaper from places like Walmart and eBay and then sell them through Amazon). Amazon allows private third-party fulfillment of customer orders, as long as it's your business name that appears on all the purchase and shipping slips that are attached to the product. According to the Amazon TOS, you have to be the "seller of record," which means that if you use a competitor of Amazon's (like Target or Walmart), they may close your account.

Here is how to go about dropshipping on Amazon:

First, you should get a professional Amazon seller account. You should pay the fee for a pro account because the free account will limit your ability to grow and scale once you have started your dropshipping business. There are also certain categories in Amazon's platform in which you cannot sell products if your account is a free one.

You also need to get UPC codes (Universal Product Codes) for all your products. There are lots of services online that can help you acquire UPC codes, so with a little internet research, you can easily figure out how that works. You also need to get suppliers, and they shouldn't be big box suppliers (big companies that compete with Amazon in the retail market).

Use a product research tool to find a great product to sell on Amazon. Remember that with Amazon, it's even much harder to compete in popular niches because there are other sellers who have been around longer and they have positive reviews, so you have to go an extra mile in your product research.

You also need enough capital to sustain your business in the first few months because it takes a while for Amazon to pay its merchants, so you can't count on the payout from your sales to maintain cash flow.

Also, make sure that your suppliers ship the products pretty fast (preferably within 5 business days). That's because Amazon customers are accustomed to fast shipping, and the platform keeps metrics of its drop-shippers which customers can see. If your metrics are poor, customers won't be too keen on buying from you. Amazon is a bit strict when it comes to quality control, and if you get a high number of product returns or cancelations, or if your metrics are terrible, they could suspend you from their platform.

As a drop-shipper on Amazon, the way you create and organize your listings will determine how many sales you will be able to make. First, to increase your chances of success, make sure that you have lots of product listings on your account. Second, you have to be well organized in the way you list your products. Make sure that you use bold and clear titles and descriptions that sound like professional sales copy. You should also use high-quality product images for all items in your listings. As a drop-shipper, you may not be able to use PPC ads for your products because Amazon prioritizes FBA merchants over drop-shippers, so your best chance of boosting your visibility is by optimizing your product pages.

You should be careful when selecting the products to dropship on Amazon because not all products are suited to be drop-shipped on this platform. You should choose a niche where people are passionate and very specific about the products, which means that they will be willing to wait a little longer to receive that particular product. If you go to a niche where products are readily available everywhere else, you may not be able to compete with merchants who use FBA, mostly because of their faster shipping times.

Most Amazon drop-shippers eventually end up switching over to the FBA program. They use dropshipping to test the viability of a product in the market, and then if it works well, they switch to FBA to take advantage of Amazon's fast shipping, advertising, and other perks. If you have the capital, you can adapt this model to increase your competitiveness within the Amazon platform. If you would rather stick with dropshipping, you may be able to offer incentives to your customers to make them more willing to wait for a little longer for their packages. You can add a small freebie to every product that your customers purchase to entice them to select your products despite the longer shipping times.

Finally, when shipping with Amazon, be extremely careful about copyright and trademark issues because you could get authenticity claims from big companies, and Amazon could shut your down. Otherwise,

Amazon is a great place to run a dropshipping business, and all you have to do to succeed there is to work smart and hard and follow the rules.

eBay

eBay is a great platform for dropshipping mostly because it adds a twist to the dropshipping model. Instead of just having a fixed price for your products, you can set up auctions for each listed item (especially if the products you are selling are rare and high-value items). It's also less restrictive when it comes to the kind of products that you can sell. Unlike Amazon, you don't have to worry too much about where you source your products, as long as you are able to deliver.

eBay is like the wild west of online retail because it allows people to sell all sorts of new and used items, so if you want to stand out and gain the trust of customers, you should be able to provide as much information about yourself and your product as you can and try to make your listings look professional. Compared to other platforms where you can start your dropshipping business, eBay is probably the cheapest because it doesn't charge any fees (like Shopify and Amazon).

To start dropshipping on eBay, go to their website and open an account. You can either open a personal or a business account, that doesn't matter since most dropshipping functions can be performed by both accounts, plus you may be able to upgrade a personal account into a business one if the need arises. The account opening process is fairly standard. You just have to fill in your personal information and contact information, and towards the end of the process, you will need to add a PayPal account to your eBay account. After signing up, you can personalize your account by adding a logo. The whole process should take you less than ten minutes if you have all your details ready.

When you start selling on eBay, you will only be allowed to list a few items at a go (about 10 items). As you make more sales, the platform will increase your limit more and more. You have to write good product descriptions with eye-catching titles for your products, indicate their prices, and then use high-quality images to show the product from multiple angles. eBay listings differ slightly from listing on personal websites or other platforms because you have to add terms of sales and shipping information within the description for each product.

For each product that you list on eBay, you have to go through the same listing process since eBay doesn't support synchronized settings across multiple listings. If you exceed your listing allowance, eBay might charge you a listing fee for the extra products. eBay listings usually expire after thirty days, so if you want yours to stay up beyond that period, you have to go to 'setting details' and set your preferred duration for that listing. The "Good till canceled" option ensures that your product stays on the site until you decide otherwise.

You will then input the price, quantity of items, payment options, buyer privacy setting, sales tax for the product, and your preferred return options. When it comes to returning options, you have to choose the length of the return window for the product, and the action that you will have to take when dealing with returns. If you feel like your customers could benefit from some further explanation of your return policy, there is a field where you can insert additional information.

You will then have to fill in all your shipping details. You can select different shipping options for different regions. You should also specify your shipping method, fees, durations, etc. You will then click the "list" button to publish your listing on eBay. In case you have left an important detail out, eBay will notify you and allow you to fix the error.

After you have listed your product, you could start promoting it on social media platforms almost immediately to drive traffic to your page. When you make sells, you will contact your supplier and have him ship the product to your customer within your stipulated time period.

Shopify

Shopify is by far the best online tool for drop-shippers who don't have the technical expertise to create their own shops. It makes it possible for anyone to sign up and start his own online store in just a few minutes. It's great for people who want to start a dropshipping business but lack the technical know-how or the resources to build their own e-commerce websites from scratch. If you want a hassle-free experience as you start your first store, you should seriously consider using Shopify. The service offers free trial periods for beginners who want to test the waters before making a financial commitment. Here is a step by step guide to help you start your first Shopify dropshipping store.

Choose a Name for Your Dropshipping Store

When creating a Shopify store, your first task will be to select a name for your dropshipping business. You want to make sure that the name you select is simple, creative, and memorable. If you already have a niche in mind, you could try to find a name that is related to that niche so that people can have an easy time figuring out what you are selling. There are some online business name generators that you could use to come up with a list of possible names before you narrow it down to one.

When you find a few possible names that you may want to use, you must check to see if they are available. Google each of your shortlisted business names to see if they are already in use. If you use obvious sounding names such as "American Watches," chances are someone has already thought of that, and they are already trading under that business name, so try to think outside the box.

Create a New Shopify Account

Shopify has made this step extremely easy. All you have to do is go to the Shopify homepage. At that page, you will find a field where you have to enter your email address to start the process. Once you have entered the address, click the "get started" button. You will then be asked to create a password and input your chosen store name. Shopify will ask you a few questions about how much experience you have had in the e-commerce sector, and then they will ask you to provide a few accurate personal details. After you are done providing those details, your account will be officially opened, and you can then proceed to optimize your settings.

Set Up Your Account and Add All Necessary Information

You have to go through your new account's settings one menu item at a time, and you are going to input the information you need to configure your account before it can be operational. You have to put in place the correct settings to allow you to receive customer payments, to create your shipping rates, and to establish your store policies.

When customizing your account, your first task will be to add one or more payment options to your store. Unless you have this in place, there will be no way for your customers to pay you for the products they'll purchase. Go to your Shopify settings page and click on the tab that has the word "payment" on it. You will have the option to add a PayPal account or to use other payment solutions.

We highly recommend that you use PayPal because it's extremely convenient and it has a deep market penetration, so most people who shop online already have PayPal accounts of their own. You can also opt for other payment systems if you find them convenient or necessary given the particular nature of your products (for example, if yours is a store that mostly sells products to offices and other businesses, you may find it more convenient to add a payment system that allows for bank transfers.

After you have all your payment channels in place, it's time to set your store policies. These policies will govern the relationship between you and your customers, so you should make sure that they are clearly stated and that they are compliant with the law.

Shopify understands exactly what kind of policies you might need for your store, so they have created a tool that enables you to automatically generate store policies that are standardized. You can immediately generate a refund policy, a privacy policy, and even a set of terms and conditions that will protect your store from legal liability in many foreseeable situations. To gain access to the policy creation tool, you have to click on the "checkout" tab, the go through the page to find each of the fields that you have to fill. You can then click on the "generate" button, and your policy will be set.

When your customers check out after making a purchase, the full text of the policy will appear, and they'll have to accept those terms and conditions before the sale goes through. If you have your own conditions that you want to include in the policy, there are some templates that you can use as guides to create your own policy.

Finally, you will have to declare your shipping rates. Many e-commerce experts recommend that you should account for the shipping price when you mark up the price of each item in the store, and then, you should offer your customers "free shipping." This is a marketing technique that works pretty well because it makes most customers believe that they are getting a great deal, so they'll be more inclined to go through with the purchase. You can click on the 'Shipping' button and select your preferred shipping options for different zones, starting with domestic ones and proceeding all the way to international zones.

Launch Your Dropshipping Store

After you are done with your settings and configurations, you should proceed to launch your new dropshipping store. To do this, click on the "sales channels" option, and then click on "Add sales channel." When you are done with that step, you will have a real online business that is up and running.

Design and Personalize Your Store

Now that you own an online store, it's time to personalize it. Here, you have to consider how you want your customers to view your site as they browse through it and make purchases. The design of your shop is going to be crucial, and it may have a huge bearing on your level of success as a drop-shipper. You want to make a good first impression when customers visit your site, and you want to project an image of professionalism. The two most important design aspects that you have to consider are the theme and the logo of your shop.

Shopify has a large collection of themes in their inbuilt theme store, so you don't have to worry about finding a theme that suits your brand. You can use a free theme option, or you can pay a little money for a premium theme. If you are working under a tight budget, a free theme will do just fine. However, if you are very particular about your branding, you may want to go for a premium theme. Try out a few themes before you settle on one. After selecting a theme, you can customize it to make it more reflective of your brand.

Logos are important for branding purposes because they enable customers to remember your dropshipping store in case they want to make more purchases in the future. Your logo should blend with other design aspects of your shop because you want to create a sense of uniformity.

You can use tools like the Oberlo Logo Maker to create a high-quality logo in a matter of minutes. All you have to do is play around with colors, fonts, and icons. If you are a skilled graphics designer, you can create your own logo and upload it onto your Shopify account. You can also hire graphic design experts for cheap on sites like Fiverr and Upwork. After you are done with both the logo and the design of your store, it's time to add your products.

Add Products to Your Store

To add a product to your shop, go to Shopify Admin and click on "Products." You should then click on the "Add a Product" button on the top right part of the page.

You will then have access to fields where you can enter the title and the description of your product. Fill the fields by either copying and pasting the text from your supplier's website or adding a description that you have prepared on your own. Make sure that you use colorful language in your product description because your customers are going to make purchase decisions based on that description.

You should then scroll down the page and find the "Images" section. Here, you have the option of adding images by uploading image files from your computer. You can also use "drag and drop" to achieve the same outcome. Make sure you upload your favorite product image first because it's the one that is going to act as a "featured image," meaning that it will appear prominently on the sales page when your customers scroll through your shop.

You should then review all your product details, particularly the "visibility" settings to make sure that your product is set to appear on the online store. You should also review the "Organization" settings and modify them to make sure your product is properly categorized according to Vendor, Product Type, and Collections.

You then have to input the price of the product. As you do that, you can select an option that makes it possible for customers to compare prices, and you can also check a box that allows a tax to be added to the final price of the product.

When you get to the inventory section, you should add your SKU, your Inventory Policy, and a Barcode. Indicate whether or not your product has a shipping price, then select the weight bracket of the product. If your product comes in different sizes and colors, you should fill the "Variants" section appropriately, and put in the different prices for each variant.

Finally, you should edit your Meta Title and Meta Description in order to improve your SEO (search engine optimization) so that customers will have an easier time finding your product online. Ensure that you save all your product information correctly and that you view your product listing from the front end to see it from the point of view of the customer. You should repeat all these steps to add more products, or you can use services such as Oberlo which can help you add products to your account automatically.

Start Selling and Cashing in

Now that everything is done, you can start making sales. Remember that dropshipping is a competitive business, so you should do everything that you can to promote your products on blogs, social media, and other websites. Advertising is also an option if you have the resources.

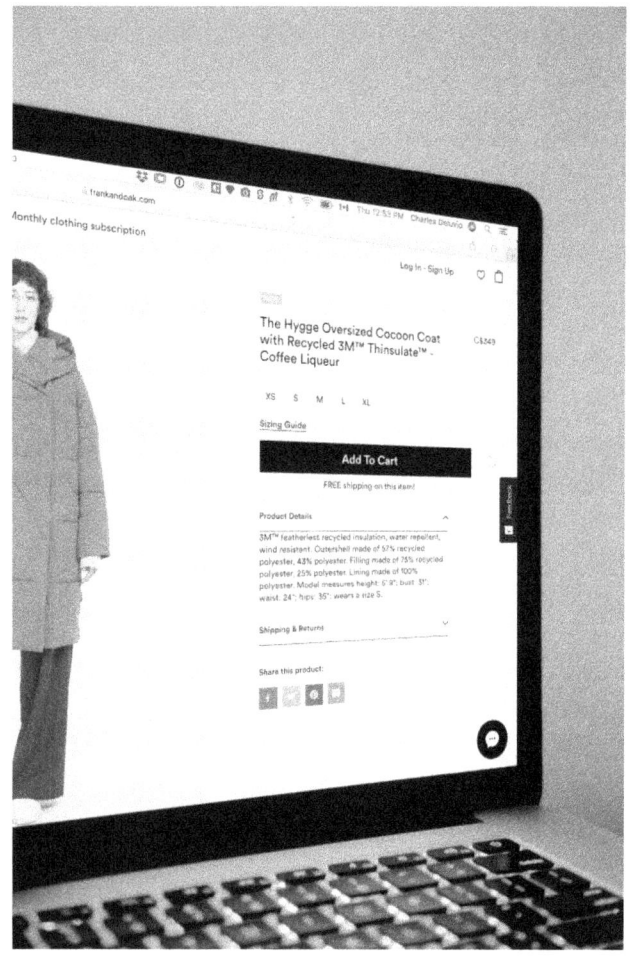

Chapter 4 Pros and Cons

The Advantages Of Starting A Dropshipping Business

There are many advantages of starting a dropshipping company, but in order to benefit from those advantages, make sure that you understand how the dropshipping model works and ensure that you stick to the model.

All retail businesses are inherently risky, but many of the risks of ordinary retail and e-commerce businesses are somewhat mitigated in the dropshipping model because they don't fall within your docket as a drop-shipper—most risks are borne by third-party suppliers. A lot of the advantages of the dropshipping stem from the fact that you as an entrepreneur are at liberty to try things out without having to risk too much.

Here are some of the major benefits of investing in a dropshipping business:

> Less Startup Capital Investment Compared to Other Models

One of the most important advantages of dropshipping is that you can launch your business without needing to put down a lot of money into purchasing inventory. That means that pretty much anyone can start a dropshipping business. Even if you are a broke student or someone without access to much capital, you won't be locked out of this business.

In traditional retail businesses, before you are able to start your shop you have to spend thousands of dollars stocking up on inventory without any guarantee that you will be able to offload any of it. For most people, starting a traditional retail business would mean taking a bank loan, or using a huge chunk (if not all) of their savings on inventory. However, with dropshipping, if you are savvy enough, you could get your business off the ground with almost zero capital investment.

In dropshipping, you never have to purchase a product until you have made a sale, and the customer has already paid you. It's like being an agent who makes a commission by selling a supplier's product to a customer without having to put his own money down. In fact, when you are getting started, the only investment you absolutely have to make will go into setting up your online shop, registering with suppliers, and marketing your brand to increase visibility—none of your money has to go into production costs.

The agreements that people make with suppliers tend to vary, but the one constant is that you don't have to make an upfront payment for your products. If you find a supplier who insists that you pay for his product in bulk, you should know that he is not the right supplier for your dropshipping business, and you should keep looking around until you find one who is suitable for this model.

Low Overhead Costs

Apart from spending a lot of money on inventory, running a traditional retail business would require you to spend a fortune on overhead expenses, most of which you don't have to worry about if you decide to try out dropshipping. In traditional e-commerce businesses, you would have to rent offices, warehouses, and transportation vehicles. If you were importing your own products, you would have to pay ocean freight fees, and spend a lot of cash hiring warehouse workers to store, sort, package, and distribute your products. It would mean that you'd have to pay for rent, utilities, insurance costs, transportation costs, maintenance costs, etc.

Many traditional retail businesses fail because they end up buried in unforeseen overhead expenses. In dropshipping, you never have to worry about any of the logistical issues and the overhead expenses. You don't have to be concerned about paying warehouse workers, being late on utility bills or not being able to make enough for rent that month.

Most people run their dropshipping businesses from their homes (although if you find it necessary, you can rent a small office from which to run your operations).

Whenever you have an order to fulfill, you essentially outsource all the duties that are involved in the process to a third party, all at a bargained cost that is manageable. Your supplier will have to deal with storing your products in a warehouse, organizing and packaging the products before shipment, labeling them properly, shipping them, tracking them, and delivering them to your customers. The supplier will give you the tracking number for each product so that you can keep tabs on it, but you don't require many resources to do that. The only cost that is absolutely necessary, is the cost of operating a customer service line (preferably one that is toll-free).

Easy for You to Get Started

Starting a traditional e-commerce retail business requires a lot of technical know-how that just isn't necessary when it comes to dropshipping. When you run a dropshipping business, you don't have to spend a lot of time learning every single detail about how to operate and manage warehouses, how to hire warehouse employees, and how to provide them with a safe working environment. You never have to learn what goes into packing and shipping your products, let alone what goes into manufacturing them. You never have to learn the intricacies of optimal inventory management. You don't have to learn the accounting mathematics that goes into tracking products through different parts of the supply chain. All you have to do is find a reliable supplier who will do all of those things for you, and you will already be in business.

Can be Highly Scalable

If you run a traditional business, you would have to increase the amount of work that you had to do if the number of orders that you received was to increase significantly. However, with dropshipping, that doesn't have to be the case. The only work you have to do is to relay the shipping order from the customer to the manufacturer, so you won't be burdened with the responsibility of having to hire extra workers to increase your production. That means that once you have set up your dropshipping business to process a given number of orders every day, the only thing you have to do to scale up by any factor is to increase your capacity to receive and submit orders, which is neither difficult nor technical.

If your sales grow significantly, the only people you will need to hire to meet the increase in demand will be customer service people. A traditional retail business that finds itself in a similar situation will have to hire more warehouse workers, purchase more packaging materials, hire more managers, construct more facilities and warehouses, and invest more in transportation. In dropshipping, none of those things will stand in your way when you want to scale up.

Dropshipping is also highly scalable when you want to upgrade the quality of the product that you are selling. The effort that it takes to drop-ship an item that costs $1 is the same effort that it will take you to drop-ship an item that costs $1000. That means that if you want to switch from selling cheap items to expensive items, you won't have to exert any more effort than you already do. By contrast, if you wanted to switch from a cheaper product to a more expensive one in a traditional retail business, you would have to invest a lot of money into upgrading your production capacity. With dropshipping, nothing changes—you just relay the customers' orders to the suppliers as you have always done. If you want to scale up by adding new products to your online shop, all you have to do is find the right product and supplier, market test it, and add it to your shop.

An increase in the number of customer orders may cause you to run out of stock more often, but that is not a hindrance to scalability. If your customer base grows, you can always increase the number of suppliers that you have in order to meet the extra demand.

You Can Do It from Any Location

If you have a dropshipping business that is already operational, you have the flexibility to run it from pretty much anywhere you want, as long as you have an internet connection. The supplier will deal with every physical aspect of your business, leaving you to handle only the digital stuff, which doesn't restrict you to a given location. When you are setting up your business for the first time, you may need to stay grounded because you may have to acquire things like permits, a tax ID, licenses, etc. (some of these things can also be done online). However, the minute that you have all things set up, the only obligation you will have is to be able to stay in communication with your suppliers and your customers.

As part of your due diligence, while you are still establishing your business, you may have to visit your suppliers' facilities to verify that they indeed have the capacity to provide the product you are looking for on a consistent basis. However, beyond that, the business doesn't require you to be physically present at any one place. Some people have been able to operate profitable dropshipping businesses while on vacation in exotic locations, or while trotting around the globe.

If you choose to travel as you run your dropshipping business, you can easily communicate with your suppliers and customers through email. However, if you prefer talking to them over the phone, it's important to remember that international or cross-country phone calls can be rather expensive, and they may put a significant dent on your bottom-line.

Ensures a High Customer Lifetime Value

In business and marketing, the term "customer lifetime value" is used to refer to the amount of net profit that a business can generate thanks to its relationship with a particular customer throughout the remainder of his or her life. Dropshipping gives you the ability to increasingly expand your selection of products by adding new ones to your online store whenever you want to. This makes it possible for you to keep your customers interested enough so that they will want to return again and make other purchases in the future. This works best when you have found a niche that is unique, and you have curated a product line around that niche in a way that your competitors haven't been able to do.

Minimizes Your Risk

Traditional retail businesses come with lots of inherent risks, some of which cannot be mitigated against. If you put your money into traditional business, there is always the chance that your product won't move, and you will be stuck with useless inventory. If you operate your own warehouses, there are risks such as accidents, fires, water damage, among others. If you ship your own goods, there are risks of breakages, damages, and lost packages. When you run a dropshipping operation, you won't have to shoulder any of those risks.

If you are selling trendy products, there is always the possibility that trends will change, and people's tastes will be different in a few weeks or months. What if you sank all your capital into the inventory of that product? Well, with dropshipping, that is not something you ever have to worry about. Even if you invest in a certain niche product only to find out that its sales volumes are lower than you had expected, you can always pivot to another product without losing too much capital (your only loss will be the cash you put into creating your website and doing some marketing).

Enables You to Come to Market a lot Quicker

If you are familiar with the term "opportunity cost," you understand that any delays to get to market can technically be considered as loses. If there are two people looking to start e-commerce retail businesses, the one who chooses dropshipping will get started almost immediately, while the one who chooses a traditional e-commerce model will have to spend a lot of time looking for capital, learning the intricacies of the business and setting things up before he can finally enter the market. By the time the other guy official launches his business, the one who took the dropshipping route will already be making money.

Another aspect of this is how long it takes to ship products in traditional e-commerce versus how long it takes to do the same in dropshipping. In traditional e-commerce, you first have to ship the product from the supplier to your own facilities, then you have to ship the same product again from your warehouses to the client. It takes a lot more time for the product to reach the customer in traditional e-commerce than it does in dropshipping and that time difference matters a lot. If the product is a trendy one that could go out of fashion at any given time, the entrepreneur who chooses the dropshipping model will get into the market fast enough, make a killing, then get out before the trend changes. The other guy will get into the market a little much later, and he'd be stuck with outdated inventory if things change.

Sell an Unlimited Selection of Products

There is no limit to the variety of products that you can sell through the dropshipping model. You don't have to own or physically possess whatever you are selling. All you have to do is list it on your website or sales page to find out if there is anyone who is willing to buy it. That means that you can list as many products as you want, and you won't lose anything by doing that. On the other hand, traditional e-commerce retailers are limited to the selection of products that they already have in stock, and sometimes, they may have to hold off introducing new and trendy products because they need to clear inventory that is backlogged.

Because of the unlimited selection of products at your disposal, it's easy for you to expand into new markets. In fact, when some suppliers introduce new products, they will allow you to add them to your website for free if you are already in their roster of registered merchants.

Access to Unlimited Amounts of Inventory

There is no limit to the number of products that you can sell. If you have a good enough marketing campaign to go along with your dropshipping business, you may find yourself selling your products like hotcakes. If this happens, you never have to worry about running out of inventory because you are getting your supply directly from a supplier who keeps enough stock to service several merchants. Even if there is a likelihood that your supplier will run out, you always have the option of having backup suppliers. In theory, your inventory is virtually unlimited, so if you are well organized, you will never have to turn a customer away for any reason.

Less Time Consumed

Most of the things that you need to do to set up and to operate your dropshipping business can be done in a hassle-free and convenient way. You don't have to deal with the hassle of storing and packaging your products in preparation for shipment. All the labor-intensive parts of the job are handled by suppliers and wholesalers. You can also add new products to your sales page with just a few clicks and begin making money almost immediately. Compared to other retail models, dropshipping is indeed extremely convenient.

Fewer Products With Little Risk

All the time-consuming activities that are involved in the e-commerce retail process are delegated to other parties in the dropshipping model. The only thing you have to do on a day to day basis is to relay the customers' orders to the suppliers and send customers notification about the current location and the ETA of their packages. That means that you don't need to spend too much time running this type of business.

This business is, therefore, a good option not just for full-time entrepreneurs, but also for people who have other obligations. You can run a dropshipping business while you have a full-time job, a part-time job, or even as you pursue a college degree. If you have a startup e-commerce shop where you do your own packaging and shipping, your business will suffer if you split your attention and focus on other things such as a job or school.

Test Products with Little Risk

Dropshipping is the only e-commerce retail model where you can get to test the viability of different products in the market without risking too much of your capital. In fact, lots of experienced drop-shippers do exactly that. They list products on their websites and sales pages, and they wait to see if there is any market out there for those products. If after a while there is no visible enthusiasm for the product, they pull it off their list of offerings and try a different product altogether, until they find the one that generates the most profit. That kind of trial and error approach isn't a viable technique in any other model of e-commerce. If you put money into inventory that doesn't sell, you can say bye to your capital.

Increases Your Favorability with Wholesalers

Wholesalers love dropshipping businesses because they expand and boost their sales to levels that were previously unimaginable. Before dropshipping came along, obscure manufacturers and wholesalers had to rely on big stores and e-commerce websites alone to get their products to the consumer, and even then, it was hard for some of those products to receive any visibility online or even in physical stores. When dropshipping came along, it changed the game for wholesalers because they now have the ability to sell more goods and to reach wider customer bases.

Wholesalers look favorably upon dropshipping businesses, and some of them have been going out of their way to make their products and services available to drop-shippers. Dropshippers and wholesalers have relationships that are mutually beneficial, and if you start a dropshipping business, you too can benefit from those relationships.

The Disadvantages Of Starting A Dropshipping Business

Like many other business models, dropshipping has its share of disadvantages, most of which we will be discussing in this chapter. You have already seen some of the advantages of dropshipping, and as you read about the disadvantages, you will realize that some of them are direct results of the advantages that we discussed earlier. Some of the things that make dropshipping attractive to many merchants also have the effect of making it harder for individual merchants to succeed as drop-shippers. In other words, some of the positive incentives that attract people into these businesses have a way of turning into "perverse incentives" and ruining the viability of many dropshipping niches.

We are not discussing the disadvantages of dropshipping in order to scare you away from this model. Instead, we are outlining all the things that could go wrong with your dropshipping business so that you can know what to expect, and you can understand what you need to do to mitigate against any problems that may arise. We will be doing you a disservice if we only talked about the positive aspects of dropshipping without informing you about its negative aspects. If you fully understand common problems that drop-shippers face, you will be better equipped to distinguish yourself, to rise above the fray, and to succeed in your business.

Here are some of the disadvantages that you may have to deal with as you run your dropshipping business:

Low-Profit Margins

The biggest disadvantage that you would have to deal with in the dropshipping business is the low-profit margins. It's extremely easy to get started in this business and that has attracted many entrepreneurs, and it has made most niches very competitive. There are hundreds or even thousands of merchants who are willing to start online shops and to sell their products at a very small profit margin, so every new entrant into the game has to keep his or her prices close to those of everyone else in order to stay competitive.

The vast majority of dropshipping merchants build low-quality sites, and they barely offer any customer service, so their operating costs are low. When customers are looking for the product that you are selling, they now have online tools that will help them compare your product prices to those of other similar products, so even if you have a good marketing strategy, you have no choice but to set your prices low in order to make any sales.

The low-profit margin also results from the fact that drop-shippers don't get to purchase their product as a wholesale or "bulk" price because they sell their products one item at a time. Compared to a traditional e-commerce shop that carries its own inventory, drop-shippers have to pay more per item, so at the end of the day, their profit margins are limited.

Wholesalers are right to charge drop-shippers more than other merchants because they go through a lot of trouble to package each item individually rather than sending out bulk orders. This costs them more in terms of packaging material, labor, and transportation costs, so they feel the need to transfer those costs to the owner of the dropshipping business.

The profit that you make as a retailer in the dropshipping business is your selling price minus all other costs, including the cost of buying from the supplier, shipping costs, and your own operating costs (e.g. the amount you pay for ads and content development). If you already have less than a 20% margin to work with after subtracting the supplier's charge, you can end up with a really minuscule profit margin.

In order to make decent profits as a drop-shipper, you have to move high volumes of the product. You can also do a lot of research in order to identify a niche that works well with the dropshipping model. We will be discussing how to find a great niche later in this book.

Suppliers Are Prone to Making Human Errors

Dropshipping suppliers tend to service a lot of merchants, and because of the high volumes of the orders that they have to fulfill, they often end up making human errors. If you have chosen to work with the cheapest supplier as a way to cut your costs, chances are that he would end up making frequent mistakes in which the customers will end up blaming you because they are doing business with you, and not your supplier.

If the supplier fails to keep his stock levels up, you may end up accepting orders from customers only to find out that your supplier is unable to fulfill them. Whenever there are bungled shipments or missing packages, you will have no choice but to take responsibility for the errors. You can mitigate against some of the human errors by having backup suppliers and backups to the backups so that if one supplier fails, you don't have to let down your customer and come across as unprofessional.

Issues with Inventory

Compared to traditional e-commerce businesses that stock their own inventory, dropshipping means that you have no idea how much stock is actually available at any given time, so you have to source your products from multiple suppliers to avoid a scenario where you run out of stock. However, even that solution presents its own problems with your inventory. Some technological solutions are available to help owners of dropshipping businesses sync up their sales records with their suppliers' stock records, but most suppliers don't invest in support systems for such technologies because they aren't the primary benefactors of such technologies. Technological solutions also fall short because it's hard to project the suppliers' inventory depletion rate since they service multiple dropshipping businesses at the same time.

Shipping Costs Can Get Complicated

Many drop-shippers work with multiple suppliers at any given time, and this opens up the opportunity for shipping costs to get really complicated and unnecessarily high. Take the example of a customer who orders a handful of items from your dropshipping business. If you source each item from a different warehouse, you will have to pay a shipping fee for each of the items that the customer receives. You will have a difficult time convincing a customer who has checked out multiple items in one cart that there is a shipping cost attached to each individual item—customers who are used to shipping deals from places like Amazon may find that ridiculous. They'll assume you are trying to grossly overcharge them for shipping, and they may even decide not to buy your products anymore. If you choose to offset the shipping costs on your end, you may find yourself actually making a loss on that sale! In a scenario such as this one, it's impossible for you to come out on top.

Competition

Because it's easy to get started, there are many people who have set up dropshipping businesses, and while this is a good thing for the consumer, it is a very big challenge for you if you want to succeed as a drop-shipper. You can find that hundreds of people are selling the same exact product, so it makes it hard for anyone person to break out from the crowd and to make extraordinary amounts of profits. In many cases, you even have to go up against juggernauts like Walmart or Amazon who won't hesitate to undercut smaller retailers whenever they feel like it. When the profit margin is already low, you have very little room to outmaneuver dozens if not hundreds of competitors.

Shipping Can Be Slow

Marketing research shows that shipping time is one of the main factors that most online shoppers consider when they are looking to make a purchase decision. When you drop-ship your customers' orders, you don't have any control over the logistics of your shipments, which means that you can't optimize shipping times. You just have to rely on your supplier's shipping speed and hope that he always keeps it up. If you had a traditional e-commerce retail shop where you do your own shipping, you would be able to provide your customers with a lot more shipping options, and you would be able to offer them guarantees when it comes to delivery times.

Suppliers aren't particularly keen on going out of their way to make fast deliveries. Faster shipping times mean additional costs for suppliers, so they are contented to do the bare minimum. At the same time, giant retailers like Amazon are doing everything in their power to cut down their shipping times, so it makes it very hard for drop-shippers to compete. Even if a supplier offers tiered delivery services at different costs, as a drop-shipper, you may find it hard to select the fastest and most expensive package because it would affect your profit margin which is already small, to begin with.

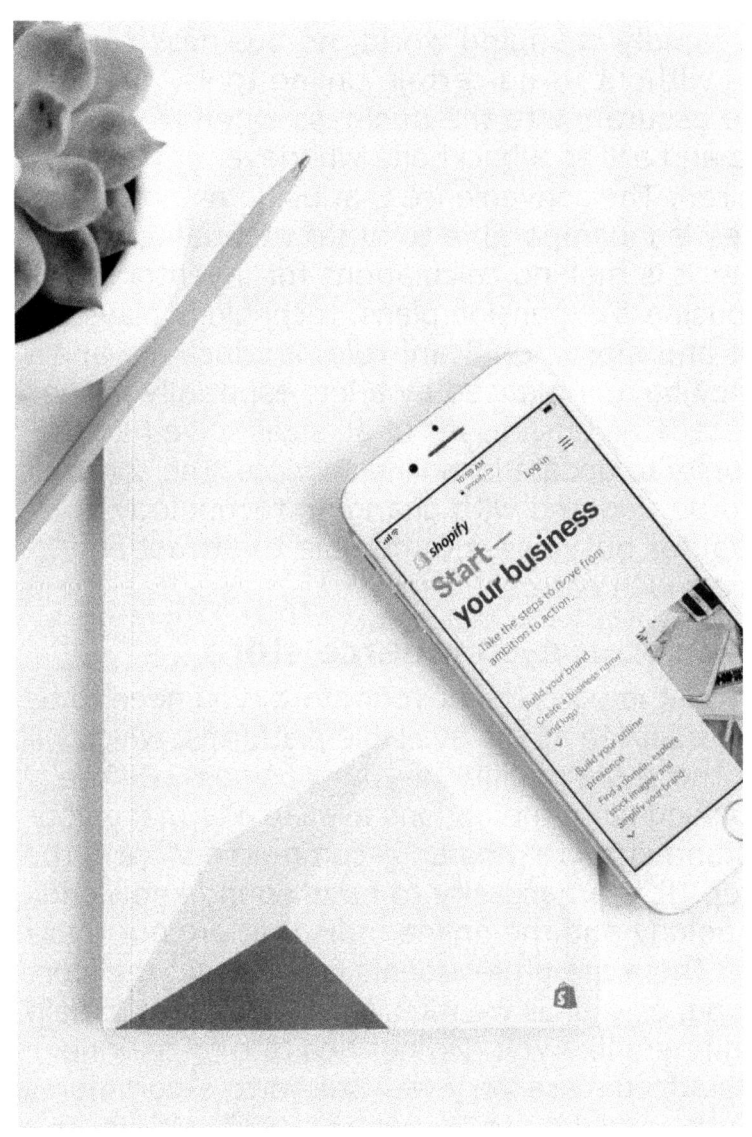

Chapter 5 Tools That You Need for Your Store

In this rapidly changing world, no business can survive without using certain online tools. These provide assurance to the business when trends change and act as a backbone whenever any support is required. The convenience that using an online tool provides is incomparable to other manual forms. Whether it is making calculations for inventory or to make business expansion plans, technology plays the biggest and most significant role. Productivity and efficiency have increased by a lot, especially in the past decade as businesses of all sizes have had the opportunity to update its online services. The constant need to be updated with changing technology is essential for businesses to be able to attract new customers with ease.

Creating your e-commerce store

To explore the potential of your store, you need to be ready to adapt to all the available platforms, which will ensure the sustainability of your business. Before even looking all of the options available to make your store stand out, creating an e-commerce store is the first step. It is a necessity to have sound knowledge in technology and the online tools that are out there to start. There are professionals who can set the store up for you, as well as websites solely dedicated to help out beginners like you. Do not hesitate to seek help! These platforms are very well suited to e-commerce entrepreneurs who are just starting out. Moreover, these applications can guide you through steps to manage almost everything when launching your store.

Picking a theme

Now comes the part where you need to focus on particular and intricate details of your niche that will define your e-commerce store. However, before this step, you need to have good knowledge of the type of products you want to work with. The very inspiration for having a relevant theme that portrays your vision comes from your product range. If you are seeking help from a professional website or application, you will find a lot of preset themes there already. These can help you in brainstorming ideas and making decisions if you are unsure where to start. More importantly, think about customizing your store and giving it a unique touch. In a lot of cases, generic designs can be a turn off to consumers, while innovative ones can entice high-end customers and turn them into returning customers in the long run.

Designing an e-commerce store

Whenever customers visit your store, the theme, color palette and the design are the first things that they notice. At times, you may wonder, "Why do I need to put an extra effort into making it pretty?" or "Isn't having a great range of products enough?" Well, the answer is simple - if consumers are not interested, they will not bother going through whatever your store has to offer. Having an aesthetically pleasing e-commerce store entices customers and also validates your business as a professional one. With word of mouth, more people can become aware of and take notice of your store. If it is unorganized or shabby, it would be very difficult for you to attract them. Hence, to have and maintain loyal and potential customers, investing your resources on building a good e-commerce store is a necessity.

Online Logo Makers

After you have designed and set your store up, now is the time to brand it. This helps to gain recognition for your products and creates a lasting first impression in the minds of the customers. It can be anything from a simple tree to an intricate design; this should depend on the type of products you are selling. It is better to be more open to ideas and new designs instead of being adamant on one. Having a professional store can do wonders and help create a buzz among customers. Hence, a logo is the simplest and best solution for you to put your business out there. If you want to experiment, do not shy away from creating your own design but if you are not proficient enough, do not shy away from help from online logo makers. Hiring graphic designers or outsourcing can be great options too, depending on the budget you have for creating the logo.

Payment processing

Due to globalization, we have access to faster services, much faster than those in the past. The systems for making online payments have developed immensely and have made it easier for us to make daily purchases. You do not need to carry cash around all the time. Their personal information and details are encrypted and have protection from credit card frauds for when businesses are willing to adopt such models. You should do research on the most common online methods of making payment among your targeted customers and make sure that you provide them with those payment services. PayPal is one of the most efficient systems in the most recent times. You can also be open towards offline payment services but the online payment methods are much more convenient in today's time.

Online business plan services

If you are happy with your strategies and find that they are working for your business, this should not be a tool you need. However, it is recommended that you explore these services. An outside perspective is necessary for you to be able to work on your shortcomings. For entrepreneurs, these online plans for your business guide you in designing a feasible and strong plan when you are making the transition from great idea to a profitable business venture. The inbuilt features and tool templates of web based applications help you generate charts on performance and goal achievement. Your financial status, depending on investments made for the business, can be studied carefully. You can be in charge of and keep track of the progress that you are making. Once you learn about what the services offer you, it would not be a surprise to see that you have started to think more critically and that your ideas for your store and product line go beyond the surface.

Using social media for your store

Whether you want to focus on Facebook, Instagram, Twitter, or any other social networking website, engagement with your customers through this platform is one of the most effective ways to draw and drive traffic to your store. Using social media is attractive as you do not have to invest a lot of money into it and you can utilize it to broaden your reach. Millions of people all around the world can engage with your store. Specialized tools on individual platforms are available to make social media users aware of new products and you have the flexibility to promote your products and content related to them. This also helps you to create a brand for your store. The best part is that as more time passes by, these platforms continue to grow and once you can get comfortable with social media, you should expect to look at great numbers!

Web hosting

The pace of the business world is much faster than what it was ten years ago. You cannot expect to apply those same strategies for attracting customers today. Hence, if you have not explored the internet yet, you will lag behind and before you realize, you will already be out of the game. A web hosting service allows you to start a website and run it. The files that makeup the website on a data server can be stored through these services and these files are uploaded to the web automatically from your web hosting service. The use of email marketing and installation of one-click supported applications are some of the many features that you can use when building your business. You can also be assigned an email address that includes the site's domain name.

Shopping cart software

When you have set up your website, there are some additional things which you need to offer your customers when they make a purchase. Shopping cart software is necessary to be able to make payments through your website. This is not only beneficial for the customers as it can allow them to feel safe when buying something online, but it is an advantage for your store too. Tracking inventory gets easier and you can keep tabs on which product to promote or communicate with the suppliers if a surge is predicted with the latest trends. This will also help you produce reports based on this data through your website's services. This software can be connected to multiple platforms for making payments. PayPal or credit card services can be offered to customers and this makes their experience more familiar as well. The purchasers can also be aware of the amount of tax they are paying and how much they are being charged for shipping costs. You promote transparency and convenience through these services on your store's website and it will help you gain a good reputation among old and new customers.

Webinar services

As your business grows, you may think of expanding and gaining new customers, both locally and internationally. Webinar services can help you connect and take orders faster and most importantly, they can help you monitor your day to day operations, especially if you have multiple offices. This will help you out if your employees are working remotely and if you have multiple working locations. Training sessions, meetings with all of your employees, either within a specific branch or all together, can be conducted much more comfortably. Webinar services are a great fit for you when you want to present your sales online and make product demonstrations for your clients too. Becoming more proficient in this helps you connect with your customers faster and you can respond to their queries in real time.

Anti-virus software

When you are using your computer, it is highly likely that you are storing information through a variety of applications. Whether you are dealing with storing personal information or you are processing orders, you need to keep all the data in an organized way. The information stored here is valuable and not having any protection programs on your computer puts you and your business in a lot of danger. Apart from the technical issues that your computer will go through, you could experience data theft, which would be a very big loss for your business venture. All businesses should have anti-virus software to guard the computer network against viruses, malware, Trojans, worms, or spyware. Since the platform of dropshipping is online where you have to constantly be in touch with your suppliers and customers, having a good antivirus software is a necessity and it is equally necessary for protection.

Receiving payments from customers

In order to deal with customers from various backgrounds, your knowledge in different modes of payment platforms is required. It reduces hassle if you can connect to multiple platforms that your customers will feel safe using. There are additional charges when you want to use these online payment platforms, ensuring to keep you safe against business fraud. You will be charged a fee for every sale you make and an additional amount to ensure protection for your store. You should check out different platforms apart from PayPal to make a sound decision, however, it is and has been the most trusted and convenient one in the market. Apart from this, there are built-in features to provide you protection if you are using platforms like Shopify.

Online data storage

Due to the ease of an online platform, storing data has become much easier than it used to be. Online data storage acts as backup storage if anything goes wrong with your computer. Of course, you can access your data online even if no problems arise instead of relying on your computer's storage. Data is stored on a cloud server which is convenient and safe. You can access the files from any part of the world at any time. Also, if you want to free up space on your computer, having online data storage is the best way to go about this. It is wiser to have online storage as hard drive failures, theft, and file erasure can occur and make these files extremely difficult to retrieve.

Business tools that you should know how to use

Google AdWords & Analytics

Google is the place we think of going instantly whenever there is something we want to know. From getting instant information about the most complicated technologies to doing the most basic spell checks, Google is our one-stop solution. For your business, you need to learn to make the most of this platform. Whenever you want to know about anything, this search engine can give you around 40,000 results per second and is definitely the most reliable search engine today. You can focus on getting on the first page of the search list and witness how this changes your income. Use an SEO (search engine optimization) strategy to try and make it on the first page. It may take a long time, maybe even months or longer, but you should keep at it. This will ensure you benefits in the long term. However, there is another way that can help you attain a first-page position faster, and this strategy includes using Google AdWords. This is a scheme of paid ads where you pay every time a visitor clicks on your advertisement. Additionally, you need to invest time into how to utilize Google Analytics and understand its importance for your website and your business. This tool allows you to understand the types of mediums through which your visitors come from and this could be a huge advantage when you are starting out or are struggling to reinvent your line. Overall, this will assist with things that are working and not working, guiding you towards better execution and expansion plans.

SurveyMonkey

Now that you have set your store up and are getting ready to attract customers to your niche, you need to know about the current market and what the trends are. This is a surveying tool available online that helps you connect with your audience. Survey Monkey already has a lot of preset questions along with built-in templates to give you a thorough insight when analyzing data. The best aspect is that the tool gives unbiased responses which can help you modify your strategies or help you create new and improved ones. The free version of this tool still provides you a lot of information through the surveys but the number of features is limited. Give it a try and see how much it helps improve your product line. If you are finding it useful, go ahead and get a subscription with a paid plan. The paid plan will provide many more useful tools for surveying.

X-Cart

For newcomers who do not have a lot of money to start out but want to give dropshipping a shot, your e-commerce website still needs to stand out. This tool is cost-effective and will not put a strain on your funds. X-Cart has a free version if you want to give it a try and see whether you find it suitable for your business or not. It helps you build your website and you can explore its various features. Moreover, free extensions will allow you to create shipping labels, slideshows, and do so much more! Your business can access these facilities and prioritize what will be more beneficial to get started on in terms of harnessing technical skills. You can get acquainted with the different themes available online and customize them wherever you feel necessary.

Tableau Public

This is a marketing tool that helps you to conduct research and lets you make a thorough analysis of your business data. You learn to make better predictions on what will work and what will not and this helps you make better decisions for the future. This tool is very effective because it sources out data from CSV files and Excel among many others. When the business venture is new, investing in high profile marketing research tools is important but expensive. This is where this tool is handiest as it can give free access to up to 15 million rows in one workbook and provide data solutions for free with up to 10 gigabytes of space.

BuzzSumo

In the modern day, social media has been the best platform for marketing. Social media is perfect for if you want to understand demographics, connect with influencers, find out what the most shared content is and much more. BuzzSumo is the best influencer marketing tool that allows you to find out what content is performing the best on any social media platform. You can choose a paid subscription but there is a free trial period too which you should definitely make use of before making a purchase. This application helps you understand what sort of content will work well with your product line; this in turn will help you connect with influencers who can help you in expanding your marketing strategies.

Designhill

Lack of personalization during the shipment process, executed by your suppliers can make it difficult for your customers to relate with your brand. In such a scenario, you can simply add your logo to the package; this will help you promote your brand.

Through Designhill, you can access countless templates for free and it even helps you create your own brand name. You can insert your store's name and pick themes, colors, icons to match your niche. You can choose a logo from the app's generated logos and purchase it to obtain the copyright. You can spend according to your budget and get started with this graphic design platform. The platform is powered by AI and allows you to design a logo on the go.

These tools should give you an idea about the factors that are important for you to be updated on to run your business smoothly. You should focus on your niche and work around it with the insight of technology. Since technology improves every day, it is useful to become proficient at using these applications as you gain more experience through your dropshipping store. It will help you explore better solutions to your needs and gain technical expertise accordingly.

Chapter 6 What Factors To Look At When Analyzing The Target Market

Demographics
Demographics is a term that relies to certain data about people, such as where they are located, i.e. their geographic location, as well as what income bracket they belong to, and other such information. Being able to gather this data and use it to define a particular market is crucial to understanding just how large your target market really is and where they are centered around, and will be extremely useful in catering the product catalog to their demand.

Gender
One of the undeniable and statistically observed differences between genders is the general shopping and spending patterns between men and women, as men and women have varying shopping patterns when purchasing things, whether online or in a physical store. Gender is not the most controlling factor when deciding on a target market, but it still offers insight that may be useful when targeting a particular market segment. Some things that can be influenced by gender is the type of content that motivates them to buy, what language to use in write - ups to make products more attractive, or even what times of day they tend to shop, all these are factors that may be influenced by gender.

Age
Age is a major factor in deciding a person's spending and purchasing pattern, especially due to the change in tastes over generations, as well as the general difference in spending capacity depending on age. For

example, millennials, the nickname given to the demographic group born in the last 2 decades of the 1900's, tend to do a lot of shopping online, but due to the relative youth of this group, have a lower spending capacity and thus rarely spend on big - ticket items online. Another example would be those in the ages of sixty and above, who are generally more unfamiliar with ecommerce and are not as comfortable shopping online, and thus are less likely to buy things through the internet.

Institution

One thing to keep in mind is what type of sales you will be making, if these products will be sold directly to consumers, to other businesses, or even to government institutions. Whether these goods are being sold Business - to - Consumers (B 2 C), business - to - business (B 2 B), or Business - to - government (B 2 G) are all factors in deciding many aspects of the business, such as what types of product should be offered, how many products they will be purchasing, and how these products and services will be marketed. However, most drop shipping businesses sell directly to consumers, using the B2C relation, but in the case that the retailer's drop shipping business will also cater to other institutions, these factors should be taken into account.

Know the Competition

Earlier we discussed how checking up on competitors is a part of market research. This aspect cannot be emphasized enough, as in order to beat the competition, one needs to know them well. For example, if the product that the retailer or merchant wishes to sell is already being sold at a high volume by established and well - known online retailers, then this is a positive sign for the retailer. However, if the retailer notices that that very same product has become ubiquitous on online markets, then it may be too difficult to distinguish the business from everyone else's, and it may no longer be a good idea to focus on selling that type of product.

Here are some tactics and tips when it comes to scoping out the competition:

Use Online Tools
While there is nothing wrong with simply looking over and exploring their website, and that is in fact the first step, in order to get a more in - depth understanding of how your competitors are doing, some online tools may be made use of. There are some site explorers such as SEMrush that allow the gathering of data such as the ranking and domain authority of a website while needing only the URL. This tool would help the retailer get a better idea of where their traffic is coming from, and how people are getting access to their website. These online tools, in conjunction with examining the website manually would give a more holistic view of how they are doing, as opposed to simply eyeballing their business.

Order their products
While this may initially seem counter - intuitive, as ordering from the competition means giving them business, ordering from competitors is a way to get valuable insights. While the general flow of ordering online tends to remain the same, there are always quirks, little things and details that distinguish one company from another, which can give an idea of what things should be avoided, or what things can be improved upon in the ordering process. Remember that in a drop shipping business, the only real interaction that a customer will have with something

controlled by the retailer is the product platform and ordering process, so it's to the benefit of the retailer to make the ordering process as smooth as they can. Note that the order process should not simply be copied, but rather used as inspiration for ideas of how to make a well - oiled and smooth order process.

Analyze their social media
In the current day and age, social media is king. Perhaps not literally, but if social media can make or break a long - term established brand, what more a fledgling e - commerce drop shipping business carried out entirely in cyberspace, the same region where social media is located. Social media is one of the best ways to get feedback and to observe how people perceive the business. Watching the social media channels of competitors gives you an idea of the problems that they have, and the things that they are doing right. Picking up tips from how they engage with customers online is a way to improve one's own social media marketing methods. In addition, looking at their content is a good way to be able to find out how to compete and design a marketing strategy that would be able to overtake theirs.

How to Find the Right Drop Shipping Supplier for You

The drop shipping business model is highly reliant on the supplier; after all, it is the supplier that will be fulfilling orders, since they will provide the product and deliver it, and without the supplier there will be no business. Of course this means that the supplier is one of the most, if not the most important part of the puzzle when it comes to establishing a successful drop shipping business. If the supplier messes up a delivery, sends defective goods, or is constantly out of stock, your drop shipping business is the one that customers will blame, so it is of paramount importance that the merchant will be able to find a reliable drop shipping supplier that is capable of communicating well and fulfilling their obligations. The following are a few tips for finding a drop shipping supplier that you can trust:

Experienced Sales Representatives
Sales representatives are the first line of communication of a company, and these sales representatives are most likely those that the retailer will be working with most of the time. If these sales representatives are experienced at their job, they will most likely know how drop shipping goes, and the ins and outs of the process, allowing them to more easily handle any issues that come up and coordinate with the retailer to handle any issues that come up. An experienced sales representative will be able to put the retailer's mind at ease, as they are adept at communicating and will be able to make things move much quicker and smoother.

High quality products
Though an ecommerce store does not have the traditional brand hallmarks, it is still a brand that the retailer will wish to develop. After all, it is key to the drop shipping platform's success that the platform be recognized as a reliable place to buy high - quality products. A retailer is judged by the products that they sell and the quality of service that they provide, and the supplier handles both of those things, though the service to a lesser extent. If the supplier has high - quality products, customers will end up more satisfied, which means repeat customers and a good reputation, and good reviews and recommendations are one of the best ways to boost business and keep the retailer afloat. A reputation for selling low quality

goods, on the other hand, is a quick way to sink any chance of success.

Technologically Capable
A good drop shipper keeps up with the times and is able to match the latest technological needs. Whether it be by having an inventory software that ensures that their stock availability is always up to date, or an efficient warehousing system to dispatch orders quickly, or even by simply having a well - automated order receiving system, it is important for a drop shipper to be capable. This will come in handy especially when it comes to scaling the business, in case the merchant wishes to expand, as they can feel secure that their trusted business partner will be capable of scaling along with their operations.

Punctuality and Efficiency
Drop shipping is not only about the products, but about a safe and efficient shipping system. If there is a drop shipping supplier that offers same day shipping, or at least shipping within twenty - four to forty - eight hours from receipt of the order, this will go a long way in making customers happy with the service. In a highly competitive market, any edge goes a long way, and a quick and efficient delivery system is a way to gain customers. One way of ensuring that the supplier is actually efficient with their order fulfillment process is to test them by ordering a few items, just to see how fast they are able to fulfil the order.

Where to look for Drop Shipping suppliers
If you happen to be an experienced businessman, or are friends with one, then most likely you will already have access to one or more reliable suppliers that are also capable of fulfilling drop shipping functions.

However, not everyone is so lucky, and in case there are no contacts available, the best way to look for a drop shipping supplier in an area near you, funnily enough, is to simply Google it. There are many websites online, among them start - up incubators that provide directories of various drop shippers that provide various products. Once the retailer finds a few promising leads in a suitable area, it is simple to send them a quick and polite email in order to inquire about their services and a possible partnership. Sending an email over calling is preferable, as an email chain would allow you to keep a record of the conversation, as well as allow you to gauge how well and how quick their sales representatives do at replying to inquiries.

Drop Shipping fulfilment
While we have already gone over the basics of drop shipping order fulfilment, some aspects still need to be taken care of on the part of the retailer, such as whether some steps should be automated or not. Some components of the process such as the receipt of the order, the shipping information, and other such details can be automated, or can be handled manually, depending on the preference and resources available to the retailer. In case of multiple suppliers, the fulfilment process will most likely include sending the orders through email but finding the best supplier per product per order will likely rely on factors such as delivery location, shipping cost, and product availability. In this case, the retailer needs to find a way to ensure that these details are dealt with, either through using advanced software, or manually sifting through the orders to match them to the best - fit supplier.

Drop shipping Customer Support
As has been reiterated time and time again, good customer support can make or break a business. By now the reader should know that the majority of the contribution of the retailer to the customer shopping experience is in providing the platform and in providing customer support. Thus, it is in the best interest of the supplier to build and maintain the best customer support system it can in order to look good in the eyes of the customer and distinguish themselves from their other competitors.

Phone Support
One of the most classic methods of customer support is having a phone customer support system. Not only is it classic, but it is one of the quickest ways to get in touch with the customer, and it also works to the advantage of the retailer. The retailer can have an advantage when using phone support as a human conversation makes it harder for the customer to get mad, and it also makes it easier for a trained sales representative to defuse and manage the situation. It is also more immediate, and it allows customers to resolve their issues quicker, and allows the retailer to receive feedback in a more immediate manner. In a lot of countries, especially the more developed ones, the landline phone is becoming phased out, with more and more households opting not to get a phone in the first place.

A retailer can still offer phone support through applications such as Google Voice or Skype, which will allow the benefits of voice communication while still remaining relevant and allowing people without landlines to call directly. However, this will take more internet infrastructure, as it will require the platform to have a messaging system in order to inform the customer support representatives that there is a customer that wishes to call.

Email Support
The phone support is the classic method of customer support, but in reality, most of the customer support interactions will most likely be done through email, due to its convenience and accessibility. In line with this, it would be best to have domain emails set up for your website, which would grant credibility and legitimacy, as it looks quite professional and helps in establishing a brand. In addition, email support is useful for both retailer and customer as it allows them to track what steps have been taken and they can keep a record of what has happened during the interaction. One useful software for email support is the Helpscout software, specially designed for customer support functions.

Social Media Support
Given the primacy of social media in our everyday lives, a lot of customers ask questions or direct complaints at the social media pages of brands and companies even before using official, more conventional channels. This includes posts on their page or direct messages, things that are done by customers because of the convenience, and because a large amount of the time, other customers have asked similar questions on the page, and they hope to find the answers there. In line with this, having a dedicated customer support representative handling social media will help with engaging the customers even during the times that there is negative feedback. A skilled social media handler will be able to do much with the company account, and this can help with the popularity of the brand and will help with establishing good faith.

Live Chat Support
Given the dominance of internet technologies nowadays, a lot of brands are including live chat functionality in their websites and platforms, allowing customers to have nearly - immediate access to a customer support representative, and this acts as a hybrid of a phone call and email method of customer support. This is because the response is almost immediate, but there is a written record, and the customer can easily forward data such as pictures of a defective product, or a picture of the packaging, or the tracking number of their order. However, having a live chat function is difficult for a start - up with limited resources, and viable alternatives that serve a similar function are using the direct messaging services on social media platforms. However, integrated live chat support is a good option to explore if ever the retailer has the opportunity to scale up.

Chapter 7 Marketing

Once your drop shipping store goes live and it is ready to be presented to its first customers, now is the time to get it in front of as many prospective customers as you can and attract them to become paying customers. This is one of the most challenging parts of starting a drop shipping business. However, without promoting your business, your chances of success are next to zero. Luckily, if you commit yourself and do it right, you will get massive results.

You can use several channels to promote your drop shipping business. While each business has a different channel that works best for it, I am going to look at five proven methods you can use to promote your online store. You don't have to use all of them; just focus on the methods that suit you best.

Social Media Marketing (SMM)

SMM is the use of social media sites to create brand awareness, create customer relationships, gain traffic, and drive sales. These can be done on major social media platforms such as Facebook, Twitter, Instagram, Pinterest, Google+, LinkedIn, and YouTube, as well as on online forums and blogs. While many people see social media as nothing more than a social tool, it is something that you can leverage to drive sales for your drop shipping business. When you create a social media marketing campaign for your business, you should avoid trying to market your business on every social media platform. While it might seem like a good strategy to gain maximum reach, it will be overwhelming for you, and you will end up achieving dismal results on each of these sites. What you should do is identify two to three social media platforms that will deliver maximum results and completely focus on them. All in all, social media is a great tool to market your drop shipping business, so it's a big risk to avoid using this tool.

Facebook Ads
Though it is an offshoot of social media marketing, advertising on Facebook deserves its own mention due to its effectiveness as an online marketing tool. Facebook is the largest and most popular social marketing platform in the world. The platform has over 1.71 billion monthly active users, which makes it the ideal place to advertise your drop shipping business. However, the effectiveness of Facebook as a marketing tool goes beyond the numbers. Unlike most advertising platforms that serve ads on query-based data, Facebook serves its ads based on contextual data. With query-based data, the advertising platform shows adverts that are relevant to what users are searching for on the internet. A good example of a query-based advertising platform is Google Adwords.

In contrast, platforms that serve advertisements based on contextual data allow advertisers to choose the demographics of the people they want to present the ads to. This makes it easier for you to target a specific audience. Are your products geared toward 25-year-old men living in California who be obsessed with sports bikes? With Facebook ads, you can target this exact group. Facebook advertisements allow you to choose your audience based on factors like age, geographical location, interests, behavior, job position, and so much more. This means that Facebook advertisements are more relevant and are more likely to drive conversions.

To make your Facebook advertising campaign more effective, you should first come up with a clear objective for the campaign. Is your aim to create awareness for your brand? Is it to drive people to your drop shipping store? Is it to increase your sales? Having a clear objective will help you craft an effective marketing campaign. On top of that, Facebook provides you with a variety of options that make it easier for you to achieve your marketing objectives.

To create a relevant Facebook advertisement, the other things you should keep in mind is to ensure that you use persuasive, relevant, and actionable copy, relevant and attention-grabbing images, and a clear and concise Call to Action (CTA).

Search Engine Optimization (SEO)
Search Engine Optimization is the process of fine-tuning your site to capture traffic from search engines like Google. In other words, it is the process of ensuring that your drop shipping business can be found on search engines. SEO is a broad topic that consists of many elements. However, to make it simpler to understand, SEO can be broken down into steps. The first one is defining the keywords that you want your site to rank for. This means that when people search for specific keywords, they should be able to find your site on the first page of Google. You will have to do extensive keyword research to find appropriate keywords that you want to rank for. The second step is optimizing your site for the keywords you defined in step one. Step three is building backlinks to your drop shipping store. Having many backlinks on your drop shipping store gives Google's algorithms the perception that your site is an authoritative one, which in turn leads to a higher ranking on the search engine's result page.

By properly utilizing SEO tactics, your drop shipping store will rank higher on search engines, which means that more people will find your store, visit it, and buy your products. SEO allows you to direct traffic to your drop shipping store without having to pay for it.

While performing proper SEO to ensure your store ranks high on search results is not necessarily an easy task, it is still doable. Defining the keywords you want to rank for and optimizing your store for these keywords is the easy part. The hard part is trying to outrank your competitors for the same keywords, especially when your store is still relatively new and has yet to build some authority. This is where backlinks come in handy. Backlinks from high-quality sources will help raise your store's authority.

You want to ensure that you are doing SEO correctly because according to data by Custora, organic search traffic drives about 26% of all orders on e-commerce stores. By improving your site's SEO, you can increase your sales by up to 26% percent. One thing you should keep in mind is that with SEO, you won't see immediate results. Initially, you will hardly see any results, but in the long run, you will reap exponential rewards.

Email Marketing
Email is one of the most cost-effective tools you can use to market your drop shipping business and gain customer engagement. Email generates high-quality leads and high-quality conversions, which is why it has a 44% return on investment (ROI). If you do it right, you will see massive results. Email is extremely effective because people share their contact details voluntarily, which is a sure-fire sign that they are interested in your products. Email marketing also allows you to accumulate your prospect's personal

data, which you can use in further interactions. By providing quality content through email, you can create more demand for your products.

To run an effective email marketing campaign, you should have an attractive lead magnet for your site. As a drop shipping business, your lead magnet can be a loyalty program that provides subscribers with exclusive discounts. You should have a well-designed email template and ensure that you regularly communicate with your subscribers. However, this does not mean constantly spamming them with sales emails, as this will only lead to people opting out of your email list. Instead, you should always strive to provide value through your email newsletters.

Video Marketing

The greatest thing about video marketing is that it makes it possible for you to create an instant connection with your audience. Posts with videos lead to more time spent on your site and increased engagement. Search engine algorithms also tend to give more importance to videos, which means that using videos will improve your ranking, increase your conversions, and have greater results on your brand awareness campaign.

The most effective way of using videos to promote your drop shipping business is to create video reviews of the products you sell in your store. These can range from amateur reviews by previous customers to professional and detailed reviews of a product's features, performance, and benefits. If you decide on using video marketing to promote your store, create a YouTube channel that matches your store design, provide information about your business on the channel, and make sure that your channel is also optimized for search engines.

Chapter 8 Dealing With Your Competitors

When you know your competitors, you have a good idea about the market standard, making it easier for you to know about the customers' expectations. Hence, if you want to survive in that particular industry you need to bring quality products and your business can stand out, eventually making your business better and sustainable. Healthy competition results in building a successful industry. You cannot stop the competition nor can you create restrictions and barriers to enter the market. However, you should learn from the strategies and policies your competitors adopt to become successful. Before implementing any plan to cope with stiff competition you should have an idea of the big dropshipping entities, how such large-scale businesses are run successfully, and what they do when they are up against competition. If you are a newcomer to dropshipping, most of the big company rules will not apply to you but that does not mean you should not take ideas from them. You can adopt and test out strategies with your store's product line and see how well they work.

Just like you, your competitors are used to following their competition and due to the internet, this has become easier than ever. You can make a list where you can keep tabs on companies that have entered the market before you, along with those which are going to be launched soon. Knowing who you are competing with helps you prepare a better plan for the battle that you are getting yourself into. Unless and until you have an extremely unique product that targets a small market, you will undoubtedly have competition. On the contrary, it will be wise to pay closer attention to the products that the other stores are selling. Do not just settle with the picture descriptions but try to analyze how they advertise, who are their distribution channels are, what their values are, and the age demographic they are targeting with their niche products. You should expect the same to happen to your store and be smart about giving out details about your products, especially when you are sharing anything on social media. Monitoring what they do and how your competitors work around certain issues will also help you make backup plans and make sure you are ready to deal with complex situations in the longer run.

Another perspective which you should adopt is to understand where your business stands and what your role is in the market. Having the ability to understand the market is a gift and can help you understand the potential of your product line. It is important to know whether the demand for a product is increasing or decreasing or remaining stable. You can make calculated decisions about how much competition you can face if you move forward with that product. If you find it too risky, try to work on finding a special niche that you feel passionate about; you can start small but grow as the market for the new product expands.

Tools For Analyzing Competitors

Google Alerts
This tool gives you well-rounded information about the industry you are involved with. You can check your status and understand where you stand through email alerts. You can receive notifications whenever your

search term appears on Google. Since it is the best and the most accurate search engine available, it is highly unlikely that you will miss any notifications when your search terms appear. This is a trustworthy and reliable source of information. You can also utilize it to stay updated on your competitors and your niche. If there are any trendy niches that your industry is following, this tool is enough to get you accustomed and keep you updated.

Utilizing SEO

Having your store on the first page of a Google search is hard and requires a lot of time and effort. When you are using SEO, you should not expect instant results to have your store be on the first page of the search results. You should try out new and interesting strategies to make the most of your situation. One way could be to not use generic images that every other dropshipping business is promoting. You can re-order the products you want to sell and take photographs by yourself or use a professional photographer that is within your budget. Customization always works in your favor. Additionally, SEO helps you understand product quality and decide whether you want to be associated with this supplier or not. All these can help you reach a higher ranking in search results but in the short term, you have to rely on paid advertisements and PPC to be able to at least break even with your direct competitors.

Understanding Your Competitors

If you are thinking of getting into the competitive market of dropshipping, you need to have sound knowledge in understanding who your direct competitors are. You cannot make assumptions and design strategies around companies that you are not competing with. If you do that, you will waste your resources, funds, and be headed towards a failed business venture, not in the near future but in the long run. You need to know who they are and what prices they are quoting for the same products that your store is also selling. You should not rest after analyzing one or two competitors, it is essential for you to list all of them in your region. You should not think of offering the lowest prices; this will result in a negative impression of the type of service you offer and quality of products you are selling, especially if you are a newcomer in the industry. This should not be your first option. When you find out the prices of your competitors, try to understand the market price that has already been set by them and then put a price within that range, depending on your niche. You can offer extra support through customer service or offer bundles when you see that your business is part of a saturated market. Think and plan creatively to be able to stand out among your competitors.

Being Aware Of Competition

The dropshipping industry has seen an increasing number of competitors, among all niches. You need to have a sound knowledge of what type of policies your competitors adopt along and understand the impact of their packaging and services they are willing to offer. The best method would be to order products from your competitors and assess how their services are. If you are unaware of the competition, it will be very hard for you to pinpoint what you should do better or what you could do in a better way to sustain. This can help you improve and also gain a broader customer base. Using search engines is the most effective way and you are recommended to start with this, but you need to know what you are looking for and who you are looking for. In short, you need to dig deep and read through multiple pages. Do not move on after looking at the first page. A lot of information can be misguided. On the other hand, you could get a subscription to a legitimate directory. WorldWideBrands is a well-renowned one where you can look for thousands of pre-screened dropshipping companies. This can help you understand and strategize region-wise. You may feel conflicted about getting this subscription as most of the directories are available online but many of those are usually of low quality and would not add much to your research. Last but not least, you can think of contacting the manufacturer - the direct source - and gain information about others who are selling the same products as you through dropshipping. Here, you can rely on getting authentic information since this manufacturer is also dealing with your products and is used to being in touch with stores with similar product lines.

How To Get Your Store To Gain More Exposure In The Market?

Everyone in today's day and age uses Google to look for products. Even if they use other search engines, the process is similar. They use keywords to look for something specific and look at the top results on the screen. Now, if you want to match up to your competitors, you need to have your store within those primary search results. Usually the links on the first page are perceived as the most reliable ones and customers find them easier to trust, regardless of if you are new or not.

Picking the right keywords

The concept of your niche needs to be precise. If asked, you should have the ability to describe your store in three words to anyone who has never heard of your store before. These words which you have come up with to define your store will act as your store keywords. The search engines try to match the keywords you have used to describe your store and niche to the search words customers are using when they are looking for any specific product. Hence, when choosing your keywords, you need to be concise but effective because these words will represent your niche and product line.

Optimizing The Website

Optimization of your website directly deals with the procedure required to optimize or design a website from scratch in order to make it rank well in search engines. This is a direct result of the keywords which you have chosen. Optimization helps you gain a higher number of visitors, leading to an increase in the number of purchases made. This is what can help you gain an advantage over your competitors as this process can help you get a much larger volume of orders from customers. In the long term, you will be able to observe the ranking of your store and how optimization has significantly contributed to its improvement. This optimization can be done on all of your pages but when done to your homepage, category pages, and product pages, the changes are more noticeable and positive results can be observed much faster.

Improving The Visibility Of Your Store On Google

Search engine optimization allows your store to gain much more exposure but it requires time. The effects of SEO last longer, but as a short-term solution, you may consider other options. PPC gives you faster and better results as the traffic in your store increases almost instantly. You can look through the websites of your competitors and find out what they are doing that you have not done yet. You can learn through this and choose the correct keywords, which in turn helps Google to attract more customers to your store. Try to be aware of strategies and techniques already adopted by your competitors.

Providing a user-friendly interface
No matter how many luxurious products your store has, if customers are unable to navigate through your store, those products will never be able to sell. When you are setting up your theme or designing your store, you should keep this in mind. Keeping in mind the idea of your product line and the age group of your targeted customers, try to choose templates and colors that fit; this will help to grab their attention for a longer period of time. Make sure the font sizes you are using are clear and that they can find where the products are, where your contact information is, where the search bar is, and so on. If they cannot navigate through your site, the whole process will be more time-consuming for them and they might prefer to make purchases elsewhere.

Providing limited-time offers
You can introduce deals on your products when you want to drive away traffic from your competitors and also during special occasions. You can set deadlines and make customers aware of the limited time offers. They can also be informed through the use of the "Recent Sales Pop-Up Plugin" that lets them know about other shoppers that have bought products with this limited time offer. They will be interested to look around for what is available for purchase as you have already ingrained the idea of purchasing in their minds. They will see an array of products that they have never explored before. Meanwhile, other

customers have been targeted the same way and are making purchases simultaneously. This cycle can be continued throughout the entire time of the limited offer and the increase in activity on your site will keep on attracting more and more customers.

Promoting Upsell
Upsell is a sales technique through which the customers are induced by the seller to make more expensive purchases or upgrades in order to make a higher percentage of profit per sale. This strategy is by far one of the most effective ones when you want your customers' attention. When they are sure about what they are looking for, they can add the product keywords in your search bar. When they are provided with the list of items, they are also presented with an extended product range. You need to put in a bit of work here beforehand. For every product that your store displays, you should have another additional list of products that your customers can access. They will make the customers feel like your store is a one-stop shop and that they do not need to look around at other stores. They will spend a more significant amount of time on your website browsing and looking for desired products and also for complementary products they may want to purchase. Upsell surely enhances your profits.

Having unique content
You should always be on the lookout for new niches that are still untouched. You can start by sorting out what your competitors do not have and this will help you stand out. When you have items that are not available on any other stores, it will be comparatively easier for you to drive traffic to your store. As long as your store is the only one, you can charge high prices as if it is something that the customers have always

needed but could not find, they will be ready to pay high prices. However, when you see that other competitors have also introduced this niche, you can regulate prices according to theirs. Availability of an alternative should not worry you since you were the first to introduce the product and customers have purchased from you before. Hence, this sense of security will enable them to keep coming back to you even if your competitors offer the same price.

Using videos for promotion and branding
A lot of other stores like you may not think of making videos or doing live sessions on social media platforms, thus, you can now provide that to your customers where you can directly communicate with them when they comment or inbox you with any queries. Of course, they can get the details of the product from the description but for example, how it fits, if it is a shirt or a pair of sunglasses, cannot be known simply by the pictures. This is your opportunity to represent your product line in a creative and unique way. You can develop an interactive relationship with your customer base and let them be more involved. You can also to product reviews to make them more aware. This will allow for healthy competition to thrive and also help the customers to identify your store as a top store.

Having active collaborations
You need to have faith in your niche and product line and be able to try out new ways to attract customers. When you are first starting out, it is obvious that big brands will not be willing to collaborate with you, but never forget the power of your local community. Depending upon your niche, look around for influencers and bloggers who would be interested to be associated with your store. However, you have to

remember that you need to collaborate with people that are not your direct competitors. If you have a clothing store, seek out makeup artists and hairdressers and brainstorm together to get mutual benefit.

Lastly, try to think of your competitors as your friends because they can be your best teachers. Each business and product line is different. You need to be conscious of that and you should try to research as many dropshipping stores as possible.The more you are aware of your competitors, the more opportunities you will get to provide better services and explore new and unique products.

The policies adopted for certain niches will not be the same but if they can be merged into your product line or have similar target customers, you can do tests and strategize accordingly.

Chapter 9 Establishing Your Brand Through A Marketing Plan

Once you have established your supply chain and your website is up and running, it will be time to establish your brand. You do this by developing a smart marketing plan and scaling that plan to fit your estimated growth rates. The last thing you want is to create a great marketing strategy only to end up overwhelmed. That can cause you, and your business, to crash.

Scaling Up Your Business

At this point, you definitely want to know what scaling is so you feel like less of a newbie.

Scaling means that you are creating new revenue at a much faster rate than you are increasing your costs. If your costs increase with every single new income stream, then you are not really becoming profitable.

Smart business owners want to scale their business just as much as they want to grow their business. To do this, you need to have the foresight to look ahead. Scaling is tied directly to your marketing plan. Your marketing plan should give you a good idea of how fast you could grow and what you will need to have optimized to ensure your business continues to grow in profitability without picking up just as many expenses.

The primary goal here is not to eliminate costs because frankly, that is impossible. No matter how you look at it, every business has costs and overhead. What you are trying to do here is to make sure that your business has more profit than costs. You also want to be careful that you aren't working so hard for so little that the business is no longer worth it for you.

In order to do that, you will need to create a system that helps you deliver your products in services in an efficient way that can be replicated and used over and over again for little cost. This will tie into your supply chain and website. Your supply chain needs to be able to keep up with order demands. If it can't, you need a new one. Your website needs to be optimized for high volume traffic. Things as simple as you create an easier system for payment can help scale your business.

Although scaling is important, and it is a key piece to the puzzle that is a successful business, you need to strategize and scale proportionately to the business itself.

To scale to quickly could be as detrimental as not scaling, or scaling too slowly. If you are only bringing in one thousand dollars a month, you aren't going to spend five thousand dollars on scaling your operations for those sales. That is a fast way to spend too much money too quickly.

What it comes down to, essentially, is that scaling allows you to run your business efficiently and smoothly. If scaled properly, there will be no need for you to be working twenty hours a day to problem solve.

You will be able to trust that your website is running smoothly and efficiently. You will know that the ads you have in place are bringing in a steady stream of customers. Those customers will be happy because you have ensured that your supply chain could handle the growth in sales.

That is the point of scaling. It makes your life easier, and your business runs smoothly. Without scaling you would end up frustrated and overworked. Your customers would become unhappy. You may end up with a lot of growth but you will not be able to sustain it because the business is not scaled to serve that many people.

Scaling vs Growing
Growth is when your business is creating new business, but also incurring costs to match. You are bringing in customers, you are making sales, and you can see clearly that your business is increasing in size.

Whereas you used to only need to check-in and see how your store was doing once a day, you are now fielding questions and putting out fires all day long. Here is the problem: in order to see this growth you have probably spent a great deal of time and money on trying to market these products.

In the Drop shipping world, you are not making or dealing directly with the products, which is already helping you to scale. However, you still need to market and your products which will require a lot of work and a lot of money. You also need to get the orders, check that the orders are correct in your system, and get the orders to your supplier. Then, you need to be able to trust that your supplier is shipping out the products as promised when promised, and with the quality promised.

You have already read how a good, solid supply chain is one of the most important aspects of your business, but as it relates to growth and scaling there are some considerations to take a second look at.

You also need to look at how you communicate orders to your supplier.

If you are experiencing high growth and gaining customers quickly but your supplier can't deliver that quickly, you could end up losing money.

Let's say you gain one hundred new customers in less than a week and they generate you another one thousand dollars. So now it is two weeks later. Fifty of your customers got their products with no problems. They got everything on time and with no defects. You don't need to worry about those customers.

The other fifty did not have the same luck. Some products may have been late or not shipped. Maybe you missed ten of them because you have not scaled or optimized the part of your business that involves sending orders to the supplier. So you refund them.

Twenty got defective products. The other twenty got the wrong product altogether. Either way, you just lost five hundred dollars, or more, because you now need to refund or replace the items.

Had you scaled, the results would be different. You would have had an ordering system in place that automated the orders and you would not have missed that first ten.

That same system would record exactly what the customer typed and/or clicked on so you are no longer attempting to manually order everything. In addition, you would have a reliable supplier who can handle large orders so the customers would have gotten the correct items.

You may still end up with a few whose items were damaged in transit, but those customers would only make up a small percentage.

Scaling Business Culture
No matter what type of business you are running company culture is important. It sets the tone for how you and your employees treat customers, vendors, and each other. Having a company culture that involves respect, kindness, and putting the customers first can make the difference between your company thriving or failing.

Company culture starts with you. What do you want the culture to look like? How do you want the employees to treat each other? How do you want them to treat customers?

Let's say you want the culture to center around respect for employees and customers. You also want your employees to be driven and innovative. That is your culture. That is what you include when you are training new employees.

This may seem simple. Drop shipping companies usually start with just one person starting their business. However, you will eventually need employees to help with customer service and marketing at the very least. You may need more than that. The first few employees may be easy to train.

It is easy to take one or two people and say hey, this is the culture. This is what I mean. This is what I want. It will not be so easy with twenty employees. It will be even harder with fifty.

So how can you maintain your companies culture and reinforce it? How do you ensure that your employees continue providing quality customer service? How do you ensure that the employee morale stays high and you don't end up with a high turnover rate or terrible customer service?

You are the key here.

The first thing to remember is that this is your company. You need to model these behaviors. Anytime you are around your employees or talking to a customer you need to demonstrate the same qualities you are asking for. Be patient. Listen to the customer. Speak to them kindly and do all you can to resolve their issue. This shows your employees that you are not only asking them to show customers respect and kindness but that you are willing to practice what you preach.

There are many other things you can do. No one thing is enough. Make sure your managers are on board. They deal with the rest of the employees more than you do, and the more employees you have the more managers you will need. Always model this behavior to them, and talk to them about doing the same thing.

Reward employees who show the qualities you are looking for. Did Jennifer in your customer service department handle a particularly rude customer very respectfully and kindly even though you could tell she was stressed? Tell her what a great job she did. Let her take a break. Occasionally have company-sponsored luncheons or parties to thank your team.

You can also put posters and graphics around the office, and set up learning materials through the employee portal. Make the company culture a priority. Happy and cohesive groups work better and more productively than groups who feel ignored and unappreciated.

Things to Look At When Scaling Your Business
There is no shortage of considerations when you are trying to decide on what to look at to scale your business. There are so many moving parts to any Drop shipping business.

It may seem simpler than a traditional business, and in some ways it is, but in some ways it actually much more complicated since you do not control the products or shipping yourself.

The first thing you need to look at is your marketing plan and your projected growth. Assume that your business with double within a month. Could you handle that? If all of your projections have you making two hundred orders a day within the next two months, how would you handle that?

Let's start with the basics.

Are you using a quality website platform? Have you ensured that your platform, in particular, has shown that it does not crash with heavy traffic? Is it fast enough?

On average, if a website takes more than two to four seconds to load, almost a quarter of the potential customers would leave the site. You need to have a high-quality provider to guarantee your site can handle heavy traffic and fast load times.

How are the payments being processed? Do you offer enough options? Do you accept all major credit cards and payment apps? The more payment types available to your customers the more likely they are to buy.

If person A only uses PayPal for online shopping and you do not have a PayPal option then you just lost a customer.

Once you have the orders and payments, how are you communicating those orders to your supplier? Do you have an automated system in place?

Having a close working relationship with your dropshipper is always the best way to handle things like this. That way, if you choose to make life easier by automating your system, you can still make sure that if there are any issues you will know about it right away.

Do all of your systems work well together? If you have an automated payment system, an automatic ordering system, and systems controlling your bookkeeping and more, do they "speak" to each other? The more automated all of your systems are and the more they can share information with each other the better.

Finally, let's talk about employees.

Will you need more? Having a tech on call is a good idea, of course. What about an assistant? Maybe someone who is more experienced in marketing? Remember, you want to scale, not just grow.

Hire who you need to for business to run smoothly, but not before you need them, and automate as much as you can so that you only need a few employees.

For example, if you are up to a thousand orders per week, you can have three employees. One tech, one marketing expert, and someone that helps you to field customer calls. Your automated systems handle the rest.

How to Scale Your Drop shipping Business

So far you have learned what scaling is and why it is important. Now you can learn what you can do to scale your Drop shipping business in a way that makes sense and works for you.

Let's assume you have already gone over all of the details in the "Things to Look at When Scaling Your Business" section. So now you want to know what to do once you have evaluated your business and looked into all of the different things you could streamline.

Start by once again combing through your marketing plan and your current growth rate. How many new customers and new sales can you expect for the next month? How about for the next six months? How about for the next year? Project your growth, and work backward from there.

Do not hire four employees to take customer calls when you won't have more than a hundred orders in an entire week. It is unlikely every customer would call, and even if they did, one employee could handle one hundred calls in a week.

Talk to your suppliers. This can not be said enough. Your Drop shipping partner is the person who supplies all of your customers with the products. They keep the stock, they take the orders from you, and they pack and ship all of your orders.

You can have every perfected system in place. You could have the absolute best advertising and the most amazing website. The entire business will fail if you do not communicate with your suppliers.

Let them know what the projected growth rate is. Make sure they know how much inventory you think they may need. Let them know that orders will be increasing so they can decide if they need to add people to their team to keep up.

Also, attempt to make your costs lower. If you are reaching a certain benchmark, try to talk to them about taking off a percentage for so many bulk orders.

Get a freelancer or hire a techie who is experienced in building entire business systems. You need someone who can optimize your website. They should also be able to set up your payment systems, your ordering systems, your phone systems, your bookkeeping software and more.

Get a professional who can automate as much as they can and then tie it all together so they work well together. Keep that person on retainer in case anything goes down. This person will be invaluable. The right systems save you time, money, and stress.

Speaking of money, pay attention to your accounts!

Some banks and payment apps will flag and block funds if they feel something is fraudulent. They don't necessarily know you are running a business. Communicating with them and heading off any problems before they start can go a long way in preventing any accounts from being frozen or blocked.

As your business grows you will need to hire customer service representatives. You cannot spend twenty-four hours a day awake and taking calls and responding to emails.

It is important to deal with customers, but you are a busy person and no matter how much you'd like to, you can't take fifty calls and a hundred emails in a day by yourself on top of running everything else.

Hire an assistant to help you manage all of this. Have someone responsible you can trust working directly with you to help with anything you need. They should be able to do anything from grabbing you a coffee to handling calls to your supplier if you need them to.

Throughout all of this, treat everyone who works for you well and always do your best to model the company culture you want to create.

Why a Marketing Plan is Essential when Scaling Your Business

Your marketing plan is probably the most important part of your overall business planning. It outlines your products, how you plan to market these products, and who you are marketing to.

The marketing plan is your go-to when trying to make decisions in your scaling operations.

Your marketing plan is created based on data. You will have done research and looked into every single detail of your business and projected growth. This data will then be compiled and analyzed at which point you will put it all together in a cohesive way.

It will include your overall plan along with sections outlining how much money you plan to make, how you plan to make it, and when you plan to make. Your goals will be set and you will have data to support your projected goals.

When scaling your business your market plan will be your most important tool. This will be your guide. It will give you a clear timeline. Scaling is a process. It is not something that you can do overnight. You need to make strategic changes and decisions based on your marketing plan's projected goals and timelines.

For example, if you have planned and projected that at three months you want your website to have two hundred and fifty thousand visitors a month then you will need to scale to meet that goal. Which means you will need to scale your advertising. You could choose to hire someone for that goal.

You can use sites such as Upwork and Fiverr to find freelancers to write your copy for you and create social media content, or you can choose to do it yourself.

In the meantime, if you have grown your website traffic by that much you will have also built your sales way up. This means you should also ensure that by that three-month mark you have also set up all of your payment and ordering systems so that the process is streamlined for you, your customers, and your dropshipper.

You would have hired a programmer to set all of that up for you and a customer service rep to help you handle any incoming customer problems.

Throughout all of this, you would have talked to your Drop shipping partner about the projected increase in product needs. That way you could make sure they can handle the influx on their end as well.

This is just an example of why a marketing plan is essential to building your business. Because for each milestone you have outlined in your plan you can already have a solid way to ensure you hit it by properly scaling in accordance.

If you do not use a marketing plan, your company may grow, but you will not have planned out how to grow all of the moving parts with it. So how do you create this all-important marketing plan?

Creating a Great Marketing Plan

A marketing plan can be time-consuming to create, but it can save you time and thousands of dollars down the line. The very first thing you need to do is sit down and detail where you are now and decide what your goals are and why you chose those as your goals.

Remember to keep these goals clear and concise because later you will need to flesh it all out. You also need to have the data to work with, such as what types of ads and content attract the demographic you are targeting.

For example, you would not write "gain a million twitter followers". This is vague and not based on any type of data set. You would write "gain a million twitter followers by hiring an experienced writer to write articles specific to "my niche" and targeted customer demographics. I will post three articles per day every day, and ensure the writer uses set keywords in the articles. I will gain one hundred thousand followers every two weeks until I hit a million"

Customer demographics will be a large part of your overall marketing strategy, so you want to include as much about them as you can. Do as much research as you can possibly afford to do when studying these demographics.

If you are selling gaming headphones, for example, you would need to do studies and research to determine the people most likely to buy them. Let's say that the research shows that these headphones will primarily sell to young males between the ages of sixteen and twenty-five.

You need to know all you can about males between sixteen and twenty-five in order to cater all of your marketing content to them. Targeted marketing works better than any general marketing you could do.

Now that you have your current standing and goals outlined, your timeline, and your scaling strategy to match, you can fill in the rest of your marketing strategy. Include demographic details.

Write a solid but to the point executive summary outlining who you are and what type of values you want your company to represent. Research your competitors and find out what works and doesn't work for them.

Outline your overall marketing strategies and how you plan to track all of your growth and changes so you can continue to scale in advance.

Ultimately, your marketing plan should be clear, concise, and informative. Make it attractive to look at so anyone who needs to see it wants to read it. Keep your executive summary to the point while still giving the reader a clear idea of what you want to convey. Make your goals and the plan of execution to those goals clear and detailed. Make sure the reader can clearly see who your targeted audience will be, and how you will keep track of all of your progress.

This marketing plan will be your guide. You will refer to it to make any changes necessary to scale your business. You will refer to it when talking to any investors or at any meetings with other business owners. You will use it to inform your employees about the overall strategy and goals of the company and what you need from them.

This plan will be something you look back and follow for years to come, and a good marketing plan will cover ten years or more. You can always go in and adjust it based on new data.

Most importantly, this marketing plan is what will help you securely establish your brand in a strategic way.

Conclusion

As you begin working your drop shipping business, you are going to begin to learn your own tips and tricks to help you master the business. However, to help you get started, we have compiled a list of some of the best tips and tricks you should pay attention to when you are starting your drop shipping business. Having this knowledge under your belt now and applying them immediately will ensure that you are prepared for everything that is to come and that you come out of the gates strong.

It is a good idea to keep a book handy so that as you learn your own tips and tricks in the industry, you can write them down. While you may remember some due to using them on a regular basis, having them written down can help you remember what works in the situations you don't tend to experience as often, such as specific situations with certain vendors. Make sure that you keep this notebook handy and that you use it whenever you need in order to make sure that you are running your business smoothly and efficiently.

As with any business, your reputation is highly important. You need to recognize what goes into creating a solid reputation and how you can use your reputation to positively impact your business performance. Your reputation is closely attached to your brand, but it is not your brand itself. Instead, it is the way people think about your brand.

Take a moment to think about a company that you haven't had such a good experience with. It is likely that many people haven't had a good experience, and for you and the rest of the population, their reputation is tarnished. People may continue to shop there, but it does not equate to them gaining as much business as they could if they had a positive reputation.

Now, think about a business that you love shopping with. Think about how positive they make you feel and the type of experience you have when you do business with them. Also, think about how other people tend to talk about that business. Since their overall reputation is more positive and they are known to serve their customers effectively, it is likely that their reputation is excellent.

With your own business, you want to be the one with the reputation that has people eager to work with you. People should be aware of how positive your business is and the type of experience they can expect to have with you well before the first time they ever do business with you. When people run into issues with their service, they should be able to rely on the fact that your company will rectify the situation quickly and in a justified manner. The customer needs to know that you are always going to look out for their best interest and do everything you can to serve them to the highest of your abilities.

Real Estate Investing For Beginners

The Best Ways To Create Wealth And Build True Passive Income with Secrets and Strategies and No Money Down, Rental Property, Commercial, Wholesaling, Family

ROBERT ZONE

Introduction

Real estate is an investment, not only in money but in time. Yes, it can provide stability, and regular returns if done correctly. But before all that can take place, you need to engage in some serious introspection. What made you first look at one deal over another? Is this something you need or want? Will this produce the monetary and potentially emotional returns you were hoping? Will this deal require any sacrifices, such as relocation, or a lot of extra time?

You don't even need to directly own real estate in order for this to happen.

Moreover, your income from real estate investments is not affected by inflation. If anything, your rental income will increase along with inflation. This means that you will be able to enjoy a higher cash flow while maintaining or improving the purchasing power of your money.

There are tax benefits too. If you have investment property, you are allowed to deduct deprecation of the building and any additional capital investments, which will reduce your taxable income. And there are other tax advantages you can enjoy based on what investment method you use.

While this all may sound a little 'woo' to you, the reality is that you have to know what you want and why you want it. Knowing these things comes with understanding who you are. Do a little soul searching to discover your true beliefs and values. What is that you truly hold dear, to run a business and understand your boundaries and belief system and values take work and a deep knowing of you who you are. If this isn't something you've ever done or considered it won't be easy. But it will separate the successful business owners from the unsuccessful ones.

In this book, we will describe the various methods that you can use to invest in real estate. Like we said before, you don't actually need to be a direct owner of property in order to make money from it. We will give you an overview of each investment method, including the pros and cons of each one.

You can also earn your ticket to financial freedom when you learn how real estate investing works. While it is true that real estate is a great investment opportunity, when you lack the wisdom and knowledge about how to operate it, things might turn sour. The game of real estate involves a lot of capital and brain. If you have the capital without the brain, you will commit financial suicide.

Yet, a brain without the capital will lead you nowhere. Therefore, you want to learn how real estate investing works and how to raise money to build a strong investment empire. This will start with your mindset, traits, and values. When you have the mental thought pattern of highly successful real estate investors, you will be able to weather the storms and do well financially.

Ideally, you can make money in real estate either through the capital gains system or cash flow. When you invest in real estate for capital gains, you buy, fix, and sell properties. However, when you invest in cash flow, you invest in buying, holding and collecting rent. The rent will be collected and then used to pay down for other real estate properties while using leverage.

Through effective property management systems, the value of the property will be increased over time. This will enable you to pay down the mortgage on the property, decrease your liabilities, increase your equity, and grow your net worth over time. Using the principles, hacks, and methods of in the following pages, you will be able to multiply your real estate holdings in a short period of time.

Chapter 1 Fundamental of Real Estate Investment

Real Estate Investment Trust (REITs) is an investment trust where a group of people invests their money in residential or commercial real estate business. These trusts use mortgages of large numbers and commercial properties and manage them. Such trusts show both shares and real estate's best features.

Invest in real estate investment just the same way an organization operates revenue-generating business assets such as hotels, warehouses, apartments, and shopping centers. While different property types are available, many of these REITs are limited and focus solely on any one type of property. Companies specializing in health care are known as REITs of health care. Such trusts were established in 1960 to allow large-scale investment in the real estate sector, which individual investors can then access. The main advantage of these trusts is that they help people pick a share to invest in a variety of a company rather than investing in a single large estate or house.

Most of these trusts are grouped into three subsections: equity, mortgage, and hybrid. The first class is the property owners and loans are also given to property owners. The second category comprises of ownership and property-generating income management. The mortgage investment trusts are the ones that provide money by acquiring their loans and mortgage-backed securities to property owners.

In several respects, these investment trusts differ significantly from limited partnerships — one of the significant differences is in how their investors disclose the annual tax data.

A company must share 90 percent or more of all its taxable income within its shareholders for a day in the year to become a real estate investment trust. Once the company is eligible as REIT, it can go through its shareholders ' dividends.

Academic concept

Real estate has been defined as land (or immovable assets) along with anything permanently attached to it, such as buildings, and investment is the use of money to purchase property for the sole purpose of income holding or renting. It is fair then to assume (combining both definitions) that investment in immovable property includes the purchase of immovable property (or investment in the immovable property) for income generation, profit-making, and assets acquisition.

The Conceptual Description

Leverage, unlike stock investments (usually requiring more equity from the investor), a real estate investment (heavily) can be leveraged. With an investment in real estate, you can use money from other people to increase the return rate and manage a much more significant investment otherwise not possible.

Investing in real estate tax shelter provides tax advantages. Annual after-tax cash flows, equity buildup through asset appreciation, and cash flow following tax on sale arc yields.

Non-monetary refunds Investment in real estate provides ownership pride, security in which you monitor ownership, and diversification of portfolios.

Nevertheless, investing in real estate is not a bed of roses. Investment in real estate requires capital, risks exist, and rental property can be intensive in terms of management. The clothes you wear requires money, on the other hand, for a car, it includes risk driving, and it certainly requires management. The difference is that a car is not a wealth source.

How to become an investor

In real estate, develop a goal of investing in real estate. What would you like to do you want to do, and by what time do you want to do it? What rates of return do you expect to earn on money that you squeeze out of your home or bank account to buy an investment property because of the risk?

Know what you need to look for returns and how to measure them. Unless you can read music, you can't succeed in music. Invest in an excellent investment course in real estate or technology for investment in real estate where you can learn how to monitor returns and calculate formulas.

Be vigilant about the schemes of Getting Rich. Many so-called gurus are ready to teach you how to make millions of property investments with real estate. But let logic be your guide; we assume a map is published by no one who discovers a gold mine.

Establish a relationship with a real estate agent who is familiar with the local real estate market and understands rental property. Spending time with the "agent of the year" will not advance your investment goals unless that person knows about investment property and is adequately prepared to help you get it right. Choose a broker who understands investment in real estate.

What Are Real Estate Investment Trusts?

Is there a secret formula for investment in real estate? Looking at property moguls, including Donald Trump, who made millions of investments in real estate, we usually think that investing in real estate needs to have some unique blueprint, but that's not always the case.

There are some fundamentals, golden rules, and unchangeable realities that relate to investment in real estate, whether you're a first-time dabbler or a seasoned professional. Most of these are common sense, only good old-fashioned.

Do Your Homework. At the time, there are plenty of shops to have on the market, as distressed homeowners scuttle to realize their investments, maintain their financial stability, and avoid foreclosure. Still, when faced with a deal that seems too good to be true, it might just be.

Making sure you leave whether substantial changes are intended in the area- a significant industrial development or a new highway extension from your doorstep could limit the profits you will make on your investment in real estate!

Find out how often To Invest. There are several reasons why people like to invest. Do you want a long-term investment that will give you rental income, or are you looking for a property that you can update quickly and sell for a profit? Do you focus on the fickle residential market, or do you prefer a more stable market for commercial real estate?

Understanding what your goals are in structuring and planning your portfolio of investment in real estate is vital for the very first time.

Know Your Risk Appetite. Great reward comes with considerable risk. Occasionally.

Understanding whether you can manage the sometimes challenging high-risk investment climate, in real estate or otherwise, will help guide you in making the right choices.

If you don't have the appetite for the pressure which follows it, there's no use opting for a higher risk portfolio of investment properties. If you think higher-risk investments are stressful, they may not be for you!

If you choose safer options, investment in real estate can still work for you, pick a property in developed areas where your rental income and steady growth are more stable.

Maybe don't extend yourself. It is maybe tempting to bite off more than you can chew when you're caught in the high that accompanies successful real estate investment. However, consider that if you invest in renting out your properties, there may be times when you cannot find suitable tenants. Can you cover all your property payments if that happens? If not, reconsider your plans, and proceed accordingly.

Real Estate Investing is a safe choice. Whichever your answers to the questions mentioned above, real estate remains a safe and profitable choice.

Understanding your ambitions, personality, or if you are in lengthy-haul real estate investment or a quick buck, will help you make sound choices, give you a balanced portfolio, and make sure your investments pay dividends over the coming years.

WHAT IS TURN-KEY REAL ESTATE INVESTING?

This is a simple concept where the buyer is buying, rehabilitating, and then reselling a property at a profit. This is also referred to as a home, "flipping." The process usually occurs remotely, as the investor resides in her or his own house, sometimes in a place where flipping does not make any sense and uses the Internet to locate and invest in opportunities. The target here is to make the process of investing in real estate as easy as possible, so all the investor has to do is flip a switch or "change the button." Usually, instead, you purchase a minor home that contains a single family, repair it to match current codes, and make sure it attracts the buyers. Below is how its work: the property is purchased by a turnkey retailer or company.

One or more investors buy a share or all of the house's stock.

To make it new and attractive to customers, the seller or company "fix-up" or rehabilitates the property.

Once the property has been rehabilitated, it will be put back on the resale market.

Once a sale is completed, the buyer gets his or her money back plus any gain gained, depending on the share of the investment he or she owns.

This could be a sound investment technique if it is done correctly. You have made a benefit from flipping the home as the buyer, and you can have as little or as much interest as you want. You can be as interested in the flipping process as you want, helping to manage the home treatment contractors, and leaving the entire process to the turnkey retailer.

Why not buy and rent a house myself?

You may think you can remove the middleman, the turnkey distributor, or company, and do all the legwork yourself. While this is what many shareholders do and excel in, there are some drawbacks. You will end up doing a lot more work in most situations than you would as an investor. Here's what you'd have to do if you became a flipper instead of using a turnkey approach and managing the operation for you by the turnkey retailer.

Finding a property: - First, a suitable property would have to be located.

Rehabilitating house:- First, the estate should be restored and rehabilitated, adhering to existing codes and also being an outstanding one-family property. It requires proper budgeting and treatment of contractors and staff, which requires a presence on-site.

Marketing this property for rent or sale: You'd have to look for a paying tenant or a buyer to live in the house once the property is ready to move in.

You'd be entering a whole new dimension when you want to rent the property. Check out our overview of that investment strategy for more details on turnkey real estate investment where you lease rather than resell.

If it sounds like a lot of effort, it's because it is. With turnkey real estate investment, you can take off your hands as much or little of the work and put it on other people. Let us have a glance at the benefits of turnkey investment in real estate.

The benefit of turnkey real estate investment is that a turnkey retailer is an investor, not a landlord or a flipper, in a full-fledged turnkey real estate investment scenario. The property should be managed for you, you are employing someone else, and all you have to do is collect on the income. Here are some of the main benefits of turnkey investment in real estate.

It does not need your presence locally. You acquire single-family property in remote locations with turnkey real estate investment. This allows you the freedom to stay where you want while maintaining a cash flow from a location with excellent property values. For example, you could continue to live in the gated community in Texas, where the flipping house may be meaningless while investing in rentable or flippable properties in Seattle or elsewhere that have a strong demand for such properties.

Easy diversification of your turnkey real estate investment portfolio could be a good move while done correctly. One element of successfully implementing a turnkey investment strategy for real estate is appropriately investing in multiple markets, which is easy to do as it takes little to no time of its own. The benefits of investing in various markets are simple: it protects you from an unforeseen economic downturn.

Since turnkey investment in real estate makes it so easy to have multiple properties, if you do it right, this is an essential advantage of the investment strategy. Don't put all your eggs in one basket, in other words.

If working with a reputable turnkey real estate retailer or company, the provider knows the real estate markets much more accurately than an outsider might. You can probably do some basic research on an area, checking out local school scores, crime reports, and price range, but a turnkey company would know all that and more; they'll see the heart of a community.

The disadvantages of turnkey investment in real estate. If turnkey investment in real estate sounds like a sure-fire way of making money, you should be aware that the strategy has disadvantages. First and foremost, you will find turnkey manufacturers trying to maximize their profits at the risk of cutting corners, but there are other pitfalls beyond that.

The "middle man" has to make money. The turnkey business is a business, and it needs to make money for that business. That means buying property at a discount and selling it to you at a higher amount of the property, often for a substantial profit margin. The turnkey company will then be able to make an additional profit by managing the sale or rental of the property for you. Though, one thing to remember about this downside is that turnkey businesses often have a marketing machine going at all times and can find incredible deals in their business, enabling them to give you a lot even as the company makes its money.

There are "shady" turnkey companies out there, and you have to trust someone. Such firms would allow an out-of-state investor to purchase a bad property in a bad location, which means more money going out of the hands of the buyer than flowing in. You have to rely on the experience, skills, and reputation of the turnkey operator to make a good deal for you. This means that you have to deal with someone you truly can trust.

As a result of this, Turn-key real estate investment, has significant benefits, and it can certainly be an enticing practice for cash flow. Nonetheless, disadvantages also need to be taken into account before making any deals. You'll need to research the turnkey provider to make sure they're both reliable and successful and make sure that the cash flow opportunity they're giving you is practical and feasible. Turnkey investment in real estate is a great way to make money as long as you're smart about it and take care of your due diligence throughout the process.

How Does Real Estate Investing Work?

Investing in real estate works best with a strategy. In deciding how you want to invest in real estate to work for you, it is necessary first to determine the results you wish to get from investment in real estate — looking to build wealth, or quick cash, or both? You could choose a brief-term strategy, a lengthy-term strategy, or a mixture of the two, depending on your desired results.

How does it work to make quick cash by investing in real estate?

Quick cash could be developed with a brief-term investment strategy for real estate, including fast turning or flipping property. Fast turning property (buying and selling immediately) can provide substantial and fast cash if you buy correctly. The estate is usually placed under a low price contract and then sold at a higher price to include again. Based on your plan, the property can be sold with or without changes. Quick turn deals can quickly produce between $2K and $30K plus depending on the contract and whether it's a sharp turn for wholesale or retail.

Wholesale Fast Turn

Wholesale fast turns involve finding a product below market value and selling the offer quickly at a wholesale price. You give your buyer, usually another shareholder, the opportunity to make a profit by selling wholesale (below retail).

Wholesaling is always a way to make zero, or little, transactions with money down. It is a means for real estate investors to get around the house flipping used for financial support. Let's presume you're seeking a motivated seller, willing to sell your house at $200K. You contract the property with the seller for $200 K and find another buyer who likes the deal and is willing to pay $110K. Your agreement with the seller would then be transferred to your buyer for $20K. In reality, the buyer closes and buys the property from the seller; and a $20K assignment fee is charged to you at the closing. The form used for retail is an alternative. You could place an option on a property and then sell the option again to another shareholder. In reality, you never have to buy the property with assignments and options to make money.

Retail Fast Turn

Short turns involve finding a property well below market value and getting it ready for retail sale. Your target customer is a homeowner rather than an investor with fast shifts in retail. You could buy a property that requires a little effort, a bit of work, or you may not need to do any work at all because you purchased it at a discount from a motivated seller. You market and sell the property at a retail price once the property is ready.

How does it work to build wealth by investing in real estate?

Wealth is created by long-term investment strategies for real estate, the purchase, and keeping of land. The investor purchases a property in this scenario and then rents it to a tenant or leases it to a tenant with the option to purchase it.

Renting

Renting is about finding a house, getting it ready for rent, and marketing it for rent. The investment strategy for rental property offers a number of prospects for profit. If the mortgage is less than monthly rental income and other expenses, cash flow is created. Long-term wealth is created through property appreciation, mortgage payment by tenants, and tax benefits.

Imagine getting ten apartments paid in full for a cash flow of $10,000 and rented for $1,000. If flats are worth only $100K each, you'd have an asset worth $1 million-plus a cash flow of $10 K per month before spending. This financial position can be reached in your timeline reasonably and easily. Some people buy one or two houses a year, while others immediately purchase several homes.

Lease Option

Lease options are provided by providing a lease property with the option to buy (usually for twelve months or more). Including revenue from the initial incentive charge, monthly cash flow from the rent, profit from the sale when the option is exercised, and tax benefits, which are a variety of profit centers with lease options.

Finally, the answer to the question, "How does real estate investment work?" really depends on how you want real estate investment to work for you. Whether you're building wealth, leaving the 9-5, early retirement, quick cash, or financial freedom, you can get it through investment in real estate. Investing in real estate, such as buying at a loss and generating instant equity, creating capital by tenants paying down a loan, appreciation, cash flow, interest, and tax benefits, has numerous benefits. Determine the strategy, lengthy-term, brief-term, or a mixture of the two, and invest in real estate that works for you.

A Beginner's Guide For Real Estate Investor

When selecting your first property to purchase and deciding to enter the current market, real estate investment for beginners involves a few things to consider. For learners, we plan to address some of the concerns that are engaged in this form of investment.

You have to understand that by making the wrong decision, most people lose money. Buying while stock prices are low and selling when they are high is the key to making money in real estate. Before you determine on your first property and enter the real estate investment field, we will give you essential tips to think about.

The number one principle of investing in a property is the location- the location is one of the first things to think about. If you think about which property you want to purchase, you need to think about areas that might be anticipated shortly to become popular locations but have prices that have not yet risen. This may indicate that they are situated in the outer parts of the city or that they may be located near a proposed resort area. If you're looking to invest in property, think about whether it's going to be better than some other real estate investment locations.

You may want to consider investing in lower-priced real estate than market prices. You may find the right property offers that an owner needs to sell due to a job transfer or divorce. This may imply you could get the property at cheaper prices than most other homes in the area, and when you sell, you will have better chances of making a profit. You can find a property that needs a few repairs, or needs a paint coat and adding a few minor details. When you start investing in real estate, these can be the best chances to make better profits.

Having land that can be leased out to fund the mortgage payment is another thing to think about. If you're paying the best price and getting the proper funding for property you're buying, then you could rent it till the demand increases, and you can make a profit. Keep in mind that you'll have to find a suitable renter and pre-screen them to find those who pay their bills on time and won't harm your estate. You do not want the additional cost of hiring an attorney and evicting renters who haven't paid rent or caused damage, but it can be part of real estate investment.

If you want a mortgage in which you invest, you must ensure that there is no penalty clause for early payment of the loan. When you buy the property and repair it to sell quickly, this can happen. You could make a profit this way, but when you sell it, you could have a penalty for paying off the loan early. Most banks understand that you are trying to repair and sell the property, but if they know you are investing in real estate, they will require a higher down payment.

Think of ways you can save money when it comes to closing costs and land charges. When you find property for sale by sellers, you can get better deals because they protect the fee for the seller. Such charges may be 7 to 10 percent of the price of the property, but it is a charge that the seller pays. Most buyers are always using agents to help them find the best deals. The critical thing to consider is that when you're investing in real estate, you get the best price on the property and don't charge the market price.

When investing in properties, do not make these common mistakes. When making property offers, think carefully, and don't rely on gut instincts because they're not always right. Before investing in properties, make sure you do your homework and find out as much as you can.

Inspect the properties and consider a professional home inspector for significant defects. Do not depend on rumors or promises in the popularization of a particular region or rising prices due to plans to grow it. Do not be emotionally involved with properties because when you are investing in real estate, it can cause you to make bad decisions that cost money.

When you intend to invest in real estate, you've heard some of the most important things to think about. There may be small things that make a big difference when it comes to making a profit for the beginners in this sector. You need to find out as much as you can about the estate you are involved in and get expert assistance before you enter the field of investment inland. To help you find the best deals and get some professional advice to help you make the best decision, you can contact a local real estate agent. Once you enter the real estate investment market, this should be your next step.

Real Estate Investing - Is it a Wise Investment?

I still find it interesting that you hear so many stories about people who made tons of money in real estate rentals, but never about regular accidents, as people don't talk so much about them. Much as you always learn about the winnings of a gambler, but never the full amount of their losses.

Among the most critical parts of owning a single property is to understand the concepts and see them as a corporation

Here are the main reasons why I don't recommend investing directly in real estate properties:

1) It's one of the few investments that can cost you considerable money and time.

Owning property like an investment include costs like interest on the loan, cost of closing, cost of locating tenants, cost of months without tenants, cost of additional insurance, cost of restoring and maintaining an investment property, and management fees to name a few. Most people don't consider all property ownership costs.

2) It is an asset leveraged to increase the risk.

Whether it's a home, apartment building, or property, most people take out a loan to purchase the investment. Their initial investment is leveraged, and they bet that the investment will be worth more. Gains and losses are magnified by leverage. (This is good on the upside, terrible on the downside.) If the price of the real estate market has plummeted, you may not be able to sell the property for what you put in, and you still have a monthly cash outflow obligation.

3) The portfolio is not diversified.

Some real estate is an investment in a particular location of one house. In this one basket, you usually put many of your eggs, which again increases the risk. (Diversification is among the most critical priority tenants. I am a fan of low-cost mutual funds and ETFs because of g on the real estate market. Even in good markets, selling and closing on a property usually takes more than two months. Anyone who owned a home during a buyer's market, like now, can tell you their nightmare and frustration over a year (or years) with the house on the market.

How about a holiday home?

Even when it comes to holiday homes, if you want to use a holiday home as your holiday home, do it if it makes financial sense to you. I see that as a little investment other than just buying a second home. The satisfaction and happiness you get from having a holiday home make up for the real estate's risks and costs. A vacation home's main objective is to be used and enjoyed differently from a property purchased primarily as an investment. (Often, renting a holiday home for several weeks a year is much cheaper and more convenient than getting the cost of owning a holiday home.) REITs- whether you believe in it and want to invest in real estate, I am a fan of real estate investment trusts or REITs. REITs are security that trades like a stock and invests directly in real estate through the ownership of a portfolio of properties and mortgages.

1) Having an expert picking up assets

2) Without the hassle, costs and responsibility to manage an individual property

3) Not incurring the risk of personal property due to lack of diversification (because the REIT may purchase many properties, mortgages and/or locations)

4) It is marketable.

5) A REIT alone is a diversified investment conclusion. Although I do not suggest buying individual real estate as an investment, real estate as an asset class usually improves the diversification of your portfolio as it has a low correlation with the general market. Therefore, I generally recommend that you devote a small portion of your portfolio to this category, not as a market call to this sector (especially now), but based

on my confidence in its potential to dampen your portfolio's overall long-term volatility.

Please note that because we are not great fans of REITs right now, mainly commercial property REITs, we must be in the potential as the economy is improving and less demand due to lower prices.

Chapter 2 Real Estate Investment Groups

Real estate investment groups (REIG) have become a popular alternative in recent years to real estate investment trusts. Both allow you to enjoy the benefits of investing in real estate without the effort and time required for direct ownership. They also allow you to start investing without requiring you to have a lot of knowledge about real estate.

However, joining a REIG provides you with an opportunity to learn the ins and outs of real estate investing. This knowledge can be valuable to you later on should you decide to buy your own investment properties.

REIGs are associations of investors who pool their money to invest in real estate, buying, and/or developing properties. They then rent these properties out to generate rental income from them. This income is shared among the investors.

These groups usually specialize in a certain property type, such as commercial or residential real estate. They may also focus on finding properties nationally or concentrate on local real estate investments.

REIGs usually hire professionals to manage and maintain the properties as well as to find tenants. Mortgage payments come from rental income. If there are vacancies, the group may put aside a certain portion of their earnings to cover the shortfall.

A real estate investment club does not invest in properties. It is simply a networking and educational group that allows members to share expertise about real estate investments. They also help each other find investment opportunities.

These groups are formally incorporated as legal entities, with each member listed as a joint owner. When the group makes a purchase, its official name is what is listed on the deed. Although there are no legal minimums or limits on membership, these groups usually only accept a manageable number, which may be around five to ten members.

They are run based on formal operating rules that the members have agreed on. Like any organization, most of them elect members as officers with specific responsibilities in the running of the group. Members will also jointly make investment decisions, voting on which properties to buy or to sell.

Pros and Cons
The main advantage of joining a REIG is that it allows you to invest in properties for a relatively small amount, although your investment will be larger than when you buy into real estate investment trusts. In exchange, however, the potential earnings will be higher.

Another advantage is that, collectively, the group is pooling its investment capital. This gives them the ability to place bids for properties that, as individuals, they may not be able to bid for.

In addition, REIGs also allow certain underrepresented groups to benefit from property investing. For instance, there are women's real estate clubs and clubs that are designed to teach minorities how to invest in real estate and to accumulate assets. This is to empower them to actually get into the market themselves.

Some groups may also provide education for their members by hosting events in which speakers talk about various investment topics. This may be useful to members who want to learn more about the subject and improve their skills. These gatherings are also invaluable for networking purposes as it allows members to meet and interact with other potential investors.

However, members may be asked to pay an entry fee in addition to their initial investment. They may also be asked to pay recurring annual fees. These fees may ultimately affect your net earnings.

In addition, your investment is not liquid. If you suddenly need to get your money back, you cannot just sell your share. You have to follow the guidelines of the organization as to how to liquidate your investment. This might require that another member buy you out. When this happens, you will have effectively withdrawn from the group since you no longer have any investment in it.

The collective way that decisions are made may also pose a problem. The various members may vote on their decisions based on emotional factors, and this could affect the profitability of the group. For instance, one member may convince the others to vote to hold on to a property that is not generating sufficient income, for sentimental reasons.

How to Choose a Group

Before you decide to invest in a REIG, you should be familiar with what your investment goals are. A REIG holds on to property over the long term in order to generate income from it. If you are expecting to see quick returns on your investment, i.e. by flipping the property, you should not invest in this group.

On the other hand, if you are preparing for retirement, then you should definitely consider investing in a group. This investment will provide you with a recurring source of income for when you are no longer earning income from employment.

When you contact the group, ask about their history. Have they been operating for some time, or are they just getting organized?

If they are a new group, ask about the other members. What experience do they have? If they are all new investors, who is guiding the group as to what investments they should make?

If they are an existing group that is looking for new members, ask about their record. How successful have they been with their investments over time? Ask if you can talk with former members about their experiences with the club.

Ask them about their portfolio of properties. They don't have to give you specifics, just what type of properties they generally invest in. Find out how much you can potentially earn by investing in the group and how often the returns are paid out.

Also consider: who are the members? Is the membership focused on a certain demographic, i.e. older adults, or are they open to anybody? How does the composition of the group affect its investment decisions?

Next, look at the costs of membership. How much does it cost to invest in the group? After your initial investment, do you have to make additional investments?

Also ask about the fees the group charges. Are there entry fees? Are there any recurring fees such as service fees? How are they charged? Are they fixed amounts or a percentage of the profits? Can you offset these fees from your earnings or do you have to pay them separately? Or do you have the option to choose?

What are your obligations as a member? Are there certain duties and responsibilities that you have to fulfill as a member of the group? Does the group meet regularly? Do you have to participate when it has to make investment decisions?

Another important consideration is the group's investment goals. Does the group invest in the type of real estate properties that you are interested in? What is their investment strategy? Is it an aggressive or a conservative one?

If the group offers you access to invest in wholesale properties, do they have documentation attesting to the quality of these assets?

What about exiting the group? What if you want to withdraw your investment? How long do you have to maintain your investment before you can exit? Are there fees and penalties for early withdrawal?

Now that you know what to look for, how do you find a group? Before you start, keep in mind that, generally, REIGs are not regulated in the US unless they have more than $25 million in assets. So, you will have to do your homework to avoid signing up with a group that is not reputable.

The best way to find a trustworthy group is to look for a trade association of investment groups. For instance, there is the National Real Estate Investors Association, which includes investors' groups among its membership. The websites of these groups usually allow you to do a search to find a group in your area.

You can also do a Google search for real estate investment groups, but this is more time-consuming. In addition, the results usually also include real estate investment clubs. But if you have the patience and the search engine skills, this can also be effective.

If you are doing your own research, you might want to check out if the group has a listing and ranking at the Better Business Bureau website. For your own security, go with a group that has the highest A+ rating.

If you know any realtors or real estate dealers in your area, you can also ask them to recommend a group. This is the best way, since you can talk to them about your requirements so that they can suggest a group that best meets them.

Forming Your Own Investment Group
If you can't find a real estate investment group in your area that suits your requirements, you might want to consider forming your own group. Of course, this will take a lot of time and effort on your part, but the potential rewards will be substantial.

Unless you already have some prospects in mind, you should start by joining a real estate investment club. This will allow you to network and find potential members of your club. You can also start to learn about how to invest and what properties to invest in.

Joining a club may also provide you with the opportunity to meet with members of existing investment groups so that you can get an idea of how they work. You can also learn from their mistakes so you can avoid them in your own investment activities.

When assessing potential members, some of the considerations to keep in mind include:

Do you feel comfortable entrusting them with your money?

Do you feel that they are responsible enough to pay their contributions on time?

Will they be able to meaningfully contribute to the group?

Are they decisive enough to 'pull the trigger' when it comes to making investment decisions?

Aside from looking for potential partners, you should think about how your group will be run. For instance, how much will you need as an initial investment so that you can start buying properties? How many members will you accept and how much will you require them to invest?

You should also consider your investment goals. What types of property do you want to invest in? What investment strategy are you going to follow? You should look for members whose investment outlooks reflect yours.

Once you have identified potential members with similar investment goals who are willing to join your club, invite them for an organizational meeting. Discuss with them how the group will be run and will be organized. For instance, what officer positions will the organization have (President, Vice-President, Treasurer, et. al.)?

You should also discuss how much each person will invest, how withdrawals or reductions of investments will be handled and how the group will be dissolved. Can a person make an initial investment and then pay smaller monthly amounts?

You should also decide how and why to accept new members. For instance, if one of the founders withdraws, will you accept a new member or just increase the remaining members' investments? Under what circumstances will you accept new members?

In addition, if you already have an investment property in mind, you can propose it to them. Make sure to provide details such as the cost of the property, how much is the down payment and how big the mortgage will be.

When you have decided on policies regarding how the group will be run, these should be written down. This document will serve as your operating agreement. All members should agree with its provisions and sign the document in order to make it binding.

Having a binding operating agreement means that you have a formal set of rules that dictates how the company will be run. Thus, you can avoid misunderstandings since you already have written specific guidelines for how to deal with particular issues. Keep this in mind when you are drafting the operating agreement.

Here are some of the things that should be covered:

What is each member's ownership share (in percent)?

What are the responsibilities of members?

What are their duties?

What are their voting rights?

How will profit and loss be allocated?

How will meetings be held?

How will the company be managed?

What are the provisions if a member wants to sell his share? What if a member wants to buy out another's share? What if a member wants to sell his share to an outsider?

What happens if a member dies?

Once you have created an operating agreement and an organizational structure, you can start preparing to register your group. Generally, investment groups are organized as general partnerships, under which all partners will equally share the assets and profits of a business as well as its legal and financial liabilities.

For the purposes of investing, it is best that you register your group as a limited liability company or LLC. Under this type of corporate structure, the partners are not personally liable for the company's debts. This means that creditors cannot sue to seize your personal assets so they can be paid back.

Another advantage of the LLC is that you will enjoy taxation benefits. Since the LLC is considered a pass-through entity, it passes on its profits and losses to the members. Each member is then required to report his profits, paying taxes at personal federal tax rates, rather than as corporate tax.

The LLC thus allows you to avoid double taxation on the rental income. In addition, if you were to dispose of the investment property after a year, it would be also be taxed at the lower capital gains rate.

Another benefit of an LLC is that it allows you the freedom to distribute profits, unlike in a corporation where they have to be given out based on the amounts invested. Thus, you can have a partner who does not make a direct financial investment, but who has agreed to handle the running and maintenance of the properties in exchange for a share of the profits.

Although it is possible to file your own LLC documents, you might want to consult with a lawyer or legal service to help you. This way, you are assured that you will not miss anything that could make your LLC registration invalid. There are many low-cost and reputable legal services, such as Nolo, that you can find online.

In addition, you will have to apply for an Employer Identification Number (EIN) with the IRS. The EIN is a unique nine-digit number that also indicates in which state the business is registered. You can apply for one at the IRS website by filling up an application form. You do not have to pay for anything as registration is free.

All businesses need to have an EIN as this allows the IRS to identify them for the purposes of filing business taxes. Financial institutions such as banks and brokerages will also not allow you to open an account if you do not have an EIN.

When you register your LLC, you should include your operating agreement in the registration papers. It is not mandatory in most states, but if you do not file one, it is construed to indicate your agreement to run your group based on your state's default rules. These are very broad since they are not tailored to a particular business and may not be appropriate for your particular requirements.

Another thing you need to do is to open a bank account in the name of the business. You will have to designate people who will have direct access to this account - usually the treasurer or other officer. The company's money will be deposited into this account and disbursed as needed.

One of the keys to the success of the group is keeping accurate records. By doing so, you can account for each members' share of the equity as well as their returns. This will help you avoid misunderstandings that can result in conflict within the group.

You can prepare your records using a Google spreadsheet with the relevant data on it. You can even make it accessible to the other members to ensure the transparency of the group's financial affairs.

If you are inexperienced, you might want to consult with a professional accountant. They will show you how to keep records, what documents you need to keep, and most importantly, how to file your tax returns. The cost of hiring one will be more than offset by the potential penalties from the IRS that you will be able to avoid.

Unless one or more of the members are willing to take on the job of managing and maintaining the property, the group will have to hire somebody to do it. You and the other members will have to decide how much to pay them and how they will be paid. If the property is not yet generating income, you will have to shoulder their salary out-of-pocket.

The members may have to make donations until the rental income starts to come in.

Once there are candidates, the members will have to approve them, unless a particular member is designated with the power to hire. Either way, once a particular person or persons are hired, there will have to be a meeting so that the members will be familiar with them.

Scoring REIGs

A. Liquidity

Your investment is not liquid since it is not easy to withdraw it if you suddenly need money. Unlike REITs, you cannot simply sell your share. Depending on the bylaws of the group, you may need to ask another member if they are willing to buy out your share.

2/10

B. Scalability

This depends on the rules of the group. Usually, however, you cannot just increase your investment unless the group decides to buy another property. If you want to increase your investment in real estate, you may have to join another group.

2/10

C. Potential Return On Investment

As with real estate investment trusts, the ROI earned with REIGs comes from both rental income and your share of the proceeds if the property is sold. Thus, the return on investment can vary depending on how much income is generated.

There are other factors that may affect your profitability. For instance, the group may impose other fees and charges, such as your share of management and maintenance costs.

On the other hand, it should be noted that real estate investments are still among the most profitable. Provided that the group chose its investment well, then you should still enjoy a high ROI even after expenses are removed. You will also be able to pay fewer taxes if you organize your group as an LLC.

5/10

D. Passivity

Investing with a real estate investment group is not passive income since it requires some effort. The amount of effort required depends on whether you join a group or form your own. However, it still requires less effort than direct ownership since you can share duties with others. In addition, once the property has started generating income, the effort required to continue earning income will be sharply reduced.

5/10

D. Simplicity

How easy is it to get into investing through a group? Again, it depends. If you are setting up your own group, then it is not simple. But if you are just joining one, it may be as simple as just attending meetings and making your investment.

Be that as it may, you do not need a high level of expertise when you invest with a group. In fact, it is designed for people who are not that knowledgeable about investing, since you will have the benefit of more experienced investors working with you.

Ten Tips for Successfully Investing in REIGs

1. Make sure that you feel comfortable with the other members of the group. Whether you join a group or form your own, keep in mind that you are ultimately entrusting the success of your investment to other people. So it is very important that you trust them and feel comfortable with them handling your money. This way, you will have peace of mind that your investment is in good hands.

2. Take a long-term viewpoint. As mentioned earlier, REIGs follow a buy-and-hold strategy that involves holding on to the investment property to generate income from it. It may take some time before you start earning the maximum returns from your investment. So you should be patient. Don't expect to start earning a lot from your investment at once.

3. Keep learning. Real estate investment clubs should never be just about making money. They should also provide an opportunity for members to constantly learn new things about investing. If you run the group, make sure that you provide educational opportunities such as inviting speakers and holding workshops. This will help them to make better decisions when you have to vote on your investments and ultimately make them more profitable.

4. Build a network. One of the most important functions of joining a REIG is not just being able to pool your money to invest, but meeting people who can help you. Through the group, you can find a mentor who will help you learn about investing and avoiding common mistakes. You can also build a support group with whom you can brainstorm ideas and talk over your problems.

5. Be disciplined with your commitments to the group. You should not view your participation in the REIG as simply a way to make money. Make sure that you allocate time to meet your duties and responsibilities. Keep in mind that the success of the group would ultimate result in greater profitability of your investment.

6. Periodically assess the strategy of the group. Take time to meet with the other members and discuss investments. Are you maximizing your investment with this property? Should you add another property or sell the one you have? Should you shift (i.e. pivot) to another type of property? Is the management strategy maximizing the returns the group gets from the property? Does the group need to change or adjust its strategy?

7. Work with an accountant. Unfortunately, our tax laws are very complicated and there is a possibility that you may miss something that will result in severe penalties later on. A qualified accountant can help you avoid these pitfalls. And the costs of hiring one will be more than offset by the savings you can enjoy long-term.

8. Make the meetings enjoyable. You should not treat your group meetings as if it was a board meeting of a corporation. Of course, there are serious parts, such as reporting on the state of the investments. At the same time, you should remember that you are also networking with the other members. Make sure that you provide snacks and refreshments. You can also schedule social activities for the members, such as going golfing.

9. Don't be afraid to leave if you have to. If the group no longer fulfills your investment requirements, you

should not hesitate to exit. Of course, this can be difficult, particularly if you have already become fond of the other members. But keep in mind that there are other ways that you can support the group, such as becoming a mentor to new members or by being a regular speaker.

10. Have an exit strategy. There may be times when the group decides that it is better to sell the property to a bigger investor rather that continue to run it. You should already have prepared for this possibility by creating a plan for wrapping up the group. How will you wrap up the group's affairs? How will the proceeds of the sale be divided among the members?

Chapter 3 What To Expect In The Real Estate Business

Starting a real estate business is a daunting task. It may not be that easy looking at those who have made it in the area and concluding it's a walk in the park. It takes a lot of hard work, good decision making, patience, tolerance, and learning. If you are ready to pick lines from the gurus in the area, you will find running a real estate an easy task. However, you may need to be more determined to get your business up by investing everything in it. For most of the people in the industry, they have experienced hardships in the first year of starting the business, and those who are brave make it higher.

Getting into the real estate business does not need you to expect more than you can offer. You need to concentrate on building it fast than thinking about the profits and how you will handle it. Rather start by learning ways on how to make it better and grow. You need not get distracted on the way as that may lead to your failure early in the business. Make sacrifices and ensure you have gained what it takes to be the best in the industry. It is not easy at first, but once you get used to it, you will grow to love it.

The real estate business is an interesting industry as you get to meet different people, locations, buildings, and so on. You first need to love it to do it. If you keep the mentality that you can do it without loving it, then this is not for you. It's also not for the fainted hearted as it requires a lot of work and sacrifices to pick up.

What is the real estate business all about?

Before going into the industry, you need to be well versed in what you are dealing with. You should understand all the aspects of real estate and how it works.

Real estate is considered as a property that includes land, buildings, natural resources, crops, roads, and other immovable things. It can also be the professional act of selling, renting, and buying land and generally houses. It also deals with human activity that is involved in making improvements to the land. On the other hand, real property deals with the rights that a property has. For instance, the interests that come from human activities.

Why choose the real estate business?

The real estate business is a fast-growing investment strategy that takes more than hard work. You need to be dedicated and sacrifices to make sure your needs are met. However, they may be affected by market changes or conflict, and you need to have knowledge of what type of real estate business you need to venture into. It is so interesting working on something you love and feel safe handling. It is always hard at first but can turn out to be the best over time.

Making a decision to embark on the real estate business takes a lot of courage and commitment. However hard it may be at the beginning, there is always a greater reward in the future. Here are the reasons as to why you have to consider real estate business:

It is so easy to get in

Unlike other professionals who take a longer time to get employment or while studying, the real estate industry does not require a lot of skills to become one. You can be a real estate agent with a limited number of skills or knowledge and learn more on the way. Once you get in, you will easily fit in. In most firms, there are a number of part-time workers or students too. It's easier to learn and adapt. The knowledge you seek is always within your reach. For example, you can acquire it from the realtors or your mentors.

There is an easier profit-making

Starting out on your business may not be that simple. However, once you have mastered how to grow your business and know how to get more clients to buy the real estate you are selling, you will automatically feel a boost in your bank. It is a lucrative industry, and working hard for profits is essential. Once you work hard, you are sure to get something in return at all times.

You will more likely work hard

As much as it is easy to work hard for your business, you may need to have a form of appreciation for what you do. You should feel and experience the results of your hard work in a unique way. The more the hard work, dedication, and determination, the easier it is to receive positive results.

It is interesting

You will not have that life of a professional who always sits in an office from Monday to Monday, getting bored and feeling like quitting all the time. There are a number of trends that change, markets, and the environment. You will most likely be at the field or place of construction to see if it's taking the right direction and so on. You may even interact with people who see life from a different perspective, and sharing experiences will make it even more worthwhile.

Types of real estate businesses

There are six types of real estate types for you to choose from. Once you select the one you need, you should not be distracted to do all of them at once. It will be better to concentrate and give your all to one that really fits your needs and interest. However, some investors have invested in different types of real estate business to make more profit. As it is, what works for you may not work for someone else.

You should ensure you do a thorough research analysis to determine the possibility of making a profit or a loss. Choosing the right type will sorely depend on your needs, goals, circumstances, and market. Getting the perfect location for all your construction needs is very important. This is because it will determine whether your business will pick up or not. Choosing the type that fits you requires you be ready to invest in a kind of property while knowing the risks involved and the amount of involvement needed. Making the right investment will guarantee your profits. Read and understand what you need and how to go about it. These include the following:

1. Raw Land

This consists of undeveloped land, ranches, and working farms. It mostly includes everything on land, which is trees and water. It can also consist of air rights, minerals, and other natural resources, for example, oil and metals. It also includes agricultural practices. Land can be used in a number of ways, from construction to farming. Choosing the right land for all your needs may not be that easy, but through research and extensive reading, you will have an idea of what is needed for that particular real estate investment. You should consider looking for a location that will attract further investors when it comes to selling the land or property. It is on-demand nowadays as it will give you the opportunity to construct something you have always looked forward to from scratch.

2. Residential real estate

Mostly fall under the category of single-family homes, townhouses, condominiums, duplexes, triple-deckers, and high-value homes. They mostly deal with houses or sites of construction as well as selling and resale of houses. It is among the most popular investment in real estate that yields maximum profits. However, for any residential real estate investments, you need to have another plan as it tends to be affected by markets. Once the market is affected, there will have a small number of investors. What you can use is the wholesaling, buy and hold and also rehabbing strategies to survive the bad business days.

3. Industrial real estate

This mostly consists of warehouses, industries, factories, power plants, and other manufacturing buildings. Most of these buildings are preferred for distribution of goods and services, production, research as well as storage. These buildings tend to be different from other kinds; thus, the zone is to be selected carefully, so is the construction. For these kinds of buildings, you should mostly consider an environment that is a distance away from residential homes, as that may have an effect on their health. It should be in an open property for more air circulation and less pollution. The location to be considered should be ideal for producing goods in the most effective way without having to pollute the environment and destroy property.

4. Commercial real estate

These, on the other hand, are considered commercial as they are used to produce income. They include shopping malls, educational institutions, hospitals, and hotels, strip malls, parking facilities, stores, entertainment facilities, and office space. In most cases, most of them are used for businesses rather than residences. They also require very little management.

5. Special purpose real estate

This kind of property is set aside for special purposes such as schools, cemetery, and places of worship, government buildings, parks, and libraries. Most of these places cannot be owned by a single person. Most properties of this kind are strategically constructed to meet the needs of the investors. You may find that it does not take a lot of time in construction. As long as the property is unique, it can easily attract the interested party.

6. Mixed-use

In this area, this type of real estate property deals with incorporating types. In this case, you can have the residential and industrial together or any other two. For example, you can have a mall and a warehouse on the same property. This needs you to have enough knowledge and the ideal location for your business. Not all of them can work together or be convenient at the same place. You need to be careful of your choices, as that may affect your investment in the future. Let's say, for instance, you construct a factory and a hospital on a piece of land. That will not work effectively as the factory will be emitting poisonous gases into the air while the hospital takes care of the sick people and help them get better. Most factory gases are hazardous to the environment, humans, and animals.

What you should expect in the real estate business

Most people make a mistake of expecting everything to turn out easy as they may have thought. This is not the case with real estate businesses. They are faced with a lot of competition, and you need to keep your business up to be the best. You need to invest in your business and strive to make it unique as much as possible to remain relevant. If you are willing to learn and sacrifice, you will surely get the deserving results.

Here is what you need to keep in mind when starting your business:

Not an easy task

Starting the real estate business may not be that rosy at first, as it will take a toll on your time and sleep, thinking about the best ways to grow and improve your businesses. You may need to research a lot on the market, the location of the property as well as the gents you will use to get clients, and so on. To ensure everything is going on smoothly, it will take a lot of hard work, determination, and sacrifice. Success and profits will not come on easily. It takes time and perseverance. You should not be faint-hearted if you need to experience success. Always keep in mind the idea that you have crossed the battle line, and you have to do everything it takes to emerge the winner.

Be creative

For any real estate business, you should expect to be more open to ideas. Learning new things and how well to solve the challenges in the real world will help you grow your business. As much as you have the knowledge and expertise in your profession, it will take more than that to come up with the right decision to help you grow. You do not have to rely on your family and friends to help you solve your work issues. Being your own boss comes with a lot of responsibilities that need you to be reliable and go beyond your comfort zone to see you grow into a successful real estate agent. You will learn how to handle your issues peacefully within yourself and use the most innovative and creative ideas to help your business improve and make the decisions right for it.

You will need help

When starting out your business, you are probably afraid of getting new experiences. At the same time, you may find yourself excited about seeing your business grow. As you may be new in the industry, you may need somewhere to lay your shoulder on. You may have to ask for help with running your business. Most real estate agents use brokers (salespeople who have expertise and experience in negotiating deals). They are a great resource for the growth of your business. They will prepare you for what you will meet on the way to your success and how you need to finalize deals or decide on the property value as they have been on the market for long. They work on a commission, and they navigate the market easily to get you potential customers.

Where you are not well versed, you should feel free to ask those who have experience in the industry. Who knows, you may learn a thing or two on how to improve your business. Before gaining more knowledge and experience, you will pass through challenges that will require you to make the right decision for your team or business. Listening to other people's experiences would help you make it right.

Make room for disappointments

Like any other business out there, you need to make room for failures. It may not be that easy to be relevant in the industry within a day. It takes a lot of time and effort to become somebody. You may feel like giving up at some point in the journey, but reminding yourself why you chose to start it in the first place may help you remain firm. You will, at some point, be disappointed by your team or the tenants you sold or rented a house to. In most situations, the tenants are always hard to handle and want to control you, but getting good ones takes a miracle. Always be prepared for disappointments will save you from heartbreak all the time as you had already prepared your mind of failures once something negative comes about. By easily accepting mistakes and learning from them will greatly help. You can learn to take things easy next time. It's simple and effective once you plan for its possibility. Choosing to ignore and handling issues amicably should keep you going. You can strive to make yourself better.

Profits

Real estate businesses are very popular with successful profits. Once you have mastered the art of convincing your potential clients into buyers, you may have to sit and wait for your bank alert. It takes a lot of time and patience, but once you have a perfect property most people are yearning for, you will easily sell them. You need to research more on the kind of location that mostly fits a particular type of real estate business and strive to get properties of the best quality. Not overpricing will definitely get you more clients. As small the profits may be at first, you can invest them in a more meaningful way to help secure your future and save you during tax payment. It is a lucrative business, and it really reaps benefits.

You need to grow your business

Once you start a business, you need to look for ways to make it grow. Consider using your knowledge, expertise, and influence to grow the leads and networks. You need to build relationships with people. The more people know you, the more there will be potential buyers. It may not be an easy task, but you need to market yourself. Let people know what you are selling or what you are into. Putting yourself out there will greatly help you make the right networks. You can simply connect with your family and friends, attend community gatherings, and use online platforms for marketing you as a brand. However, it may not be simple as you need to sacrifice a lot to get what you are looking for.

Stick to your plan and budget

This is an important part of the real estate rule. Once you make plans on how to run the business, you should not mostly dwell on how to get clients while forgetting what you need to do to make a great impression on your business. That being said, your budget should not exceed your ability. You should not forget your needs and invest everything you have in the business. Ensure you have a budget that covers all the areas of your life, not leaving anything behind and sticking to the budget. The more times you add money to the already formed budget, there is a possibility you will have a shortage in other areas. Be disciplined when handling money and not forgetting you and your business needs as well. A good plan will always yield good results. Always being prepared will help a great deal.

You need a license

For you to become a qualified real estate agent, you need to be a qualified broker for you to open your own business. There is a broker exam that takes up to months to complete or work under a broker to gain knowledge on selling a property. Brokers are highly experienced in the business as they help get potential clients and getting commissions in return. For different states, there are varying broker tests that should be done to make you an experienced real estate agent.

Chapter 4 Types of Rental Properties to Invest

When investing in real estate, you have to know the type of rental properties that you are investing in. The main reason for this is that different properties have got varying ways in which they offer returns on investment. Some are ideal for long term purposes whereas others are preferable if at all you are looking to earn profits within a short period of time. Experienced investors will also argue that knowing the type of rental properties is essential simply because they differ in value. Thus, you ought to determine whether the properties you are going for are within your budget range. This section takes a look at the common rental properties that you will find. With this information, you will end up making sound decisions on the best properties that are worth investing in.

When you are in the market for a new rental property to purchase and fix up, there are a few options that you can go with. It often depends on how much you want to invest, how much work you want to do, and how much you would like to make in the process. Each of the rental property types is going to have their benefits and their negatives, but being open to each one and looking at them can make the difference in whether you choose one over the other.

Below are some of the types of rental properties that you can consider investing in.

Family Homes

The first option that you can consider is a single-family investment property. This is going to be either a condominium or a house that was purchased by the investor to rent out to one single tenant (or a family that lives together). Only one tenant or family will live in the property at a tIme. This has many benefits, including only needing to watch after one property at a time, and the fact that many of those who rent these properties are willing to stay in them for some time.

Some of the common ways that you can invest in these kinds of properties include buying fixer-uppers, foreclosures, or other types of properties that are undervalued for one reason or another in the area. Your goal is to purchase the undervalued property and then fix it up before renting it out to a single-family or tenant. You want to make sure that the actual value of the property is higher, as high as possible, compared to the purchase price.

Small multifamily investment properties

The next type of property that you can consider investing in is the small multifamily investment property. These are usually going to be either a two-unit or a four-unit building. The small multifamily investment is one of the best places for a beginner to start. It allows you to get more than one rental income in a month, which means more profits for you. Even if one of the parts is vacant, you are still able to make an income on the other parts, which can be a lifesaver when you first get started.

There are a few ways that you can work with this one. First, you can have the tenants occupy all of the units. This means that if the property has four units in it, then there are four different tenants that can pay you each month (unless there is a temporary vacancy). This is the way to make the biggest amount of profit each month, and you should be able to cover the mortgage easily if you can keep the property filled.

Another option is to occupy one of the units. If you have four units, you will live in one of them, and then three other tenants will live in the other units. This can be a great option if you want to keep your debts and your risks down during the time. You are effectively having your tenants pay for the mortgage and your living expenses as well, which can help you get started. Make sure that you can charge enough for the rent on the other units to cover you before you decide to do this one.

Large multifamily investment properties

You can also decide to take the step above a bit farther and work with a property that has five or more units. Sometimes, this goes so far as to have hundreds of individual units that you will manage. You will most often see these as apartment complexes. This type of property can sometimes be owner-occupied, even though this is not as common as you will find with some of the other options. But mostly these units are all going to be occupied by the tenants.

The Mixed Use Investment Property

This is another type of investment property that you can choose to work with. It is usually going to be used by the landlord for both commercial and residential purposes, and you are most likely to see this property type in some busy urban areas.

If you see this one, it is going to include a combination of stores and apartments. For example, you may have a restaurant in the bottom part, and then a handful of apartments in the top part. It could also be a combination of apartments and offices. The way that it is used will depend on its layout and how the landlord decides to split things up. But the point is that part of it is used by businesses in a commercial manner, and the other part is used as living arrangements for tenants.

While it can make you a good deal of profits, it could limit the number of tenants you have. Many people may not want to deal with the noise of the commercial business being there, and the commercial business may not feel like that is best for them and their customers either.

Retail Investment Property

The next type of property that you may want to consider working with is a retail investment property. This could include one tenant, such as a small ice cream parlor or a larger store like a grocery store. You may also find that things like strip malls that have four or more companies using them can fit into the retail investment property category. Usually, this will include a good deal of space for the tenant but can bring you a nice income if they choose to be there.

There are a few benefits that come with this type of investment. First, you will find that retailers tend to sign longer leases. This allows them to stay in one spot and makes it easier for their customers to find them. This also provides you with a level of stability with the amount of money that you can count on with the property.

However, these are hard to find tenants because most of the tenants are going to be picky. And once one of your tenants move out, it can take a long time before you can get anyone else back in and using the property. The success of these retail investment properties will depend on how healthy the economy is, as well.

Industrial Investment Property

This is a property type that only one tenant is likely to use at a time. In most instances, it is going to be something like a distribution center, storage garage, manufacturing plant, or a warehouse. It is going to be used for a very specific need, and it is likely that once you find a tenant, they are going to be around for a long time.

There are a lot of different types of investment properties that you can choose to work with, and it often depends on the area you want to invest in, the potential that you see in each building, and the amount of work and the amount of profit that you would like to receive from each one.

Now that you have learned real estate trading, it is time to learn the types of properties in the real estate sector. Well, as you already know, this is not a small market, rather this is a broad market that consists of a lot of choices. And this is a beneficial sector, but that doesn't mean you can make profits if you are not cautious. When you are making a decision, you have to consider all the possible aspects of real estate trading. A buyer, an owner, or an investor all must have an understanding of the type of investment. They should understand the significant difference in the types of properties. Since you are a beginner, you wouldn't have the experience, so learning the types of properties in detail is essential. If you have an understanding of the kinds of investments, you would be able to select the ideal investment as per your needs.

Commercial Rental

You may have talked to an experienced investor, and they too would have shared their experienced, but how can it be a guarantee that you will experience similar things on this journey? You wouldn't get the experience, but you can learn from their stories. But you don't feel the pain until you get it. Similarly, you have to try Investing In commercial rental to know what it is. You can still target success by feeding your mind with relevant tips, points, and ideas.

Multifamily home

This is not similar to a single-family property; instead, you would need a particular investment that suits multifamily property. As a beginner, you wouldn't understand the ways to find the right lender. But, with this guide, you can get some understanding of the multifamily home. The whole process will take three weeks or less if you are aware of the process. There are many lenders that offer loans for this kind of property so that you can get their help. You can be prequalified quickly with the support of lenders.

Vacation rental

Vacation Rental is like the two-in-one benefit because you own a second home that generates income when you are not using it. The best thing about a vacation rental is you will be able to earn profits and offset it to the ownership cost. When you manage your second home with a business touch, you will be able to create a steady income. However, certain factors make rental ownership a lucrative business. Of course, location is essential; meanwhile, there are many more factors that must be considered as well. Your primary goal must be to provide convenience, comfort, and ease to the travelers. In other words, you must make them feel at home. If you do so, it will be easy to find more clients as previous clients will leave positive ratings on the websites where your property is displayed. The effectiveness of word of mouth marketing has not gone out of the market, so you can still hope for it to work for you. So, here are some of the tips you can consider to make your investment worthwhile.

Turnkey

Turnkey investment trading is an exciting type of trading because you would be able to trade from afar. This is the specialty in turnkey investment. You can make passive income in different ways, but this is something out of the box because you gain rentals without actually being there on the property. This means "turn the key." It might sound amazing. But, you shouldn't directly enter the market without learning it. The turnkey market is about the outside local market; you would be exposed to a wider range of opportunities. If you do not know the definition and other details, the turnkey investment may look scary. But, once you learn the details, you can easily master the investment method. The definition in detail:

The definition is flexible and simple because it is "turnkey." The definition means you will be purchasing a property that you have no attachment to or involvement in. Hence, there are different terms, such as:

A company will manage the fixed property, so your role is to invest and receive income concerning profits.

Apartment Rental

What about apartment rental? How well are you aware of it? Do you think it is profitable? Well, let's check out the detailed information on the apartment rental along with the pros and cons to get the best out of it. Who doesn't like an additional income? Nowadays, people don't stick to one income source; rather, they look for a few sources. So, apartment rental is an option to make additional income.

Of course, collecting a steady income from apartment investment is a great idea. There is a high demand for apartments, which means a higher opportunity to make a steady income. People prefer relocating to a place near their workplace. So, you have to be considerate about the location of the apartment that you are planning to invest in.

Action Plan

In this chapter we discussed the types of rental properties; now that you know the types of rental properties, it is the high time to move forward toward your dream (Investing in rental properties).

Which Property Makes the Best Rentals?

We all know that mistakes happen; accidentally saying the wrong thing, bumping into someone, or dropping what you were holding. But while these mistakes are pretty small and can be overlooked, choosing the wrong rental property can mess up your new real estate company. It can mean a lot of unnecessary stress, be very expensive to fix, and even cause you to feel ill. So how do you make sure to choose the best property? There's so many out there, and there's a lot of different questions you can ask yourself to help.

What to buy, what to not buy, how many bedrooms, should the property have a garage, what are the neighbors like, what's the color of the property, how old is it, how big is it. Keeping these basic questions in mind will help you to find the best property for your business.

Multi-Family Homes

The ultimate goal is to find long-term tenants, which is hard to do with single-family homes, depending on the family. When there are only one or two bedrooms, tenants might stay for a year or two but eventually move out. Think about it - people usually end up getting married and having kids and need a lot of space for their future plans. By choosing three or four-bedroom houses for your rentals, you're ensuring that your tenants will stay for at least five years! And if you ever get to the point of needing to sell, three to four-bedroom houses sell best because, again, of all those families looking for the perfect home.

Single-Family Homes

These homes probably make the next best rentals. They're the easiest to manage, mainly because those renting them tend to treat these types of houses as if they are their own homes. While some people like living in apartments, most would prefer a house with a yard. However, most people also don't want too big of a house or to buy a house outright, which is why they're renting. You can find tenants that would prefer to stay renting a single-family home for decades, which would benefit you. Since the renters see the home as theirs, they also usually do some of the repairs needed and take better care of the yard. And unlike apartments, in single-family homes, the tenant pays all of the utilities, which makes it much easier for you.

Apartment

Two-bedroom apartments are pretty good and liked by a lot of people. People seem to be moving slightly away from suburban life and wanting to live closer to the city. It can be difficult for families because it's hard to find a two or three-bedroom house in a city. So many families compromise and look for a two-bedroom apartment. The type of person can affect your rental business, too; you want to rent to a professional, someone you know that will be able to afford your rent. And typically, a single professional person prefers a two-bedroom apartment over a studio or one bedroom. It's extra space for their office or a work out room. Studios and one-bedroom apartments usually have a high turnover in their tenants, even with a 12-month contract. So, renting out a two-bedroom apartment is a good middle-ground for someone looking to rent a place for a few years. You can try investing in and renting out a one-bedroom or studio apartment, but you run the risk of a high turnover rate. Of course, it's possible to find a single person that is professional and wants to stay in the apartment long term, but the norm is typically the opposite.

Chapter 5 Choosing the Best Location for Your Real Estate Investment

We have all heard the expression "Location! Location! Location!" when it comes to real estate investing. From simply buying a family home to purchasing a multimillion-dollar investment property, the experts all agree, the number one determiner of if you have a sound investment is, you guessed it, location. But what exactly is a prime real estate location? Can you still make money while buying in prime locations? Can you make money by using a different model, buying in sub-prime locations? In this chapter, we will attempt to answer these questions and many more.

Why is location so essential in real estate?

"Location! Location! Location!" the cardinal rule that is preached by every real estate agent and investor. So many things factor into the decision to buy real estate and where to buy it. Why is location the most important consideration when buying?

The truth is the biggest importance to location is that it is the one thing about a property that you cannot change. You buy a house that has horrible orange shag carpeting from the 1970's. That's not a big deal. Laying down new flooring is an easy and relatively inexpensive fix. But if you buy a house next to a busy airport, major highway and that has railroad tracks that have trains running all day and night. Those are things that you can't fix. It can be a luxury mansion with all the upgrades, but you still can't change the fact that there is a cacophony of trains, planes, and automobiles all day and all night. Obviously, this is an extreme example (though I did see a property like this once), but the principle is true. You can change a lot of things about a property, but you cannot change the location. Therefore, location is one of the most important factors to consider when buying a new property. But how do we determine if a location is a good location or a bad location?

Factors that Determine a Locations Value

There are many factors that are used to determine if a property has good or bad value. Sometimes those factors aren't as cut and dry as you would imagine. Sometimes what you consider good or bad depends upon your investment strategy. In this chapter, we will first look at things that traditionally make a property a good investment. Then we will explore what makes a property a good investment for some less traditional investment strategies.

Neighborhood

Before buying a property, drive around the area. Look at the condition of the other properties in the neighborhood. This is particularly important when investing in residential real estate. Are the homes generally well maintained? Are there a significant number of vacant lots or vacant properties? Talk to people who live in the area. Are the police often called to this neighborhood? Do people generally stay for at least five years once they buy? Or are properties a revolving door of buyers and sellers? You can learn much about an area simply by asking questions and listening to the residents of the area. You can also find out good information by visiting the local library. They usually have reference materials and statistics on local neighborhoods.

Wealth

It is good to look at an area that has some degree of wealth. Having a wealthy "part of town" for lack of a better term, is important because it having wealth in the area helps to offset any overall turn down in the economy   For example, if there is an economic downturn in manufacturing, the wealth of the area will ensure that much of the retail and restaurant business remain viable, protecting the overall real estate value of the area.

Job Market

If an area has a strong job market, people are going to want to live there. It's as simple as that. Jobs increase the value of properties in an area. For example: In 2018 a major car manufacturer moved its US corporate headquarters and some manufacturing to Plano, Texas. For six months before their opening and for a year after their opening the housing values for homes for a 45-mile radius around the newly opened offices increased by an average of 20%. New jobs meant the need for more housing. More people in the area brought more restaurants and shopping in some of the smaller towns. These long-term improvements to the towns increased their property values for a much longer time. They became more enticing to new home buyers as places to live.

Attractions and Convivences

People like to live where there are things to do for entertainment, convenient shopping, transportation, and public services. It the area you are looking at has these things, your property will keep its investment value. Look around the area. Is there a choice of restaurants, convenient grocery and clothing stores?

Are there easily accessible medical facilities? Are there fun things to do: movie theaters, restaurants, bars, sports arenas, or concert venues? All of these will increase the value of your investment property and the value of the area that they are in.

Crime Rates

It is important to know the crime rates and statistics of the area that you are looking to invest in. People are looking to live where they feel they and their families will be safe. It is logical really. If you find an area where there has been a string of house robberies in the past months, the housing values will suffer. If the neighborhood is a known gang area or known to have drug houses, this will affect the value of your property and the chances of finding good renters for it (if you are going the rental route of investment).

Neighborhood Future Prospects

This factor is a bit more difficult to quantify. This is where experience and a good gut instinct come into real estate investment. You can buy a house in one of the best neighborhoods in the area, but if that neighborhood is on the decline, your property will lose value over time. However, you can buy a property in an area that is not in the best neighborhood, but if that neighborhood is up and coming, your investment will continue to increase in value. As a beginning investor, this is a hard call to make. But there are some practical things for you to look at that can help when making this call.

- Research the housing prices over the last ten years. Is the overall trend increasing or decreasing property sale prices? It is important that you look at the overall trend over the ten years and not focus on "micro" upturns or downturns in the market.

• Look at the overall business trends over the last ten years. Are there more business opening or closing? How long does a new business stay open in general? You want to see the business opening and staying open as an overall trend.

• What is the average time a property stays on the market? In a strong market, the properties don't last long when they are put up for sale.

• What is the vacancy rate of the area? If there is a high vacancy rate, there is a likelihood that your property will sit empty for a while.   This is an investment killer when in the rental investment business. Also, rising vacancy rates show that people are leaving the area, not moving in. This is a good indicator of a declining market.

"Find out where the people are going and buy the land before they get there." -William Penn Adair

Vacant Lots, Lots of Open Land

If you are looking at buying an investment property and there is a lot of open land of vacant lots available for building, keep in mind that you will have more competition in the future. This isn't necessarily a deal killer as new construction is the sign of a growing economy. However, it is important to remember that all that new construction means that, soon, you will have a lot more properties competing for the same renters and buyers. You can check with the town or county to determine how many new construction permits have been issued and the forecasted population growth. This will give you a better idea of what factors you will be contending with from the new construction arena.

If you are a beginning real estate investor, I encourage you to look at properties in several diverse areas and then compare these facts on each property. This will give you a good idea of where your first property should be bought. For a first or second investment property, I encourage investors to be more conservative in their approach towards buying properties. It is good to have a couple of steady earners in your portfolio before investing in more risky ventures. For your convenience, I have put together a table where you can see all this information at a glance.

Location Facts

Neighborhood Crime Rate

Job Market Neighborhood Forecast

Wealth Available Land

Attractions/ Conveniences New Construction

Non-Traditional Investment Strategies and Location

There are some investment strategies that rely on different location factors or put more emphasis on one of the above factors more than the others. Although I do not necessarily recommend these strategies for new investors, I would be remiss if I did not mention them.

Investing in an "up-and-coming" neighborhood There are many investors that focus their investment strategy on predicting where the growth is going to happen, rather than in already established areas. This is a risky strategy because if you forecast the growth of an area incorrectly, you will get stuck with low-value properties that you will have trouble unloading at the best. Or a worse scenario is that you invest a lot of money into property renovation only to end up upside down on the property and unable to sell it except at a huge loss. However, when this strategy works the profits can be massive. This is the draw of this strategy to investors. You buy properties in a low value or formerly industrial area at rock bottom prices, put money into renovating them, and then sell them (or rent them out) at a large profit as the property values increase. This strategy is part science, part experience, and part good luck. If, as a new investor, you are looking to invest this way. I cannot stress enough the importance of talking to more experienced investors and getting their thoughts. I encourage new investors to find a mentor who is an investor that is where they would like to be in ten years. This is an area in which such a mentor would be important. You can also research the town and city plans for the area. Is there a large company coming to the area that will push up the demand for properties? Has the city started an improvement initiative in the area that will bring new businesses and city resources to the area? Is the city changing the zoning ordinances from industrial to residential? All these are good indicators that an area will be an "up-and-coming" neighborhood and a good prospect to make money. However, remember, there are no guarantees. More than one investor has lost his or her shirt using this strategy.

Flipping Houses

This is related to the above investment strategy but not quite the same. When flipping houses, you look for homes that are in need of renovation and repair, put the work into doing that renovation, and then sell them for a profit. The best houses for flipping are the ugly duckling houses on the block in prime location areas. The risk in this investment is that you will spend too much on the renovation and will not make a profit. Another risk is that you bite off a project that is more involved than you have the time or ability to handle, and you lose steam partway through the project, having to sell the property for cost or a loss. However, one strategy when flipping houses is buying ugly duckling houses in "up-and-coming" areas. The risks to that are the same as both investing in "up-and-coming" neighborhoods and the risks inherent with flipping houses.

Here are some tips for flipping houses.

• Hire a qualified contractor to assess the renovations needed before buying the property

• Be sure you have the necessary skills to do the renovations or the money to hire professionals to do the things that you do not have the skills in

• Research the building codes and the process for getting building permits in the area that you are looking to buy property in before you purchase the property

• Do not underestimate the time commitment that this project will take from you. Be prepared to say goodbye to your nights and weekends until the project is completed.

"Location! Location! Location!" has been the mantra of real estate agents and investors for good reason. Getting the right location for your investment strategy will bring you one giant step closer to realizing your real estate investment dreams.

Chapter 6 Financing Investment Properties

Whether you are independently wealthy, have a lot in savings or simply plan to have a mortgage for each property, you need to decide how you are going to purchase your properties. I will cover a few of the different ways that you can go the route of financing if you don't have enough cash at the beginning.

Leveraging vs. All Cash

Leveraging is using other people's money to make more money for you. Instead of paying out of pocket for them, it will free up cash for you to do other things or save for future repairs and maintenance. The reason for this is so that the lender can free up their money to re-loan to others. As with any other mortgage lender these two entities will have their own loan amount ranges and borrower score credit minimums among other things.

Within Canada you would typically just go through a mortgage broker to get the best rate deal or straight to a bank or credit union. There isn't a lot of competition between the lenders as the rates are set by the Bank of Canada. I believe a the time of purchasing my condominium in 2009 the rate difference between a couple of the lenders was 0.25%.

There are things to consider when leveraging:

- 15 or 30-year mortgages
- Fixed interest rate or variable

Always try to put enough money down to keep the cash flow positive. This accounts for margins of error if something unexpected occurs. Also, be prepared for more money down and a higher interest rate as it's not your primary residence.

Shop around for the best rates. Places like LendingTree will compete for your business, so you get an excellent deal. Don't forget to be open and assert negotiation. Even knocking 0.5% off the interest rate will save you big dollars in the long run.

Consider this. If you own stocks, it's 100% of your money, and you control 100% of that investment, but in real estate with leveraging, you pay around 20% of your money to control 100% of a property. Who doesn't want that? When you sell, hopefully, your returns have multiplied because you were making money each month on the full value of the investment.

Look at it this way. Two people both have $100,000 to invest in real estate. Person A decides to buy one piece of property for $100,000 in case outright. After expenses, the property generates $500/month in cash flow. At the end of one year, they will have made $6,000 or 6% ROI. Person B invests $20,000 into five different properties. After expenses are paid, the properties generate a $200/month positive cash flow per house. At the end of one year, they will have made $12,000 or a 12% ROI. Person B not only makes more money than Person A, but they control more real estate, approx., $500,000 worth compared to $100,000. Diversification is better in the long run.

Now, there are generally two camps of people, the ones who leverage and the ones who believe in only using cash. As the example above shows, leveraging does provide a better ROI, but there is also something to be said for "no debt," as long as you can carry the costs if the property remains vacant for any amount of time.

All cash is the easiest way to complete the transaction as there are typically fewer complications. Still, the reality is that for most investors, especially first-time investors, all cash isn't going to be an option.

Pros for Leveraging
- Low-interest rates - help keep mortgage payment low and maximizes cash flow.
- Longer terms - up to 30 years for a mortgage repayment, which helps keep payments low.

Cons for Leveraging
- Loan amount maximum - a bank will never lend out more than ten loans to one person in the US, but even getting that many could be tough due to debt-to-income ratio.
- Slow process - loans are not fast to obtain and can take 30 days or more to secure.
- Property condition - banks tend to only loan money out on properties that are in good shape, sometimes ruling out "fixer uppers."
- Not entity friendly - banks don't like loaning money to LLC's.
- Market drops - the real estate market can be volatile, and the value could drop. If there is a steady decline in the equity, then you could end up owing more than the house is worth, which eliminates any profits made.

Pros for All Cash

- Easy to buy and sell - it's easier to negotiate with cash in hand. It cuts out any need for a bank that could otherwise affect your credit rating and whether you get a reasonable interest rate.

- No mortgage - extra money you would have typically spent on a mortgage can be diverted into repairs, savings, travel, or other investments.

- Sense of security - if you lose your job, you wouldn't have to worry about the bank foreclosing on your property.

- Available equity - you can tap the equity in times of hardship by getting a home equity loan, which is like taking out a second mortgage on your home. This involves refinancing your house for a larger amount and getting the balance in cash. A home equity credit line is similar to a credit card where you have available cash to take out if needed. However, you never want to use either option as an ATM; it can severely ruin your credit.

Cons for All Cash

- Loss of liquidity - cash tied up in real estate is not easily accessed except through a sale, so it should only be considered if you have a comfortable cushion of cash for emergencies.

- Lack of leverage - debt in real estate is not a bad thing; it can be a good thing because the more leveraged you are, the harder it is for someone to consider suing you. Think of it this way, if you don't have any debt against your property and a tenant slips and falls and feels it's your fault because maybe the stairs were icy, they then hire a lawyer to sue you for negligence. They can sue for your property appreciation amount or more. But if you are fully leveraged on your property, there is no equity to touch, and a lawyer is unlikely to take the case.

- No tax advantage - buying a home with cash offers no tax deductions.

Portfolio Lenders

Unlike conventional lenders, some banks within the United States choose to hold onto their loans and keep the money within the community. These are typically called portfolio lenders. They don't always play by government rules, and this 'allows' them to be a little more creative with their lending. That doesn't mean it's any easier to get a loan here; there are still qualifications that need to be met with approval. What it could mean, however, is flexibility, and by building a relationship with one or more of these lenders, you may be able to avoid the ten loan maximum. Caution: this leniency can also be met with stricter terms of above-average credit ratings and non-negotiable money down.

These portfolio lenders aren't everywhere. You have to search for them, focus on small community banks or credit unions that have less than 20 branches. You will have to ask if they offer these services as they are not usually listed. But beware of balloon payment requirements. At the 10-year mark of a 30-year loan, they may expect a large "balloon" payment, usually done through refinancing.

Private Lenders

It could be a friend, family member, or a person who is looking to invest in the real estate market short-term. Sometimes they want to invest longer-term opportunities if you happen to find one of these people hang on to them and treat them well. They don't come around often.

Typically they will charge between 6-12% interest on the loan. Consider offering on the higher side once you find someone who is willing to do this for you. Yes, that is higher than a bank, but there are a lot fewer hoops to jump through. It makes sense to consider private lending when wanting to purchase an older home that is not move-in ready, and the banks don't want to work with you.

Private lending allows for more time to fix up the property and get it rentable while paying them the mortgage. Once it's ready to rent out, you have a better chance with the bank to get a long term loan at a lower interest rate, so you pay back the private lender any additional money owed.

You might wonder why would anyone hurry to pay back a lender instead of pocketing all the money. As a lender, they will receive a promissory note from you agreeing to pay back the money, and put a lien against the property through the title company or lawyer. This stands until they receive their full payment, so if you don't hold up your end of the bargain they can claim the house through foreclosure. They should also consider being on any insurance you have like title insurance and hazard insurance, depending on your state's requirements.

So, how do you go about finding a private lender? Mention you're looking to invest in polite conversation with new acquaintances. You never know when you could be talking to someone interested in getting involved. If you don't, how will anyone know? This includes posting about it on social media.

Ask your competition. You will find that some real estate investors want to invest in other deals because of the opportunity to turn a profit without putting in the work is gratifying. Second, you need to have a perfect deal; otherwise, how can you pitch the lender? You need to be able to bring something to the table for them to see, so they know they will be getting a profit. The most important part is the pitch. It may be intimidating, but it helps to have a short, simple presentation ready to go.

Getting Creative

Home Equity
If you own your own home, you might be able to use some of the equity to purchase your rental property.

The spread between what is owed on your home and what it's valued at is what can be borrowed. Home equity loans or lines of credit have very low-interest rates. While they are similar, they do have some differences.

The home equity loan is based on what your house is worth and what is left owing on the mortgage. You can then take out the balance for whatever repairs or renovations are needed or as a down payment on a new piece of property. The home equity loan is typically taken out all at once and paid back in monthly installments, as you would a car loan or mortgage.

Same as a home equity loan, the home equity credit line is the balance between what the house is worth and what is left owing. But in this case it is a revolving account that can be used as you need it. You borrow as much or as little as you need, up to the limit, pay back the minimum interest payment, and then borrowing again. Credit lines generally have the lowest interest rates.

Partnerships

These can be a valuable tool for real estate as two or more people can work together to cover or counter each other's shortcomings. Knowing your weaknesses in a business can help you find a partner who excels doing the things you're not good at and can take the pressure off of tasks that you don't enjoy doing.

Never pick someone based on convenience. This is an important decision, take the same care with this that you would take in choosing a spouse. Choose carefully and with great consideration, maybe because they would be fun to work with or they have something you lack, and vice versa. Make sure your goals and work ethic are compatible, then have a lawyer draw up an agreement to protect you both.

House Hacking
Finally, there is house hacking. For those of you just starting on a real estate journey or not sure if being a landlord is for them, this could be one of the best ways to get started and finance your deal and see what it means to be a landlord.

House hacking refers to combining your primary residence with an investment. You can accomplish this one of two ways:

- A live-in flip - you buy an older, single-family home to fix it up and resell within a couple of years. You complete the renovations while making it your primary residence.

- A small, multi-family property - usually a two- to four-family unit; you live in one unit and rent out the others.

This can be a smart option because of the relatively easy financing given to homeowners, and since it will be your primary residence, you can apply for the homeowner's grant at tax time. Consider it this way, you find a duplex or triplex you like, with a Federal Housing Administration (FHA) loan, and you are only required to put down around 3.5% down. On a $200,000 property, that is just $7,000, plus closing costs. Depending on the market value at the time, you could potentially live mortgage-free until it's time to buy your next property.

Just keep in mind that you can only have one FHA loan at a time. So if this is something you would like to continue doing, you will have to consider refinancing the original property to a different loan or mortgage before moving on to the next property.

There are other benefits to house hacking, such as great cash flow because, in the case of buying a small multi-family building, the likelihood is the tenants will be paying your mortgage payment and splitting some of the other bills, while you live rent-free or almost rent-free.

Going this route, it is also a fairly low-risk way to introduce yourself to the world of being a landlord. Yes, you will be onsite, so they may contact you more than if you lived off-site, but then you will start to understand boundaries and how important they will be now and in the future, as your portfolio grows.

As with other properties, do your due diligence. A bad deal could wind up costing you more, and then you may as well continue only renting. Do your homework, shop around. It may not be the secret to success, but house hacking can be a powerful tool to start building your financial freedom.

Once you have decided which route is best for you and your finances, it's time to get pre-approved. It makes sense to do this before any deals come up, that way you will know ahead of time which property to start the offer process on and which one you have to walk away from because it's out of your price range. Don't let this dissuade you as prices are always negotiable. Now you're ready to start making offers.

Chapter 7 Getting the Right Property to Sell

Now that you have got into the business of real estate wholesaling, the next vital step you need to make is to get the right property. Remember that the property you get is what will determine the amount of profit that you make at the end of it al.

While this is the simplest method for you to make much money in the real estate market, it also presents you with a challenge because you need to have the best property for wholesale. We have different tactics and levels of flipping houses this way, including the different types of properties that can be wholesaled.

As a real estate wholesaler, you have various options when you decide to sell houses on wholesale. Here are a few options to choose from.

Single Family Homes

This is most probably the most popular type of house for wholesalers. Here are a few reasons that make these houses the best for wholesale purposes:

The prices of these houses usually appreciate faster than multi homes, and they also have a higher rental rate which means that you will attract investors much easily.

These houses are usually cheaper than other types of units that you will opt for. They are therefore lighter on the market and ideal for people that are just getting into the rental business. They will allow you to have more disposable income that you will get to spend on other things.

These houses are relatively easy to maintain and manage, especially when you compare them to multi-apartment buildings. Tenants that are in the houses tend to take them as their own, and this means you won't have to spend a lot of money on renovations. As a property owner, you have an easy time looking at the tenants because they aren't so many like in multifamily apartments.

These rental properties bring in higher rental prices as opposed to every unit in a multi-unit facility. The tenants in these homes enjoy many advantages that will make them be able to pay the high amount that you ask. So, while waiting to flip the house, you can as well make some more money from them.

These houses have a specific tenant base that isn't interested in living in apartment units. The appeal of these houses is in their privacy and the freedom to make use of the garden areas the way someone pleases. You are targeting a market segment that is the biggest - people that are after their own privacy and that need space. This means that the demand for these houses usually remains steady the whole year-round.

These houses are easier to finance compared to other homes. This means you can get a loan for buying the home faster than you can get one for multi-apartment homes. The loans also have a lower interest rate compared to other homes.

Condos and Townhomes

The benefits of buying condos are definitely dependent on what you plan to do with the condo or the townhome. Now that you plan to sell it after a short period let us look at the various benefits that you gain when you invest in condos for wholesaling:

Cash flow - when you buy a condo, you will enjoy some income as you look for a buyer to flip the property. The aim of buying a condo is to try and sell it off in the shortest time possible. But while you wait for this time to reach, you will benefit from the cash flow, which represents the difference between what comes in and what goes out. Additionally, the rents on condos are high, which means you will recoup a small portion of your investment as you wait for the property to sell.

The condos appreciate in value, and this means you will be able to profit in the form of passive income. The growth in value is a good way to make more profit compared to letting the property sit and wait.

If you hold onto the condo for some time, you will be able to pay off your loan in the shortest time possible. This is because the property will give you the income that you can use.

While you hold onto the property, you will be able to decrease your tax obligations to a large extent. You will be able to write off a portion of your tax obligations.

While waiting for the property to get a market, you will benefit from the passive income that comes with the entail income from tenants. With the help of a property manager, you won't have to do anything - just sit and wait for your income to grow.

As urbanization increase, the condos and townhouses are in very high demand. This is also due to the fact that Millenials and the younger generations love the city and they are attracted to these types of homes.

The demand for these homes is very high, which means that you will sell them off faster and make your profit more easily.

Mobile Homes

Though commonly overlooked, these homes can be as profitable as the other homes that you flip on the market. Let us look at the reasons why mobile homes are ideal for wholesaling purposes:

Compared to single-family houses and multifamily properties, the cost of these mobile homes is lower. This means you can acquire more units at a lower cost.

Since the mobile homeowners are responsible for the repair and maintenance of the homes, and you will not have a lot of work when it comes to renovating the home for sale.

Since you are buying a set of units, you get to spread the risks out, and the risk for losses reduces significantly.

With the demand for these homes hitting all new highs, the need for mobile homes has also increased in equal measure. This means that you will be able to sell off the homes faster than ever. People are now opting for more affordable housing, which means you will be able to sell the house off faster than if you had a different unit.

Not many people have learned the secret of investing in mobile homes, which means that the competition will remain low. You won't have to fight for the available units.

Apartment Buildings

Apartment buildings are some of the top investments for real estate investors. They are usually on demand even if the economy isn't going their way. Here are a few reasons why you need to invest in apartment buildings:

Before you sell it off, you will be able to enjoy a steady source of income. However, you need to choose the apartment in a good area and location, and you will be assured of a steady source of income.

These types of buildings usually provide an affordable housing option that will allow people to enjoy affordable housing, something that they are all after. Apartments will always remain on-demand at all times.

The property can easily appreciate without investing in the property at all. You don't have to invest in new carpets, windows or sidings and paint.

These apartment buildings provide you with tax benefits. One, you will enjoy depreciation expense when you purchase the property, and you can reinvest the proceeds into a new property, and you won't pay any taxes due to the appreciation.

The demand for multifamily houses is steady and doesn't experience the dramatic changes that we see in office and retail.

You have access to a host of multifamily loan products that you can choose from to finance the purchase.

Commercial Real Estate

You can also wholesale, retail malls, office buildings, and other mixed-use properties. Here are a few reasons why commercial real estate is an attractive investment for you:

While you wait for your investments to generate interest in the market, you will be able to enjoy the cash returns that come from using the property for rental purposes.

Commercial real estate doesn't fluctuate in the price as compared to other types of investments in the market such as stock and more.

Commercial real estate is less volatile compared to other types of properties. They remain valuable even when the prices rise in the market. This helps to protect you against inflation.

The property enjoys a steady level of appreciation compared to other properties on the market.

When you invest in real estate with the aim of flipping it, you are able to diversify your portfolio the right way.

Vacant Lots and Land

You can sell these vacant lots and land fast because many people are looking to develop their own properties the right way. Here are a few reasons why you can invest in land as a way to make some more money:

When you have a vacant lot, you don't have to do anything on this property at all. It appreciates without investing more money in it.

You don't have to deal with stubborn tenants, leaky roofs, burst pipes, or broken furnaces when you handle the land. Once you buy it, all you need to do is to wait for the land to appreciate.

As a wholesaler of vacant lots, you have little competition to deal with in the first place. Everyone is investing in rental properties, but when you decide to invest in land, you are one among many other people to do this.

When you learn to research and find the right property to sell, you will be able to buy and sell the land without having to see the land yourself. You can make the purchase and sale of the land virtually without leaving home at all.

How to Find Properties for Wholesale Real Estate Investment

Now that you know the kinds of properties that are available for you to invest in, the next step is for you to locate these properties. Remember that you need to find properties that you will sell then make a profit. Here are the top ways to get the property that will make you a hero in wholesaling.

Foreclosure Listings

For you to get the property to sell, you can explore foreclosure listings online. When you decide to go for foreclosure listings, you will be able to achieve a fast purchase, which will give you a better profit compared to others. You, however, will have to do repairs on the property. The good thing is that you will be able to know the price of the property as well as the history, which makes it easy for you to estimate what is required before you put it on the market.

When you buy a foreclosure listing, you have the ability to do all the standard inspections, including research of the title during that period.

When using a foreclosure site, you will only be able to see late-stage foreclosure, which means that you miss out on properties that are in pre-foreclosure, which is the stage where the borrower has already defaulted on the mortgage, but the bank hasn't officially performed the foreclosure.

Property Auctions

Another good place that you can get distressed properties for wholesale auctions. We have various auction sites online that you can use to get the property that you need. You can also check your local newspaper for planned auctions.

If you wish to get more options, you can go for other auction sites that are out of your target area. Many of the auction sites are always updated to give you the latest on the properties that are available.

The good thing is these sites allow you to bid on properties so that you can post the best price you need the property for. Just like other auction sites, they also have a buy it now an option for a few properties.

The competitive bidding process is fast and gives you a chance to bid on houses that you would normally fail to find at a better price. Auctions require you to put down a deposit, usually between 5 and 10 percent and then the remainder in 30-45 days that is if you win the auction.

You can opt for financing from a series of companies that offer to finance specifically for borrowers. These financiers can prequalify you in a few minutes so that you can compete with all-cash buyers.

Real estate auctions will give you a wide range of properties at different price points and will include things such as multi-family units, single homes, as well as commercial properties. Auctions can be online or in person.

These auctions happen in real-time or over a few weeks, and they usually start with a minimum price. From here, the auctioneer will allow the competitive bidder to put up a price for the property until a single person remains. When the auctioneer realizes the price, they will close the auction and then award the property to the winning bidder.

The objective and the investment timeline that you have will dictate what financing options that you have available for you. Cash is the preferred method of payment for the auction. However, you can use lenders to finance the process of paying for the property.

When you get into an auction, you need to budget for the following costs:

Down payment of between 20-35 percent depending on the purchase price of the property as well as any other lender fees.

Holding costs, which are monthly costs that will help, keep the property such as taxes, mortgage, and insurance.

Repair and renovation costs, which vary according to the condition of the property as well as the area.

Marketing costs, which is the amount that you need to spend to put the property on the market. This is usually a percentage of the property and is paid out on the sale proceeds.

Where to Find Auction listings

There are various ways to get real estate auction listings:

Real Estate Auction Sites

You can visit real estate auction sites that offer both online and physical auctions. Some of them offer both types of auctions, while others only offer a single type. You need to check out these sites and browse what they have on offer, they r requirements and more, then start looking for houses that you can bid on.

Real estate Professionals

These have a lot of information regarding upcoming auctions for real estate properties. They include brokers, real estate agents, and trustees. Bankruptcy accountants and lawyers are also good people to engage when you are looking for such opportunities.

You can find these professionals through referrals from friends, investors, and other family members.

You can also decide to join a real estate investment group in the area or search for a real estate agent and ask for personal auctions.

Real Estate Classifieds

These are somewhat outdated, but you will still find listings in local newspapers. Some of the newspapers have an online presence as well, and you can get your properties on them.

Abandoned Houses

Another strategy that you can use to get the right property for wholesaling is to go for an abandoned house. An abandoned house is one that no person is living in, and the signs will tell you that the house has been abandoned for a long time. The owners will be paying annual taxes as well as mortgage payments, and so they will be interested in letting it go. You can approach the homeowner directly and make an offer to purchase the home.

If you don't have the time to move around looking for such property, you can go ahead and visit sites that list these properties in the community. These platforms have a search platform that allows you to choose the property type, kind of ownership, and attributes. Most listings come with a phone number attached.

Drive-bys

You can also locate a property for wholesale by moving around the neighborhoods in which you wish to purchase the distressed property. If you see a house that has mail accumulating with the landscaping neglected, it is highly likely that it is abandoned. The house could also belong to a child of a homeowner that is deceased or has gone into a senior facility.

However, you need to approach the home with a lot of caution, because these kids might have an attachment to the home, or they cannot agree to the terms of sale of the property. They might also be avoiding the costly repairs that come with owning such a home and will want to dispose of it. Offering to buy the property will seem to them as an attractive option that they will take up willingly.

While moving around, don't forget to contact the local people that have information on homes that are vacant. These can be mail carriers or real estate agents. Remember that real estate agents will find these homes to be a liability because their clients never want to stay near such homes.

Pre-foreclosures

These are homes where the borrower has defaulted on payment, and they have gone at least for 90 days without paying. Though the agents have in place a process that will help the owner to pay the mortgage, in most cases the property usually goes to foreclosure just because the homeowner cannot afford the amount needed to redeem them.

When you identify a property that is in this state, you get to eliminate most of the competition, and thus you stand a better chance of getting the property. You also have the advantage of negotiating directly with the lender or the borrower while you still have a lot of options on the table.

Attorneys

You will be surprised that you might find a good property from your attorney. Many attorneys run the wills of their clients, and they know when the property is to be sold or not. They also handle divorce settlements, and they know when a couple is undergoing a foreclosure at the close of the divorce, so they will know when a property is on the market or not.

Chapter 8 How to Get The Best Offer

Real estate wholesaling can be a profitable venture if you do it the right way. However, many first time investors find it a big hurdle when they realize that a lot has to go into the process. One of the major hurdles that make real estate wholesaling fail is the lack of negotiating skills.

This is understandable because for you to be a real estate wholesaler, you have to talk to sellers that are motivated to sell the property off. The seller usually seeks to get as much as they can from the deal as possible, which puts you in a corner when it comes to making sure you get the best price.

Talking to Sellers the Right Way

So, if you are finding it hard to get into the murky waters of talking to sellers, then you need to read the following tips:

Perform the Right Research

Before you can perform well in front of a seller, you need to perform due diligence about the property. First, you need to join a local investment group that will give you an idea of what is trending and what isn't. Learn to ask questions about the property that you are interested in, and sure enough, you will know what you need to do so that you can get the best deals in the area. Most of the people that are on these investment groups tend to have experience with what you are planning to do, and they will give your ideas on how to approach a seller.

The next step is for you to build a rapport with the real estate agent. At this point, ask the real estate agent to give you a list of the properties in the area and how much each of the properties goes for. This gives you an idea of what to expect in terms of price.

When armed with the right information, you will get over your fear of investing in these types of houses, because you have all it takes to face the seller.

This means you first have to know every aspect of how the wholesaling deal works, as well as knowing all information regarding the seller that you are making contact with so that you don't end up getting surprises when you are in the middle of a conversation.

It is also vital that you know what the other party wants from the deal. Dig some background information on the person so that you know whether they are having financial difficulty or are going through a divorce. Depending on the situation, you will be able to know what to say or do, especially when the negotiation isn't going your way. Remember that you have to know what the person wants so that you play with their emotions during the deal.

Practice

If you have a fear of speaking in public, you need to know that you aren't alone. It is a common aspect of negotiations. Fear usually is a result of a lack of experience that makes you fear expressing yourself in front of other people.

So, how do you go about a negotiation when you don't know how you will negotiate? Similar to any skill, you need a lot of practice in order to make things work for you. Before you meet the seller, take some time to practice in front of your friends or even the mirror. You can also take part in mock negotiations when the pressure is off.

If you have a team that you work with, try and practice the negotiations with them. This also gives them the capacity to handle negotiations when you aren't around. You can visualize a normal conversation then write down the things that you need to say, and then keep visualizing them so that you have an idea of what to expect at all times.

When you have information, and then you rehearse, you will walk into the negotiation when you are full of confidence. Confidence usually makes deals go your way.

Know What You Want, and Express It

Don't be afraid to know what you want in the negotiation. Make sure you have goals that you follow when you go to negotiation and then go for them. Achieving goals in a conversation are all about looking for a way to get what you went out for, at the price you can afford.

Don't look at the whole experience to be a confrontation at all. Instead, you need to understand that it is all a process that you have to handle the right way. Think of it as a process that is normal to you, and that you have all it takes to make it work no matter what happens. Motivated sellers are those that are out to make sure they sell the house and get what they are after - the money.

Don't look at the seller as an enemy, rather view them as someone that you need to work with so that both of you get what you want, which is a resolution to the problem at hand.

Build Rapport

People love working with other people that they like. They like working with people that are open and honest, anything contrary and the person will not work with you. Creating a rapport doesn't mean that you and the seller become very good friends, rather you need to have a certain level of respect that will cement your relationship with the home seller and give you a platform to present the message.

This means you need to focus the first few minutes of the interaction on building rapport. Ask the seller about what they do, their background, their hobbies, and interests so that you get a common playing ground. Most of the times, you will get to determine the outcome of the negotiation not by the ability to negotiate the right way, but by establishing and maintaining a rapport.

Learn

When negotiating, you are trying to tell another person about your point of view in all that is happening. You are presenting your side of the story so that the other person can give in to what you want. It is all about knowing what the other person wants from the negotiation and then finding a way to work with them.

You need to learn various aspects of the seller and the property. Here are a few things that you need to understand:

Is the seller currently living in the property?

For how long has the seller lived on the property?

Is the seller the real owner, or is he selling on behalf of another person?

When is the seller planning to move out of the property?

Why is the seller disposing of the property?

When is the ideal closing date for sale?

What will the seller resort to if the property doesn't close?

These questions are hard for the seller to answer, so you need to find a way to get the responses without triggering any suspicion. What you need to tell the seller is that you have the capacity to solve their problem immediately and this is why you need as much information as you need so that you facilitate the process.

When you focus on getting the right information the best way, you will be able to get the deal at an attractive position.

How to Identify Motivated Sellers

You have heard of this term used in this section before, and you will come across it in upcoming sections as well. We need to understand what it means to be a motivated seller and how you can find one.

Without having a source for motivated sellers, you will waste a lot of time trying hard to get a deal when in reality, it won't come your way. The best idea is for you to work with sellers that are willing to sell and who are flexible in their dealings.

The challenge that many investors have known how to get these motivated sellers.

First, we need to know what it means for someone to be a motivated seller. A motivated seller refers to a person that seeks to get rid of a property that they have in their possession. A motivated seller is willing to sell what they hold at a price that is within the prevailing market range. This means that the seller is willing to sell their property at a price that is between 10 and 30 percent below the market value.

A motivated seller is also willing to sell to you the process at favorable terms, for instance, no deposit and 0 percent interest. For many people, the ideal motivated seller is the one that has all these facts in tow, but even a single one is enough to make one a motivated seller.

Motivated sellers make it easy for you to get the property on time because they are clear with what they want and how they want it. They know that they have to talk to you favorably for them to resolve an issue that they have, which is disposing of the house.

So, how do you find a motivated seller for a property that you want to sell? Here are a few pointers:

Come up with a List

You need to come up with a list of motivated sellers that you can work with at any time. You don't need to have so many people for you to make it in real estate wholesaling, start with a few, such as two and then build on the list. The list needs to include attorneys. Absentee owners, realtors, landlords, homeowners, foreclosures and many more that you can add to your list.

You can come up with your own list, but this will take a lot of time and effort. What you need to do in this case is to find a company that specializes in making lists and then have a targeted list that you can use. Make sure that you filter everything so that you get the right form of property for you. Common filters include property size and zip code.

Have a Marketing Page

Once you have a list, you need to come up with a marketing page that will attract other sellers that have something to offer. You also need a direct mail piece that you will send motivated sellers that have something to offer. Additionally, you need a webpage that will give your contacts. Motivated sellers will use the page to contact you or to share their contact info with you.

Send Your Mail

Once you have a list of motivated sellers that are willing to handle your business, you need to introduce your self-using direct mail. This is the first contact with the sellers that will tell them that you exist and that you are ready to do business with them.

A single mail won't do the trick; you need to send out several emails in order for you to get the right response from the seller. Make sure the marketing message is convincing and compelling enough to make the seller want to give your business.

Remember that the response rate is usually about 5 percent, so know that if you sent 100 emails, you are looking at five responses.

Try and make the message as personalized as possible. Look at what the seller is looking for then create a message depending on their goals. This means that even if you are going to send 100 emails, you need to make sure each mail is customized to the needs of the seller.

Once you get a few leads, you need to follow them out the right way. Tell them what you need and then let them know your budget.

Negotiating Tips for Wholesale Real Estate

You need to be a good negotiator for you to strike the best deals. You will to really negotiate so that you get a good deal and then get profit from the deal.

Create a Win-Win Situation

The best negotiators know that they have to create a situation where both the seller and the buyer will win. Just because you are trying to close a deal doesn't mean that the seller doesn't know what to do. When you are negotiating, don't do it just for any small issue, rather look at the bigger picture. The costs that you see to be small might be big for the seller.

Successful sellers don't negotiate over small costs - they have a lot of topics that are ready to go in their queues. This way, they make sure everyone gets what they want at the end of it all.

Compromise

You might be hard up with what the seller is suggesting, but when it comes to making a deal, you need to learn to compromise. When looking at the contract, seek out the areas that you are willing to knock off the contract so that you end up with a quicker purchase. You might be willing to add a few thousand to the buying price so that you don't lose out on a lucrative deal.

Be Ready to Walk Away

The biggest skill set is getting to know when to let a deal go. You don't have to get things going your way each time - at times you have to let them go. Even if the property is all you have been dreaming about the whole time, it is a bad idea to try and negotiate with all the cards on the table.

No matter how good the deal is, try and maintain your focus when you enter a negotiation. Show the seller that you are ready to walk away at any time you feel like especially when you don't get what you wanted.

One of the best ways to avoid losing your footing before the seller is to make sure you still have a few properties that are lined up for you to choose from. If you really want to be confident in all you do, then have the courage to walk away. When you find that the seller is adamant not to agree with your conditions, then you need to move on to the next property that you have in your list. While the other properties might not be as good as the one you had chosen, they are crucial to act as backup plans.

Be Direct

The best negotiators on the market will be direct and decisive. The statements you make needs you to be direct and show assurance and confidence. You also need to anticipate other perspectives from the seller. Try and write a few things down that will make the deal go forward, and then incorporate affirmative language in the negotiations.

Do the Negotiation in Person

When you desire to get the best deal, it is always good to do this yourself. A face to face negotiation will make sure that everyone is on the same page in whatever the two of you do. If you cannot meet face to face, it is better to speak over the phone. When you talk face to face, you will get to learn the body language of the seller and the reactions from them. The phone cannot be a substitute for face to face interaction, but it allows you to read the tone of the person.

When given a choice between email and the phone, go for the phone because it makes for a better conversation and negotiation. You also need to remember that negotiation doesn't need to be completed in a single conversation; you can continue it later on in separate meetings according to the need to do so.

Be a Good Listener

The worst-case scenario in any negotiation is for one of the persons to lose their temper and storm out of the room and out of the deal. This puts an end to the deal and also becomes harmful to the reputation of the investor. It also hurts future deals that might come your way as well. Make sure you have your ego in check when entering the deal and be a good listener before you can react to some statements.

Once you listen and understand, you will be confident and speak well in the negotiations. However, this doesn't always go for all the people in the negotiation.

When you have a chance to respond, do it honestly and in a way that the other party will understand. Additionally, allow other people to respond to statements fully before you can counter them.

Real Estate Negotiation Pressure Points

These are those areas that you can focus on so that you can control the deal. Here are a few pressure points that you need to be aware of:

Time

Under pressure of time, many sellers become flexible, and they are willing to sell. The pressure makes the seller motivated to sell fast, for any reason and you will be able to get the deal that you want, even better. Some of the time pressure points include when a property is near foreclosure, relocating to a new station, probate and more.

Knowledge

In any negotiation, the side that has more information is always more successful compared to the side that doesn't have information. The more information you have about a seller or the property, the higher the chances that you will clinch the deal. This is why we talked about research earlier on when you are looking for a seller. Armed with this information, you have the ability to sway the decision towards you. The information you need can come from various sources, so make sure you get the right information when you are negotiating.

Options

The person that has a few options to explore will always have the upper hand in the negotiation. This is because when you have options, you get the ability to walk away at any time you feel like.

Chapter 9 Common Mistakes to Avoid In Real Estate Investing

Each retail investor dreams of beginning a real estate investment business, making money, and enjoying the "good life." What so many fail to realize is that investing in real estate can be incredibly complicated and expensive if you don't know what you're doing. When you take it slowly and know how to do it properly, it can be very lucrative to invest in real estate. I'll clarify eight common mistakes in this chapter that a new investor typically makes and how to prevent them.

Mistake #1 - Failure to Invest in Education

Attempt to invest in infrastructure before you start paying your rent, and you need to take time to learn the fundamentals of investing in real estate. It does not mean that you need to spend thousands on training or courses related to "guru;" it means that you have to spend time researching the various investment strategies to understand what you need to do to succeed.

Mistake #2-Failure to set up a business. Several people begin investing with their cash, name, and credit on a small scale. What they cannot know is that any mistake could cost you all you've worked so hard to make. Use your homework and produce a business entity that best suits your needs before you start investing. In most instances, the most appropriate company to use for your corporation will be an LLC or a Company. In creating a business company, if something goes wrong down the road, you can cover your assets.

Mistake #3 —Depending on the type of assets you own, and what you plan to do with the property, the type of coverage you will need will be decided. If you're planning to buy a single-family home for sale, you'll need to get a rental agreement. If you are planning to buy and sell "Flip" property, a General Commercial Cost Plan may be the way to go as many will cover the cost of the deal. For best practice, make sure that when determining which type of insurance you will need, you talk to a professional insurance agent.

Mistakes#4 - Failure to Strategize & Plan

Real Estate Investing is like any other company, so why don't you treat it like one? You need to build a clear plan of action on how you will proceed if you want to be successful. Decide which strategy(s) works best for you before you start investing. Don't panic if it takes a while to determine the right plan, but make sure that you stick with it when you find it out.

Mistakes#5- Failure to find and manage a budget

One of the first things you need to do is find out how much cash you need to spend. If you only have enough money for a condo, don't try to buy an apartment complex. Once you've worked out how much money you've got to spend, concentrate your time and energy on a budget that fits your needs. If you're over-budgeting, your growth potential may be reduced. If you're under budget, you're most likely going to get into trouble, resulting in a large amount of debt.

Mistake #6 - Failure to Correctly Estimate the Cost of Repairs

Not only will this mistake cost you time, but it can also cost you the whole deal. Invest in a local contractor to inspect the property to provide you with a list of improvements that will be required and the cost of completing every repair if you are looking to purchase a house. This move will save you time on the back end and thousands of dollars.

Mistake #7 — Failure to create a team. Everyone heard the saying, "You're just as good as the weakest link." If you're trying to invest in real estate and you don't have a strong team behind you, you're going to be the weakest link. It is essential to surround yourself with a great group of people and to continue to have an excellent working relationship with these people. Developing your team can take a lot of time and energy, but when you're finished, demonstrate your progress.

Mistake #8- Failure to take action. After educating yourself, starting a business, securing insurance, defining a strategy or project, developing a budget, and establishing your team, there is nothing left but to put everything to work and take action. At first, it might be daunting. You might make little mistakes, but if you don't take action, you're never going to make money and be successful.

It can be challenging to invest in real estate, and if you go wrong, it can be costly. Investing in real estate, on the other hand, can be very professional and financially beneficial. Don't be afraid to ask a specialist for assistance. If you know what you're doing, most of these errors can be prevented. The more information you acquire and research, the fewer errors you make.

Residential Real Estate Investing

This is the flip side of homeowners who, during the depression, we're unable to pay for their mortgage payments. Most individuals with tools and knowledge like residential property investment have been able to capitalize on the situation. Real estate has been one of the most significant asset instruments for many people in history for a long time. In the United States, more millionaires were created through real estate investment than in any other industry.

Since the start of the recession in 2012, real estate investors have taken advantage of every opportunity to invest in residential property across the United States. At discount prices up to 55% off the value of the property market. How can you ask how these prices are made? When the recession began, most companies reduced their workers in large numbers, creating a domino effect on the marketplace. Most homeowners started to stop making monthly mortgage payments on their homes after several months of unemployment. Banks and mortgage companies suddenly found themselves more able to manage all at the same time and massive amounts of unpaid mortgage payments on their hands. In an attempt to solve this issue, these mortgage companies and banks started issuing notices of default to homeowners to get homeowners to begin paying back on their loans.

That initiative was unsuccessful, and in fact, many loans occurring some years before the downturn had interest rate changes built-in to the mortgage which was immediately scheduled to raise the mortgage payment to buyers by about $2,000 or more per month, causing more distressed mortgage payments because homeowners were unable to pay the increased mortgage payments. This almost brought the financial system of the United States to a complete standstill that hadn't happened since the 1930's Great Depression. So, with banks and mortgages pursuing their standard hedging practices on delinquent homeowners, this created an ample supply of homes for the property market as a whole at a bad time.

With an unstable housing market, new homeowners were reluctant to take the chance to get wrapped up in the devalued real estate market, property values that had risen from 2004-2008 took a significant drop in value almost overnight. This is where prospects for investment in residential real estate presented themselves. Many of these people had purchased and restored homes through the 2004-2008 boom period and made a lot of money in the process.

So, we are happy to take advantage of this down market with cash new. Banks had to sell this oversupply of properties as they are forced to get these default loans off their books by the US government bank regulators. As the only real buyer in the market, banks started one by one to sell stock to residential real estate investors at high discounted prices. Such buyers, in effect, made home renovations, and as months passed by some prospective homeowners, they began to hear that there were lower prices available on the markets, so they agreed they should take a chance at homeownership. Residential real estate developers began selling their assets to these new homeowners, which they had purchased from the banks at discounts of up to 50%. The new homeowners were pleased because they were able to buy homes that were far cheaper than they could buy the same house just a year before. Now they were getting new updated features that the real estate investor had thrown in like-new stainless steel appliances, improved cabinetry, freshly painted property through the building, and new floors that were used to encourage the homeowner to purify themselves.

The investment segment of residential property started to put more money into the market to buy more discounted properties from the banks. Some houses are sold for profits of up to $300,000 to $400,000 per unit depending on where the apartment was in the state, making an insane profit amounts of money. For such investors in residential property, this was good for the company. This trend holds to this very day, but the banks who figured out how much they made these investors have changed their ways of selling the assets. Massive profits are still open, but in 2009 through 2011, they aren't quite as big as the starting days. Once the word came out how much money was produced for distressed real estate properties, new investors in the reselling real estate market joined the group, many of whom had never been in the real estate business before the recession. If you've ever dreamed about making money outside of your current job, there are still ways in this field to make money at times without the need for your cash or credit.

How to Automate Your Real Estate Investing Business

One thing you'll see quickly when you invest in Real Estate is that there's a lot of work to do to get a deal done, and the weather you're a rehabber or a wholesaler, and you've got to do a lot of work before it's sold. You usually have more time than cash at the start of most shareholder companies, and you end up doing everything yourself to keep down your costs and increase your profits. Heck, marketing itself is costly enough, and if you have little or no money to start with, you're forced to do all you can to get your first contract.

That's fine, and nearly everyone starts that way, but you don't always want to stay that way, even if by doing so, you can make a more significant piece of the pie. But why is this? If I could save money and make more per deal, why wouldn't I want to do it all myself? There's a straightforward reason why you want to pay someone else to do certain things and why working on others is essential to you. The simple answer is not the same as all the tasks of an investment real estate business. Saying the same word in another way, some jobs are simple enough that anyone can do them while others need the ability to think, invent, lead, and communicate.

When you look at any company, the lowest-paid workers are usually the non-skilled workers where there is no specialized training for them to do their job, and those positions pay the least. Anyone can be taught how to clean a toilet: P The middle class of workers usually requires some degree or a unique skill set to do their jobs, and as a result, these workers are paid more. Any corporation's top tier is the people with innovative ideas, management, and communication skills to make it happen. We get paid the most as a result. Your real estate business is the same as any company, so treat it like that!

And back to my original question as to why you don't want to do this on your own. Focusing on essential tasks and contracting out the bottom and eventually, middle-level tasks for others to do is simply more productive. This is attributable to something called "hourly pay." When you spread your time doing all aspects of the business, you take your hourly wage and average it from the whole pie. If, on the other hand, you only perform the essential tasks and contract the rest at a low price, you will produce more, and your hourly wage will rise. This is the main difference between a sole owner and a businessman and why the businessman ends up making money. I don't know about you, but I got to make money and have a ton of free time in this business!

Let me give you an excellent example of what I'm thinking about. My husband and I primarily sell the MLS and Craigslist in two different locations to find all of our offers. Both of these places are necessarily free to market (yes, I know the MLS costs money every year, but let's say it's free from there... deal? after the fee is paid). And, every day we can spend hours sending lowball deals to the MLS and advertising on Craigslist to get people to call in. Then every day, we can spend hours dealing with Realtors ' answers and sellers ' calls. All you need to find a deal, and that's when it all happens at once! Now you're having to do daily tasks like putting up advertisements and making offers on the MLS, coping with emails and calls in addition to putting together the deal so that you can either sell or rehabilitate it. What's most likely to happen is that the lower tier activities cease while you're focused on the tasks that make you money, and when you make that money, you've got to start all over again... blah: P!

So that's what I suggest ;) Hire a Virtual Assistant after you make your first or even second deal, and you've got some money to play with now! When we did that our production skyrocketed and there was a decrease in the amount of work we had to do... and all that work was the tedious work we hated doing! Now we have a lady over in India who works for $2.25 an hour with a Masters' degree making offers on the MLS. Have you heard me there... she's got a Master Dang, and she's working for $2.25 an hour!

Try to see if you can get a homeless man to work for the cheap one. Ha! Even if you could bet a month's wages, he wouldn't put in the same effort and enthusiasm as the lady with her degree we have in India;) She's extraordinarily productive and very smart and can send 50-60 offers to the MLS within 2 hours. We started working 10 hours a week with her, and she was worth her gold weight! Think about it, and we've got about 250-300 deals for about $25 each week. We made her do more research as time went by, while we focused on the creative tasks (which are also more enjoyable and take less time)... high!

Necessarily, Virtual Assistants are people who can perform any function you request of them that can be done on an internet-connected device. Someone who sends an offer to the MLS or places an ad on Craigslist does NOT have to be in my office, nor do I have to see them know they are doing their job. We let her use our company email to send deals, and we can track her progress by merely checking the sent folder to see what she's doing... so limited oversight. So, anywhere in the world, this person can be! How many of us wanted to work with our jobs from home, but it never seemed that the bosses were on board for it?

We can now be the "hot" boss and as a result, reap the rewards! You can do all the menial tasks once you have someone on board and let you concentrate on the things that will make you money, like bringing together buyers and sellers! The larger you get, the more tasks you need your Virtual Assistant to delegate. You can eventually get an "apprentice" real estate investor who can do everything you need, including managing your Virtual Assistant. A wage plus a percentage of profits can be paid to him.

Mortgages For Real Estate Investments

If you need to obtain a mortgage for your first real estate investment property, take your time to look at the various options available. Of course, having great credit helps. The good your reputation is, the more likely you are to get the loan you need. Here are some options for securing a mortgage loan for your property:

Fixed mortgage

A fixed mortgage usually lasts 30 years and does not adjust, hence the name "fixed rate." This is the mortgage loan's wife. Real estate investors have only been able to obtain this kind of loan for a long time. When they get a fixed mortgage loan, if they pay it off sooner, it comes with a fixed rate that will continue for the term of 30 years or less. The loan will be deemed to be paid in full by the end of the e30-year term. The monthly loan payments are applied to the interest of the loan in the early years. We are finally added to the inner balance as the years go by. This is about investors ' most manageable loan to manage as the terms are plain.

Usually, as you continue to pay off, you will not find anything unexpected down the road. Perhaps real estate investor will for a long time with a lot of debt.

The real estate investment wealth, not having financial investors gain wealth from they will enjoy it as they properties. emphasis is on creating liabilities at all times. As investing in real estate, keep investing in more

Zero Investment (No-Money Down Loans)

This is another type of mortgage loan that property investors can use. They're not going to have a problem trying to get information about this type of loan because they're always being advertised somewhere. Sometimes it can be claimed as one of the best loans since bread has been sliced. It is critical, however, that borrowers are aware of the risks involved in obtaining such a loan.

Investors in real estate can obtain this type of loan by securing a 100% mortgage, or they can accomplish what is called a "piggyback" mortgage. A piggyback loan is when two mortgages are backed and brought together by the lender at the same time.

The investor gets a bonus with a piggyback mortgage by not having to downplay at the closing process. The shareholder can also benefit from earning the highest amount of interest allowed to be included as a deduction in their taxes.

Being a borrower, you're not always sure to get the whole amount funded for the loan. There are many banks and other creditors that do not provide the full 100%. If some want to provide the entire lot, by including higher interest rates, they will get their share. That way, because you wouldn't have made a down payment, they would protect themselves.

The mortgage payments will be higher than usual, as with anything else that is zero-down. This kind of loan can hurt you in the long run if you don't have a lot of money as a financial backup. Getting a stable cash flow would take you longer because you'd pay a more significant amount of mortgage payments. So, you might want to think a little harder than others about this loan opportunity.

A zero-down loan, however, could still work to secure an investment property for you. Whether or not you are willing and capable of taking the risk is up to you.

Adjustable mortgage rate

Adjustable mortgage loans or ARMs are almost as popular as fixed mortgages, as they are commonly known. Investors in real estate are also likely to use these. When you agree on this mortgage, a fixed interest rate can be guaranteed.

A variable rate of interest is the rate paid by borrowers, and it often fluctuates. The rates change following the market interest rate increases or decreases during that period.

It would continue for a couple of years with a fixed rate. Then it would go into a cycle of the parameter. This ensures that your loan rate (and monthly payment) is subject to change each year after the fixed-rate duration is over.

With that, many ARMs have a stopping point as to how much they can adjust. With this loan, as long as you have it, the rate may increase or decrease to a certain amount.

Initially, this form of loan may include a low-interest rate. This would appeal to some real estate investors as they may not want to hang on to the property for an extended period.

Often, investors can take the opportunity to get in on them if interest rates fall. This loan, on the other hand, is very risky. The investor will have to go with the flow when interest rates rise.

The bad thing about this is, when the rates will rise, they won't know in advance. In reality, ARMs can be an uncertain thing because you don't know how much money you're going to keep paying because of the fluctuations that is constant.

Interest Only Loan

Another credit in the interest-only mortgage loan that is right for the real estate investor. Investors can use this fund when it is difficult to obtain a positive cash flow. Typically this occurs when the property's price. Has increased.

Some investors usually receive interest-only loans if they don't want negative cash flow, if they're going to use the cash for something else, or if they're planning to flip into the property for a future date.

If an investor has this kind of mortgage loan, for a certain period, they can hold off on principal payments. Usually, it's not more than 10 years, but it might be less. During this period, the investor will only pay the interest and nothing else.

The debt will be amortized again to get rid of the balance in the future after the time of paying only the interest has passed. The investor ends up paying a higher payment for mortgage loans. The borrower can handle this situation in several ways: selling their assets, sticking to the higher payment, or attempting to refinance.

Balloon mortgage

Using a balloons mortgage are not one of the most popular types of mortgages loans, then the real estate investor has used it. Using more time than the actual loan term, this mortgage increases. The investor ends up paying less.

At the end of the term, though, there will be a balance to be paid in full by the lender or to refinance the loan. If the buyer is unable to pay the total lump sum or seek refinancing, the investor must ultimately sell the property.

Although, in the beginning, the investor may end up being the loser if they are unable to pay off the entire refinance or balance. Plus, the borrower would have to cope with an increase in interest rates with refinancing, plus costs of refinancing. That's just more money coming out of your wallet than you need.

Conclusion

Congratulations! You have gotten to the end of this fantastic journey. This says a lot about how serious you are about becoming a real investor, and you've made a good choice by trying to know more from this book. All that you've read will help you succeed in the real estate industry. The level of commitment and interest you have shown so far will help you throughout your journey into the real estate world. You'll come across various challenges and difficulties, but your determination will get you going. You'll also be exposed to some risks, but you'll scale through since you're well prepared for them.

Ensure you come up with a good plan and make necessary findings before buying any property to avoid problems later. Challenges will always come up, but they will be minimal when you do your due diligence.

If you're a first-time investor, do not rely on your knowledge alone, as this can be disastrous in the long run. Work with the right set of people to save yourself from various problems that may arise along the line. Do all you can to get good hands and employ the help of professionals. As you work with them and invest in more and more properties, you'll have a better understanding of what works and what doesn't work.

Read, understand, and digest the information in this book and repeat the process. Apply it in your real estate experiences and see yourself succeed in this beautiful world of opportunities.

Real estate investment isn't a new trend. It has been around for a long time and is one of the most popular businesses around the world these days. You probably have heard about it a lot of times. It is a simple means of making cash, especially when you are flipping properties. Your interest in real estate might have been triggered by an advert on TV, or from a close friend earning quite an income from investing in real estate. Okay, so you have developed an interest in it, but now the problem is: you don't know how to go about it or where to start.

You are not alone in this. Many have been and are still in your shoes or worse; they were not successful when they first tried investing in real estate, while others have started hitting it big. So, where did they go wrong? What was their mistake? Why did some succeed where others were unable to? How can one be successful in real estate?

If you are here, you are on the right route. There are many books on how to invest in real estate, but for some reason, you have chosen to read this book. You are in luck! This book answers all of the questions above and covers all of the vital information for anyone who wants to begin investing in real estate. By reading this book, you are taking a giant leap towards being successful in this venture.

In this book, you will learn everything about real estate investment; Its pros and cons, everything! You will be provided with insights on the various forms of profitable real estate investments, how to source for finance, and how to make offers. You will gain the knowledge needed in investing in real estate for profit. You will also learn about some of the popular real estate myths that have managed to stop many individuals from being as successful as they are supposed to be. While there will be hurdles and obstacles ahead, you will be armed with a detailed understanding of everything you require to scale through them.

CPSIA information can be obtained
at www.ICGtesting.com
Printed in the USA
BVHW082034010321
601388BV00004B/455